THE

EACOTT

NAME

HISTORY

by John Eacott

ISBN - 978-0-9878227-7-2

Orders for copies of this book or permission to quote or reproduce may be submitted to the publisher, John Eacott at eacott@execulink.com or to his current address 465159 Curries Rd. Woodstock Ontario Canada N4S 7V8

My web sites: www.eacott.info   or   eacott.weebly.com

Version 2.2

❊

There was a larger companion version of this work with similar information except it includes material now in another book.

This work is the effort of John McBride Eacott, born July 19, 1937 at Timmins, Ontario, Canada.

The research began in 1980 and continued until publication. In 1981 I made a library inter library loan request for the Victoria History of Gloucester England. 27 volumes arrived on a two week loan. I had expected a single book. I corresponded with a lady in England with weeks between each letter. Then came the internet and the access to huge amounts of material. The search as to who were the Eacotts took on new dimensions and a study of hundreds of years of history meant sifting through a lot of material. A few families were able to add some information. I would like to have had more Australian material but there are no national census records for Australia.

This is an eclectic work which shows sample information about a handful of people. I tell the stories of people who lived ordinary lives and some exceptional ones. Like an archaeologist I have found the footprints and fossils in the layers of history that enabled me to craft information and stories about individuals, who they were and what they did and the time in which they lived. It is pretty much as true as I could write it. You will find examples of the weather on a certain day, what a person wore, and what really happened to them. Lastly there is research material which anyone who has an interest in genealogy will find interesting.

Hopefully someone in the future will find more material to add to this work?

This book is dedicated to my remarkable grandchildren:
Aven, Mackenzie, Nathan, and Tessa
who I hope will read it someday!

John Eacott
Curries, Ontario, Canada

April 2019

THE EACOTT HISTORY NAME BOOK

This work is a study of the Eacott name and its variants.

The Eacott Family

The Eacott family more properly should be called by an earlier version as the Eycott family, or Eycote, Ecot, or perhaps simply R-Z36. The thing of it is these names are the common element in what identifies a small group of people scattered across the planet earth. We even share that "ea". The name is ancient and the users of it likely hardly know anyone else with the same name. So it is something of a status symbol to be an Eacott and after reading this book you will understand in your own way the Eacott clan and how they are like a lot of other people. In fact they are a lot of other people who by following the rules of the time simply were given a different surname. These people, when they search the records, find an ancestor who answered to one or another form of Eacott which makes them an Eacott also.

We are not exactly the chosen few but when someone tries to call our name, we can at least say "Here". So this book is about some of those who in the past said "Here".

The Origins

"For what is the worth of human life unless it is woven into the life of our ancestors by the records of history." These were the words of the Roman historian Cicero in 55 BC.

Nemomnius Vercundus[1] had died. He was 75 years old and a citizen of Rome but had lived his life in Corinium (Cirencester) on the island of Britain. The funeral outside the gates of the town was a large one. He had many friends and relatives. The family talked of the stone they would erect over his grave. A stone that was found nearly 2000 years later. Nemomnius, apart from being wealthy, was also a learned man. Like others he had been given a good education and used it to prosper. His son who had married a

---

[1] *His tombstone is in the Corinium Museum at Cirencester. The rest is all fiction.*

local Dobunni girl had built a new villa north of the town along the Churn river. After the funeral the family returned to the villa and they spoke of how Nemomnius' father Alpinus had come to Britain as a legionary.

Alpinus had joined the Augustus legion as a young man. He was from a village north of the Po river near the Alps and had presented himself to the recruiter with a letter of endorsement from his family's patron, proof that he was a Roman citizen and was literate. After his medical examination he was told he was accepted and swore an oath of allegiance. He then went home to prepare his weapons and wait for his summons to gather with the others recruited for the campaign to subdue the Britons. He looked forward to the adventure and excitement as he made his way to the assembly point on the coast of the English Channel where the legion was assembling and training. He had never been on a ship and he liked to recount how he crossed the sea without sight of land for some hours. Alpinus had fought against the armies of Caratacus and the great woman leader Boadicea. He had been stationed at the fort of Corinium when his unit was demobilized because the Britons locally were no longer causing rebellion and he had served his time. He had been in Britain so long he decided to remain, not in the least because he had met a charming girl from the nearby Bagendon community. Alpinus knew nothing of his ancestors other than they were Cisalpine Gauls who had been given Roman citizenship in his grandfather's time. He didn't know that the woman he had chosen to be his wife was also Celtic but from the north side of the Alps and her family had been in Britain for hundred of years.

Now with the funeral of Nemomnius over and work to be done in the morning Comitinus went to say goodnight to his children. He remarked to his wife, who was nursing a newborn child, something about the cycle of life passing from generation to generation. She was unsure what was going through his mind at that moment. That night Comitinus lay awake pondering the nature of life and the stars in the heavens.

He did not understand that he too was made of the same stardust as the stars, as old as the universe and yet part of the family of living creatures that had arisen on earth passing on genes mutating from creature to creature until one became a human.

The Genetics of the Larger Eycott/Eacott Family

A baby boy was born perhaps 25 hundred years ago to a family of Celtic settlers living on the south slopes of the Alps in the Po valley of what is now Italy. He was a La Tene Celt part of the Hallstadt family of Celts. Two facts are known about him. He was the first male person born with a new genetic mutation that set him apart from his siblings and every other person. No one in his family thought him any different than any one else because only an analysis of cells taken from his saliva could have shown him to be different. He was the first person with a new haplotype family and is the clan father of all the Eacotts as well as many other families. His DNA haplotype was R1B1B2A1A2D or U152/28 which in 2016 was redefined and simplified as R-PF 6570 with a further sub group refinement classification known as R-Z36 which makes it even more specific. So R1B1B2A1A2Dis R-PF 6570/ R-Z36. This is confusing because as this was written the research is but a few years old and the data is increasing rapidly and the standards are constantly shifting. Simply put, a marker on a male Y chromosome has been passed down every generation since this boy was born to every male who descended from him.

The second thing we know for certain about this boy was that he grew up and was father to sons of his own. Today his descendants are concentrated in the Po valley of Italy between Modena and Lake Garda and in Corsica where today over 50% of the population are his descendants. However they did not remain in those places and some made it to England where possibly 10% of the men there today can identify themselves as R-PF 6570.

Haplotype R1B1B2A1A2D requires some explaining. Each part tells the history of someone. That someone left DNA markers that every male Eacott carries. A calling card that says I was here. The first "Y chromosome Adam" of the Eacott lived about 60 to 80 thousand years ago in Africa. An unbelievable short period of time. If one of each generation of Eacott grandfathers names were known and we typed them in a book, the book would have fewer than 500 pages. There would be about 210 thousand entries. If all these "Y chromosome" grandfathers were alive at once they could fill 2 large football stadiums.

Scientific research throughout the world has shown that all our paternal lines are connected somewhere in the past and that these connections can be traced by reading the male yDNA. As with maternal genealogies which is defined by mtDNA, men tend to cluster into a small number of groups, 18 in total, which can be defined by the genetic fingerprints of their yDNA. In native Europeans, for example, there are 5 such groups, among Native Americans there are 4, among Japanese people there are 5, and so on. The men within each of these groups are all ultimately descended from just one man, their clan father. Obviously, these ancestral clan fathers were not the only men around at the time, but they were the only ones to have direct male descendants living today.

The other men around, or their descendants, had either no children at all or only daughters. These clan fathers also had male ancestral lines and these ultimately converge on the common paternal ancestor of every man alive today.

So let's take R1B1B2A1A2D apart and see what happened to the children of Y Adam.

As of this writing the R1B1B portion of the DNA represents people who 5 to 6 thousand years BCE were an early neolithic tribe known as the Hassuna who originated in Anatolia and lived in what is now eastern Turkey, Iraq and Syria. Subsequently they migrated northward between 3 and 4 thousand BCE to the north eastern end of the Black Sea where they became the South Yamna, Maycop, and Kura-Araxes peoples. These were cattle herding people. Another group, the RIB1"A" people originated in the caucus steppes and a R1B1 "C" group moved to the Levant or the coast area of what is now Israel and Lebanon. The R1B1 "B" group were concentrated in Anatolia (Turkey). The Eacott ancestral Yamna (or Yamnaya) people were the first who developed wagons and they began to move toward the Danube river in Europe.

About 3700 BCE the Yamna become the Maycop culture who developed the first bronze age society. By 3500 BCE the migration into Europe was underway and the culture was now known as the Unetice culture. These were also known as the beaker people for they made beaker vessels. There were several waves of these people moving westward.

The R1B1B2A1A2D (R-PF 6570) subset became settled in the region of the Alps by about 1300 BCE where they became known as the Urnfield-Hallstatt Italio Celtic culture on the north side of the Alps and the La Tene culture on the south side by 450 BCE. This final bit of information Z36 makes it pretty clear the original Eacott ancestor male was a Cenomani Gaul who lived in the vicinity of what is now Brescia at the foot of the Alps in Italy about 2400 to 2800 years ago. He is the founder of the Z36 clan. Other Celtic groups were known as the Belgae who moved up the Rhine, Moselle, and Meuse River valleys.

At this time it is not known if those who bear the full subset of R1B1B2A1 and the A2D ending came to England up the Rhine as Belgae or over the Alps from Italy. But the Eacott to be from the Italio Celtic or Cisalpine Gaul Cenomani Liguri tribe made his way to England. There appear to be two choices.

The Eacott ancestor likely arrived in England either as member of the Belgae or similar Celtic tribe such as the Dobunni or much more likely as a Roman soldier/settler. He arrived somewhere between 2000 and 3500 years ago, more likely the former. Elsewhere in this book it can be learned that the Eycot manor was adjacent to both Roman and Belgae culture centers. Demographically, as a Belgae tribesman, he likely came before the Romans and would have been a member of the Dobunni tribe but as a La Tene celt he was likely to have been a Roman soldier/settler. Whichever one he was his descendants would eventually have come from both sides.

Very few names of anyone who lived in Roman Cirencester (Corinium) are known. Nemomnius was one. His ancestors were Roman but his descendants would have the genes of anyone who had lived in southern Britain. Statistically, he would have been an Eycott relative, factually who knows. While it would be expected that all those with Eycott/Eacott surnames would have the same R-Z36 marker, such is not the case.

Some Eacotts have a different heritage and many who could claim to be Eacott have been given different surnames. Simply stated some Eacotts have had their last name given to them because they were adopted or because a parent wanted them to have that name or because the person themselves chose to have it. Being an Eacott does not always mean that they share the same genes. In fact only 8 or 10 generations back we share almost no genes to identify us as the same family. It is a tiny amount.

Humans arrive in the Cotswolds

The river Churn comes down from the escarpment of the Cotswold hills and flows through some fairly steep valleys to meet the Thames south of Cirencester, Gloucestershire. The area is known for its stone. Oolite limestone is a yellow grey rock much prized for its use in building. Along the river valley are soft deposits of Fuller's earth which was used to clean oil from wool. This may have been part of the attraction to settle the area.

During the upper Paleolithic times, the stone age, more than 200 thousand years ago there were 250 to 5000 people in Britain. In other words not very many. This increased a little during the Hunter Gatherer times to between 3 and 20 thousand people. There were modest increases in the Neolithic period, up to 40 thousand, and again doubling in the Bronze age to between 20 and 100 thousand. Finally the Iron age saw the population range anywhere from 50 to 500 thousand people. These early people whose height was under 5' 6" used hand axes and flint spears to kill rhinos and mammoths which roamed Britain.

Later on, Roman Britain had about 4 million people but the population dropped by the year 600 AD due to disease to under 2 million. There would not be 4 million people again in England until nearly 1700 AD.

Homes with hearths for fires were used 6000 years ago. At that time Avebury, Stonehenge, and Windmill Hill were built. Wiltshire and the Cotswolds were the most densely populated part of England. The soil in those areas was light and easily tilled. The inhabitants were the people who were there before the Eacott male ancestor arrived. Statistically these people would also be related to all who came after.

In Neolithic times, 3000 to 1700 BC, long mounds or barrows were built and used for collective burial sites. One exists at North Cerney. Another ancient site of a village exists at Woodmancote. Little is known of these people. A Neolithic mace head, "Thames Pestle" was found at Eycot Wood. It was made of polished green stone. (Now in Cheltenham Museum) The land has been farmed in some areas for 4000 years.

The Beaker folk, named so because they made clay beakers, arrived around 1900 BC from the Rhineland in Germany. Many arrowheads were found in their graves which indicated an unwelcome reception. The beaker folk were also noted for having quite round heads. Iron age people, Celtic tribes, began moving westward from Persia about 3000 BC and came to Britain around 500 BC. They arrived in the Churn valley about 150 BC. They established a pattern of square fields.

The Dobunni

The name derivation may come from a fertility goddess but that is speculative. They occupied a large area centered on Gloucestershire.

Around 25 BC an iron age group known generally as the Belgic people arrived. The local group around Bagendon/North Cerney were known as the Dobunni, Dubunni or Belgic Dobunni. These were a Celtic people. Another view is that the Dobunni were a dark haired people from Iberia having come from Spain or Portugal by way of Brittany. At any rate their territory was centered in Gloucestershire. The hill forts and pottery at Bagendon may link to these people known as Corosolites. The Dobunni coins carried the word Corio. The name Dobunni might in old Irish mean people with dark hair in contrast with the fairer celts or their name may or may not be derived from a fertility goddess. The Dobunni group set up a tribal capital at Bagendon and traded with France and Rome. The Eacott ancestor may have been in this group.

The Dobunni were fierce rivals of the Catuvellauni and seem to have lost some eastern territory to them shortly before the Roman invasion. Although they initially submitted to the Romans, their area was later rife with stubborn resistance to Roman rule and a legionary fortress was founded at Gloucester/Glevum. During Boadicea's Revolt the Roman commander here felt unable to bring his garrison to the aid of the hard-pressed Roman forces, which brought the Romans close to losing the whole island.

The Dobunni minted their own coins, one of the few groups to do so in England. They later appeared to have been pro Roman and readily accepted a role in the Empire. Their leader at the time of occupation was Bodvoc. About 10 AD Bagendon was established. A series of earthworks combined with a wooded scarp enclosed some 200 acres three miles north of Cirencester. It was an important center for trade in metalworking. The inhabitants lived in huts with stone floors and the walls were half timbered with wattle and daub walls. The roof was thatched. Glazed ware and glass were imported. This group had an alliance with other local tribes at

Salmonsbury and Bourton-on-the-Water which broke up about the time the Romans came. Within the next decade Bagendon was abandoned and the Roman camp of Cirencester was set up. Any person with an Eacott name may have genes connected back to these people since Eycot was adjacent to Bagendon.

The later Roman capital of the civitas was Cirencester/Corinium. This seems to have been a case of the Romans relocating a center from an earlier, easily defensible site, (in this case Bagendon, an Iron Age hillfort) to a more easily controlled lowland site, often retaining the old name. So the site represented is Bagendon, slightly altered to a more Keltic Bagendun.

The later Roman capital of the civitas was Cirencester/Corinium. However, this seems to have been a case of the Romans relocating a center from an earlier, easily defensible site, (in this case Bagendon,) to a more easily controlled lowland site, and retaining the old name.

The Romans

Roman armies and settlers came to the area between 43 and 49 AD. Aulus Plautius invaded the Cotswolds in 43 AD and at a large battle at the Dobunni tribe fortress, which was possibly Bagendon, defeated the locals. Later, nearby Cirencester became an important Roman town, the district capital for western Britain. A large number of wealthy Roman villas were established in the area. This area was prosperous and stable until well into the fifth century.

Cirencester started off as small *vicus* settlement, first outside, then within the defenses of the Roman fort which was built here in the early first-century. By the second century the town had expanded to become the largest in the province, in terms of population, with perhaps 12,000 inhabitants. The town was likely among those visited by the emperor Hadrian during his trip to Britain in the early second century and the tribal council marked his visit by building a *macellum* or covered market in the center of their principal city. In the third century *Corinium* was surpassed in size only by *Londinium* and covered in its heyday an area of 240 acres, its civic buildings and town houses being of an almost uniformly high standard and it also had an impressive amphitheater built outside the town defenses.

After the Roman military left, the civil center of the *Dobunni* expanded. New houses sprang up in a characteristic grid-pattern and the civilian population flourished. *Corinium* was located in an extremely favorable position in the highway system and soon became the center of the richest area of villa estates in Roman Britain with numerous villas within a few miles and several temples within a days journey. Within a ten mile radius of Cirencester there are ten known Romano-British villa's, a temple complex (Chedworth, Gloucestershire) and half a dozen substantial Roman buildings. The town owed its eminence to its development as a center of the wool trade, hosting a large market. In the fourth century the town probably became the seat of a provincial governor, attracting the wealthier class of citizen to the area which became famous around this period as a prominent center of the mosaic industry, helped no doubt by the plethora of rich villa estates in the neighborhood.

A Roman Christian word square was discovered at Cirencester and is thought to be from the second century making this one of the earliest known Christian sites in Britain.

We know that when the Roman army was removed from Britain the empire became more and more unstable and finally the island was invaded by the Saxons.

The Saxons

In 577 the Saxons from southern Denmark and nearby costal Germany, between the Elbe and Wesser rivers, invaded and captured the kingdom of Hwicce, a part of the kingdom of Mercia. Both of these ancient Teutonic people came as Aryan people from somewhere near ancient Persia. The valley of the Churn along with Cirencester was now also settled by the Saxons. Bagendon, Andoversford, and Withington all now became Saxon settlements. The British Celts were supposedly driven into Wales or forced into slavery. However the reality may be that there were not all that many Saxons, and while they ruled, the core of the population, according to recent research, remained mostly pre Saxon Britons. They didn't go anywhere. Since Eycote was in this area it seems likely it was also a Saxon vill. Saxon foundations, barns, and churches still survive in the area. Miserdene and Winstone churches, in the same area, have Anglo-Saxon features. Yet, genetically the main core of the people were probably still of Romano - Briton stock.

The Saxons Kinric and Ceawlin defeated the local Britons at

Beranbyrig which was possibly the river crossing at Perrot's Brook (see development of this name) near Bagendon. Thereafter the Saxons lived in peace here for over four hundred years. They became Christian and they set up local governments. The people of the Cotswolds in the year 700 were some of the 7,000 or so households in the lands of the South Saxons. In 750 the church diocese of Worcester centered at Malmsbury had ecclesiastical (religious) control of most of the area. Winchester diocese had control of some areas and the area around Cirencester itself was part of the Ramsbury diocese. Eycote was under the bishop of Worcester and at one time was owned by the bishop. In 680 AD the Bishop of Worcester was given his first See. (Area over which he had authority)

The Vikings briefly occupied the area, capturing Cirencester and held it for a year in the 800's, so they had little effect on the genetics of the area.

Eycote or Eugkote, a manor given under an ancient Saxon charter, likely traces back to the mid 800's or early 900's and probably came from the Bishop of Worcester. It was probably a deal the Bishop made with some landowner. To date the source has not been located.

About 1000 AD the common administrative unit was the hundred.[2] It was set up in 945 - 961 AD. It was a group of vills (Villagers) organized for defense purposes and to help each other out. The Saxons kept slaves but they also practiced a form of democracy since they elected their leaders. Once each month there was a meeting of the Hundred under the chairmanship of the hundred man. Eycote was in the center of Rapsgate Hundred and would normally be the meeting place for the hundred. However, at some time it was attached to Bibury hundred and so was not at all an important location.

The Normans

All the Saxon organization was swept away when William the Conqueror set up a feudal system and gave the lands to his followers. All the lords owed their allegiance to the king and lesser ranks owed allegiance to them. Slavery was done away with however very few people were actually free. Most had to perform duties for their lords. Most of the Saxon bishops were replaced by Frenchmen but the bishop of Worcester was not. He

---

[2] *See appendix D about hundreds*

retained his land holdings in the Cotswolds.

By the time of the Domesday census the Churn valley was fairly evenly populated with more people in the valleys than on the higher ground. There were a higher than usual numbers of slaves in the area. Twenty five per cent of the people were slaves when the Normans arrived.

The churches at Rendcomb, North and South Cerney, and Bagendon were early Norman churches. The 12 century church at Eycote was built at the same time but was later closed. At Domesday, 1086, Ulward was the Thane of Bagendon, and there were 5 yeomen and 5 slaves. Until 1792 there were still 5 freemen holdings. The land was in long narrow Saxon style strips until the enclosure of 1792.

At the time of Domesday 1086 there were 83 listed inhabitants between Eycot, Rendcomb, North Cerney and Bagendon. This figure more likely represents households. So there were between 200 and 300 people spread along three miles or so of the river valley.

An Imagined Account of the Collection of Domesday Records

See appendix "C"

Ordric was standing with a group of his neighbors in front of his manor house watching the approaching entourage come down the hill from Rendcomb. Flags were fluttering from the staves of the escort knights who were accompanying the commissioners of the king. It was the spring of 1086 and twenty years after the William and his army had occupied the land. Now the commissioners were coming to take a great census. None of those present were happy about this but this French king was not a man to be denied. The Domesday record was the source of a bitter joke. The English called it the doom and gloom book because it was clearly meant to help decide what taxes the king would demand. The penalty for not being truthful in reporting was high and the assembled Anglo Saxons and their French lords were resigned to dutifully answering the commissioners questions.

The call to Eycot had been sent and from Bagendon, North Cerney, Upper Rendcomb (Mardsden) and Lower Rendcomb the tenants had come to tell the king's men what they possessed. Fortunately the commissioners spoke the local language but conversed among themselves in French. Ordric saw they were writing in Latin as he recognized a few words. He wondered if they were making up what they were being told but his neighbor said no. He could understand the numbers. The knights took the horses over to the stream to water them while the agents began questioning Ordric.

"Whose land is this?" they asked.
"Mine" he said "I hold it from the Bishop of Worcester."
"And who held it when William became king."
" My father Alric from the Bishop"

He went on to explain he held other lands in other places but the agents only wanted details on Eycote. The commissioners wanted to know if Eugkote was the center of the local Rapsgate hundred as they expected but it was explained that the correct name was Eycote and it was part of the
Bibury hundred. The agents thought that surprising as they had thought otherwise.

"So what is it you have here?" Ordric was asked while the others listened. There was no point in fabricating as all could hear his answers and there was no way he could omit something because the agents would ask the next owner the same questions and he would be found out. However Ordric had cut a deal with the 3 riding men or Radmen to exclude their 4 hides as he had subleased the land to these fellows who lived at Rendcomb. Eycote was actually a 600 acre farm not a 120 acre one.

" I have 1 hide of land (about 120 acres) and own 2 ploughs and the oxen to pull them. These two are my yeoman villagers who each have 12 acres." He pointed them out and they nodded. "The villagers each have a team of oxen and a plough and they each had a slave to help them. There are also 4 small holders with their own cottages and a garden. We all share a meadow of 8 acres by the river which floods from time to time. You can see my mill over there." The commissioners made some discussion and valued the mill at 64 d, just over 5 shillings and considered the entire property had been improved since the takeover. The land was reasonably useful so they said it had been worth 20s and now was worth 30s. Did Ordric agree? He nodded.

The land while it had increased a third in value in 20 years was still less than a third the value of Rendcomb and only 15% the value of North Cerney. In all, North Cerney was 10 times more valuable than Eycott and Bagendon was 3 times more valuable. Eycott was a very modest possession of the bishop. The bishop was one of the few landowners not removed by the Normans so his ownership remained constant from 1066 to 1086.

One of the escort knights made a motion to the commissioners to speak. He said he was subletting two hides from Ordric and named two others who each had lease of Eycote land. All three lived at Rendcomb. After some discussion these hides were included with Rendcomb. These Radmen were persons who had a higher status than a villager. Originally they were escorts or messengers for the king. They were found on royal or church lands and were entitled to work their own holding free from the demands of the lord. They did have to give work to the lord but did not have to provide full military service.

While the discussion about what to do with the land of the Radmen was taking place another knight came riding down from Rendcomb. He was Gilbert, son of Thorold[3] and he was there to make his deposition. The conversation now was all in French and most of the neighbors did not understand the discussion. Gilbert however was a Norman and the king had awarded him part of North Cerney and Upper and Lower Rendcomb. He was

---

3

Land of Gilbert, son of Thorold (52)
In Rapsgate Hundred
North Cerney. 7 hides, 2 thanes - Elaf and his brother, held it as two manors and could go where they would.
In lordship Gilbert held 4 ploughs, 7 villagers, and 6 smallholders with 5 ploughs, 6 slaves; a mill at 8s; meadow, 6 acres; woodland 2 furlongs long and one wide. 4 of Gilberts men-at-arms with their men have 7 ploughs and a mill valued at 8s. Value of the whole manor before 1066 was 14 pounds now 12 pounds.

Rendcomb. 5 hides which pay tax. Aelfric held it. I lordship 1 plough; 3 villagers and seven smallholders with 3 ploughs. 7 slaves; a frenchman who holds the land of 2 villagers. 4 continued : A mill at 8s; meadow, 4 acres. The value was 7 pounds now 100s.

Rendcomb. Walter holds it from him (Gilbert). 3 hides which pay tax. In lordship 2 ploughs; 4 villagers, 3 small holders with 2 ploughs. 6 slaves; a mill at 5s; meadow 3 Acres. The value is and was 6 pounds

(Gilbert was also Gilbert of Bouille. North Cerney also included Calmsden and Woodmancote. Rendcomb was classed as Upper (later Marsden) and Lower (later Rendcomb)) Rendcomb in earlier times was also spelled Rendcombe.

the principal landlord in the area.

Bagendon which was in Cirencester hundred was under the lordship of Hugh Donkey but he had leased it to Gilbert of Thorold who in turn had leased it to the Saxon Wolfward. So most of the churn valley north of Cirencester was controlled by Gilbert but the actual farming was done by the Saxon tenants. The one exception in ownership was Eycote which belonged to the church.

The name Eycote was composed of two Saxon words The Ey stood for water or dry island in a marsh. The Saxons also used Ea and Eg interchangeably for water and/or island. A cote or cott was the Saxon word for a small shelter for sheep, animal or especially bird. In England it was also a small house or cottage. So the name most closely means a small house by the water.

Presumably the original Saxon charter was given to some Saxon thane or lord by the bishop for land that would be used to graze Cotswold sheep. The land by the river was flat and fertile and a small house was built which later evolved into a manor house. [4]

Through all of this time, century after century, the DNA of the family of the La Tene celt that would become Eycott remained in the vicinity of Cirencester and North Cerney and Bagendon. Everyone had names but the notion of a family name had ended with the Roman time. Now the Normans occupied England and surnames began to be used again. The same Normans were inclined to keep records and ancient documents piled up in storage for hundred of years.

~~~~~~~~~~~~~~~~

" It is not without pleasure, and perchance it may not be without use, that we rescue some quaint old document from the dust of ages; and that we arrest the floating memories of men and things, as they pass down the stream of time toward the ocean of oblivion"
- B.H. Blacker 1879

---

[4]

See appendix on the Eacott name.

Early Eycott/Eacott Locations

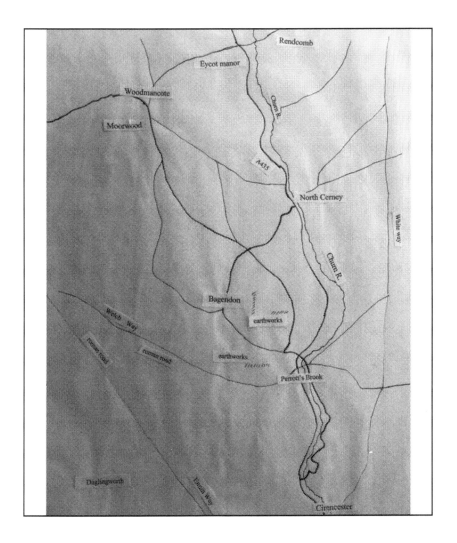

The First Identifiable Eycott

Two hundred years after the Domesday census we meet Simon de Eycote, an educated clerk who finds himself part of the action in one of the more unstable periods of English history. He is the first Eycote whose story has some supporting evidence although parts of his story are fiction based on fact.

Simon is working at the abbey of St. Mary in Cirencester, the same place where he was educated.

Simon wandered into the kitchen of the abbey to speak with the senior cook who was busy stuffing a duck to roast over the open fire. He greeted the cook in their native tongue. " Me thinketh it acordaunt to resoun to telle yew al the condicioun ....." The cook like most of those who worked at the abbey were not able to converse in French, the language of the educated, but could read material in the language that was becoming English, and to be truthful Simon was happier to use his native language when he could.

There were to be travelers for the night ..."was come into that hostelrye". Perkyn the cook was only half listening as his mind was on this new dish and he wanted the recipe correct. Simon leaned over to read the recipe. It was in the native language now becoming popular with even learned men.

"Stwed Beeff.
Take faire Ribbes of ffres beef, And (if thou wilt) roste hit til hit be nyg ynowe; then⁻ put hit in a faire possenet; caste þer-to parcely and oynons mynced, reysons of corauns, powder peper, canel, clowes, saundres, safferon⁻, and salt; then⁻ caste there-to wyn⁻ and a litull vynegre; sette a lyd on⁻ þe potte, and lete hit boile sokingly on a faire charcole til hit be ynog; þen⁻ lay the ffless, in disshes, and the sirippe there-vppon⁻, And serve it forth."
- A Boke of Gode Cookery

That looked simple enough. Beef of course would only be served to the higher ranks at the abbey. He inquired if the cook had all the needed ingredients as it was part of his job to see that the provisions were ordered and paid for. Perkyn said that his last request for supplies had included enough to last for some time. He knew Simon was the sort who would always verify his information.

Simon looked about for a bit of bread or a bowl of porridge for himself. He found some leftover pottage made of ground capon with almond milk and some pomegranate pips tossed on top. It was a cool April morning. " Aprille with his shoures soote," he remarked. It had been a cold long winter and the previous summer had been very hot and dry and the crops had suffered greatly. He hoped that this year would be more like the gentle green summers he remembered as a boy.

Simon had been born around the year 1284 to Roger de Eycote and his wife Agnes. [5] Roger had been educated at the abbey school in Cirencester[6] where Simon and his brothers had studied and where Simon was now working as clerk of provisions for the abbey. Like his father he had a talent for figures and a good organizational sense. Roger who was born at the manor of Eycote was a yeoman, a free man who lived at the manor as had his father and grandfather and presumable everyone of his ancestors since who knows when.

Eycote [7] was not a large manor and it held both bottom land along the churn river and the hillside pastures as well as some ancient woodland.

Roger had been able to increase his land on which he had a flock of magnificent Cotswold sheep. A series of good sales of wool had prompted him to engage in some other trading activities in Cirencester and some deals

---

5

.Roger may be the earliest known person with the Eycote surname. He is mentioned as the father of William. There are no other details about him. From the evidence of the later Eycotes there must have been a person or persons who might have resembled the person portrayed here. There is no evidence he is father of Simon. Simon is however, a real person. The recipe and speech is contemporary to the 1300's. The weather is from the best records of the time. From this point on there is a period of about 30 years where there are serious effects of the fluctuating bad weather including a mass famine.

6

Alexander Neckham a great scholar saw that the abbey school taught grammar, rhetoric, dialectic, music, arithmetic, geometry, astronomy and science. All cathedrals had schools by 1100 and taught in French.

[7] *Eycote manor and it's history is in the appendix "E"*

with Florentine and Flemish traders had enabled him to go into business as a wool merchant. At about this time he moved up the hill from Eycote and acquired some land by Woodmancote near where the roads from Bagendon and North Cerney converge. Simon and his brother William were born here.

At the market in Cirencester people had begun to call him Roger de Eycote as there was another merchant by the name of Roger as well and more importantly he needed to be better identified on the documents he was now signing with other merchants. Like the Norman lords who used surnames, Roger thought he needed to keep up with the times. His educated sons kept up the tradition. He was no lord but he was no simple peasant either. Learning to read and write and more importantly to study arithmetic, geometry, rhetoric, dialectic and grammar had proved most useful to him. Music and astronomy were not his best subjects but a new study of logic appealed to him. His father had sent him to the school attached to the Augustinian abbey at Cirencester because he had known Alexander Neckham, a very learned man of science who was abbot there from 1213 to 17. The headmaster he had appointed would do well for his son Roger. Roger had also made good use of the skills his father had taught him about raising sheep and tending the soil. He had become prosperous beyond his wildest dreams. From time to time he would say, " I praise God and ever shall, for it is the sheep hath paid for all".

As his fortune increased, he was able to gain other lands at Woodmancote, Bagendon and North Cerney as well at Bernham (Barnham) near Chichester. This land he left to his son William. William had used his education to good advantage. He had left Cirencester and worked with Bishop Gilbert and Henry de Gulford at Chichester. They had been his mentors. Both of these men had helped him gain a position at the St. Alban's abbey. The Abbott of St. Alban's was the senior cleric in all England and was the Pope's representative. It was a most prestigious abbey. The royal family frequently stopped by the abbey since they held a palace at nearby Langley. For many years William was the Seneschal or chief steward of the Abbey.[8] He was responsible for all the employees and for the overall management of the Abbey.

---

8 *Gesta abbatum monasterii Sancti Albani: A. D. 1349-1411: Introduction ...*
By Thomas Walsingham, Matthew Paris. He is listed as Senesechel under the Abbott
Thomas de la Mare.

William had little time to attend to his land holdings at Barnham. So on July 2nd of 1324 he decided to give land and a house to the parish church at Barnham for the use of a chaplain on the condition the chaplain was to celebrate divine service daily and pray for the souls of William himself, his dead wives Maud and Cicely, his father Roger and mother Agnes and his benefactors Bishop Gilbert and Henry de Gulford.[9]

It was through his brother that Simon, who had his mind set on following a similar career, went on a visit to St. Albans on Wednesday, December 13, 1290. King Edward's queen, Eleanor of Castile had died in the north of England and a huge funeral cortege was slowly making its way to London. Her body rested at St. Albans because she had property near there and visited the abbey often. She was well known by the staff. William had recently obtained a position at the abbey so did not know the royal family at all. Roger had taken Simon to witness the procession and William had arranged for them to stay on the premises. During this event Simon age 6 met another 6 year old who was eager to have a playmate. The young Edward had broken away from all his sisters to play tag with Simon. Together the two boys explored the abbey and discovered some common interests. It would be another generation before they met again but the memories had been made and the King had need of people he liked to work for him.[10]

---

[9]

„Also in 1324, William de Eycote has this patent roll recorded on July 2nd.
Licence for the alienation in mortmain (to give land to church) by William de Eycote of a messuage, 17 acres of land, 3 acres of meadow, 10s. Id. of rent and pasture for one plough beast (afrum) and 2 oxen in Bernham and Walburton to a chaplain to celebrate divine service daily in the parish church of Bernham for the souls of the said William, Maud and Cicely sometime his wives, Roger his father, Agnes his mother, Gilbert, sometime bishop of Chichester, Henry de Guldeford and all the faithful departed. (Bernham (Barnham) and Walburton are just east of Chichester. A Psalter of 1300 from Chichester has notes of obits of 3 Cirencester men.
Roger de Eycote, Williams father Roger may actually be the earliest known Eycote likely born around 1260-70. We do not know if he was related to Simon. It is not clear why Gilbert bishop of Chichester who died 1305 (likely born in France) and Henry de Gulford, appointed justice in 1305, are remembered in this gift. There is no evidence this is the same William who the story makes as Simon's brother nor is there any evidence to prove he is the same person as the Seneschal. In fact the seneschal tenure is known to exist in 1349. We can conjecture him born about 1275.

[10]

This is a fictitious meeting but the funeral was a big event and Edward was a curious person described as being interested in the work skills of the common folk and enjoying rowing and swimming. He also had his allowance terminated as described.

Simon left Perkyn and went to find the abbot to learn more about the expected visitor. The visitor and a friend and a small retinue had already arrived and were having their horses attended. Simon recognized this event as something important and as he approached he realized it was the crown prince. What was he doing here? Royalty never came to Cirencester without a huge entourage and ample warning. In this instance Simon was to learn that the prince and his followers had been banned from the kings court and that he had his funds cut off. The prince needed to make amends and was consulting with the abbot, who was friends with Bishop Langton the royal treasurer, about ways he might apologize to the bishop with whom he had an altercation over his living allowance. The prince needed to get back into his father's good graces. Simon standing nearby, as the party spoke to the abbot, wondered if the prince would recall their previous encounter. He wondered if he would even get to speak with the prince.

The prince had been rowing on the Thames and was now interested in seeing some famous Cotswold sheep being sheared and perhaps try his hand at it himself. Although it was not shearing season, exceptions could be made. The abbot knew Simon had been raised on the land and called him over to meet the prince. He observed that they were very similar young men , strong, witty, with sharp minds. The new junior official at the abbey had the opportunity to speak of their earlier meeting which the prince definitely remembered. Soon they were off like old friends to try their hand at shearing sheep.

With the passage of time Edward went on to become king and Simon gained a reputation of being a clever and capable clerk able to deal with all manner of issues at the abbey. Some of these tested his allegiance. The old abbot Henry had sent out his bailiffs in the fall of 1305 to break into the homes of several men in Cirencester and take or destroy their illegal millstones which they were using to grind grain that was supposed by right to be ground at the abbey mill. Simon personally knew many of these men and empathized with them and he thought the abbot to be a vindictive arrogant old man. However Simon was principled enough to keep his mouth shut and when the people complained, he knew he did not have any authority other than to remind them of the law that said the abbey had the right to demand all grain be milled there. If they did not like the law, then they should approach the king. The towns people knew Simon could do nothing for them but he was local and even though the relationship with the abbey was usually pretty terse Simon was someone to whom they could express their feelings. The town wished to be free of the control of the abbey and this was just another vexatious incident although an expensive one since the illegal millstones cost them a substantial fine of 100 marks. The abbot duly noted the young man's circumspect, shrewd and loyal behavior and considered that he would go far in life.

Edward became king in 1307, a job Simon knew he did not particularly want. The next year Edward was pushed into a political marriage with a 12 year old. The barons did not like the kings friends, nor did they much like Edward. Edward was no military leader and in 1314 Robert the Bruce of Scotland soundly defeated his army. England was a political mess and to make matters worse the crops were not what they used to be.

Simon gave a lot of thought to an offer he had been given by a personal courier of the king. He had a good career and did not need to make any changes in his life. Still he considered the king a friend and one who could use someone as loyal as himself. The king seemed to need all the friends he could get. Simon accepted the offer to become the kings clerk.

The spring of 1315 was cold and wet. The rain never seemed to stop. Worse it kept raining all summer long and the wheat could not be planted and what was planted went moldy. The hay rotted, the sheep caught murrain and the salt could not be harvested because the pans would not evaporate. As a result meat could not be cured. In August the king himself went hungry as there was no bread to be had when he visited St Albans on August 10th. By September it was clear that there would be no bread anywhere as the warehouses, having suffered from other recent poor crops, had no reserves. The coming winter was going to be very hard on everyone. Simon and everyone at court knew it. The faces of people showed the strain as the awareness sunk in that many would not be alive in the spring. A great famine swept the land and 10% of the population died. Draft cattle were butchered, seed grain eaten, children were abandoned and old people refused food. The next three years were not much better as the rains continued and famine was everywhere. However Simon had used his skills and business connections to keep the royal court fed. It was not until 1325 that food supplies returned to normal.

The chapel at Woodmancote built in Chapel Field had fallen into disuse and needed major repairs. No one was available to do the work and there just were not enough people there to keep it open. Simon arranged for the North Cerney Church to get some of the material from the chapel which was made into a part of the churchyard cross at North Cerney. The wheel cross was given to Bagendon church where it was placed on the vestry. Many of the children had died in the famine and food was so scarce that no one had any energy to do the work needed to keep the farms going. Discouraged tenants could no longer pay their rents. One bad crop simply led to another and another. This disaster was something no one could remember ever happening before.

The northern part of the kingdom was being harassed by the Scots and Edward's barons there were untrustworthy. Edward needed some astute person to be his eyes and ears in the north. When the Bishop of Durham died, the Sea being vacant, Edward saw an opportunity to act as the Bishop and increase his own power. He called on Simon to become the new master of the Hospital of St. Giles at Kepier near Durham effective Oct 17, 1316. The incumbent master Hugh de Montalto was displaced and made a clerk of the royal court. A job swap.

The mandate of this appointment [11]was made to the brethren and sisters of the hospital. There never seemed to be any sisters attached to the place. Hospital had a different meaning in those days. It was essentially a place for the poor, an almshouse and sometimes a hotel for pilgrims going to Durham Cathedral. It resembled a monastery as it was self contained. There were 13 brothers and a master. Six of them were chaplains. The chaplains each got 2 new boots each year the others got 1 pair of shoes with thongs. The accommodations were not very good but the queen had stayed there a few years before Simon had his appointment. Isabella, the queen left a 20 pound gift to pay for her nights lodging and support the refurbishing of the place.

These were nervous times to get such an appointment as in the months before he took over, their lands had been raided by Scots who claimed the area as part of Scotland. Robert the Bruce's men has trashed the hospital. At any time Simon was apt to be attacked. The hospital was founded and funded by Bishop Flambard in 1112. The hospital held substantial lands before it was closed in 1546 by Henry VIII when he dissolved the monasteries. The master was exempted from some church duties as his main

---

[11]

See appendix B, http://www.british-history.ac.uk/vch/durham/vol2/pp111-114

focus was management and not ecclesiastical duties. Simon ruled over the hospital for 4 years at which time the appointment was withdrawn and Montalto was reinstated. At the same time Montalto gave Simon £10 worth of land in Amerston, Harworth and elsewhere as some sort of compensation. Simon returned to the King's court.

On his return he found the political situation to be even more chaotic than when he was Master. Of course he knew all this but still to be back in the court was to be involved in all the ever mounting intrigue.

After the routing of his army by Robert the Bruce in 1314 Edward had his hands full with the barons and he was still looking for ways to avenge the killing of his friend Gaveston by Earl Lancaster. Lancaster had himself placed as head of the Royal Council in 1316 and was pushing for greater enforcement of the ordinances of 1311 which put strong controls on the king. For two years the King and Lancaster had been at an impasse in running the country. A treaty in 1318 was supposed to clear that up. In addition the royal court was busy trying to requisition enough food to feed itself and the army Edward raised in 1319 to chase Bruce and his Scottish raiders out of England where they had come as far south as York. His army was suffering from malnutrition. On the plus side Edward's general had defeated Edward Bruce, brother of Robert, who had tried to establish himself as king of Ireland. The compromise with Lancaster falls apart and by 1321 the barons were after Edward's key supporters the Despensers family. Civil war erupts and in May 1321 the Despencers are captured and the king, fearing being deposed, is forced to agree to their exile. Edward then forms a small coalition of his half brothers, some earls and some senior clergy and goes after Lancaster who he captures and executes on March 10 1322. During this entire period of time the country is under extreme stress due to the famine[12] and people are attacking each other for food and stealing animals and crops and timber. A disease among horses creates a huge die off of these animals. The government was too distracted and totally unable to deal with the collapsing society. The King needed help.

12

The winter of 1305/6 was very severe; in 1309/10 the Thames froze over at London and people were dancing on the ice; 1314/6 were very wet years and the crops failed, over ½ million died of famine;1315 there were no crops; 1320 was another cold wet summer with no harvest; after 1324 the weather began to warm. Centuries later it was established that a series of volcanic explosions created this cold period.

During the turmoil of 1318 and 1319 Simon is called upon to come to the aid of the king. Simon has been called away from St. Giles. During late 1318 through late 1319 the Scots had been raiding northern England while Edward was trying to deal with the Earl of Lancaster and his allies. There are essentially 2 parties at war with the king. Lancaster is refusing to help the king against the Scots. The queen is nearly captured at York and the angry Bishop of York organizes his own army of clerics to chase the Scots. These men are not soldiers, poor fighters, and at the battle of Myton Sept. 10 1319 a great many clerics of England are killed. Simon has been issued a letter of protection on April 25, 1319 which is good until Michaelmas (sept 29). He is given security from a wide range of legal actions which might be due to his engaging in acts of war. Clearly Simon is expected to go fight for the king. On July 20 a great many clerics are called to defend the king. Clerics were normally exempt from fighting but the situation was dire. Simon reports for duty and survives the humiliating defeat. He and the Bishop of York and others are routed and chased back across the river getting well soaked but saving their necks while others are slaughtered by the Scots. Simon thought the whole enterprise was foolish but somebody had to stand up to the Scottish raiders. Simon is a priestly cleric and manager not a fighter but he has gone to defend his king.

The king must now be aware of Simon's loyalty because he is now selected to be a member of the king's personal party of 26 going with the king on a planned trip to Ireland. He is listed as Simon de Eycote, clerk. A John Hacluyt also went and either a second Simon de Eycote or a repeat of this Simon is listed as part of the royal party.

Feb 23, 1320 Westminster. The king accompanied by his brother Edmund of Wodestok, the Earl of Richmond, each of whom is with their named parties in addition the king also has his own personal party of knights to accompany him.[13] The names are listed below.

13

Persons going with the king to Ireland.
John de Chisenhale, clerk, William de Tilkhull (sic,) clerk, John de Sancto Albano, John Sperman
William le Baud, Richard Lovel, Roger de Sancto Albano, John Jolif, Thomas Cokliko, Walter de Wytheresfeld, Robert Romayn, William de London, Simon de Eycote, clerk, John Hacluyt, John de Knotingle, William de la Legh, Thomas Hobbode, John de Caiieford, Laurence de Elmhame,
William de la Chaumbre, Thomas de Derby, Philip Dewias, Henry de Pennebruge, Hamo Quarel

This trip never actually took place as events that year moved quickly. The king was at the palace of Westminster but headed off to Canterbury and then circled to Rochester but ended up at Eltham before going back to Westminster briefly before being on the move again. Wherever the king was the government was and so was Simon. The king's entourage always included his personal knights and several officials such as Simon. Tents, cooking gear, cooks, horse grooms and assorted other help went on these perpetual travels. The king was hardly in any spot for more than a few days, except at York or Westminster. It was not a life for a homebody and the king was not only restless but afflicted with too many emotions in an ongoing state of anxiety. Simon no sooner gets back to St.Giles when on June 5th 1320 he is called back to Westminster.

He departs St. Giles and hurries to London only to find the king is as usual elsewhere. Simon is surprised to learn that he will accompany the king on a journey to France with the senior dignitaries of England each of whom have their own entourage. The logistics of these operations is huge. Every movement is that of an army constantly on the march. Simon is to be in the kings personal party as one of 19 intimates of the monarch. The purpose of the journey to France with Isabella his wife is to convince her brother to give help. He has recently become King Philip V. Edward owes fealty to the French king but has been loathe to give it. Now it is politically necessary as he needs support for his cause to help reign in his rebellious nobles. Simon learns the former master of St. Giles will be returning to his old post as the king wishes Simon to be at the palace for other duties. But first it's a trip to France. On June 18th 1320 the royal party departs Dover for France. Simon will be attending events at the court of Philip V. It's no holiday but Simon is spared the need to find food to keep the hospital operating and the french court at Amiens is a lavish place to spend some time. He is able to socialize with a celebrated company of dignitaries and learned men and take part in a major medieval pageant. Over one of the banquets he learns that the Bishop of Norwich intends to put a clock in the new cathedral tower being built at Norwich. Such a thing had never been done before but Simon thought it an excellent idea even though he had never seen a clock. The royal party is back in England on July 20 but proceeds to various places including Stratford before being ceremoniously welcomed back at Westminster by the Lord Mayor of London and citizens dressed in

---

Oliver de Burdegala, Simon de Eycote, Richard de Hale. (Patent Rolls, Edward II vol 3 p 419)

their appropriate clothes of office who turn out to greet and welcome Edward and Isabella and the entourage back on the 2nd of August.[14]

Although Simon has been Master of St. Giles since 1316, he has spent a lot of time away from the hospital. His position of master is surrendered on November 22, 1320.

Simon is now back at the palace in Westminster where in addition to official clerks duties he has been engaged in a profitable side business of loaning money to knights who have had financial difficulties. Unfortunately not all were able to meet their obligations to Simon who was forced to haul some into court.

Nov 24, 1320 Simon is at Westminster where in court John de Denum and Roger de Esse owe Simon de Eycott, clerk, £ 100 and John owes another £ 10 which they had to pay or forfeit some of their lands. [15] The matter was however resolved when they paid up.

Things have not gone well across England as another bad summer has ruined the crops once again and provisioning the army has been a problem. Simon is put to work once again to find provisions.

Simon continues in his whirlwind travels with the king who is almost always with the army these days. The lands of the Despensers, his key allies, are seized by Lancaster. The Earl demands reform, fearing he may be deposed. Edward agrees to banish the Despensers. The opposition occupies London and the Royal court is more or less on the run. Simon wonders how

---

14

These are the people who personally accompanied the king to France; Richard Pilk; Isambert de Langa Villa, dean of Thameworth; William le Harpour; John de Rythyr; Nenry de Braundeston; John de Grey; William de Cressy; William de Boteler; Richard de Lusteshull; John son of Robert Pecock, the elder;John Sturmy; Simon deEycote, master of Hospital of St Giles, kypier vacated because of otherwise below.; William de Monte Acuto; master John de Strulford, archdeacon of Lincoln;John Hakelute; William de Herlaston, parson of Ibestok; Donald de Mar; Bartram de Mounborcher; Hugh le Despencer, the younger and his 2 aides; Also the Earl of Richmond; the Bishop of Norwich, chancellor; Archdeacon of Middlesex, Robert Baldok; The Bishop of Exeter.

15

Calendar of the Close Rolls Preserved in the Public Record Office By England. Court of Chancery, Edward ll pg 343

he got mixed up in all of this. The king simply can not keep his friends around without the barons objecting to anything poor Edward does. Simon is quite uncomfortable and concerned for his own welfare. All through 1321 Edward has faced nothing but misery. Walter de Stapleton has been appointed Lord High Treasurer. He has many good ideas and works well with Simon but it takes the king to implement things if he ever would or could. The king is all but on the run for his life. Christmas of 1321 is spent at Cirencester. After marching from Purton they camp and from Dec 20 to 28 Simon is able to spend time with his family who he seldom sees. His children are growing up. Many of those he has known have died or suffered greatly. There are very few people now at Eycot manor and Woodmancote. He meets with Margery LeBrun who he knew as the daughter of John Rusell lord of the Eycote manor and his friend Thomas Neel of Purton who describe how difficult the past several years have been. [16]

The King has been reorganizing and setting plans. He organizes a small core of supporters, his half brothers, and some senior clergy and in the spring of 1322 Edward has two rapid successes in March. The Earl of Hereford is killed and the Earl of Lancaster is captured and quickly executed.

In anticipation of victory in his efforts the newly energized Edward has given instruction to Simon and a sum of money to find food and necessities for the Marshalsea prison where Edward has been putting those whom he has recently arrested in his drive to control England. The money is to come directly from the king's funds and not from parliament. [17] Simon is in effect the jailer of the royals who have been rounded up and those who have

---

[16]

See appendix on Ownership of Eycot.

[17]

Then Feb 16 1322 at Gloucester the king has provided a writ of aid for one year to Simon.
"The like for one year to Simon de Eycote, king's clerk, whom the king is sending to purvey necessaries for the Marshalsea of the Household, to be paid for in the Wardrobe" by bill of the Wardrobe. (Patent Rolls, Edward II , vol 4, p 71) At this point the King is about to be victorious over the Duke of Lancaster in battle and confiscates the dukes wealth. The Wardrobe traveled with the king and administered the royal expenditures. The Keeper of the Wardrobe had 2 deputies, the controller and the cofferer. The exchequer was in the state apparatus with parliament.

committed crimes as employees of the royal court. These people, being important, will be needing special treatment. This is no problem for Simon since he is an experienced manager. The king's liberal purse will also mean some extra money left over for Simon if he manages things well. For now it's only for a year but it may continue.

Over the summer Edward has an unfavorable battle again with the Scots. He sues for peace and that year the crops are finally better. England has suffered greatly.

During 1323 there are improvements in the situation. De Stapleton has reorganized the treasury, the government records and financial rolls. Simon finally feels he has been able to contribute to some important improvements. He likes working with Walter de Stapleton. New subsidy tax rolls will be implemented once things settle down.

In 1324 Simon continues his loans business and collects. Richard de Perers, a knight, owed Simon 40m (Marks) and Simon sued him to get it back. (A Chancery Inquisition record.)

1326 is a year Simon wants to forget. In September Isabella lands in England with an army. She has had it with Edward and has lined up help to go after him. On October 15 Simon's friend, the treasurer, Walter de Stapleton is murdered and Simon fears for his own life. Stapleton, the Bishop of Exeter, had founded Exeter college at Oxford and rebuilt the cathedral. Such a great man torn down. In November the king is captured and Simon jumps ship and heads back to Woodmancote. What was to become of him? The King abdicates in January and rioters attack St. Alban's abbey.

On January 20, Edward II was informed at Kenilworth Castle of the charges brought against him. The King was guilty of: *"Incompetence; allowing others to govern him to the detriment of the people and Church; not listening to good advice and pursuing occupations unbecoming to a monarch; having lost Scotland and lands in Gascony and Ireland through failure of effective governance; damaging the Church, and imprisoning its representatives; allowing nobles to be killed, disinherited, imprisoned and exiled; failing to ensure fair justice, instead governing for profit and allowing others to do likewise; and of fleeing in the company of a notorious enemy of the realm, leaving it without government, and thereby losing the faith and trust of his people."* Edward, profoundly shocked by this judgment, wept whilst listening. He was then offered a choice: he might abdicate in favour of his son or he might resist. The King, lamenting that his people had so hated his rule, agreed that if the people would accept his son, he would abdicate in his favour. The lords, through the person of Sir William Trussel, then renounced their homage to him and the reign of Edward II was ended by himself.

On March 27th 1327 [18]under the rule of queen Isabella acting for her minor son Edward III, there was a rush of charges laid against many people who were believed to be supporters of the former king. These charges were designed to take the supporters of the king out of circulation and as a result Simon and 10 others were charged with stealing. Edward II was no longer king so his supporters who had been under his protection were left to fend for themselves. His troops still acted as they had before in supplying themselves with victuals and firewood which were obtained by night raids on previously identified properties. Suddenly these actions were no longer legal and the owners wanted restitution so it's a toss up whether anything was actually taken or not. What makes the complaint seem to have no substance is the positions of the people charged. Oliver was a wool tax collector for the king, Richard Foxcote was Sheriff of Gloucester, Anneford was bailiff of Cirencester, Broughton was a clerk and lawyer and Simon a clerk.

A three man commission was appointed to look into the "complaint of Robert de Ruyton, parson of the church of Duntisbourne that Stephen Dunheved, Simone de Eycote, Robert Oliver, Richard de Foxcote, Thomas de Foxcote, John Le Marescal, Roger Somer of Cirencester, Walter de Anneford, John le Carter, James de Broghton, and others took away five horses, six oxen, two cows, a hundred sheep and fifty two swine of his worth 40*l* at Duntisbourne co. Gloucester, felled his trees there, and carried

---

18

http://sdrc.lib.uiowa.edu/patentrolls/e3v1/body/Edward3vol1page0080.pdf
March 2. Westminster
The like to John de Annesle, Elias de Godele and Peter Fiz Waryn, on complaint by Robert de Ruyton, parson of the church of Duntesbourn, that Stephen Dunheved, Simon de Eycote, Robert Oliver, Richard de Foxcote, Thomas de Foxcote, John le Marescal, Roger Somer of Cirencestr', Walterde Anneford, John le Carter, James de Broghton, and others, took away fivehorses, six oxen, two cows, a hundred sheep and fifty-two swine of his,worth 40l., at Duntesbourn, co. Gloucester, felled his trees there, andcarried them away with other goods.

them away with other goods." Richard Foxcote was sheriff of Gloucester and remained so later in life. Stephen Dunheved was lord of the manor of Dunchurch and brother of Thomas who was a Dominican friar and the king's valet. The Dunheveds organized a rescue attempt to free the detained ex king from captivity at Berkeley Castle in September. Was Simon part of this plot? Thomas was imprisoned for life. The problem was there was a new king and new rules. Bishops, Sheriffs and others of high rank were being accused of being common thieves. The new regime had the opportunity to bring these people over to their side by using the commissions that investigated to decide on these cases. The laws of England were being used ahead of the right of the king. Not much likely came of these charges since the knight in charge of the investigation John Annesley knew many of the people who came before his commission and realized the objective was to silence Edward's supporters.

What happened to Simon we do not know. Was he simply detained for a time and let go? Or not even that. Had he been imprisoned or fined there would likely have been a record. There is no further information specifically about him. For more than 10 years he served the unfortunate king, Edward II. Edward met an unenviable fate. He was " sleyne with a hoote broche putte thrro the secret place posteriale". Fortunately, it appears Simon may simply have retired from public life. However his family remained influential at Cirencester.

In 1327 Eycot had a population of 8, 5 of them were freemen, (likely 8 male adults) and 12 in 1381. (Subsidy Roles for Cirencester, Bagendon, Woodmancote 1327, 1381) A few people were still there in 1442 the last time a record existed for Eycote. The plague arrived in 1348-49. The Black Death spread quickly all over England. The death toll was very high. Two rectors of North Cerney church died from it in 1348. A huge depopulation took place and many farms were abandoned. The economy collapsed and the survivors of the plague, which came repeatedly over the next half century, were in no position to engage in trade. The poor marginal lands were no longer farmed. There was no one to buy the crops. The plague struck badly in 1348-49, 1361, 1369 and with lesser outbreaks every few years until 1480 when a severe outbreak reduced the population to less than half what it had been in 1348. The population did not recover to the pre plague level until 1600. Peasant farmers who survived increased the size of their farms from an average of 12 to 30 acres. They also became more prosperous as the demand for their skills increased. The Eacotts who survived the Black Death may have been from only one family. The village of Eycote, not on the best land was abandoned. The church was destroyed and the stone cross from it was relocated to North Cerney churchyard.

Johannem De Eycote, Merchant of Cirencester

Johannem De Eycote, more familiarly known as John, was engaged in an interesting conversation with the scribe who had been to Westminster and seen the documents.

"A Saxon charter was it?" John had said. There was much to remind John that the Romans had lived here and the Saxons as well. The great Norman King William the Conqueror had collected a vast amount of important tax information known as the Domesday book. That's why John had asked the scribe to go to London. He wanted some background so he could understand his new position better.

The manor of Eugkote or Eycot from which all Eacotts, Ecotts etc. take their name[19] was created by a Saxon charter nearly 1,300 years ago at a place which had probably been a Roman villa. Even before that the land was part of the capital area of the pre Roman Dobunni tribe which was located on the banks of the Churn River near Bagendon,[20]

19

Eldon Smith in " New Dictionary of American Family Names" 1973 says that Eacott means "Dweller in a cottage by the river" Old records show EA and EY interchangeable in the name. This was possible in Old English because EA, EY, and EG all refer to water in some manner and the use does not change the meaning.

20

Like other names the Eacott name evolved over hundreds of years. It was the product of the whims of the spelling of the writer and the perceived accent of the speaker in the days before spelling was regularized. This is the record of how the name evolved. The earliest record of the name is in the form of EUGKOTE. In a manuscript of Worcester (Hemming's Cartulary) from the late 11th century the name of the manor now known as Eycott is recorded as EUGKOTE. That name was given to an area granted in a Saxon charter from the late 800's to early- mid 900's which was identified later as the same place as Eycott. The Anglo Saxon charter was in effect a deed of a parcel of land to someone. The charter was in a book. Anglo Saxon land was either "Bookland" recorded in a book or "Volkland" which was common land held by the people. Since it is recorded in a book of the Bishop of Worcester it may be assumed the church granted the original charter. The church could do this because the Bishopric of Worcester

Most of this information was not known to John but no matter. The Domesday records would help John understand his new roll. John was now a tax collector for King Edward III. Only a wealthy man, usually a merchant, would be entrusted with this job.

It had been nearly 250 years since Domesday and much had changed. As John studied the scribe's information he wondered if he was related to Ordric or Alric who had held the manor of Ecote.

He learned that at Domesday there were 2 villagers, 4 small holders or 2 slaves living at Aicote. The Bishop of Worcester owned the Manor of Eycote. Alternatively it could have been Ordric and or Alric who sub let from the church. Alric however controlled other lands, some presumably more desirable. Perhaps, John reasoned, his ancestor was one of the 2 villagers.

These villagers were likely descendants of long settled families with genetic ties to Saxons, Romano- British, and Celtic ancestors.

At the time of Domesday there were 367 settlements in Gloucester. Eyot or Eycott, or Eycote or Aicote or Eugkote was one. There were about 8,000 people in Gloucester. In the Churn valley the population was relatively high at 10 per square mile. John had realized that in his grandfathers time there had been many more people in the area but the previous 25 years had seen many properties abandoned as so many had died. Things these day were fortunately a lot better and his wool trade was really prospering.

John turned his interest to the subsidy roll information from 1327. Simon had told him that the old king had planned to implement these tax documents.

---

extended back as far as the 600's. The bishops were inclined to pass out charters for small estates so that the lessee would be available to help the bishop in case he needed to defend the church lands.

Eycot thus was an ancient manor along the river Churn in the county of Gloucester, England. It was recorded in the great census ordered by William the Conqueror in 1086 AD. The name was then recorded as Aicote. However for many centuries since the

location has been known as Eycot. The name has identifiable Saxon roots.

In 1327, the following persons were listed for Eycote as being on the subsidy roll: John Acton, Richard Walker, Richard Geffrey, Richard Cave, Simon Dauwe, Agnet Drois, Richard Page, Richard Dygon. There were no Eycotts. The Subsidy Roll of 1327 was a poll tax to raise money from people who might have some. It is about the earliest document to record surnames so as to identify people. There were 8 adult male persons at Eycott. Only reasonably well off adult males, yeomen, clothiers, craftsmen, merchants and others of some wealth would be on the roles. The Eycott name occurs only in North Cerney and Cirencester in that year. No variants on the name existed in England. There were also 7 taxpayers at Woodmancote in 1327.

John had read enough background for now.

He needed to get back to North Cerney and see how the sheep were being sheared. As a wool merchant he wanted to be sure his wool was clean, dry and properly bailed. He wanted to maintain the quality for which he and the other guild members had become renowned. With negotiating the future sale of his crop he hoped to do better than 12 marks for a sack of his best wool.[21] The upcoming fair at Cirencester would see merchants from Flanders, Florence, Venice and several places in France. Cotswold wool was premiere quality and demanded top money. He and the other guild members wanted to keep it that way. John was a leading merchant in Cirencester and by any standards a wealthy middle class yeoman. Apart from his wool trading he was able to deal with the Florence merchants in gold florins and found that money lending in gold was a profitable sideline. During the early years of the Hundred Years War in the 1330's and 40's great fortunes were made and lost. Some was due to the collapse of the Florence financial system and some was due to opportunities to make money off of the king by financing his war spending and providing for his army. It appears that John was one of those whose fortunes soared and then waned.

Now that he was one of three commissioners elected or appointed to collect taxes for the king he was anxious to compare notes with Richard Skarnynge and Rico Dyeare the other local commissioners. While John was

---

21

In 1318 wool sold for 11 ½ marks a sack. In 1381 ten Cirencester wool merchants sold wool to Florence Italy. The weavers fraternity funded a hospital for poorer members. Two fairs a year and two markets a week were held in Cirencester. Cirencester had been a wool town since Roman times.

not considered the wealthiest man in Cirencester in the year 1330, he was pretty well off. As tax collector he had to pay a nominal 12d for his own taxes. Luke Chapman the wealthiest merchant had to pay 3s 1d. Fewer than 100 people in the town whose adult male population was around 600 had to pay any taxes. These wealthy men, educated at the local abbey, had developed a work ethic and were among the earliest industrial capitalists in Britain. The Cirencester weavers had power and influence. King Edward III had engaged in some serious warfare with France and the royal treasury was in need of all the cash it could raise.

The king decided to call in his Cirencester tax collectors. Our John, Johannes de Eycote of the town of Cirencester, was called to the King Edward III's parliament at Westminster on 26th September 1337 as the representative of the town to advise the king on tax matters.[22] The idea was to find ways of getting more taxes out of the 600 or so adults who lived in Cirencester.

Meanwhile back in Cirencester the prospering townsfolk were once again distressed over the power of the local abbot who in effect owned most of the town and insisted on collecting all the taxes he could from the fairs and the ownership of buildings in the town. The burgesses of Cirencester wanted a free town with its own charter and to not be beholden to the abbey.

Early in 1342, (Jan 28) John de Eycote, collector of wool taxes, was with others accused of negligence as they had hitherto levied little or nothing on the wool and were not considering the king's needs. He was given until March to answer or have his lands forfeited. This accusation led directly to the following petition.

In 1342 Johannem de Eycote was a signer of a petition to King Edward III on 15 March 1342 given at parliament at Westminster. This information comes from documents of the Abbey at Cirencester known as the Cartulary of Cirencester. The records of the Cirencester Abbey began in 1131 and

---

22

Commune Country and Commonwealth: the people of Cirencester 1117-1643
"Town of Cirencester accordingly elected John de Eycote, Richard de
Skarnyngge, and Richard le Dyere. They were not however Members
of Parliament, but merely merchants or prominent burgesses summoned
to advise with the King upon special matters in Parliament."

ended in 1539 and were in Latin or French.

Sometime during 1169 King Richard gave the Abbey considerable land holdings. In the 1200's the Abbey made deals with others holding land in the vicinity to come before the Cirencester court for a fee. Both the king and the church held courts. Both wanted the tax money.

In the 1300's a bitter dispute broke out between the townsmen and the church officials which eventually involved the king. The town was a prosperous wool trading center and the abbot got involved with taxing the wool trade and claimed the right of tallege over his tenants whenever the king himself levied a tallege. In 1214 the barons compelled king John to recognize that he could not take tallege in Cirencester because it was the right of the church to do so. By 1312 the king was again taking tallege and so was the church. So double taxes were collected. The townsmen got the king to charge the abbot with wrongly collecting the tallege. The matter was resolved after discussion in Parliament and the king, Edward II, backed off. He recognized the church's claim on the land.

However, the controversy between the townspeople and the church continued. The townsmen wanted to have a measure of self rule and argued that the church had never legally been entitled to own the town. In 1342 resentment broke out and a group of men drew up a petition to take to the king. At first they appealed to his own self interest by suggesting that past and present abbots had wrongfully taken revenues belonging to the king. They also accused the abbot of moral turpitude and malversation of endowment intended for the poor.

The dispute with the Abbott of St. Marys with the prosperous wool men of Cirencester who wanted a guild was a standoff because the abbot did not need to borrow funds from them as did the king so the merchants were not able to force him to grant a charter giving them a mayor and council. They were a wealthy group and had various land holdings. The Weavers obtained Bagendon for a brief time but turned the church holding over to the control of the church at Cirencester. Johannem de Eycote was one of the guild.

In a revision these charges were dropped and 42 townsmen including Johannem de Eycote were called before the king and council. The main purpose of their complaint was to make the point that the abbot had suppressed the borough and had illegally enclosed the sixty acre pasture called the Crundles which had been the common pasture of the borough. They said the abbot had suppressed their Reeves Court, hounded his critics and had by means of trickery obtained and destroyed a charter given them by Henry I which made them a free town.

Robert Barbast accompanied by 42 others including John Eacott appeared before the king with their petition. In April the abbot was summoned to appear and make answer to some of the grievances which were listed in the summons. There was considerable evasiveness on the part of the abbot who did not produce all of the required documents. The evidence today seems to indicate the abbot and the abbey did not have a good claim to owning Cirencester. However at the time the wealthy abbot was able to make a deal with the king. The townsmen remained unhappy for generations and when Henry VIII dissolved the Abbey, the destruction was particularly thorough.[23]

Although John had signed the petition in March of 1342 he had a lot of other issues to deal with that spring. The king had called a parliament in 1341 during which he agreed to cease trying to collect taxes which had been assessed in 1340. The conditions in England were such that he could not effectively do so. Besides he had illegally tried to collect taxes from the clergy. Land all over England was going out of production because the king had called so many up to help his army there were too few to work the land

---

[23]*REF: [Vol I Cartulary of Cirencester by C.D. Ross, Oxford University Press 1964, items before and after # 125.] Called before the king at Westminster by the Sherrif of Gloucester 15 March 1342 were, among others, Robert Barbast, John of Weston, John Estoft, John Canynges, Willelmum Erchebaud, Thomas Payn, John of Yeuele, John Brymesgraue, Willeimum Rothewelle, Robert of Cerne, Reginald the Harpour, Peter of Derham, Lucam le Chapman, John the Smyth, Robert Langford, John of Cricklade, William Somer, Nicholas the Coyffestere, William Edmond, Peter of Stratton, Walter Caumberlayn, John of Otynton, Richard of Scarnyngge, John the Peyntour, Thomas the Valk, Reginald the Goldsmith, John of Eycote, Richard the Deghere, John Waleys, John the Deghere, John Lucas, Robert of Auebury, Thomas the Gussh, William Cotyler, Thomas the Coteler, Richard of Stonehouse, and several others. The list shows where these residents hailed from or what they did as well as persons who did not use "the" or "of".*

At this time there were only about 500 people living in Cirencester. So it was actually only a small village, one in which great issue of the day was the appearance of the plague that would depopulate it and lead to the the abandonment about this time of the manor of Eycote. The petitioners were likely most of the influential adult males of the area around Cirencester.

and he had seized too much for his supplies. Consequently, still needing to support his war effort, he cut a deal with the parliament. Parliament would give him 30 000 sacks of wool and permission to go to war. Once parliament had been dismissed the king reneged on the effort to collect taxes and went after his wool tax collectors to get the 30 000 sacks.

By January 28 1342 Johannem de Eycote, or John Eycot as he was sometimes called now was caught up in an impossible dilemma, low wool production and a demanding king. The king said that John and others had levied little or nothing in taxes and that would not do. On March 15, 1342 at Westminster John and others were called to come before the king to be informed of certain things to be set forth and further to do what shall be enjoined upon them by the king's council.

What this meant was made clear the same day at Eltham where the king stated he was going to seize the lands, goods and chattels of all the wool tax collectors in every county if they did not come up with the goods.

" *To the sheriff of Gloucester. Order to attach Reginald de Abehale, John de Berkeleye of Duresleye, Robert de Prestebury, Richard Shot, Robert Handy, William Crisp, Roger Norman, Henry de Brokworth and Alexander le Hattere of Gloucester, so that he shall have them before the king and his council at London on Monday in the first week of Lent next to answer the king for their contempt, and further to do and receive what shall be ordained by the council, as Reginald and the others with John Estof, John de Eycote, William Belle, and John Athelam, collectors of wool in that county, have borne themselves negligently and have hitherto levied little or nothing of the wool, not considering the king's great necessity or the orders by which he directed them to cause the wool to be levied speedily, wherefore the king ordered them to be before the king in chancery on the morrow of Hilary last to answer upon the premises, and further to do and receive what should be ordained by the council; and John Estof, John de Eycote, William Belle and John Athelam came before the king on that day, ready to do what they ought, but Reginald and the others refused to come. The king has given a day to John, John, William and John to be before him there to answer in the form aforesaid. The sheriff shall cause all the lands, goods and chattels of Reginald and the others to be seised into the king's hand, and shall answer for the issues of the lands and for the goods and chattels at the exchequer, and he shall not omit to do this upon pain of 100l. By King and Council*"

Poor John and his other wealthy merchant friend tax collectors were being threatened because the king assumed they were dodging their responsibilities. In fact the collectors were between a rock and a hard place. Obviously, enough grief was caused to the poor tax men that the next month the king who had a reputation for being temperamental on the one hand but quick to grant clemency on the other had a change of heart. The king informed the sheriff of Gloucester and other counties not to intermeddle until further orders.

April 20 1342

"To the sheriff of Gloucester. Order not to intermeddle until further order with attaching John de Byrkeleye of Duresleye, Robert de Prestebury, John Estof, John de Eycote, Richard Shot, Robert Haudy, William Crisp, William Belle, Henry de Brokworth and Alexander le Hattere of Gloucestre, whom the king appointed with others to collect wool in that county for the past year, or with taking their lands, goods and chattels, restoring to them any issues received from their lands, as although the king lately ordered the sheriff to attach them and take their lands, goods and chattels, and have them in chancery on Monday after the quinzaine of Easter last to answer the king for a certain disobedience, and further to do and receive what should then be determined by the council; yet they have been attached by the sheriff, and on being brought before the king in chancery on the said day they have undertaken to certify him concerning the collection of wool fifteen days from Trinity next, at their peril, and for that reason they are licensed to return to their own. By Council."[24]

By this time the king was busy organizing his invasion of France and the tax collectors were hard at work inspired no doubt by their recent close call with the king.

In John Eycote's case there was the issue of the Abbot of Cirencester collecting the same tax as the king. So he was eager to have his name attached to the petition because not only was he a tax collector he was also a merchant trying to get the king to understand the situation. The spring of 1342 was a very vexing time for John who had a king demanding money to go to war and an abbot who was entitled to tax in addition to what the king wanted.

---

[24] *Calendar of the Close Rolls .Edward III..: Preserved in the Public Record Office ..., Volume 29*

We know the petition went nowhere. We don't know how the tax collectors came to satisfy the king's demands. We don't know what happened to John.

A few years later in the spring of 1349 the bubonic plague arrived in western England and in a few weeks the dead and dying were decimating the population. The population which began to decline with the great famine now accelerated and landowners who survived had few tenants to farm. The depleted ranks of skilled craftsmen resulted in such severe labour shortages that costs of labour and food skyrocketed. The manor of Eycote basically ceased to exist as no one lived there anymore.

Meanwhile a few miles away at the Monastery of St. Albans north of London, William de Eycote was another educated member of the family who had done well for himself. He would have spoken English, French and likely Latin. Under the abbot Thomas De La Mere, the 30th abbot of St Albans 1349- 1396 William had become the Seneschal of the Abbey, the senior member of the staff in charge of the abbey. The De La Mere family was known to him as they held lordship of land around North Cerney. This may be the same William who earlier donated land to the church near Chichester. The time when he was in charge is not clear but it may have been in the later years of the abbot. The St. Alban's abbot had great connections with the royal family and was designated by the Pope as senior cleric in England. The abbot sat in parliament during this period in history as the senior clergy in England. During De La Mere's long life Richard III had the captured King of France locked up here in 1356. Jack Straw attacked the monastery during the Watt Tyler rebellion 1381. St. Albans history is written up during the middle ages and William is listed in the appendix as having significance on pages 413, 414, and 415. These are in Latin and are concerned with the finances of the monastery which had the rights to much land and also the ownership of the local mills. (Gesta abbatum monasterii Sancti Albani: A.D. 1349-1411By Thomas Walsingham, Matthew Paris).

In 1381 a Poll Tax return for Cirencester listed 574 adults, 62 of the surnames are not readable, no Eycote is listed although one name Richard Yaneworth is also bracketed as Enekot. Apart from labourers(36), there were 19 brewers, 10 merchants, 9 cobblers, 11 tailors, 5 weavers, 5 smiths, 4 bakers, 4 fishermen, 3 butchers, 2 goldsmiths, 2 tilers, 2 masons, 2 skinners, 1 clerk,, 1 carpenter, 1 draper, 1 harper, 1 bagger, 1 glover, 1 inn keeper, 1 spicer, 1 mercer, 1 saddler, 1 wool monger, 1 draper, 1 tanner.

(about 90 listed occupations) A number of the surnames are directly linked to the occupation. Wives and domestic servants (55) were also tax listed. The occupations say a lot about the nature of the town at that time. Presumably the Eycotes were now living at North Cerney and Bagendon and they frequented the town for their beverages, shoes, fine clothes, and hired the skills of others when needed.

The next known Eycote was Robert who owned a messuage (or estate) according to a deed from 22 May 1383. The location is not certain as he was simply noted as holding land adjacent to another property. Robert Eycote was however a person who had escaped the plague.

Wardstaff Duty

A little later, still very much in feudal times, 1394, we learn of another John Eycote. He appears on a duty list for persons who had to serve wardstaff, an obscure custom in which persons, knights of the lord, were appointed to stand guard duty. This list of names, their village and place of duty is listed.[25] It is not clear why this was an event because in 1394 Richard II, the king was at the time in relative harmony with his lords and there was no indication of any local unrest that might have called for service.

John wandered down to the bridge holding his staff. It was a wooden pole he had made some years ago that measured 5 foot, 6 inches tall, about his own height. He mostly used it when walking but he had been trained to use it in battle if need be. He supposed he could still use it against any trespasser or highwayman who should approach the bridge he was delegated to guard. John uncoiled his rope, tied it to a small tree and anchored the other end on a sturdy stake across the road so no one could pass without stopping. For the first couple of hours no one came by. Finally a rider on a horse approached and stopped to pass the time of day. A couple of men with some tools were going to work on a barn and stopped to share some ale. Later the rider came back and in passing John raised his staff in greeting. Some children stopped to ask why he was standing by the bridge. All he could respond was he was doing his duty. He showed them where his staff

---

25

Cartulary of Cirencester item # 741 under a "View of Wardstaff in the Seven Hundreds of Cirencester 1394".

had been notched by his lord as evidence he had done his duty before. He wondered himself what the point of the exercise was since other than report to his lord the events of the day and getting his Lordship to put a ceremonial notch in his staff after which John would pay him token 2p, there was nothing more to the ritual. John had given his obedient service to his overlord, a vestige of the feudal days. As darkness approached, another rider in an obvious hurry was unhappy to be stopped and investigated so John had no time to socialize. If there were highwaymen or thieves about, they were not going on this road or over the bridge. There had been some stories of people waylaid leaving Cirencester but he thought they had been caught. He sat down by a tree and was trying to determine if it was late enough yet to go home. A half moon was rising and there would be some light to help him find his way home. He still had a bit of bread and munched it as he looked up and down the dark road. He decided to go home although he was supposed to remain at his post until sunrise. He had done that once, got really chilled and had never seen a single person once it was truly dark.

This means that John Eycote of Bagendon had to stand guard duty at Bear ford bridge (Perrot's Brook). It shows how names got rearranged. Bearridge or Bearford became Perrot. This John was a yeoman, a freeman with land usage held under his lord. The land would have been at Bagendon and thus he may have dwelled at Woodmancote. Was he the son or grandson of Johannem of fifty years before? The one who had survived the plague? Another couple of decades later we learn that a John Eycote dies and leaves his land to his son Thomas.

In 1421-37 [Cartulary of Cirencester # 740] in a list of suitors in land transactions. Listed under Bagendon for this time " To Thomas Eycot for the term of his life the house and land of Johannic Eycot lately of Hunfridi atte Mere of Boyndene - presented in writing." This meant that John left his property to Thomas. John owned his property with the permission of his lord Humphry More of Boyndene. He may have been the same John Eycote who had to stand guard duty 20/30 years before.

[item # 740 pg 628]

Bagyndene
" Thomas Eycote ad terminum vite sue pro terra et tenemento Johannis Eycote nuper Hunfridi Atte More in Bagyndene per scriptum. "

The medieval system of keeping the peace was known as frankpledge under which all males over 12 were allotted to groups of about 10 known as tithings who were collectively responsible for the good behavior of one another. Each such group had a chief, the 'tithing-man', and periodically the tithing-men were summoned to the *court leet* of whichever feudal lord held 'View of Frankpledge' for his tenants. Taken from a View of Frankpledge in the Seven Hundreds of Cirencester (probably early 1400's).

In this instance there is a memorandum that the hundred of Respigateis owed payment twice a year from the place beside the wood of Eycote called Respigate. (Rapsgate)

> *" Hundredum de Respigate"*
>
> *Memorandum quod visus hundredi de Respegate debet teneri bis per annum in quodam loco juxta boscum de Eycote vacato Respegate, videlicet, ad terminum sancti Martini et ad terminum de Hock', per summonicionem ballivorum abbatis de Cirencester per eosdem ballivos. Ed ad eundem visum venient omnes decennarii villarum subscriptarum bis per annum cum eorum decenis ad presentanda omnia que ad visum pertinent, videlicet"*

The fortunes of the Eycotes who survive the Black Death are still made in the hamlets of North Cerney, Bagendon and the town of Cirencester. They are no longer tied up in the affairs of the royal court.

We know that about 1430 the Eycote family passed land from John to Thomas at Bagendon. Whether the family was spreading out from North Cerney, we do not know although a prosperous wool merchant would be looking to provide his sons with farms or a good position.

John Eycote, Curate

John Eycote saw the smoke rising from what looked to be the North Cerney church. His father Thomas was called and the two men raced down from Woodmancote to see what was happening. When they arrived, a few people were still carrying leather buckets of water but the fire was too far advanced. The church tower was acting like a giant chimney sucking air in the damaged windows and creating a great inferno. The Norman roof beams were blazing and their 300 year old church was a ruined mess.

William Whitechurch rector of North Cerney was beside himself and welcomed the arrival of his assistant John Eycote. John was the curate of the church a position that pleased his wool merchant father.

It was several days before the exact extent of the damage could be assessed. During that time Thomas and Whitechurch had lengthy discussions about what to do. It was not a large church and some suggested they tear it down and merge with Bagendon or Rendcomb. Thomas was not pleased with those ideas because the Woodmancote church had been closed and this would mean it would be farther to travel to attend services and in addition there was a question about further employment for his son. Whitechurch was able to get Thomas' support for a large donation to rebuild and in addition he would speak with the influential Tame and Rich families. Other wool merchants were also approached.

The fire of 1465 led to some intense rebuilding including a new addition. Thomas thought it would be appropriate for a commemorative window to be placed in the repairs.

He went searching for a glass artist who could do this and other work for the church. Foster glass, made from potash from burned Beech tree ash, lime and silica, was being produced in Burgundy and Flanders. It would be no problem to import some sheets for the windows. The new windows and church repairs were completed in 1470. Unfortunately the hard of hearing artist who crafted the window of the supplicant John Eycote had misspelt John's name as Bicote. And so until this day that is the name on his window. (In the north transept the east window was the gift of John Eycote, curate here, and his figure appears under the crucifix. This window was releaded in 1732 by a Cirencester glazier, inside out, with the pigmented surface exposed to the weather; hence the loss of most of its drawing. It was releaded and reversed in 1912.[26])[27]

John was so pleased with the results of his efforts that he decided to take his wife Johanna on a pilgrimage to Rome in 1469. He obviously had the wealth to enable him to do this. It was a big undertaking but since the jubilee of 1350 when a large delegation from England had travelled to Rome to celebrate, there had been a new hospice built in 1362 to care for English travellers who were able to afford a pilgrimage or who simply went for business purposes.

His journey began at Canterbury and he crossed the English channel to Sombres, France following the marked pilgrimage route of the Via Francigena which took him from abbey to abbey bypassing hostile towns and areas. While the hospice and the abbeys would look after John and his wife, he was obliged to pay for all the expenses of getting there and for housing and care for their horses. A cash gift was appropriate at each abbey as well. Each day John and the others on the entourage would travel about 20 km or 12 miles a day although some days required 30 km and longer treks. The journey of 1,100 miles took them over 80 days. The route led into Switzerland and up to the St. Bernard's Pass hospice before winding down to Aosta and then finally on to Rome. It was an exciting journey that only the very wealthy could afford. Since the assistant curate was a lowly paid position, he obviously relied on his family fortune to finance the trip.

He signed the hospice register sometime between 1469-71. He and his wife had finally arrived in Rome! He was surprised to find all sorts of English persons living at the hospice, tailors, goldsmiths, carpenters, cobblers but mostly rosary sellers and merchants. The pilgrims on the other hand were more or less tourists. The pope was now back in Rome having left Avignon and John planned to attend Papal mass as the highlight of his journey. St Peter's and St. Paul's graves were here in Rome along with many other important religious sites. This was sufficient enough for him. John had determined he would bring back something for the church to add

---

[26] *Pg 335 Gloucestershire: The Cotswolds by David Verey 1979*

[27]

The author of this work, did in the 1980's after visiting North Cerney design, craft and donate to two churches a memorial book stand. These stands are in Curries United Church, Norwich, Ontario and Old St. Paul's Anglican church in Woodstock, Ontario, Canada.

to the chest[28] the family had donated after the fire. Symbolically, his trip also marks the end of the outbreaks of the great plague although no one at the time knew it.

We also connect Eycots to Cirencester, Bagendon, and North Cerney at this time. As the 15th century comes to a close we enter a period with very little information about the Eycote family. What we do know is they likely began to settle in other places outside of the original places. We also know that at least some of them, likely most, were educated to some degree. At least they were literate.

After the pilgrimage of John the world and England changed greatly in less than a lifetime. Columbus discovered America and Aboriginals from Newfoundland were brought to Bristol. Printed books and a printed English bible come into common use. England becomes a Protestant nation. Copernicus proves the earth revolves around the sun. English families are more prosperous and the population after two centuries of decline is growing again. Henry the VIII is king for many years. Many large homes are constructed and schools are plentiful.

In the mid 1500's the Eycotes have become Eycott and Ekot and Ecott.

Wyllyam Eycott of Bagendeyne witnessed the will of Thomas Foxely in 1525. He could have been the son or grandson of John the curate. We know that he was a man who could read and write in order to be able to witness a will. He would have been well aware of the great events happening around the world including Henry VIII's attack on the church whereby he dissolved all the monasteries and seized their lands and sold off their property.

In 1540 with the dissolution of the abbey the ownership of Eycott was taken from the church and sold to Edmund Tame of Fairford and his wife Catherine Stafford. A few years later it is resold to the Berkeley family. After this Eycott becomes part of Rendcomb Park estate and essentially it disappears as a separate entity. The monasteries were all destroyed between 1536-40. Feudal laws on land holding were abolished. However somewhere someone, to this day, holds the lordship of Eycott. There is no coat of arms

---

[28] *Pg. 336 Gloucestershire: The Cotswolds by David Verey, 1979. The medieval chest belonged to the Eycote family.*

for Eycott because the College of Heralds was not yet established when the manor ceased. [29]

The Eycotts were no exception to the general rise in population. From this point forward there are many family lines some of which can be traced back to North Cerney. Many others have untraceable gaps. From here forward the Eycotts are not as easily connected on paper to each other. The church records before 1538 were spotty and after that time birth (more precisely baptisms), marriages and deaths are well recorded because it was ordered for churches to do so. It was a double entry system. The parish church made the original and the bishops' office made a back up copy sometimes with different spelling.

Church records for North Cerney exist from 1568. This is a few years after the dissolution of the abbeys and like other churches North Cerney was now Protestant, Church of England. If there were older records that were destroyed is not known. However, it had only been in the past 150 years that churches had become active in promoting church weddings and baptisms. Marriage customs had been based on the consent of both parties but until about this time many people got married in a pub or wherever by simply stating to each other they agreed to be married and it was useful to have someone around to witness that they had agreed. It was a pretty informal situation that annoyed the church who had made efforts to have the ceremony made into a sacrament a couple of hundred years earlier. For many the old traditions still applied which explains why there are so few records from earlier times.

The population for North Cerney hamlet was about 36 in 1086. In 1327 twenty six were assessed for the subsidy. In 1381 forty five were listed for poll tax. In 1551 there were 145 communicants in the church and in 1563 there were 18 households. By 1603 there were only 110 communicants. In 1650 there were forty families. In 1710 there were 190 inhabitants and 42 houses. Currently the parish has about 600 people. The high price for wool and good prices for crops allowed the construction of many fine stone houses in the Cotswolds during the 16th century.

What the reader has so far discovered is the Eycott history that is

---

[29] *I personally visited the college about this. Anyone selling a coat of arms is making it up on their own. There is none.*

hardest to trace is what has just been read. It's this which makes the Eacott history extremely rare, a lineage that goes back to the 1200's. What is covered next is the way the family began to migrate out from North Cerney/Bagendon.

In 1563 North Cerney had 18 households, and Bagendon 7. Both were very small places.

During 1572 Thomas Eycott is the church warden at Bagendon. He has a growing family and is prospering. This means the wool was selling at a good price. He likely lived at the "Moor".

It is now the 1580's. Elizabeth 1 is on the throne, English explorers are circumnavigating the world and William Shakespeare is about to write his plays. Catholics are socially out, Protestants firmly in.

Two Wills

The Eycotts are writing wills and leaving a cast of characters and personal information for our consideration. There are the wills of Mary Ecott 1588 of Elkstone, Thomas Eycott's will of 1594 at Brimsfield, and the marriage in 1577 of John Ackett and Jane Parnell at Purton Wilts. What is of special interest are the wills of Richard of North Cerney and Thomas of Bagendon both from the early 1580's.

Richard is perhaps the son of Wyllyam Eycott of Bagenden. He has prospered at the farm at Woodmancote and his crops have been regularly harvested and he had his grain ground at the mill in Cirencester.[30] He has a variety of animals sheep, ewes, cattle both milking and draft. His brother Philip is incapable and needs care. His son Thomas is a responsible person with his own family. Richard is able to bequeath his children more than

---

30

Technically, people of the parish had to have their grain ground at the Trinity Mill in Bagendon or pay a fine. The mill was on the same site from the days of king John and was for some time owned by the Cirencester Weavers Guild. By Richard's time the mill was owned by the Thynne family and may have become a fulling or clothing mill. The miller in 1580 was John Deynton. So when Richard says Cirencester he likely means another mill 2 miles further on in the town.

forty pounds of silver coins. This would be a sizeable amount likely worth about $50 000 in current money. A days pay would be in the range of $10. Both of these wills give an insight into life of the times. Brass pots and pewter are the goods of well to do people as the common folk ate out of wooden bowls. Bedding is a commodity worth handing down as are items of clothing all of which are handmade. These goods were not handed down for sentimental reasons but because they were practical and useful. One must wonder about the specifics of the sums handed down. Good bookkeeping is evident but why the specific amounts so articulate right down to the penny. However a penny then was worth a lot.

One thing that is not mentioned in either will is land. Everything is possessions. The land lease may have been of a nature to pass on or it may not have been. It was not theirs to deal with in a will. The record of to whom their fees were paid is likely available but not known. One English pound in 1583 would be worth about £ 180 in 2005, but this does not indicate the real worth of Anthony's £ 4 being £ 700 plus today. The official price of gold then was about £ 3 an ounce so compare to today's value. A bushel of barley in 1630 was worth about 4 shillings or 36 US dollars in 2005. A pence (penny) from then was worth about 75 cents in 2005. A days wages would be around 8 p or 6.00 dollars a day. When daughters Elizabeth and Katerin got their inheritance, it was nearly a year's wages. John and William getting but 40 shillings indicates that they were in fact given use of land to farm and didn't need cash. The girls however needed dowry money and goods.

Richard has four sons Anthony, John, William and Thomas? However Thomas Ekot 1583 has several brothers, John , another John, Edward, Richard and William. So is the Thomas of the will of 1583, son, brother or cousin of Richard who died in 1581?

Thomas has a young family. His youngest girl, Alice born 1578, is 5 years old and his only son Joseph is not of age either. He is entrusting other family members with his children's inheritance. So Hugh Cowles and John Cherington are likely married to two of his older daughters although no reference is made to any of them being married. Four of them are entrusted with a variety of animals which it would not be likely they tended themselves. His wife is likely about 40 but he is concerned for any future child of his that might yet be born. Thomas was not expecting to die so young but he knows he is pretty sick. From the will of Thomas Ekott of

Bagendon 1583 we learn that he had six daughters by his wife Elizabeth. Their baptisms are recorded at Bagendon.

He makes reference to his brothers:
Robert who, I conjecture, may have been the father of Ellen in 1575 and whose will may have been the lost will of 1629 of Robert Eacott ; John the elder who may have had 7 daughters; John the younger; Richard who may have been the Richard of the other will noted here but more likely is not since the family names do not match; Edward who is probably the Edward of Winstone who became Eacoote. William is likely the father of Richard 1590 who may have become the Richard Eacott Sr. and father of Thomas etc. We know that Thomas lived at Bagendon and more specifically likely at Woodmancote (field reference). He was a fairly well to do person. He was a farmer and at that time farming was prosperous especially for those in the sheep and wool trade.

Thomas is looking after all his brothers with token gifts and while unlike Richard he does not have a bundle of cash he is able to provide a dowery for each of the girls. He refers to Thomas Vyner as his brother. In the future this proves to be an important family connection. His sister(Margaret ?) had married Thomas Vyner of North Cerney. She may have been the grandmother of Sir Robert Vyner wealthy goldsmith of London who was Lord Mayor of London and stepmother of sir Thomas Vyner also goldsmith and also Lord Mayor of London. It was also a time when the Eacotts generally did very well economically.

Is Thomas' brother John the Younger or John the Elder the John Ackett who married in 1577 at Purton? Is Mary Ecott of Elkstone his sister in law or aunt. Is the Thomas of the will of 1594 at Brimsfield Richard's son?

The Will of Thomas Ekot of Bagendon,1583

In the name of god Amen, the nineth day of Julie 1583,I, Thomas Ekott of Bagendon in the countie of Gloucr,husbandman, being sicke and weake in bodie but of perfect memorie doe make
this my last will and testament in manner following.
I geve my bodie to be buried in the churchyarde of Bagenden

Aforesaid.
I geve to my daughter MARGETT twenty shepe and one cowe.
I geve to my daughter MARIE twelve sheepe and one cowe.
I geve to my daughter KATHERINE fyfteen shepe anf a heyfer or a bullock of three years olde.
I geve to my daughter ELIZABETH fyfteen shepe and a heyfer or a bullock of three years olde.
I geve to my daughter EDITH tenne yewes and one cowe in the keeping of Hugh Cowles of Winston.
I geve to my daughter ALICE tenne yewes and one cowe in the keeping of John Cherington of Winston
To everyone of my forenamed daughters a flock bedd a bolster a pare of sheets a pare of blanketts. My will is that these my goods be delivered to them either at their day of marriage or at the tyme of their mothers marriage or her decease.
To every one of my daughters a brass pott, a brass pan, and a half dozen of pewter to be delivered at the time above named.
To my sonne JOSEPH twenty sheep one yoke of bullocks and ten pounds of current money, to be delivered to him when he reaches the age of twenty years.
Itm yf yt shall happen that my wief to be with child I do geve unto it ten pounds of currant money
Unto my brother ROBTE myne yron bounde waine as yt standeth a yoke of bulls and four acres of barley in Woodmancote.
To my brother JOHN the Yonger two acres of barlie in Bagendons field.
To my brothers EDWARD and RICHARD two acres and a half of Barley.

To my brother JOHN the Elder my modley coate my jerken, my workdaie lether dublett.

Unto his children one shepe. Unto my brother WM. ten pounds that is in his own hands.

To every godchild I have xi jd.

Unto THOMAS BIDLE of wodmancote the money that he oweth me

I forgive RICHARD ELDER of WINSTON the debt he oweth me.

Itm EDMUND CAWDLE of Bagendon oweth me six shillings and eight pence, half of which I forgive him, and the other half I give to his brother JOHN CAWDLE of the parish of Winston.

All the rest of my goods I give unto ELIZABETH my wief whom I make my sole executrix.

I make my brother THOMAS VYNER of North Cerney, RICHARD BURTON parson of Badgendon and HENRY BALDEN of wodmancote mine overseers

and give to every of them ten shillings.

(no witnesses named)

By me THOMAS EKOTT

proved 6th August 1583

<u>The Will of Richard Eycott, North Cerney, 1581</u>

In the name of god Amen, the xxiii th daie of aprill in the year of our Lord god 1581, I Richard Eicott of Woodmancote being of whole mind and of good remembrance I make and ordain this my last testament in manner following.

In the name of god Amen, the xxiii th daie of aprill in the year of our Lord god 1581, I Richard Eicott of Woodmancote being of whole mind and of good remembrance I make and ordain this my last testament in manner following.

ffirst I commende my soule unto Almighty god and my bodie to be buryed in the churchyard of North Cerney.

I bequeath to the reparacons of the churche two bushells of barley.

I will that my deptes be discharged by my wieff whom I make mine Executrix.

Unto my sonne JOHN ffortie shillings.

Unto my daughter ELIZABETH six pounds thirteen shillings fourpence.

Unto my Daughter KATERIN a like sum.

Unto my sonne ANTHONY four pounds.

Unto HENRIE BALDEN the younger ffoure sheepe.

Unto my sonne WILLIAM ffortie shillings.

Itm I will by this last my last will and testament that my brother
PHILLIPPE shalbe kepte during his Lief at the cost and charge of mine
Executrixe during her Lief and after Executrixe
deceasse I will that my sonne THOMAS shall kepe him beinge an
Inocente, In Consideracon wherof I geve my sonne THOMAS after my
Execitrix decesse my hole teme and the hole Crops of corne in the barne
or on the grounde Payinge out the same to my Children Twenty
pounds within the space of two yeares thence next ensuinge, at the
discrecons of my overseers to my children then lyving.

Itm I will that mine executrix shall geve to every of my god children
xi pence. And to RICHARD BAULDEN one shepe and also I will that if
my wieff shall marrie after my decesse that she shall lose the haulfe of all
her goods. And the remaining haulfe to be divided amonge my children in
manner and forme aforesaid besides the payinge of the legacies.
I make mine overseers of this my last will and testament

William Walker
Thomas Eycott
Henry Balden and to every one of my overseers I geve a bushell of barley
a peece.

I do owe to John Teritt xx shillings.
I do owe to Thomas Hawkins of the mill at Cirester townes end
xxxvi shillings vii pence.
Richard Eycott his mark
proved 29th January 1581

These two wills inform us that in the 1580's these six : Thomas, Robert, John, Edward, Richard and John the elder were brothers and Richard had 4 sons: John, Anthony, William, Thomas. He also had one brother Phillippe. This means Richard of North Cerney was not the brother of Thomas who dwelt at Bagendon. It also indicates that Woodmancote is seen as distinct from North Cerney and Bagendon. So Richard and Thomas are cousins. At this point there are a lot of relatives living in the same area and there clearly is not enough farmland nearby for each son to have a farm. From a genealogy perspective it now becomes difficult to determine lineage since we don't know for certain who the common ancestor was for Richard and Thomas. Nor can we yet create a certain descendants chart as there are too many options and incomplete records. The various name spellings also confuse the issue as they are still very interchangeable at this time in history. However all the Eacotts, Eycotts etc. seem to still be living in the same small area.

At the close of the 1500's virtually all the known Eycott families live north of Cirencester, Bagendon, North Cerney, Rendcomb and Winstone. The one exception is the marriage in 1577 of John Ackett and Jane Parnell at Purton.

So what is the connection to Purton? [31] As far back as 1386 there was a connection. John Pouger who owned the Manor of Eycote, with 2 houses, 80 acres of meadow and other land also owned 10 acres of wood at Purton in Wiltshire transferred the ownership to Thomas Beerton. Thus there was an historical connection although the later significance of this is not known. So John Ackett could have gone to Purton as a consequence of this property relationship. Then again no other Ackett was known in those days. Did he come from North Cerney?

The Eacott spelling of the name was not known until Edward of Winstone had a similar spelling. Ekot, Ecott was used by a few but most were known by Eycott. At Bagendon Eycott was the only form ever used. North Cerney families used several variations. The Eacott version began in Wiltshire after the middle of the 1600's at Warminster in 1665 and similarly

---

31

This is a reference to the document that links Eycote to Purton in 1386.
CP 25/1/289/54, number 146.
Link: Image of document at AALT
County: Gloucestershire. Wiltshire.
Place: Westminster.
#30 continued Date: One week from Holy Trinity, 9 Richard [II] [24 June 1386].
Parties: John Pouger, querent, and Thomas de Beerton' of Eycote, deforciant.
Property: The manor of Eycote in the county of Gloucester and 2 messuages, 2 carucates of land, 80 acres of meadow and 10 acres of wood in Puriton' in the county of Wiltshire.
Action: Plea of covenant.
Agreement: John has acknowledged the manor and tenements to be the right of Thomas, as those which Thomas has of his gift. For this, Thomas has granted to John the manor and tenements and has rendered them to him in the court, to hold to John and his heirs, of the chief lords for ever.
Warranty: Warranty by Thomas and his heirs.

Standardised forms of names. (These are tentative suggestions, intended only as a finding aid.)
Persons: John Pouger, Thomas de Bierton, (variant Beerton, Burton)
Places: Eycote (in Colesbourne), Purton

north of Bristol.

Until the end of feudal times families stayed near the property where they were born. By the time the above wills were written families were much more on the move. An examination of different rural communities has shown that after about a 50 year time span more than half the family names known at the outset were no longer seen. Young people left home to find work on farms or as domestic servants. In the 1600's one third of British homes had servants. Poor laws helped keep track of the movement of some. An indigent person was the responsibility of the parish where they were born. (See appendix P) Marriage licences were relatively expensive so only the reasonably well off would have gone to the bother of a legal marriage. These were the same people who would undertake to have their child christened. So the search for ancestors is mostly a search for those who had done fairly well in the society of the day. The fact that a person may have been christened and becomes known to history and then never found again may represent anything from an early unrecorded death to a person who grew up married and had children and moved about the countryside looking for work in the poorer levels of society. This was especially true in the sixteen and seventeen hundreds. Along with the migration came alterations in the surname due to local dialects and spelling styles. Eycott in the middle ages could have been pronounced roughly as Egg cott which would lead to recasting the spelling to Eacott. People knew their names but only those who could read and write would have a convention for spelling. The literacy level was unusually high in the 16th century but declined continually into the 19th.

The Eycotts of Woodmancote

It is not really known when the Eycotts came to live at the hamlet of Woodmancote which is on top of the hill which drops away to the old Eycot manor and to North Cerney and Bagendon. However it could be guessed that they lived there from the 1200's. The early references to the family locates them in respect to the churches at Bagendon, North Cerney and Rendcomb. Woodmancote is located at the place where three parishes meet. This location included an ancient plot of land deliberately claimed by no one. A form of no mans land at the point where the parishes met. The Eycotts had strong connections with Bagendon and North Cerney churches but not so much with Rendcomb across the Churn because it was less accessible in the old days.

According to the book, History of Bagendon, 1932, by Rev. Geo. Edward Rees a minister of Bagendon church for many years, the Eycotts lived at The Moor or Moorwood as it was also known. They were yeoman gentry and went by the names Mister and Mistress. That is they were not titled but did hold their land freely. The Moorwood farm also held a woods which was mentioned in a document from king Johns reign. It was held at one time under the lordship of the Marquis of Bath (Thynne family) and was the last property over which he relinquished his lordship. The farm, The Moor was held by the Eycott, Agg, Small, Haines, Longworth and today by the Robinson family.

The feudal lordship of the land at Domesday 1086 indicated that Hugo L'Anse (Hugh Donkey) held Bedwedene (Bagendon) and Gilbert (son of Turold) sub held it from him. They rebelled against the king and the land was taken from them and given to the de Chandos'. In 1283 Richard de Bathenden (Bagendon) held it from Robert de Chandos. In 1346 (Testa de Neville) Roger de Chandos held the land. There was a double ownership, perhaps father and son. The division of ownership separated Bagendon and Moorwood manors. LLanthony II shows that at an earlier time the parish had been divided in two. King John's charter, July 30,1199 refers to Robert making a gift of wood from Moorwood and Roger the Younger joining in the gift of wood to the mill. In 1383 Sir John Chandos was the lord (a baron).The De Bagendon were the knights. By 1543 the lordship was taken over by the Marquis of Bath, Sir Thomas Thynne.(said as thin).

Woodmancott in the middle ages had its own chapel. The church was located in chapel field. At an unknown time it was abandoned. The wheel cross from it is located on the vestry of Bagendon church and a part of the North Cerney churchyard cross is made from a fragment of the chapel.

The Moor was not the only manor house at Woodmancote. The Moor belonged to Bagendon parish. The second manor went with North Cerney parish. It was dated to the 16th C. The hamlet of Woodmancote was recorded in the 13th C. There were 7 taxpayers in 1327. In 1710 there were 13 houses. The Woodmancote manor house was bought by Thomas Taylor in 1566 and was claimed by his descendants and by the Stafford family. Lady Mary Stafford was named lady of the village in 1608. Later the Pooles and Guises lay claim to the lordship. A third part of Woodmancote, also called the

Manor of Woodmancote, went to the De la Mare family and subsequently went to Rendcomb at the time of the Tames ownership.

Thus when references occur about the Eycotts, it is uncertain just where at Woodmancote they lived, other than at the Moor and possibly a residence known as North Court.[32] In Rees' book he reports Eycotts living there until at least 1776. (Francis Ashmead lived with an Eycott at the Moor until her death that year). She had lived at Perrot's bridge before taking up with Mr. Eycott. She was known as madam and was refused burial in the normal location thus raising a question about her nature. By 1832 the Haines lived at Moorwood. The existing house at Moorwood dates from 1750-90, was extended in 1820 and 1920. This indicates that the Eycott residence there was likely torn down.

Thomas Coots and the Early 1600's

Thomas Coots appears in history in 1608 in the book "Men and Armour" by Smith who was directed to take a record of all men from age 20 to 60 who were fit for military service in Gloucestershire. He was the only person in Rendcomb, North Cerney, Bagendon, Woodmancote or anywhere who came close to being recorded as an Eycott or Ecott that was fit for military service. So why was he the only one?

Thomas was a sturdy fellow of about 40 years of age and he was fit and suitable to be a cavalier which meant he would be a soldier mounted on a horse. We know that 20 years earlier there had been lots of Eacotts around the area. And there still were. Thomas Ecott had baptized two daughters in 1603 at North Cerney. Thomas Ecott and Joseph Eycot were also born in 1607. A Thomas Ecott was buried there in 1604. Nearby at Winstone, also in 1607, William Eacoote son of Edward and Margarie was baptized. Edward died in 1612.

At this time Lady Mary Stafford was the Lady of Woodmancote and Lady Eleanor Berkeley was the Lady at Rendcomb. These ladies had

---

[32]
There are several existing old buildings from 1700's and earlier which may be connected to the Eycott family. These include Dortley Farm; Scrubditch farm cottage, North Cerney; Old park house at Woodmancote; Bagendon House; Bagendon Manor

entertained the late queen Elizabeth in 1592 when she visited Rendcomb. The Eacotts who lived in these parts would have seen or met the queen who died in 1603. James I was now king and he was very much a Protestant. There was opposition and Guy Fox tried to blow up parliament. Adventurers were setting up a colony in Virginia. The Earls were driven from Ireland. Shakespeare was still writing plays.

The Eacotts of 1608 included Joan Ecott and her brothers William, Thomas, and Richard whose son was Thomas and their families who were living at North Cerney and Rendcomb. Joan's sisters were Susan Chamberlain and Margaret Broade. Her mother in law was Susan Jefferies. She had been a doyen of the community as her will indicated. Edward and Margerie Ecott of Winstone lived a few miles away. Some of the people appeared dedicated to the old religion and were catholic in their sympathies or had taken up the Puritan cause which a few years later was greatly supported locally in the civil war. At the very least they were not considered loyal enough to the king to be documented as men suitable for military service. Then, perhaps Smith was just not a very accurate keeper of records for his book!

John Eicot was churchwarden at Bagendon in 1623.

In 1630 John Eacott was born to Richard Eacott, a rough mason, at North Cerney. At this time surname interchanges were quite common. This is the first instance of a brief use of Eacott as the surname. John Eacott likely was Eycott later in life. Parish and Bishops registers were even at variance with the same person and event. Alse and John Eycot lived at the Moor in the 1630's. Alse (Alice) died in 1631. This is also the time period when the father of Berkeley Eycott was living.

The Last Hundred Years of Eycotts Along the Churn

The following is an account of some land transactions which show what became of the land held by some Eycotts, who were at the time thought to be, and some were, Roman Catholics.

In 1680 Thomas Eycott gave his lands to Richard. He gave land between Cross Piece and Moorcomb Piece which was bounded on three sides by land owned by the Stevens. In 1708 Thomas secured a mortgage for

700£. At the same time Berkeley Eycott held other property at Bagendon. In 1723 John Eycott gave up his rights to Thomas, his brother (these were likely sons of Berkeley.). In 1747 Robert Saunders bought the land from Thomas Eycott and at the time Robert married Thomas' daughter Elizabeth Eycott. In 1753 Elizabeth Eycott gave to her daughter Elizabeth Saunders her share of the estate. The marriage to Saunders took place at Tyndale but she later lived at Little Farringdon, Berks. The land next passed to Wm. Bolt in 1777 and back to Robert Saunders of Little Farringdon in 1807. In 1812 Wm. Croome purchased parcel #809 and in 1832 he is listed as owning a farm house. In this way the Eycotts ceased to live at Woodmancote where they had dwelled since at least the 1200's.

It would appear from this that Thomas in 1680 left his land to his son Richard who passed it on to his son Thomas. This man had two sons John and Thomas and two daughters. John may have lived at Chedworth and arranged to place his share at Woodmancote in his brothers hands in 1723. Thomas was to have no sons but did have a daughter Elizabeth, named after her mother. She married Robert Saunders in 1747 and the Eycott name left the property. Other Eycotts may have lived at Bagendon for a few more years but by 1778 there were no more Eycotts on the church rolls renting seats. A little farther along it is shown more in detail how several wills showed how the ownership passed along to various Bagendon properties.

In 1715 the Jacobites, who take their name from Jacobus, the Latin form of James, were supporters of having James II of England and James VII of Scotland (same person) be the new king instead of George I, a German prince from Hanover. George was chosen because he was a Protestant while James was a Catholic. Parliament did not want a Catholic monarch. An uprising took place, one of many, supported by the Presbyterian Scots, Catholics and others who wanted the Stuarts. One of the results was a requirement by Parliament for all Catholics, then called Papists, to register and sign an oath of loyalty or fidelity to king George I or forfeit their property.

At the time of the registration of papists in 1717 this record exists:

In Woodmancote John Eycott held two houses and several arable parcels of land, meadow and pasture ground with appurtenances in Chedworth plus 1 yard lands of common pasture of diverse sorts and cattle. He held two closes in Woodmancote. One field was called Dorothy's Leaze and one was called Linkham's Piece. He was required to pay his sisters Robertta and Martha 3£ each for these until they are married and subject to a mortgage made by Thomas his late father with Jonathan White for a principal of 100£. This was signed by John.

Another registration by a Thomas Eycott of Woodmancote who held four yard lands of arable meadow and pasture as well as a house. His sisters Robertta and Martha held a cottage which was apparently rented to a William Sherrall. So John and Thomas are brothers. There was a mortgage on the farm for 700£. This Thomas or another of the same name was constable of Bagendon in 1715. That means he was appointed to keep the peace in the community and was really the only local government official.

The will of Thomas 1715 says that he had two sons, Thomas (the eldest) and John. John was the executor of the will and Robert Moran of Fairford was the trustee. Thomas had three daughters, Rebecca, Elizabeth and Martha. Thomas's wife was Mary. John was given a house and grounds in Chedworth and was also given Dorothy's Leaze and Linkham's piece. Thomas (the eldest) in his will of 1740 says he was a catholic, a bachelor and he gave his possessions to William Eycott of Cirencester his nephew. Thomas also gave his sisters Rebecca and Martha a freehold estate at Woodmancote with a cottage there until they were married.

John Eycott of Cirencester (son of Berkeley sr.) who lived at 35 Dyer St. was a Catholic Goldsmith with an estate at Bagendon. His mother was Mary Shewell widow of Berkeley and was still living in 1737 (age then about 67). When he wrote the will, his wife was Elizabeth and sons were Richard, Thomas and John. John had a freehold estate at Chedworth. His son John is the executor of his will when he dies in 1751. He gives his sons Richard and Thomas 250 pounds each when they become of age and they each are to gain an estate at Bagendon. The will was witnessed by Henry Timbrell and Richard Worstlar.[33]

In the late 1600's and early 1700's those who were not Church of England were pressured to conform. They could not marry or otherwise have official status so these dissenters, Nonconformists, were forced underground

---

33

This will is listed with the records required of Catholics in 1715 and onwards in a document published in 1889 listing English Catholics.

or participated just enough to get officialdom off their backs. Some were Catholics but others were various form of Protestantism of which Quakers would be loose cover for some of them. Cirencester had from the 1660's an active Unitarian, Presbyterian and Congregationalist community. This was before Methodists appeared.

There was a series of rebellions in 1715 by the Catholics under the new king George because they wanted another person to be king. Since Berkeley was active with the Bagendon church, he may have been a closet Catholic or not one at all. Berkeley was married in London at the Fleet prison gates which clearly meant he was a non conformist of some sort. His son clearly was a Catholic although other Eycotts at North Cerney were not or hid the fact. Certainly the constable would not have been a Catholic. There is some room here for speculation that the family was divided in their religious affiliation.

In 1730 the will of Thomas, made and read that year, listed his son Thomas as the executor. He had three daughters Dorothy, Rachelle and Hester. This Thomas also lived at Bagendon and may have been the one listed as constable in 1715. The father of this man might have been a Richard (if he was in his 80's(84)) or it may have been Berkeley (if he was 35) or it may have been another person.

John Eycott of Cirencester (son of Berkeley and whose wife is Elizabeth) in his will of 1751 leaves his estates in Bagendon to his son John who is executor and gives his son Richard 250 £ when he reaches age 21 and the same to his son Thomas when he came of age also. These boys would also gain estates in Bagendon. Henry Timbrell and Richard Worstlar were witnesses.

Elizabeth Eycott daughter of the above John also inherits property at Bagendon.

Elizabeth granddaughter of Berkeley and daughter of John Eycott, Goldsmith of Cirencester never married. She died about age 38 in 1757. In her will she notes her brothers John, Jones, Joseph, Thomas, Richard all of Cirencester. She has property at Bagendon which is leased from Lord Weymouth. She leaves all her properties at Badginton (sp) all houses, barns and outhouses to her brother Richard who is also executor. Richard in turn dies in 1772 without any children. He leaves his estate to his brother Jones who gets Badgendon. Brother John is still alive. When Jones dies in 1779 six years later, his wife has already died in 1775. She had no will and neither does Jones. John claims he is next of kin as the only surving family. John lives in Withington. He dies in 1789 and leaves his lands in Bagendon to John Gregory Rupell of Withington, Gregory Rupell of Daglingworth and Richard Savory of Withington. There is a carved memorial to John Eycott by Franklin in St. Michael church Withington. Such a monument indicates that John had led a prosperous life and in passing he had no direct heirs. We don't know the connection to these three men. But the transfer of the property to them concludes the tie to the Eycott/Eacott/Ecot name to the places of it's origin Bagendon, North Cerney and Woodmancote.

The Eycots did not leave the Churn valley until after 1600. Their first regular appearance outside the valley was at Warminster in 1665, then South Cerney 1696 and Cromhall 1697. The Rev. Nathaniel Eycott was preaching in Thuxton, Mitford Hundred, Norfolk in 1655-7 for the sum of 22 £ per year. He may have been brother of Joseph b. 1607. In early 1700's Eycotts spread more into Wiltshire and a few other areas such as London. The Eacott name as such became common at Cromhall and the parishes which adjoin it to the south and around Warminster.

An increasing population meant more people had to go searching for work. Having connections for farm work was a big help. But overall the reasons for the movement out of the Churn valley and the locations where they appear is difficult to determine. However when examined, there are local lordships connected to the places where Eacotts went. The Berkeley family around Cromhall and the Thynne family at Warminster. In addition other names which are associated with Bagendon and North Cerney such as Croome, Guise, and Stafford show up in the same places where Eycott/Eacott are found.

Over the next few decades several families flourished and multiplied. The descendants of Thomas Ekott tended to use Ecott and Eacott rather than Eycott during this time although after 1650 Eycott became the most common spelling again. William and Joan lived at Stratton, John and Ann at Colsbourne, Richard went to Brimsfield and Thomas to Bisley. Others stayed closer to home. Edward and Margerie of Winstone had 3 sons, Richard, Thomas and William. By 1665 John and Edward Eacot are householders in Warminster. And in the 1680's and 90's Samuel, Nathaniel and Berkeley were living in Cirencester.

Family connections of note from this group include William Ecott of Cromhall who married Sarah Guy, daughter of Philip Guy of Gloucester. He was a descendant of John Guy the colonizer of Newfoundland. From his will of 1625 we find that this Governor of Newfoundland and former mayor of Bristol (1618 - 19) had a farm at Gauntes Earthcott in Almondsbury Parish, a tenement in Bristol, land known as Seaforest in Newfoundland and 1/16 part of the prisage wines of Bristol.

William and Sarah had a son William who married Mary Drew in 1767. Their son William born 1776 reportedly went to the West Indies.

A William Eycott, age 30 and a stone mason, and his wife left Gloucester in March 1774 bound for Jamaica. Not finding the place to their liking they returned the same year to Bristol.

All told the Eacott records for Cromhall 1697-1849 include 90 persons with another dozen at Wickwar and Charfield. At Alveston there were 47.

The Eycott Goldsmiths

Earlier in this work the wills of the Thomas Ekott and Richard Eycott who are discussed below something of their lives is explained.

Thomas Ekott in his will of July 1583 says he was not a well man. In fact he was to depart the world within the month. In August his will was proved.

Thomas was a husbandman at Bagendon. That is he was a farmer, raising principally sheep. There was a status layer. The title farmer connoted that he was a man paying rent for his land. A husbandman mostly held his land as a copyholder, later a freeholder. They were the successors to the medieval villeins and typically farmed 30 acres of arable land and also had grazing rights. He could pass the copyhold to his son. Still he was obligated to pay a little something to the lord of the manor. Finally, a yeoman was a substantial farmer owning outright some of his land without obligation to anyone.

He had 6 daughters all unmarried and a son, Joseph all under twenty years of age. In addition his wife was still of child bearing age. It could thus be guessed that he was between 35 and 50 years of age. Thomas had 5 brothers, Robert (his will 1629), John the Younger, John the Elder, Edward and William. John the elder had children. His wife was Elizabeth. His will includes references to Henry Balden or Baulden.

Richard Eycott of North Cerney, ostensibly in good health, set forth his will in 1581. He had 6 children 4 boys and 2 girls named John, Anthony, William, Thomas and Elizabeth and Katherine. Richard has a brother Phillipe who has some severe difficulties and needs to be cared for. His son Thomas has been delegated that responsibility. What is the relationship between Thomas and Richard? Father and son? No, Thomas has other brothers than in the will. Brothers ? not likely, since Richard entrusts his brother to his wife and son and does not mention other family. Richard must be uncle or cousin to Thomas.

Thomas in his will says this " *I make my brother THOMAS VYNER of North Cerney, RICHARD BURTON parson of Badgendon and HENRY BALDEN of wodmancote mine overseers and give to every of them ten shillings.*"

During the 1500's the price of wool increased rapidly and Cotswold wool was in great demand in Europe. Literacy was also on the rise and by mid century the old feudal rules on land ownership had been abolished. It was a time of prosperity for the yeoman farmers, particularly in the Cotswolds. The wills indicate ownership of some modest property. They own pewter dishes not wood or clay as most people would have used.

Families by and large didn't stray far from their origins and Bagendon and North Cerney were adjacent villages on the road along the Churn river. Everyone pretty much knew everyone else.

Thomas Vyner of North Cerney is married twice. First to a sister of Thomas Ekott , Margaret born about 1533. They have several children: Richard 1566, Joane 1568, Katherine, Robert, Mary, Ann including a son William (31 Jan 1568) then Margaret dies in childbirth. Afterwards Thomas remarries Ann Ellis (born 1554) also of North Cerney. There are several more children born including on the 15 of December 1588 a son also Thomas born at North Cerney. Thomas senior has a sister who has married and moved to London. At the age of 13, in 1601, Thomas Vyner junior is apprenticed to Thomas's brother in law Samuel Moore who is a London goldsmith. This is a trade with great career connections and available only to the favored child who has access to these connections. In 1604 Thomas junior continues his apprenticeship with William Terry. From 1623 to 1665 he lived at the "Vine" Clements Lane, Lombard St. Lombard street is the home of the money managers of London. Thomas moves in a select society and became a goldsmith, banker, and national financier for the Commonwealth and also the monarchy. He was able to get his hands on an entire shipload of Spanish treasure which made him quite rich. In 1646 to 1651 he became an Alderman for Billingsgate. In 1648 he was Sheriff of London. The next spring the king was beheaded. An active supporter of Cromwell, he was made Lord Mayor of London in 1653 when Cromwell took full power of the government. This was real power at the highest level that only great wealth could command.

His nephew Robert Vyner, son of his half brother William whose mother was Margaret (presumably Ekott) became an Alderman in London for Broad St. in 1666. He had been an apprentice of his uncle in earlier years. He had gone into business with his Uncle. Born at Warwick in 1631 he died at Windsor Castle in 1688. He was lord Mayor in 1674. In 1662 Thomas and Robert were the King's goldsmiths and were asked to supply the East India Company. He also was a partner in the Hudson's Bay Company and reputed to be the wealthiest man in England.

With the Restoration of Charles II to the throne Thomas changed sides like many other influential people of the day and became a supporter of the monarchy again. He floated the king a very large loan. His reward was instant as he was created a baronet in 1660 for his support. (He had also been knighted by Cromwell).

Thus when Thomas Vyner died 28 May 1665 his funeral was a major event. He had been a leader of the realm and one of his clients was Samuel Pepys' who attended the funeral. Thomas was buried at St. Mary Woolnoth. Thomas' brother Robert is also buried there. Robert erected a statue to Charles II on Lombard St. that is now in Newly Hall in Yorkshire. A third brother George Vyner was given building contracts in London after the great fire in 1666 and worked under the supervision of the great architect Wren. Robert became deeply involved with funding the frivolities of Charles I such as lending the king great sums, erecting a huge bronze statue to the King and personally creating the crown and most of the regalia for the coronation. (

We know these today as The Crown Jewels of England.) Unfortunately the king later defaulted on the loans and financially ruined Robert who died in 1688 at Windsor castle.

In the shadow of these self made giants there were opportunities for relatives. Among these were Richard Eycott (born 1640). Two boys who were nephews or great nephews of Sir Thomas and Robert Viner seemed to have benefitted greatly. William Eycott who was born about 1654 and Berkeley his brother born about 1655 were chosen to train as goldsmiths in London. Fewer than 30 or so children a year were able to do this. Berkeley in particular bore a prestigious name perhaps in honor of a Berkeley who lived at Rendcomb. This was sometimes done as a form of flattery.

Berkeley and William Eycott had a birth that gave them a future. They were born after the great upheaval of the 1640's when the Puritan power was ascendant, when Roundheads fought Royalists, when parliament stood against the king and prevailed in the 1650's. The boys were reared in a community with strong links to Cromwell the Puritan leader who became ruler of England. Bagendon parish had clergy appointed by Cromwell and had many Puritan style names in the baptisms. Considering the influential local people who rose to prominence, it can be assumed this was a Cromwell supporting community.

1660 saw the end of Cromwell's commonwealth and the restoration of the monarchy.

Richard Eycott of North Cerney may have been Berkeley's father and his grandfather may have been Richard the rough mason. There was problem recording information during the Cromwell era. Berkeley's other brother may have been Samuel also a Cirencester goldsmith.

I wrote Richard may have been Berkeley's father. The question is which Richard. In the 1600's there are 24 references to Richard. Several may be the same person repeated. A Richard was born 1635,40,45 and there were others in 1664,1658,1668 whose father was Richard. A similar problem exists with Thomas of which there are 25 references, and William 27 and finally John with 31 references. (See Appendix T for Eycott- Vyner connection and R For Berkeley's family tree)

Young William and Berkeley, when about 14 years of age and having had some schooling, were sent to London to be apprenticed to the goldsmiths. This may have been arranged by Sir Thomas himself. Their apprenticeship began just after the great fire, during which their great uncle Robert had been the Sheriff of London. The city was undergoing much construction in the rebuilding of London at the time. The Goldsmiths new hall had just opened. The guild of Goldsmiths were at the peak of their power. They controlled not only the making of gold plate and jewelry but the coin of the realm and the flow of currency. The boys would learn to make and sell plate, to buy foreign coins of gold and silver and to melt them and to make small wares, cutlery, salters, cups, chafing dishes etc. and to complete their 7 year training they would have made a masterpiece of their own.

The Goldsmith Hall, the guild of craft workers in gold, was at the time also the assayers of the gold for England and acted as bankers before the Bank of England was created. Goldsmiths were people of real status. It was before the creation of modern banking and around 1670 the goldsmiths of the city were engaged in the nearest thing to being bankers and money lenders that existed. To be apprenticed meant a secure future. William Eycott served his apprentice under William Harrison. He began it on July 29, 1668 and gained his freedom Aug 5, 1675. William then set off to Gloucester City where he set up his own business.

On Thursday, July 23rd 1668 just after five in the morning, young William Eycott set forth from North Cerney accompanied by his father. William was dressed in knee length trousers, long stockings and a new pair of boots. He wore a linen shirt under his doublet which had a cape on it. A new cap and purse completed his outfit. He had bundled in his blanket a clean new pair of trousers, shirt and stockings, a loaf of rye bread, and some cheese and onions.

By six they had reached Cirencester and turned east toward London. The day was pleasant enough but as his father wanted to waste no time, they kept up a brisk pace until the sun was high overhead. By now his new boots were hot and he was dusty from the riders and carts that had been passing. His father had said that the traffic would be a lot worse as they neared the city. After finding a tree that offered some shade they took their lunch and then were off to reach the home of a friend near Lechlade which he hoped to reach in time for an evening meal and a bed. His father had been carrying a flank of mutton which had been cooked the day before as a contribution for his being a guest.

The next morning, Friday, under a cloudy sky they were on the road almost as early. This day there was no specific destination and they had expectations of sleeping along the road. However by late day it had begun to rain and they were avoiding carts and riders more carefully and not making as much progress as was desired. Finally an inn came in view and it was decided to stop for a meal and a space to lay down. Others had the same idea and William and his father found themselves crowded together with some men who smelled of body and beer. There was groaning and snoring and the strange place meant that William did not sleep much in spite of his tiredness.

Saturday, July 25 dawned with pouring rain. After buying some breakfast his father sat at the table and looked out into the rain. He advised his son to take his time as there was no way they were leaving until the rain slowed. In London Samuel Pepy's was commenting in his diary on the foul weather this Saturday.[34] Past noon father and son set off and soon were soaked. Their boots were slipping in the mud and they were taking great precaution not to fall and become even more muddied than they were. By nightfall the rain had ceased and a carter who had needed help freeing his cart took them a good distance and offered them a space in his barn near Brightwalton.

On Sunday morning they were up with the rooster and making good time as there were not many about this day. The road was drying out and their boots while still wet were more comfortable. It was hoped they would be near the city by nightfall. This would mean the journey could be completed by the next day and there would be a day before William was to meet his future master.

Along the way William was told many thing about the city. He had heard of the plague and the great fire and was told there was much

---

34

"Up, and at the office all the morning; and at noon, after dinner, to Coopers, it being a very rainy day, and there saw my wifes picture go on, which will be very fine indeed. And so home again to my letters, and then to supper and to bed."
Pepy's diary entry July 25, 1668

construction work. He has seen some Berlin carriages, closed boxes suspended over the wheels with leather straps, and was told there were many of these vehicles for the rich to travel in. Some people were being carried in sedan chairs. A few people were elegantly dressed and wearing wigs and he was surprised to see men with no beards, all clean shaven. He was getting excited about the new life he was about to lead far from the sheep and hills of North Cerney.

London was no large Cirencester. It was huge with many large buildings and people in all manner of dress. The river was full of boats carrying people and goods. There were theaters and plays, eating houses, and wide streets, great cathedrals and bridges. At night there were oil lamps along the main roads to brighten the darkness. There were street after street of burned and ruined buildings. The fire of two years before had been huge. Many people still had difficulty finding accommodation. That was not Williams concern because William Harrison his master had a room and a bed for him.

William shifted awkwardly in his clean clothes and scrubbed boots. His father and Harrison were discussing his future and he was trying to decide if he liked the man who had control of his life for the next seven years. The scale of the city and the hub bub of human activity there was intimidating him and he spoke weakly almost mumbling in his embarrassment.

The contract had been settled and after it was signed, Harrison was anxious to offer something he himself had recently been served. Harrison had acquired some tea and wished to offer it. The beverage was prepared and poured from the cup onto the saucer where it was sipped. Harrison extolled its benefits as an elixer as they enjoyed the taste of this newly imported product from Holland. The men discussed a play called "The Slighted Maid" which Harrison had seen on the same day as Pepys at the nearby Duke of York's Playhouse. The boy marveled at the wonders of his new life.

Afterward, it was time to part.

Harrison eyed young William kindly and told him to say goodbye to his father. William wanted to cry and hug him but instead held out his hand and thanked him for bringing him here. He had rehearsed this brief speech every day on the journey. His father smiled and turned quickly away.

Harrison handed William his contract of indenture and asked if he understood it. William nodded.

A few years later Berkeley would sign these same papers.

When the boys became apprentices in London, it was required that they gain the freedom of the city admission papers. This was the formal document that allowed the boy to live in London and was also the contract of indenture that formally made them apprentices.

There was a standard form. This is what the City of London form said.

This INDENTURE WITNESSETH that _____ son of _____ in the county of _____ doth put himself Apprentice to _____ citizen and _____ of London, to learn his Art: and with him (after the manner of an apprentice) to serve from the _____ unto the full end of the term of _____ years, from thence next following to be fully complete and ended. During which term, the said Apprentice, his said Master faithfully shall serve, his secrets keep, his lawful commandments everywhere gladly do. He shall do no damage to his said Master, nor fee to be done of others, but that he to his power *shall let, or forthwith give warning to his said Master of the same. He shall not waste the Goods of his said Master, nor lend them unlawfully to any.*

He shall not commit Fornication nor contract Matrimony within the said term. He shall not play at Cards, Dice, Tables, or any other unlawful Games, whereby his said Master, may have any loss, with his own Goods or others, during said term, without license of his said Master, he shall neither Buy or Sell. He shall not haunt Teverns or Play-houses, nor absent himself from his said Master's service day or night unlawfully. But in all things as faithful Apprentice, he shall behave himself towards his said Master, and all his, during the said Term. And the said Master his said Apprentice, in the same Art which he useth, by the best means that he can, shall teach and instruct or cause to be taught and instructed, finding unto his said Apprentice, meat, drink, apparel, lodging and all other necessities according to the custom of the City of London, during the said term. And for the true performance of all and every the said Covenants and Agreements, witherof the said parties bindeth himself unto the other by these presents.

In WITNESS whereof, the parties above named to these Indentures, interchangeably have put their Hands and Seals the _____ day of _____. Anno Dom 16____ and in the _____and ____year of the Reign of our Soveraign Lord King CHARLES II.

Signed

Young Berkeley, two years after his brother, thus signed himself up for seven years commencing 16 November 1670 and entered his new career as apprentice to William Cowland.

However it appears that Berkeley never quite got around to petitioning for his freedom and thus technically did not become a master smith. It is not known how long he remained an apprentice although 7 years was the usual time it took to reach the level of master by the creation of a masterpiece. He did however become a goldsmith in Cirencester setting up his business by 1698.

In the year Berkeley went to London, 1670, Robert Vyner was becoming a partner in the Hudson's Bay Company and thus part owner of nearly half of Canada. Then 2 years later he was to be involved with creating the Royal African Company, a slaver organization. While the boys were still apprenticing, Robert became Lord Mayor of London (1674.) Robert Vyner's famous family portrait of 1673 by J.M. Wright now hangs in the National Portrait Gallery, London[35]. Robert had a son Charles named after the King. Charles died in 1688 shortly before Robert. His daughter Bridget became the Duchess of Leeds. The Eycott boys lived in London at a very favored time and perhaps from time to time met their famous relatives who no doubt had a part to play in their careers.

After completing his apprenticeship William began his career in

---

[35] *NPG # 5568*

Gloucester city.[36] Until the 1500's a goldsmith was considered an artist but during the 1600's they had access to gold and silver and started to become money lenders on the side thus becoming the foundation of the banking industry.

There were 52 goldsmiths in the county before the civil war - 14 in the city, 4 in Cirencester, 4 in Tewkesbury and the rest in other places. After the civil war there were only 2 goldsmiths left in the city. So William began work with much opportunity. As a goldsmith he had a seat on the city council. His seal was a 5 point star over the initials WE with a six point star under that. William's work is known at Withington church where he created a paten cover and a pair of cups. (Eycott descendants lived at Withington) and paten covers by him are also at St. Michael church in Gloucester.

Berkeley was born during the Cromwell era when few records were kept of births so his birthday is somewhat contrived. He is reportedly born in 1655. Sometime before he was born Maurice and Richard Berkeley were still at Eycott/Rendcomb but the land had been sold to the Guise family. These men were supporters of the king and fined by parliament in 1644/5 for not paying fees to parliament. The Berkeleys continued to live at Eycott until the 1690's. The connection to these Berkeleys may have some connection to the young Berkeley Eycott's given name.

When Berkeley marries Mary Shewell in 1688 he is about 33 and she around 18. Their marriage for whatever reason was identified as a clandestine marriage. At the time a couple who wanted a cheap or quick marriage without the formal banns or licence or who were married away from their home church had to find a preacher who would marry them outside of the regular rules of marriage in place until 1695. Sometimes these were performed at the Fleet prison where a different set of rules applied. As a prison, the Fleet was claimed to be outside the jurisdiction of the church. Disgraced clergymen (and many who pretended to be clergymen) lived there and marriage houses or taverns carried on the trade, encouraged by local tavern keepers in the neighborhood who employed touts to solicit customers for them. There were also many clerks who made money

---

36

The History of the Goldsmiths of Gloucester county from 1500 to 1800 was published in 1990. William and Berkeley are included.

recording the ceremonies. Many thousands of couples used this loophole in the law to get married there. During the 1740s up to 6,000 marriages a year were taking place in the Fleet area, compared with 47,000 in England as a whole. One estimate suggests that there were between 70 and 100 clergymen working in the Fleet area between 1700 and 1753. It was not merely a marriage center for criminals and the poor. However, both rich and poor availed themselves of the opportunity to marry quickly or in secret. All people had to be married in the church of England but the Fleet prison clergy made it easier for Catholics and non conformists to marry. Berkeley and Mary took advantage of this loophole in the law.

Mary was likely from the Shewell (or Sewell) family who were clothiers in the Stroud area. There is also a Shewell Wood in the vicinity of North Cerney.

Berkeley returned to Cirencester and apart from being a goldsmith, and possibly a mortgage lender, he became an important person in the small church at Bagendon. He arranged for a land transfer to the benefit of the church and was a warden of it. His responsible connection with the church makes one wonder what sort of non conformist he was. Perhaps it was Mary who was Catholic or other Protestant dissenter and did not want an Anglican wedding.

The venture into being a money lender turned sour for many goldsmiths in the early 1700's and when their clients defaulted, they lost heavily. We don't know if this affected the Eycotts much or not. In his will Berkeley is noted as a Gentleman of Eycott House, Rendcomb Glos. He was wealthy by the standards of the day and his legacy is reflected in the lives of his descendants for several generations.

However the Goldsmiths Company did not always find him to be the most honorable of men as he was fined on the 20 June 1706 by the Goldsmiths Company for selling substandard wares. In contrast to his brother we know nothing of his craft work. In 1703-5 he was church warden at Bagendon. In 1713 William Huntington M.A. became the curate of Bagendon and before his induction Berkeley Eycott and William Chandler were sequestrators. In 1714 an attempt was made to exchange five acres of Berkeley Eycott's land in North Field with some church land held for the benefit of the repair of the ancient Trinity mill. Berkeley died 15 March 1718/19 and is buried at Bagendon. He likely lived at the Moor. Berkeley had a family of 5 boys and 2 girls. Several of his sons and grandsons were John, Samuel and Jones.

John Cowland, perhaps son of Berkeley's master William Cowland, was of reputable parents, apprenticed to a goldsmith. He got into fight over a women and killed a man near Drury lane theater in the year 1700. Berkeley would have taken an interest in this crime and likely had many conversations after learning of it.

When Berkeley died in 1717 he left an interesting will. Sons John and Richard got a token 5 shillings. Why? Because they were established and had their birthright already. Son Thomas gets £ 30 plus Berkeley's living (rental property) at Coates. This was a place he owned and rented out with enough income to live on. Berkeley may have been awarded this after Thomas Eycott of Coates died in 1714 or it may be the same Thomas was already there and had a will drawn up that year. Daughter Sarah not yet 20 would get £ 200 as would Joseph and Berkeley Jr. when they reached 21.

James was included in this as well for he got an additional £ 30 to buy out his apprenticeship. He was apprenticed to Joseph Shewell, likely a relative of his mother. Shewell was a wax chandler who dealt in candles and soap. So James was being trained for business. Later we find James living in London as a merchant, a mercer at Covent Gardens where in 1730 he is registering a lad to become his apprentice. James is also active in the Cirencester Society of London helping apprentices in London from Cirencester. He was a wealthy merchant and died in 1746. He is mentioned again later.

In today's terms Berkeley left each child roughly half a million each. John's male heir was to get the Moor if there was to be one otherwise Berkeley Jr would get The Moor or would be paid a sum to equal its value.

In addition to Berkeley and William, John Eycott and Richard Eycott were also skilled trades persons in the late 1600's. These may have been other brothers. John was also a Goldsmith in Cirencester and Richard was a silversmith in Dublin, Ireland. Richard apprenticed his son William to Edward Barrett also a Silversmith in Dublin Ireland in 1712. Then Richard Eycott took on a registered apprentice on 15 Nov 1717 at Cirencester. John Eycott, a cordwainer (a person who made new shoes, a cobbler repaired shoes) had registered a boy on 1 Jan 1760 to be his apprentice at Ampney

Crucis. This was a family with a foundation of potential wealth whose children and friends were given the best opportunities.

We can trace several of Berkeley's children and grandchildren and even some great grandchildren who were affected by his legacy. They are also the most traceable of the Eacott family. John (born1689) died 1751 was also a goldsmith at Cirencester. He in turn had 5 sons. He left his estates in Bagendon to his sons Richard, Thomas and John. John the son was the executor and John the deceased had a wife Elizabeth. The boys Thomas and Richard were neither of age((under 21). They were to get £ 250 each along with their own estates in Bagendon. This John (1689) had a number of sons and daughters of whom only three are noted in the will. The significance of this is unknown and should be examined. The family must have owned a lot of property around Bagendon.

John's other sons were Joseph (1716), John (1717), Jones (1721), Joseph (1723), James (1725) and Richard (1730) . Of these Joseph stands out because he relocated to property at Yattendon, Berkshire, where presumably he was able to acquire land and with his wife Elizabeth had 3 sons Joseph Eccot (1745) Thomas Eccot (1746) and John Eacott (1748). This family branch at Yew tree, Chaddleworth, Brightwalton all in the same locality in Berkshire was to be henceforth known by the surname Eacott. Some of these descendants became preachers. Up to this point the grandchildren of Berkeley were doing quite well.

John Eacott (1748) of Yew Tree, Berkshire married Rebecca Rafe in Oct 1774 and had several children. Of these Abraham 1781 - 1865 married Martha Wiggins and sired at least 8 sons, Aaron, Caleb, Abraham, Matthew, Mark, Luke, John, James. With so many sons born in the early 1800's a large genealogical tree of Eacotts was created. More comments about this family grouping appears elsewhere.

One son of John (1689), Jones Eycott (1721) was also known as Eccott. He married in 1758 and died at Cirencester in 1779. There was a notice in the Gloucester Journal 31 Aug 1756 revealing Jones was also a goldsmith. Jones was listed as owning a house in Cirencester. There was no family known for Jones. He was also an elector for the Knight of the Shire in 1776.

In the same election of 1776 Samuel Eacott owned property at Bisley,

Gl and John Eycot owned a house and land at Badworth but lived in Cirencester.

In addition there were Berkeley's other sons Thomas (1695) and Berkley (1710) who marries Esther Cane July 10 1751. This marriage is also a little unusual because it also was identified as a clandestine non conformist marriage.

Although Bartley (1756) may have been Berkley's son. We have some evidence Berkely Jr. may have married before at the Fleet prison on July 6 1733 to Mary White. But that may not be so because Richard Eycott of Dublin, Ireland, the silversmith, had a Barkley or Berkley who was christened July 22 1712. To make it even more complicated Jonathan Ecote and Elizabeth residents of Chedworth christened Barkley Ecote on October 17 1705 in Chedworth. Barkley Eycoat and Mary were the parents of one John Eycoat. All of these events took place in the records of Clandestine Marriages and Baptism from 1667 -1754. They may have all been Catholic or Non Anglican Protestants.

However Thomas (1695) was reputed to have married Penelope Ebsworth but there was another Thomas Eycott married to a Mary living also at North Cerney in 1715. Thomas Eycott, yeoman, of Bagendon, his wife Mary and children Thomas Jr, Elizabeth, Rebecca, and Mary were reputed to be Papists who took the oath of Allegiance to king George I in 1715. Thereafter Thomas Eycott was appointed constable of Badgington (sic). This meant he was the primary government official for the parish and thus was sworn not to be a Catholic which would have denied him any government position. This oath was an oath of loyalty to the new king George I and was taken by every constable, rector and other official in the land so the reputed to be Papist assertion may be pretty weak. It's not likely Thomas (1695) was the same person as he would have been 20 and unlikely to have all the children listed for him. So the Constable is yet a different Thomas. Is the reader confused? (The Berkeley tree is appendix R)

Let's go back to Berkeley and his son Richard (1692). Richard had a son with an unusual name, Slaughter Vicarage Eycott and he moved to Berwick-on-Tweed and later Nottingham. Slaughter is a family name. His sons were George (1754)and John (1755) and daughter Eleanor. Nothing else is known of this group although he may have been a preacher and was buried in London. Richard also had a son John who went to South Carolina to become a trader. His story comes later in this book.

Berkeley's son Joseph Eycott (1703) married Mary Freeman in 1730 and lived at Cherington Gl. He had 5 sons. There seems to have been some money with this family. Joseph's eldest son Henry Charles 1736-1801 married Elizabeth Stanton and they had fabric mills at Stonehouse Gl. from 1780. His son Henry 1765-1821 enlarged the mills and his son Frederick 1803- 1884 was also involved in the business. Again Berkeley's wealth may have had a role to play in this family branch. Their story also comes later in this book.

So son John is a goldsmith in Cirencester and one of his sons, John, moves to Berkshire. His family story also comes later in this book.

Thomas returns to own land at North Cerney where he may have been the constable of North Cerney.

Berkley junior married and had educated children. The question becomes how many had this same name of Berkley, Bartley etc. The original Berkeley who started this pattern of given names was held in high regard.

James, as mentioned earlier, moves to London and joins the Cirencester Club in 1727. The club aids apprentices who come from Cirencester. Members who had to be born in Cirencester included several Shewell family members from its earliest days and Robert Berkeley Freeman a cousin. James was likely a mercer, a merchant dealing in fabrics at St Paul Covent Garden, London. A James married Mary Constantine in 1732 at Newgate, London. A child Peter Eakett is baptized and died in 1736 at St. Paul. James died in 1746.

This leaves Berkeley's two daughters and it is hard to determine who Sarah and Mary wed, if anyone.

In Summary, Berkeley died March 12, 1716. In his will he indicated he lived at the Moor in Badgington,(sic) and was a goldsmith. He left 5 shillings to John and Richard. John and Richard were established tradesmen. Thomas was paid £ 30 and a living (right to dwell or rent) at property Berkeley owned at Coates (west of Cirencester). Sarah, James, Joseph, Mary and Berkley were given £ 200 each or the equivalent of 10 years wages for the average worker of the day. These children were not yet of age.

He also instructed John, his eldest, that if he had a male child he would also be given the right to live at the Moor during his lifetime and if not Berkley should have that right. John was responsible for the young Berkley. The impact of Berkeley was significant on his descendants. That influence on the ancient Eycott property ended by 1832 as Moorwood was occupied then by the Haines family and the mansion was rebuilt around 1750.

This brings into focus other land holdings by the other Eycotts around Woodmancote. What follows in the next page is a repeat of earlier material in this book as it is needed to help sort out the relationships.

When references occur about the Eycotts, it is uncertain just where at Woodmancote they lived, other than at the Moor. In Rees' book [37] he reports Eycotts living there until at least 1776. (Francis Ashmead lived with an Eycott at the Moor until her death that year. She was called Madam a term with dual meaning. It is recorded she was not buried in the normal portion of the cemetery, but on the north side an indication that in those days she was living unmarried with a man and thus living in sin and so buried as a sinner). The families who lived around North Cerney, Woodmancote and Bagendon in the 1500's included Baldwin, Baradale, Brood, Broadhurst, Brown, Coxe, Crump, Cherington, Dean, Eycott, Hall, Large, Painter, Perry, Rich, Savery, Smith, Sparrow, Stockwell, Teale, Telling, Tombs, Townsend, Wilson, Vyner. Some of these including Wilson, Tombs, Savery and Vyner are know to be connected to the Eycotts. Studies of surnames in an area show that there is a considerable turn over within 50 years. So the Eycott name was unusually durable before 1800 in these Churn valley parishes.

In 1680 Thomas Eycott gave his lands to Richard. He gave land between Cross Piece and Moorcomb Piece which was bounded on three sides by land owned by the Stevens. In 1708 Thomas secured a mortgage for 700£. At the same time Berkeley Eycott held other property at Bagendon. In 1723 John Eycott gave up his rights to Thomas, his brother. In 1747 Robert Saunders bought the land from Thomas Eycott at the time he, Robert, married Thomas' daughter Elizabeth Eycott. In 1753 Elizabeth Eycott gave to her daughter Elizabeth Saunders her share of the estate. The marriage to Saunders took place at Tyndale but she later lived at Little Farringdon Berks. The land next passed to Wm. Bolt in 1777 and back to Robert Saunders of Little Farringdon in 1807. In 1812 Wm. Croome purchased

---

[37] *The History of Bagendon by G.E. Rees, 1932*

parcel #809 and in 1832 he is listed as owning a farm house.

At the time of the registration of papists in 1717 this record exists:

Woodmancote[38]- John Eycott held two houses and several arable parcels of land, meadow and pasture ground with appurtenances in Chedworth, also one yard lands of common pasture of diverse sorts and cattle. He held two closes in Woodmancote, one called Dorothy's Leaze and one Linkham's Piece. He was required to pay his sisters Robertta and Martha 3£ each for these until they are married and subject to a mortgage made by Thomas his late father with Jonathan White for a principal of 100£. This was signed by John.

Another registration by a Thomas Eycott of Woodmancote who held four yardlands of arable meadow and pasture as well as a house. His sisters Robertta and Martha held a cottage which was apparently rented to a William Sherrall. There was a mortgage on the farm for 700£. This Thomas or another of the same name was constable of Bagendon in 1715. That means he was appointed to keep the peace in the community and was really the only local government official.

It would appear from this that Thomas in 1680 left his land to his son Richard who passed it on to his son Thomas. This man had two sons John and Thomas and two daughters. John may have lived at Chedworth and arranged to place his share at Woodmancote in his brothers hands, 1723. Thomas was to have no sons but did have a daughter Elizabeth, named after her mother. She married Robert Saunders in 1747 and the Eycott name left the property. Other Eycotts may have lived at Bagendon for a few more years but by 1778 there were no more Eycotts on the church rolls renting seats.

The will of Thomas 1715 says that he had two sons Thomas (the eldest) and John. John was the executor of the will and Robert Moran of Fairford was the trustee. Thomas had three daughters, Rebecca, Elizabeth and Martha. Thomas's wife was Mary. John was given a house and grounds in Chedworth and was also given Dorothy's Leaze and Linkham's piece. Thomas (the eldest) in his will of 1740 says he was a , a batchelor and he

---

38

QRNC 1 (22) ;QRNC (21)

gave his possessions to William Eycott of Cirencester his nephew. Thomas also gave his sisters Rebecca and Martha a freehold estate at Woodmancote with a cottage there until they were married. William Eycot, tailor of North Cerney died 20 Aug 1748. Was he the recipient of Thomas' estate.

William Eycott of Cirencester might have been the son of John Eycott of Cirencestor who lived on Dyer St. a Catholic Goldsmith with an estate at Bagendon. His mother was Mary, his wife Elizabeth and sons Richard and John who had a freehold estate at Chedworth. John was brother to Thomas and his freehold estate at Chedworth was subject to his paying £ 3 to each of his sisters. So both brothers had care of their sisters. In the nave of the church at North Cerney is the following *"Here rests the earthly part of Thomas Eycott ob. Sept 6 1715 age 60."* and in the same church yard *"Thomas Eycott died 17 Sept 1750 age 75.* [39]

In 1730 the will of Thomas, made and read that year, listed his son Thomas as the executor. He had three daughters Dorothy, Rachelle and Hester. This Thomas also lived at Bagendon and may have been the one listed as constable in 1715. The father of this man might have been a Richard (if he was in his 80's(84)) or it may have been Berkeley (if he was 35), or it may have been another person. (Sorting this out is a project for someone else, not me!)

John Eycott of Cirencester in his will of 1751, whose wife is Elizabeth, leaves his estates in Bagendon to his son John who is executor, and gives his son Richard 250 £ when he reaches age 21 and the same to his son Thomas when he came of age also. These boys would also gain estates in Bagendon. Henry Timbrell and Richard Worstlar were witnesses to the will. However Richard and Thomas don't seem to factor into any land at Bagendon. There is no further evidence of their estates.

In 1710 the defunct Eycott manor becomes Eacott farm in land assembled to become Rendcomb Estate. What Berkeley knew about this is not know!

In Dublin Ireland in 1712 Richard Eycott, silversmith apprentices his son William to Ed Barrett. Is this Richard a brother of Berkeley and William? How did he become a silversmith and where did he apprentice?

---

[39] *Bigland:187*

When did he arrive in Dublin?

William Powlett Eycott on July 7 1791, late of Cirencester, cabinet maker, dealer and chapman (a peddler or also a dealer in raw cotton and wool) declared bankruptcy. Then in 1796 he declared bankruptcy again. After which on Sept 15 1796 he decided to emigrate to America. William was the son of Joseph Eycott and Jane Powlett. They had 3 daughters and he was their only son, born 1767 in Cirencester. In turn Joseph was the son of William and Beata Eycot of Rendcomb. William's mother was Sarah who lived at Woodmancote and died in 1755. Her husband was likely Joseph Eycott 1714- 1734. Young William was apprenticed to Ebenezer Brown in 1783 in Bristol. In later years he was an upholsterer and when he died in 1843 he was buried in the family vault at North Cerney with his wife Martha Godson. I don't think he was immediate family of Berkeley.

If he emigrated to America, he eventually came back and established himself as an upholsterer in Hammersmith, London where he died in 1843 leaving a will. There were no known children.

We now have moved the development of the Eycott family from the mid 1600's to the mid 1700's where they take their leave of Bagendon and North Cerney and Woodmancote. There is an earlier record of John Eycott of the Moor being married to Alse who died in 1631. So a case can be made that the Eycotts lived at the Moor from earlier than 1400 to 1750.

Our story now moves into the 1700's. America has been settled and John Eycott is in South Carolina working as a trader with the Creek Indians. England has an Empire and life in rural England is much unchanged but trade and the cities are beginning to grow. It is the eve of the industrial revolution but we are not there yet.

A great many people were still independent small farmers who grew enough food for themselves and sold their surplus. There were large tracts of common land where such small farmers could graze their animals. The enclosure acts were starting to reduce the amount of common land.

London of course was the biggest town and was the centre of fashionable life for the upper classes. The cities of Bristol and Liverpool were very prosperous as a result of the slave trade.

Factories did not really exist as such. Most production was carried on on a small scale. People worked in their own homes. A weaver, for instance, would have his loom in his own house and his wife and daughters and other female relatives would spin the wool or flax that he wove into cloth. Many women made a living from spinning.

Servants were commonplace. Almost everyone who could afford a servant would keep one. You didn't have to be rich. A quite ordinary family might employ a single maid for housework and a wealthy family might employ dozens. Servants usually lived in their employers' homes and one of the advantages of working in service was that you got food and accommodation. Most servants were quite young. It was a job people often did until they had saved up enough to get married.

Clothing was handmade and therefore buying clothes was expensive. Most women could sew and could make their own and their families clothing. There was a great trade in second-hand clothing for poor people and the upper classes often had their clothes made by dressmakers and tailors. Hats were an important fashion accessory. Nobody would go out without a hat in those days. In 1750 very elaborate hairstyles were the fashion and wigs were still being worn by gentlemen though they would go out of fashion about twenty years later.

The main meal of the day, dinner, was eaten at around noon and for the wealthy it might consist of two or three courses, each consisting of several different dishes to choose from. The dishes would be set out on the table for people to help themselves, rather like a modern buffet. The custom of just eating one dish at a time, as a separate course, was not introduced until the 1840s. Roasts, pies, pastries, tarts, syllabubs, and jellies were all very popular in this era and dishes like jugged hare were served. Preserves and pickles were very important because there was little fresh food available in winter so preserving food was an important skill for the Georgian housewife or cook. This was the way the Eacott families lived then.

Sending Out New Roots

The Eycotts under various name variations were dispersing about the world now. Let us take a look at some of the new communities where they were found. In many cases there is a link with the lord of the local manors and the Churn valley parishes. In general people moved where they had some connections for employment. It was not allowed to just simply move away from one's parish as there were requirements to be made. Starting about 1601 the Poor Laws were established and each parish had an overseer of the poor laws.

The laws dictated who could live in the parish. These laws in one form or another persisted until about 1930. For a person to have the Right of Settlement they had to meet certain qualifications. These included birth, marriage to a resident, renting accommodations costing £ 10 or more and paying the poor law tax which was the fund that paid the upkeep of the indigent. A person completing an apprenticeship could also be a resident. Here is an example when a spouse died.

Thus it was that Esther Eacott born 1816, recent widow of James, mother of 5 young children, James 13, Esther 11, John and William 7 and Sarah 4, who had lived in St. Leonard Parish, Shoreditch at 10 Berkeley Court in London in 1853, learned that she was no longer able to get welfare from St. Leonard parish because her husband had only lived there for 3 years not the required 5 before he died. She had no income so she was to be deported to another parish around the corner only a few streets away where she had previously lived. Esther was forcibly deported down the road with her children to St Luke's parish to get welfare. The family physically had to pack up and move and be escorted by a police constable. This was an example of the Poor Laws in action all across England.

Relocation for work even in one city was not an easy activity.

A most interesting question is why did an Eycott/Eacott suddenly appear in certain communities?

Two groups can be traced back to Berkeley Eycott as their common ancestor. The Yew Tree and Stonehouse groups are founded by his descendants. A third descendant went to trade in America.

Most of the rest of the descendants of the Eycott/Eacott can not be directly linked back to North Cerney. The trail to the other locations is fragmented and broken. Furthermore the reasons for relocation are also not at all clear. However there are tempting clues!

The most plausible answer is that in many cases it is a young person moving to find work.

In 1630 John Eacott was born to Richard, a rough mason, at North Cerney. At this time name interchanges were quite common. Parish and Bishops registers were even at variance with the same person and event. Alse and John Eycot lived at the Moor in the 1630's From 1430 until the late 1700s there were 141 Eycot and variations recorded at North Cerney, 15 at Rendcomb, 56 at Bagendon. From after 1683 there were 46 Eycots (only Eycots) at Cirencester. Records went back in most places to just before 1600.

The Eycots did not leave the Churn valley until after 1600. Their first regular appearance outside the upper valley was at Warminster in 1665, Cirencester in 1683, then South Cerney 1696 and Cromhall 1697 although the Rev. Nathaniel Eycott was preaching in Thuxton, Mitford Hundred, Norfolk in 1655-7 for the sum of 22 £ per year. He may have been brother of Joseph born 1607. In early 1700's the family spread more into Wiltshire and a few other areas such as London. The Eacott name as such became common at Cromhall and the parishes which adjoin it to the south and around Warminster.

How did the Eacott name become connected to lands near Berkeley Castle?

The Eacotts of Southern Gloucestershire

Between Gloucester city and Bristol area there are a number of rural hamlets where the Eacott/Ecott name became known. This Gloucestershire group lived in a collection of communities near the hamlet of Cromhall. Within a 6 mile radius (10Km) of Cromhall are Iron Acton, Wickwar, Tytherington, Itchington, Yate, Thornbury North Nibley, Stone, Charfield, and Alveston. These 11 villages plus nearby Bristol comprise the Eacott/Ecott settlements of southern Gloucestershire. In the same area there are a total of 36 small villages. The 2 main locations were Cromhall and Alveston where the the Ecotts seem to have been predominantly farmers. In this area lands have become known with Eacott names. Eacott's Moor is located near Alveston and a place called Earthcott is also at Alveston. The name first appeared in Cromhall in 1697 then in 1700 in Charfield because of recorded baptisms. The will of John Ecott of Iron Acton in 1711 connects him to both of these places.

John Ecott was likely born in North Cerney/Cirencester in 1666 to Richard Eycott. (Berkeley's father?) He was a tenant on land at Iron Acton that belonged to the Croome family who also held land at Woodmancote in North Cerney. This logical connection explains why when he needed a farm for himself, he was able to find a location for his relocation. John Eacott married Hester (Esther) Heaven at Charfield/Cromhall and his descendants are those found in southwestern Gloucestershire.

This area of Gloucester was quite rural. Most of the places were and are small villages. Today most are part of the Thornbury district. Cromhall is a community extending a mile along a road. Nearby Charfield is a more nucleated village. Alveston was another farming community. During the ages when the Ecotts lived in this area, the wool industry was in decline and dairy and mixed farming became more prevalent. Wickwar was a local market village. The essence for all of the Ecotts who lived here was farming and its associated crafts. Some mining was done at Iron Acton and some quarries existed in the area. Although this area is close to Bristol, only 3 or 4 Eacott families chose to live there in olden days.

The Cromhall Registry of Baptisms from 1725 to 1787 begins with the baptisms of John Eacott son of William and Sarah Eacott in 1735 followed by the baptism of Ann daughter of Samuel and Elizabeth Eacott in 1736. Then for the next 15 years the name is mostly recorded as Ecott but not always for these same two families. William's sons are John, William, Philip (1739) and Robert. Samuel's son is Josiah. After 1751 John, Josiah, Philip, Robert and William are recorded both as Eacott and Ecott when they baptized their kids although by late 1770's the Eacott spelling prevails.

Young Samuel Eacott in 1767 apprenticed as a mason to Samuel Winstone of Bisley Gl.

The will of William Ecutt of Cromhall born 1705 d. 1776 left his farm, a tenement house and two cottages to his eldest son John. John was not a young man and he had remarried. John has 3 brothers, William born 1744, Robert 1751 and Philip 1739. Philip Ecott of Wickwar left a will in 1811. William Eacutt was born at Wickwar 1779 to Philip. So it may be concluded that Philip or his father established the Ecott name at Wickwar. Around 1850 the Ecott version declines and the Eacott version appears, perhaps in only two families.

At Alveston the Ecott name begins with the marriage of Betty Drew and John Ecott of Charfield in 1765. John appears to have relocated to Alveston and established his family there. Although Earthcott (Herdicote at Domesday, later Erthcote, Ercut) and Eacott's Moor are both located there, no connection to a name creation from either is known. Again about the mid 1800's the Eacott spelling seems to be replacing the Ecott. Also Eacotts more recently at Alveston had heard that the Eacotts were Flemish, land drainage experts who were French Huguenot. There is no evidence of that here except the fact that Acott's of Shoreditch London and likely Kent were Huguenot and the name was Acourt in French.

At Frampton Cotterell the first Ecott may have been Robert b 1811 from Cromhall and he used the Eacott spelling which is the only version known at this place. His sons William Charles, William Arthur and Albert Charles dispersed to Sutton Coldfield, London, and Manchester. Grandsons also went to Wales.

At Iron Acton John Eycott died leaving a will and John Eacott born 1666 may have been the same person.

At Thornbury Josiah Eacutt married Eleanor Trayburn in 1760 and had several children but the family did not carry on after that time.

At Yate there were several marriages but only Percival Edward Eacott lived there and he was born at Iron Acton.

At Stone and North Nibley a few female Ecute, Ecott, Eycott marriages take place but no Eacott /Ecott families are established. However a John Acott was born at North Nibley in 1645 to John.

Later wills were of Jemima Eacott of Alveston 1869, Robert Eacott, 1875 of Frampton Cotterell, and Philip and John Eacott 1879 of Alveston. All seemed to have started life as an Ecott earlier in the century. The persistence of the spelling change across the area takes place about the same time literacy becomes important again. The other common factor is nearly all of these people were farmers and not trades people.

The Cromhall, Alveston and Frampton Cotterell families, it appears, were all related and may have descended from John of the 1711 will who may have lived at Cromhall and Iron Acton where he made his will. In 1776 Freehold voters list for Knight of the shire for Gloucestershire showed that another William Ecott of Cromhall was a tenant on land of Thomas Croome. As was noted, the Croome family held land at North Cerney, some of which may have come from the Eycott family. Nearby John Ecott was a tenant at Earthcott of Samuel Taylor. A John Ecott was living on 1 acre at Wickwar as late as 1873.

Family connections of note from this group include William Ecott of Cromhall who married Sarah Guy, daughter of Philip Guy of Gloucester. He was a descendant of John Guy the colonizer of Newfoundland. From his will of 1625 we find that this Governor of Newfoundland and former mayor of Bristol (1618 - 19) had a farm at Gauntes Earthcott in Almondsbury Parish, a tenement in Bristol, land known as Seaforest in Newfoundland and 1/16 part of the prisage wines of Bristol.

William and Sarah had a son William who married Mary Drew in 1767. Their son William born 1776 reportedly went to the West Indies. He would not be the only Eacott to go to the West Indies.

All told the Eacott records for Cromhall 1697-1849 include 90 persons with another dozen at Wickwar and Charfield. At Alveston there were 47.

The descendants of these Eacotts still live in the described area.

At Nearby Bristol a few Eacotts appear. In 1820 William Eacott born about 1790 is apprenticed as a cordwinder. His son born about 1805 becomes a bookbinder and perhaps operates a lending library in 1845 in Bristol. Nearly all the families in Bristol use Eacott. Although John Eckitt born 1834, and James Eckett 1831 are variations. There were never many Eacotts in Bristol. In a northern suburb Wetbury on Trym in late 1800's there was each a family of Eakets and Eccott and a few other single folk Ecott and Eacott.

We now examine some descendants of Berkeley Eycott are quite traceable for a few generations.

John Eycott, Trader to the Creeks

Among the Eycott's in the 1700's a few left for destinations abroad. One of these was an adventurous person known as John Eycott who was a commercial trader to the Indians in the southern American colonies. John Eycott was the grandson of Berkeley Eycott and son of Richard Eycott born 1692. John was born 01 April 1714 in Cirencester. His brothers were George, Richard, and Slaughter Vicarage. His sisters were Sarah and Mary Ann. He must have had a good education and may well have visited to docks at Bristol. Here he would have become aware of the trade with the colonies and some where around the age of 25 decided to emigrate.

The colony of South Carolina starting in 1710 began licensing individuals who wished to trade with the Indians.

The largest English city on the southern coast, Charleston, South Carolina, became the center of trade between colonists and Indians from the time of its settlement in the late seventeenth century. In 1670 English settlers from Barbados founded Charles Town, capital of the new Province of Carolina. Traders from Carolina went inland to Muscogee settlements to exchange flintlocks, gunpowder, axes, glass beads, cloth and West Indian rum for white-tailed deer pelts for the English leather industry and Indian slaves for Caribbean sugar plantations. English products such as woolens, tools, and weapons were cheaper and better than comparable Spanish and French items and became indispensable to the Indians. Carolinians not only amassed wealth through trade but also created economic and military alliances with Indian trading partners which helped them stave off Spanish and French control of Atlantic and Gulf Coast mercantile networks.

A licensed trader was a sharp businessman. The fur of beaver, bear and other creatures as well as the hides of deer were staples of his trade and a red woolen blanket made in Stroud, Gloucestershire was a particularly popular trade item. It may have been this wool that set Eycott into business for he had relatives in the weaving industry. He traveled with a group bearing his sales goods and carrying his purchases back and forth from the interior to Charleston.

In 1750 John Eycott was given a formal licence to trade in Little Okfuskee, one of the places where he had been trading for some years. This district was southwest of the current city of Atlanta near the Alabama border. In general relations with the Creeks was good. The traders valued their association and had to cement good relations because the French were also after the loyalty of these people. The traders risked their lives not with the Chickasaw Creeks but with the French traders and their Indian allies the Choctaws. This territory was now part of the new Georgia colony which was a buffer between the Spanish in Florida and the French in Alabama and as such required keen observation by the British who were fearful of losing control of this territory.

At some point John made his way to America likely sailing out of Bristol. What he did to enable himself to set up in the trading business is not known. However he would have needed some funding to get his cache of items to sell, some ability in keeping records and some understanding of how to negotiate. John was likely an educated man with some cash behind him which would be consistent being related to Berkeley. It was also a requirement that those who got a licence to trade were men of worth as these were also the ambassadors of the king to the natives. They had to be men who could be trusted. John was able to set himself up in the business of trading with the native people. In his case he was licensed to trade with the Creek Indians and so became one of the first white men to travel into what became Tennessee and Georgia.

The Creek more properly known today as the Muscogee were probably descendants of the mound builders of the Mississippian culture along the Tennessee River in modern Tennessee, Georgia, and Alabama. They were considered to be one of the five civilized tribes, who through contact with Europeans, undertook to adopt many of the European ways. They took up farming, established towns, and invented an alphabet and learned to read and write. It was these people allied with the English with whom John Eycott traded.

On 29 July 1741 he married Mary Jeys at St Philip's church Charleston SC. The name Jeys is English from Gloucester or Oxford and there were other Jeys family in Charleston. Her father may have been Peter Jeys. John would have been about 27 years old and just nicely establishing his career. A fur trader was no farmer and he would be frequently away from home for long periods of time. His wife would have managed their properties around the city. There is no evidence of any children. There were about 6000 white people and 20 000 slaves living in Charles Town at that time. It was still a frontier community.

Governor Glen of South Carolina was fully aware of an impending situation between the northern branch of the Creek Indians backed by the French and the Southern branch allied to the English. The Chocktaw uprising of 1746 resulted in the Governor calling a conference of Indian chieftains and offering some proposals. In addition he was asking parliament in London for additional troops. While in conference awaiting the decision of the chiefs he was influenced by several letters sent by traders. One was from John Eycott dated Sept 10 1746 who was at the time in Tallassee Town. (Presumably Tallahassee today) On the basis of these letters the governor's council decided the time was right to strike a stroke against the French settled among them. They wanted the Indians support or a least their neutrality in striking against Fort Alabama. Apart from trading the interior traders were the eyes and ears of the colony. They served an important communication function and while information was in part hearsay the traders were the only people whom authorities could consult.

Eycott was a one time resident trader in the 1840's in the Creek town of Ecunhutke where he served the Creeks and the Savanoes. So he was in south, east and western Georgia at different times. The affairs of the backwoods of colonial day were full of intrigue. One instance is a letter from John Dobell to the Trustees in which he attempts to apologize and explain he was not part of some sort of scheming against Mr. Eycott. It is not clear what the actual issue was. Dobell was school master at Savannah and registrar for all grants of land in Georgia and his word was significant. He had come from Charleston. He was anti slavery. He was a frequent commentator to the Georgia Trustees. At the time of writing this letter he was also Secretary of Indian Affairs and thus empowered to grant trading rights to people such as Eycott. Just what the issue of the day was that put Dobell in the situation below we don't know. It does illustrate that Eycott was pretty well known.

Letter From Mr. John Dobell To The Honourable
THE Trustees FOR ESTABLISHING THE COLONY
Of Georgia At their Office In Queen Square Westminster—27 Dec.
1744. rec'd 27 July 1745.

May it Please your Honours!
I want no addition to my Happiness nor any thing to sweeten every Enjoyment but the Promotion of your Honours Interest to see it flourish

in the Prosperity of this Place by whatsoever Means you in your Wisdom by the Divine Assistance should think meet; that you might reap from Georgia some Satisfaction suitable to your laudable and painful Endeavours in Labouring to Establish it. It is from this Principle, may it please your Honours that I have taken all those Liberties that I have taken in Writing to you, and setting forth the Wrong dealings of Men, and in so particular a Manner as relating to myself, because it may serve as a Specimen of their Conduct to some others, which otherwise I should have been ashamed to have harped so long upon.

I do not think my own Conduct Free from Faults, because I am Conscious to my self of many Imprudencies, and of none greater than the writing so smart a Letter to Mr. Eycott, not that I am apprehensive he will make any ill Use of it, being as I judge a Well-wisher to Georgia. But save in that Letter I have never Opened my Lips to Expose the wrong-dealings of those Men except to your Honours, to whom I have held it my Duty so to do, but have received their Evil Treatment with that quietness and Resignation as if they were so many Instances of real Favour. But when I was informed by one Mr. Smart, who heard Mr. Watson and another say to several Indian Traders of Mr. Eycotts Acquaintance that I was Corrupted in Jordans Favour, and had of him taken a Bribe to the Detriment of Mr. Eycott, it did but too much Effect me, in which Discomposure of Mind I writ to Mr. Eycott that Letter to free myself from the Odious imputation of Guilt which I found myself loaded with, not only here but Propagated too in the Neighbouring Province; and especially as knowing no Shadow of reason that Mr. Watson had to Mete my Corn by his Measure: who for ought I know assisted the most of any to Mis-lead the Commissioner in the original transacting of that Affair. Therefore I humbly crave, and hope, that your Honours will be pleased to Pardon this, and every other of my Miscarriages, whilst it is natural for an Infant to Stumble, that is left to Walk without a Guide or Leader— The reason of my taking and sending to your Honours the enclosed Affidavit, is, because I was informed the Gentlemen had reported that I came to — Morel's as an Eaves-dropper, and assigned at that as the reason of their Evil-treatment: But I had not the least Knowledge before I went thither of their being there.

May it Please your Honours! I want no other Satisfaction from these Men to beget a Reconciliation, but only that they forbear Using me so any more: For I know that Mr. Spencer, who was the Principal, was led *into it by Mr. Watson and another, or two.*

Once more I beg leave to render your Honours my most Humble and Hearty Thanks for your great Goodness towards me and to assure you that the best of my poor Endeavours shall be Constantly employ,d in Obeying your Commands in the Promotion of the Publick Good, which by your Pious Endeavours you have Manifested to the World to be your most desired Honour.

      I am your Honours most affectionately
      Devoted Servant
      John Dobell
Savannah
    the 27 Decem'. 1744.

As a result of his trading efforts John was able to establish himself as a citizen of the wealthiest town in America with a home on a major street. In 1748 his home was across the street " at the corner opposite Mr. Eycott's" from the shop of a major cabinet maker Thomas Elfe. Elfe had trained with Chippendale in England and was equally his peer as a cabinet maker. It was believed the Eycott's may have lived at # 52 King Street. Over a period of about 10 years John had well established himself not only in Charleston but he also had contacts in Savannah where the Georgia colony was headquartered.

There were other traders and they kept an eye on each other. One trader family was that of the Bosomworths.

In 1749 Mary Musgrave, an aboriginal princess, married an Englishman and became Mary Bosomworth who also assumed the title of Independent Empress. She and her husband were traders and ran a store as well as a cattle business. They had many dealings with the colony of Georgia. The following incident in part explains why Eycott was reporting on her to the Trustees and why they were interested in her whereabouts.

"Mrs. Bosomworth putting herself at the head of a large body of warriors, set out for Savannah to demand from the president and council a formal acknowledgment of her assumed rights. The militia was ready to receive her. President Stephens put the town into the best state of defense possible and received the Indians boldly. Jones' History of Georgia says: "The militia was ordered under arms, and as the Indians entered town

Capt. Noble Jones at the head of a troop of horses stopped them and demanded to know whether their visit was of a friendly or hostile nature. Receiving no reply he commanded them to ground their arms, declaring that his instructions were not to suffer an armed Indian to set foot in the town, and that he was determined to enforce the order at every hazard. The Indians reluctantly submitted. Later, at their solicitations, their arms were returned to them, but strict orders were issued not to allow them any ammunition. When at last an amicable adjustment of existing difficulties had been effected, Mary, drunk with liquor, rushed into the Assembly and told the president that the Indians were her people and that he had no business with them. Mary had been arrested and locked up and had just been released. The president calmly threatened to confine her again. Turning to Malachte in a great rage, she repeated to him with some ill-natured comments what the president had said. Malatche thereupon sprung from his seat, laid hold of his arms, and calling upon the rest to follow his example, dared any man to touch his queen. In a moment the whole house was filled with tumult and uproar. Every Indian having a tomahawk in his hand, the president expected nothing but instant death. During this confusion, Capt. Noble Jones, who commanded the guard, with wonderful courage interposed and ordered the Indians immediately to surrender their arms. This they reluctantly did. Mary was conveyed to a private room, where a guard was placed over her, and all further communication with the Indians was denied her during her stay in Savannah."

From A History of Savannah and South Georgia, vol 2 by William Harden, 1913

In July of 1750, John Eycott was sending information to the Trustees of the Colony of Georgia who were concerned about what Mrs. Bosomworth was doing. This is a copy of the minutes that record John's reporting.

At a Meeting of the President and Assistants in Council assembled for the Colony of Georgia on Sunday the 2nd Day of July 1750

William Stephens President
William Spencer/ James Habersham / Assistants

This Day two Indian Traders, Mess" Eycott and Millim, both from the Upper-Creeks came here, and reported, that they learnt from the Indians, where they resided, that Mrs. Bosomworth was
daily expected in the Upper Creek-Nation, where they apprehended, she intended to carry on Designs, that might endanger the Peace and Welfare of the Colony.

— This Report occasioned the Members of the Board to assemble, though on the Lord's Day, as Captain Pearson was then at Tybee, and was expected to Sail this Night or to morrow Morning, by whom they might give the earliest Notice to the Trustees if found necessary of what should come to their Knowledge of Mrs. Bosom worth's extraordinary Journey, which they did in a Letter to Mr. Secretary Martyn of this Date.

From the letter it appears that Mr. Eycott was providing an opinion about a competitor. Mrs. Bosomworth was the biracial daughter of the Creek emperor and wife of John Musgrove another trader. She was important as a successful trader and translator and a very important ally of the Georgia Colony. However she was also a force to be handled with care as the above quote shows. Mrs. Bosworth had been present at the founding of the colony and later wanted compensation from the trustees for her services and as Princess she also had land claims.[40]

John Eycott and his wife, in addition to a town home, also had property just outside the town where they stabled and pastured horses. This was located in the neck area meaning it would have been along Broad street the main road into town that was on the high ground above the swamp. It brought in a nice addition to their income and his connections with the legislature and the natives meant that he was the person to whom the legislature paid to stable the horse of any official delegation of Indians coming to Charles Town. Payments were regularly made to both Mary and John in the late 1740's and up until his death in 1751. The sums involved usually ran from£ 20 to £ 30 although his estate was paid a final settlement of £ 67 It was a supplemental income for the family and when John was away Mary ran the business as some of the payments went directly to her.

---

[40]

See book "Lachlan McGillivray, Indian Trader" by Edwin J Cashin 1992. This trader was a contemporary of John Eycott and so his story will be similar. These men knew each other and may have worked together.

In September 1750 Mary died after only 8 years of marriage. She was buried 13 September 1750 in St. Philips churchyard. St. Philips was the establishment church in Charles Town. We do not know the cause of death but yellow fever was a common disease in the city at the time.

In his grief John had to contend with the fact that about the same time he was placed on a jury list for 1750. We don't know if he had to perform his jury duty or not.

He was not destined to long outlive his wife because John Eycott died less than a year later on June 14th, 1751. He was 37 years old. He was also buried in St. Philips Parish graveyard. John Eycott died on the same day that Charles Town was divided into two parishes, St Philips north of Broad and Str Micheals to the south. Since up until their demise they were actively running their horse stabling business, it would appear they both met untimely ends however we know nothing for certain about the circumstances of either of their deaths. On June 12th 1751 realizing he was not long for this world John Eycott wrote his will stating he was weak in body but sound of mind. His wishes were simple, pay his debts and funeral and the rest of his estate was divided equally between his brother Vicarage Slaughter Eycott in England and his sister Ann Wooley wife of John Wooley of Withington Gl. He appointed his trusty friends Francis McCartan and Martin Campbell both trader merchants of Charles Town to administer his estate. The next day, the day before he died, John Eycott, gentleman, was still very much in charge of his affairs because he sold one of his slave girls, Bella to Mary Campbell another citizen of Charles Town. She was likely the wife of Martin Campbell. Francis McCartan became his executor. [41] McCartan and Campbell were partners in one of the largest Indian trading companies in Charles Town and Eycott may have worked for them before gaining his own trading permit. McCartan died in 1768 and it is not known who administered the estate after that.

Since John left his estate to brother Slaughter and sister Ann, we may conclude that his brothers George and John and sisters Mary and Sarah were perhaps no longer living.

The sale of Bella in South Carolina took place just a few months after the Georgia Colony, after much controversy, legalized slavery in the

---

[41] *Charleston probate and Will book 1747-52, vol 006, pg 428*

colony. This no doubt had increased the demand for slaves to work on plantations there. Previously the white settlers of Georgia had resisted because they feared the loss of employment for themselves. The list of slaves he owned shows this was where his wealth had accumulated. The inventory is matter of fact. He was part of a world where buying and selling of people as commodities was normal. Later we see where other Eacotts were abolitionists.

The law required an inventory of the deceased John Eycott's possessions so we have some intimate details about his estate as the state of South Carolina made an inventory of these goods. In examining his possessions it should be noted what is not included. This would indicate that some of his goods went elsewhere. His estate heirs continued ownership for 30 years after his death. There are no pots and pans or cooking items. There are no carts or wagons. There are no bonds or cash owed to him. While there are silver items, there were no candlesticks which at the time would have been a likely item. So someone had access to his property and the sale inventory represents what was to be sold. The slaves he owned , there were over a dozen, were of average values. All were better than the price of a good horse but none considered highly valuable. He had 4 good men and 4 good women and several not so useful other men and women including some younger children. Likely some were household staff or helped with the stable business. Some may have been hired out to make more income. Many of the goods listed were his and his wife's personal wear items. Some were furniture items but in all his furniture was not extensive. Most of his property value was in his slaves. His total estate was in size similar to others who had died around the same time. They had been an average white establishment Charleston family.

The inventory is now preserved in the South Carolina archives. This is what the estate of a Charleston resident looked like in 1751.

"Inventory of goods belonging to the estate of John Eycott, deceased. [42]

1 negro fellow named Spander		*200*	*£ Pounds*
1 ditto	*Prince*	*180*	

---

[42] *South Carolina Estate Inventories and Bill of Sale vol R1 1751-1753 #56*

1 ditto	Harry	200	
1 ditto	Warrick	160	
1 ditto	Florra	160	
1 ditto	Dinna	180	
1 ditto	Betty	120	
1 ditto	Gloster	70	
1 ditto	Sarrah	90	
1 ditto	Cloe	100	
1 ditto	Phillis	60	
1 ditto	Sam, a child	60	
1 ditto	Dinna, child	30	
1 ditto	Woolich	240 £	

1 sadle		3 £
1 ditto furniture and pistols		10
1 bed, pillow, 2 blankets & pavilion		10
1 desk		5
1 coat, weaved coat & breeches (black)		8
1 black coat		6
3 coats & 1 pr breeches		5 £
1 pair pumps, and remnant Oznabrig & remnant stuff		2 £
1 coffee mill, 2 trunks and parcel old books		3 £
1 silver tankard 27 3/4 oz		48.11.3 £
1 set silver buttons 7.30		12.13.9 £
1 silver watch		20 £
1 hatts	5 £	
1 set silver buckles		5 £
1 pair silver shoe buckles		2.10 £
??? gold buttons & 2 gold rings		4 £
1 snuff box with 1 pr old silver buttons and clasp		1.10 £
1 shag green case with 6 spoons, tongs and strainer		7 £
Brought Over		£ 2008.5

~~~~~~

1 salt seller, 7 spoons, tongs and strainer		4 £
1 pr spurs, L5, 1 silk gown		10
4 old silk callico gowns		5
7 check shirts		4
4 stocks & 4 cravets, 6 caps		2
10 white shirts	12	
8 stockings & 7 old handkerchiefs		3.10
2 weast coasts & 1 callico gown		2

1 bed quilt & 2 old sheets	1.10
6 chairs, 1 table, 1 looking glass	1.10
1 case with 4 bottles	1
a hamper Bristol water	2
a 4 wheel chaise	10
1 old safe	10
3 pictures	6
a clothes press	3
a parcell books	2
a parcell sheets ans 1 pair stays	2 £
Deer skins	25 each
lightly damaged at	2/6 each
a wigg, 1 pair old boots & 1pair trowsers ???	2
	£ 2081...

Signed   William Carwithem
William Glen, Stepn Carter"

Osnabrig is a German linen cloth. A bed pavilion is a frame. Bristol water was casked drinking water shipped from England.

Was any of the silver of family significance, especially the tankard? The tankard other than the slaves was the most valuable thing he owned.

In addition to his Charles Town possessions there was his country property. In 1742 Thomas Brand sold property to John Eycott outside of the town in Berkley county. John Eycott and his wife mortgaged to Brand for 32 acres which he later expanded. It was here he stabled the horses for those who came to visit at Charles town. His contract with the assembly included delegations of natives who came to do business with the colony.

The disposition of this property languished from 1751 until 1754 so someone was caring for the property. An inventory of this part of John Eycott's estate was taken 22nd of August 1754.

A True Inventory of Sundry Effects belonging to the Estate of Mr. John Eycott Deceased taken an acc't of and Appraised by James Parris, John Fitch, John Goldwire and Patrick Clark who being duely sworn for that purpose the 7th day of August 1751.

17 Horses v £ 40   *£ 680*
2   Ditto v £ 25   *£ 50*
19 Pack Saddles Wantrys (?) and 3 covering skins to each Saddle
        £ 66.10

1752 19 May
Sold   brass kettle   *£10*
Sold   Housen (?) and bag almost worn out
Sold   Bearskin coat   *£ 5*

11 horses and mares w their colts   *£25.15*

Signed John Fitch, James Parris, Patrick Clark his mark PC
Recorded 22 day of Aug 1754.

This portion of the estate was valued at between 800 and 900 pounds. So in total his disposable goods were valued at about £ 3000. At that time the cost of living in Charles Town for a family was reckoned at 100 pounds per year.

The land and house in his estate continued on in absentee ownership in England. Just who managed it in America after the executor died in 1768 is not known.

In 1769, Jan 14, Thomas Pike made a memorial petition to the legislature to gain 80 acres on the Charles Town Neck in Berkeley county from the estate. I have not been able to locate the total size of the estate land holdings.

Who looked after the estate from 1751 to 1783 when it was seized as loyalist property? What was the personality of John Eycott like? What became of his slave property? His possessions tell us part of his story.

An affidavit respecting the birth of John Eycott was made by James Savery and confirmed in 1774 with witness Ann Wolley, nee (born) Eycott, John's sister, who was married to John Wooley of Withington Gl. There is a potential connection that Savery was involved with the estate as he may have been in South Carolina. Ann Wooley born 1711 was daughter of Richard 1992 and grand daughter of Berkeley.

The new State of South Carolina enacted laws in 1782 to confiscate the property of those who remained loyal to the British crown. There were several classes of such property. The heirs of John Eycott (also listed as Egecott) were among the 60 or so Class 1 who were British subjects who had property in Charleston county and who had never submitted to the American government. In this case Mr. Eycott was listed as an absentee deceased loyalist and the report said his property should be confiscated. If it was, it never appeared in the report of sales from the Commissioners of Forfeited Estates account book, 1782-1783 (34/405) South Carolina Historical Society. Some one had controlled the estate for more than 30 years by the time of the confiscation law. However in 1815 the state makes a note that the sale was omitted from the account book. Possibly the property was quickly sold by the heirs. His sister and possibly his brother, if still alive, lost control of what remained of their American possession.

Not only is John Eycott the first known Eycott in America he is the first about whom we have personal details of his living.

Slaughter Vicarage Eycott, John's brother, had taken a different path in life. He did not have the adventurous spirit of his brother but instead married and perhaps became a preacher. He lived at Berwick on Tweed, Northumberland and in Nottingham. His children were Eleanor 1752, George 1754 and John 1755. He may have died in London buried under the name Slaughter Eacott about 1778.

The Berkshire Branch

Another family line can be traced from Berkeley. This line firmly established the change in the spelling of the name from Eycott to Eacott. Berkeley's son John a Cirencester goldsmith has several sons, John, Jones, Joseph, James and Richard. Joseph is born in 1723. Joseph marries his wife Elizabeth at Yattendon in Berkshire. Their children Joseph Eccot born 1745, Thomas Eccot born 1746 and John Eacott born, 20 March 1748, are all born at Yattendon.

John Eacott married Rebecca Cooper Rafe of Wickham Berks. On 09 Oct 1774 at Yew Tree, Berks and settled down at Brightwalton. Here John and Rebecca raise their family John 1775, Elizabeth 1777,William 1779, Abraham 1781, Rebecca 1784 and Martha 1787.

John marries Jane and his children are Hannah 1799 and Abraham 1800.

William marries Hannah and son William is born 1805.

Abraham marries Martha Wiggins and they have a large family. Abraham sired 11 children 8 of whom were boys. Being a religious man he worked his way through the bible. Abraham born 1800, James 1805, Elizabeth 1808, then Matthew 1819, Mark, Luke and finally John 1823. However Caleb 1816, Aaron 1817, and Martha and Ann altered the pattern.

Abraham is 80 years old in 1861 and living at Chaddleworth not far from Brightwalton. He was listed in that census as an agricultural worker.

His son Caleb at Chaddleworth is married and a grocery porter. Moses his oldest at 19 is a tallow chandler who by the age of 40 is confined to a mental asylum where he lives until 1918. Caleb's other children in 1861 are John 17, Mary 14, James 12 and Caleb junior 10.

The above Eacotts have documented descendants to the 10th Generation in the year 2000.

Abraham's son James born 1805 had a particularly interesting and well documented life. As with the life of John Eycott the trader, a single reference item sent me on a search for more details. In this case the reference was a photo in the collection of the New York Public Library, a digital collection of old prints and photos. Image ID 1227482 is an imposing engraving of the Rev. James Eacott. I thought at first it was of an American preacher but the photographer was in London, England. The engraver was J. Cochran who took the engraving from a photograph by John Watkins of Parliament St. London.

John Cochran or Cochrane (active 1821-1865) was a Scottish portrait miniaturist, a stipple and line engraver and a painter of watercolors. Cochran contributed steel plate engravings to The National Portrait Gallery (four volumes, 1820), Wilson and Chamber's Land of Burns (1840) and Wright's Gallery of Engravings (1844–1846).

Cochrane painted portraits of many famous people such as Queen Victoria at the age of 18, King William IV, the Duke of Gloucester and

Edinburgh, the Duke of York and Albany, Viscountess Beresford, the Viscount Nelson and the Earl of St Vincent. At the National Portrait Gallery they list 61 portraits by Cochran. To have been painted by Cochran represented status.

An engraving was created to produce multiple copies so the Reverend James portrait was created for distribution. It was likely included in the Wesleyan Methodist Magazine like other prominent preachers. The photographer John Watkins had a studio on Parliament St. from 1867 to 1871 but may have had a studio there earlier. So the famous engraving was likely from 1860's.

James spoke of his parents as godly people and at the age of 18 he joined the Wesleyan Methodist Society. This was in 1823 when the Anti Slavery Society in England was formed. James seemed to be passionate about ending slavery. The society was very active in lobbying parliament and convincing the general population to turn against slavery in the colonies. Methodists were particularly involved in this work. Three years later James *"believed with his heart unto righteousness"* and soon after began to preach. In 1835 he was received into the ministry and decided that he would like to become a missionary and volunteered to go abroad. The British Empire was in full flower and James, an adventurous young man, decided to take up the British Christian white man's burden and go abroad to save souls. It may be assumed because of the destination and his work with the freed slaves that he was there to help because of the termination of slavery.

First, however, he had a more important task at hand.

His wedding to Mary Jones of Westbury, Wilts. took place on Aug 31, 1835 at Westbury. James was 30. Rev. Mark Cooper, lecturer, officiated. James was mentioned as being a Wesleyan minister to the Bahamas. He and his bride at the time of the marriage were evidently also preparing to leave England. They did so less than two weeks later on September 12th. His children were born at several places in the Bahamas. Isabella 1838 at New Providence, James 1839, Mary 1841 both at Turks Island, Jabez 1843 at Grand Cay, Caleb 1844 and J. at Bahama Harbour. All of his sons went on to become ministers as well.

During the summer of 1837 a hurricane swept over the islands. From the 29 to the 31st of July 1837 the storm did much damage. James was on

Pear Cay but his wife and child were at Rock Sound. He no sooner got home to find them safe when a second storm raged from the 4th to the 6th of August. The locals said it was the worst in memory. The newer sturdier buildings survived and while most provisions were lost, the Indian corn while having been knocked down was ripe and so could be harvested.

It was necessary in his work for him to go from one settlement to another and during one of these journeys he and his horse were attacked by a large dog and driven into the sea to escape. A large wave tossed him into the water. He recovered his horse but found he had miles to ride in wet clothes to find a miserable place to lodge, with no change of raiment, no fire to dry himself and much rain from the storm. As a result he fell ill and was detained in Nassau for nearly ten weeks. On arriving home he found his wife ill and she was confined for four days. But later in a letter he says they both had recovered and he remarked that his wife had suffered much but not as much as the natives who had been much afflicted since the gales. He hoped that the visitation of the storms would awaken more to be concerned about their souls. He went on to say he was encouraging the people to build. At Savannah Sound the chapel was blown down and the chapels at Tarpum bay and Palmetto Point were unsafe and unfit for worship. The chapels at Governor's Harbour, Pear Key, and Rock Sound needed repair. He felt he had formidable work before him. (Taken from a letter dated Sept 10 1837 to Wesleyan Missionary Society.)

In 1841 at Salt Cay, James Eacott, minister, laid the cornerstone to a new more solid church. Over the next century the Salt Cay Methodist Church, Balfour Town, Salt Cay was heavily damaged by hurricanes. Although currently not operating as a church, this surviving circa 1830s Methodist church is one of the defining examples of the British Bermudian Colonial inspired architecture on Salt Cay and as such is now a historic building and tourist attraction. Salt Cay in the 1800's was more populated as there was a thriving local industry in harvesting sea salt for export. Salt was raked into ponds to be evaporated, baled and shipped.

James was often away from home as his ministry took him to a large number of islands. His arrival in the islands was just after the emancipation of slaves in the Empire. In August 1833, the Slave Emancipation Act was passed, giving all slaves in the British empire their freedom, albeit after a set period of years. Plantation owners received compensation for the 'loss of their slaves' in the form of a government grant from a fund set at

£20,000,000. James was active in the Bahamas while these changes took effect. During the transition period following the emancipation his discretion and firmness, his kindness and suavity gained him many friends and secured valuable co-operation.

Slavery was officially abolished in most of the British Empire on 1 August 1834. In practical terms, however, only slaves below the age of six were freed as all slaves over the age of six were redesignated as "apprentices". Apprentices would continue to serve their former owners for a period of time after the abolition of slavery though the length of time they served depended on which of three classes of apprentice they were. The first class of apprentices were former slaves who "*in their State of Slavery were usually employed in Agriculture, or in the Manufacture of Colonial Produce or otherwise, upon Lands belonging to their Owners*". The second class of apprentices were former slaves who "*in their State of Slavery were usually employed in Agriculture, or in the Manufacture of Colonial Produce or otherwise, upon Lands not belonging to their Owners*". The third class of apprentices was composed of all former slaves "*not included within either of the Two preceding Classes*". Apprentices within the third class were released from their apprenticeships on 1 August 1838. The remaining apprentices within the first and second classes were released from their apprenticeships on 1 August 1840.

The Act also included the right of compensation for slave-owners who would be losing their property. This compensation was paid for from the fund mentioned earlier. Under the terms of the Act the British government raised £20 million to pay out in compensation for the loss of the slaves as business assets to the registered owners of the freed slaves. The names listed in the returns for slave compensation show that ownership was spread over many hundreds of British families, many of them of high social standing. James was present at the time all these changes took effect and obviously was recognized for his handling of the situation. The transition from slave to free came with a certain amount of social upheaval and the presence of people like James was important.

After 11 years in Bahamas and Antigua James returned to England with his family. He was minister at Fen Drayton in the 1860's but also was a superintendent over several important Home circuits.

At the age of 74 James had a stroke and had to learn to walk and speak again. He died in Leicester on October 25 1882.

His sons James Weeks Eacott ministered from 1870 to 1907. Son Jabez was ordained in 1869 and died in 1906 and Caleb was the long time rector of Galby, Leicestershire until 1911. All were Methodist ministers. His daughters Isabel and Brena served as missionaries in India and China respectively. In addition the Reverend William Eacott ministered. James Weeks Eacott. was buried in 1923 at Barnard Castle, Durham. Caleb graduated from University College, Durham with an MA in 1870. He served as vicar of King's Norton and was curate of the Chapel St. church at Bottesford, Leicester.

James Weeks Eacott's son William was a minister with the Methodist Church who died in South Africa. His other son James went to St. Catherines ON Canada and his children were leaders in the Salvation Army. James Clinton Eacott was a missionary in China and after retirement he enhanced his education and graduated with a Master's Degree from the University of Western Ontario at age 78. He once visited our family in Tillsonburg Ontario. His siblings lived in Windsor, Ontario and worked as Salvationists. His sister Emily lived to age 104. His Daughter Amy Homewood also was a professional Salvation Army worker. This line of Eacott descendants shows a remarkably devout strain for several generations and their life details are also interesting. However my efforts concentrate on those who lived before 1900.

The Eycotts of Stonehouse, Early Industrialists

Yet another family line from Berkeley is traceable to the Eycott's of Stonehouse. Berkeley's son Joseph born 1703 in Cirencester married Mary Freeman (1712) of North Cerney at Quedgeley Gl. just south of the city of Gloucester in 1730. At first they lived in Cirencester but soon moved to Cherington a small village between Cirencester and Stonehouse just north of Tetbury.

Joseph and Mary lived at Cherington from 1734 to at least 1760 where they were parents to 11 children - 5 boys Thomas, Henry 1735-1801 , Joseph, Nathaniel 1746 - 1805 and William. The girls were Sarah, Graciana, Lucy, Mary (2) and Sarah again. Nathaniel and Henry were known to have survived childhood.

Nearby, another Eycott, born about 1710, of unknown relationship lived at Oakfield. He was a mason and his given initial was F. (Frederick?) He was hired to repair the toll booth at Cainscross which was destroyed in the riots of 1834. These riots were in objection to the tolls and the treatment of local weavers. A century later Frederick Eycott was living at Oakfield so he may have been a clearly known relative at the time.

Nathaniel born 21 April 1746 at Cherington grew up and lived in London where he leased a house in George Yard near Snow Hill in 1786. He was buried at Stonehouse in 1805. His name is on the Eycott memorial in the Stonehouse Church. So he is connected to this branch.

Ecotts, and Eycott and Eycott lived in nearby Tetbury in 1735 but their relationship is not known. William Eacott left a will dated 1751.

Cherington was not a large place. After the closures act of 1730 there were only 5 estates and only a couple of dozen families. How Joseph supported his family is not known but he may have been a tailor as it seems Berkeley ensured his children had skills.

His second son Henry born 1736 acquired an education and had some resources behind him because as an adult he entered the clothiers business of manufacturing cloth. Henry's grandmother Mary Shewell may have come from Stroud where Shewells were a major clothier family. We now take a closer look at Henry's life.

At some point in his life Henry purchased a 3 volume book "The Works of the Most Reverend Dr. John Tillotson, Lord Archbishop of Canterbury 1752". It was chiefly through Tillotson's advice that the king appointed a commission for the Reconciliation of the Dissenters. Tilloston was very close to the royal family of the day. He died in 1694. The agents to sell these volumes in 1918 said Henry was from a prosperous and influential family. Eycott was an active clothier owning and operating mills in the Stonehouse region, near Stroud. The first volume has a page with Henry's family history. So why did Henry want this book and why put his family information in it? The family assets were advertised for sale in 1918.

I think, because we know, either Berkeley or his wife were Dissenters and his children chose differing religious views. Berkeley had married outside the Church of England and Henry was interested.

Henry prospered and by the time he was about 40 years old had enough resources to purchase the Bond's mill at Stonehouse in 1774.

Henry married Elizabeth Stanton on 8 Feb. 1768 at Shoreditch, London. She had been previously married and had a son John who died age 51 in 1806 and another son William Stanton who was a clothier in Stroud. The marriage to Elizabeth connected Henry to the landed gentry. Elizabeth's first husband, Joseph Stanton of The Thrupp, died and Henry became the father surrogate of William and John. William Henry Stanton was MP for Stroud 1841-52 and his son Alfred John Stanton was MP for Stroud 1874 to 1880. Elizabeth was the daughter of Richard Page Esq. of London. Henry married well.

Henry and Elizabeth's son Henry was born 1773 and died 1821. Henry was married to Catherine Holmes daughter of Robert Holmes, Blacksmith. This is what the memorial in the Randwick church says.

"In Memory of Robert HOLMES, of Pagnanhill in the Parish of Stroud, Blacksmith, who departed the Life, the 12 day of Novr. 1793, Aged 69 Years".

There is also a memorial to "Catherine, his daughter, and Wife of Henry EYCOTT Clothier, She died 12 day of March, 1793, Aged 27, and lies interred at Stonehouse, Likewise of Susanna his daughter, who lies here interred, Aged 3 Years."

The younger Henry remarried Mary. He and his wife had several children who died as infants or as small children. Six in all died between 1798 and 1812. His domestic life could not have been very happy with all these misfortunes. Their lives are noted on the family memorial in the Stonehouse church.

The cloth industry had been at Stonehouse for three centuries or more because local conditions made fulling mills profitable and it persisted even though Cotswold wool alone could no longer supply the quantity or quality of raw material required. Cloth was produced on a 'putting out' system. The clothiers bought the wool, then paid workers in their own homes and workshops to prepare, spin and weave the yarn. The rough cloth then came back to the fulling mills to be processed, then went to be dyed, if required, and finished. The clothier then sold it at cloth fairs locally in

Bristol or increasingly in London. The production of 'white' cloth was declining but colored cloth was on the rise. Dyeing was mainly done 'in the piece' after fulling which retained the color. Most dyes were of vegetable origin but cochineal dye from Mexico had recently been introduced to Europe as a result of Spanish colonization. This 'fixed' especially well in the local water, producing the first 'Stroudwater Scarlet' cloth. Almost every family was involved in these cloth processes in some way, in addition to farming and whatever other occupation the head of household had.

Bond's mill was an ancient mill established before 1496 and was likely purposely built for fulling and not corn grinding. It was run by the Fowler family until the early 1700's when in 1724 the mill passed out of manorial ownership into the hands of John Peach and Daniel Webborn In 1750 it was sold to William Pitt and then his widow in 1774 sold it to to Henry Eycott. During this same time The Eycott's were leasing the Stonehouse Upper mill.

Henry was in the right place at the right time. A very important development that boosted the Eycott situation was the opening in 1779 of the Stroudwater canal beside the mills. This canal enabled transport of merchandise directly to the sea and although coal was the principal product shipped, textiles were also moved. The mill owners benefitted from this. Bond's mill became one of the major woollen mills in the Stroud area. New inventions were changing the making of cloth. Crompton's spinning mule, a composite machine combining Arkwright's water frame and Hargreave's spinning jenny, came off patent in 1783 thus allowing anyone to construct this machine. The spinning mule gave the spinner great control over the weaving process and many different types of yarn could be produced. This machine spun textile fibers into yarn by an intermittent process. In the draw stroke, the roving is pulled through and twisted. On the return it is wrapped onto the spindle. The mill had four pairs of fulling stocks in 1787. Water power was used to work fulling stocks which was a machine with two large wooden hammers raised on tappets. The cloth was contained in a trough – the stock – and was repeatedly beaten by the rising and falling hammers. Such hammers did generate heat and heavily felted cloth was produced. It took several hours to get the right degree of felting. The piece shrank by about one third of its length and one quarter of its width. Then in 1793 a Stonehouse clothier adapted the flying shuttle used in northern cotton mills to work with narrow looms. The mills were hiring more people and less piecework weaving was done in the home. After the peace with France in

1802 demand for military cloth dropped and the home weavers were out of work. Some mills closed. Yet overall from 1790 to 1835 innovation and risk taking improved the Eycott fortune. By 1820 Bond's was one of the largest mills in the area. Country squires wore blue on Sunday and Stroudwater Scarlet on Monday. Now all the cotton, wool and worsted cloth was spun in mills. Children with nimble small fingers were a major part of the workforce. Weavers in the Eycott factories had long hours and poor pay but the plus side was that there was stable employment for the mill workers.

From the founding Henry through his son Henry and grandsons Henry Charles and Frederick the Eycott's of Bond's mill occupied a leading position in Stonehouse and the clothier trade for some 60 years. Being enterprising industrialists in the new age enabled Henry to dabble in other activities.

In 1797 Henry Eycott, presumably the younger, was appointed an officer in the city of Gloucester, Troop of Gentlemen and Yeomanry, a cavalry group organized to defend England against an invasion by Napoleon. He was not listed in an 1803 reorganization.

The Manor of Frocester, just south of Stonehouse, was put on sale in 1803 by George, Earl of Warwick. Leonard Parkinson bought the manor and much of the land. Henry Eycott of Stonehouse purchased another part but sold it to Parkinson in 1806. Another estate at Nostend was owned by Henry Charles from 1813 to 1830. Nostend was mostly Clutterbuck land. Frederick Eycott had 139 acres at Nostend. [43]

Henry Charles Eycott, (Henry III) born about 1792 married Ann Clutterbuck Fryer of Eastington, born 12 March 1783, and married there, 23 May, 1818. Samuel Clutterbuck was a business partner of the Eycott's. Henry's father died in 1821 and the mills became his responsibility. After about 10 years he removed himself from this responsibility of managing and operating the mills so in 1832 it was leased to William John Wood who had married Catherine Eycott of Bond's Mill in 1823. Wood may have been Henry's sister Catherine's husband. (Kate 1798-1865) . Their son Henry Eycott Wood 1827-1865 became an attorney.

In 1843 Henry relocated from Eastington to London where he was

---

[43] *Victoria History of Gloucester Vol 10*

employed at the Tithe Office, Somerset house. His brother Frederick assumed leadership over the mills and installed a steam power loom in 1837. This loom eliminated the need for weavers so they were laid off. Frederick who now lived on his estate leased the mills to William Wise in 1840. In 1843 both Frederick and his brother were trustees of the Stonehouse School. In 1876 Frederick was associated with the legal firm of Lea, Carpenter, and Co. of Cainscross. In 1839 and 1853 Frederick was living at Stonehouse Court with his wife Sophia. Sophia married Frederick in may of 1839 at Cainscross. She was the daughter of another clothier Edward Davies. In the census of 1871 his occupation is described as parlourer. No definition can be found but perhaps it means public speaker. He and his wife were also patrons of the Arts. They were listed as paid subscribers to some books most notably one on the Roman ruins at Cirencester which he knew as the original family home. Later Frederick lived at Oak Field where he died in 1884. His estate was valued at over 45 000 pds (roughly a couple of million today). His wife Sophia died in 1896 at Oakfield. In 2016 Oakfield was listed as a charming holiday house for rent, capable of sleeping 18. With Frederick's death there were no more male Eycott heirs in this family line around Stroud although a Frederick Charles was born in 1844 to a Henry Charles Eycott.

The woollen mill continued in business until the factory was closed in 1934. Bond's Mill then became a property of the Ministry of Defence where secret munitions work was done. During WW2 Bond's Mill housed Sperry Gyroscope's "shadow factory" which produced instruments for aircraft and searchlights. Today the property is a commercial and manufacturing complex.

Frederick's older sister Mary Ann married Richard Martin in 1822. Their children bore a hyphenated Eycott-Martin name. William Eycott-Martin who was close friend to Frederick and Sophia became a Minister and their great grandson Harold Ross Eycott-Martin distinguished himself in WWI. Harold Ross Eycott-Martin was born in Haywards Heath, Sussex, England in 1896. He was the eldest son. His father Douglas born 1866 was a civil servant in Bechuanaland and his grandfather was Reverend Canon William Eycott Martin who married Sarah Jemima Hodgson daughter of another Reverend. He was a M.A. graduate of Oxford in 1853, served as librarian of Rochester Cathedral 1858 to 70 and from 1870 was vicar at West Farleigh, Kent where he died in 1896.

Captain Harold Ross Eycott-Martin MC began and ended his military career in the Royal Engineers. While seconded for duty with the Royal Air Force as a pilot, Eycott-Martin would end the war as a flying ace credited with eight aerial victories. He flew a Sopwith Camel aircraft.

Eycott-Martin was commissioned on 27 October 1915, at the age of 18, as a second lieutenant in the Royal Engineers from the Royal Military Academy, Woolwich. After being seconded to the Royal Flying Corps, he was appointed a flying officer on 29 March 1917. In May 1917, he was posted to 41 Squadron in northern France. A week after joining the squadron he crashed a Royal Aircraft Factory FE.8 during takeoff. On 24 May 1917, Flight Newsletter reported Eycott-Martin had been wounded but no date was given for the wounding. It seems likely he was injured in the takeoff accident.On 1 July 1917, Eycott-Martin was promoted to lieutenant in his home unit, the Royal Engineers.

On 7 February 1918 he was reassigned to 66 Squadron in Italy. In short order he won his first two aerial victories. Then on 30 March 1918 he and Alan Jerrard were wingmen to Peter Carpenter on the occasion when Jerrard won a Victoria Cross. In that same action Eycott-Martin was credited with two victories and on 5 April 1918, he was subsequently awarded a Military Cross for his role in this combat.

Eycott-Martin's victory string culminated at eight on 22 June 1918. On 13 July, he was temporarily promoted to captain. He almost certainly simultaneously became a flight commander.

Eycott-Martin's Military Cross was finally gazetted on 16 September 1918. His citation read:

Lt. Harold Ross Eycott-Martin, R.E., R.A.F.
For conspicuous gallantry and devotion to duty. In a patrol with two other machines he attacked nineteen of the enemy. Of the six enemy aircraft destroyed on this occasion he destroyed two. On two other occasions he destroyed an enemy machine.

Eycott-Martin remained in the Royal Air Force post-war but had a turbulent career. On 17 January 1919 he reverted from temporary captain back to lieutenant. From 27 January to 30 Apri, he was re-employed as a temporary captain. On 27 June 1919 he was re-rated from lieutenant (Ad.)

to lieutenant (A.). On 14 October 1919 he gave up his commission in the Royal Air Force; however, he retained his commission in the Royal Engineers.

In the midst of this career turmoil, on 10 April 1919, it was announced that he was engaged to marry Muriel Horner. However, it is unknown if the marriage ever occurred.

On 14 May 1920 Harold Ross Eycott-Martin, mistakenly characterized as still an RAF officer, was reported as residing at 9 Trebovir Road, Earls Court, London, as well as the Maiden Head Hotel, Uckfield, Sussex. This information was contained in a declaration of bankruptcy. On 5 August 1920 Lieutenant Eycott-Martin was removed from the rolls of the Royal Engineers for being absent without leave. He then disappeared into the mists of history.[44] Not even an obituary can be found.

Other records exist of Eycotts in the 18th and 19th centuries who were also in the cloth manufacturing and milling business. How they got into this line of work is not clear. One clue is that Jonathan Eycott born 1736 was a miller at Woodchester. The proximity of the following places indicate likely family ties. They are all within 6 miles of each other: Stroud, Eastington, Stonehouse, Woodchester, Leonard Stanley, King's Stanley, Minchinghampton, Horsley. Just east are Avening, and Cherington which might also connect to the Tetbury Eacotts.

Henry Eycott was a known figure in the milling business. However in the 1770's they were referred to as Messers Eycott so there were other family involved. Possibly Thomas Eycott who lived east of Cherington near Cirencester at Coates was involved. He may have been an older brother(his will). A number of the people, who ran the Mills after the Eycotts, were connected by marriage or descent from the Eycott family. Unfortunately not enough evidence exists to do convincing connections.

We now take a look at other Eacotts in the general vicinity. Some can be linked back to North Cerney others not. Also notably they are not often Eycott but the Ecott version.

There are records of other Eacott families in the immediate vicinity of

[44] *Taken from Wikipedia information online*

Stonehouse. Within 10 miles the following locations had families. Most of the recorded events were marriages with no further association. So it is not possible to construct a story of their lives.

At Cranham and Gloucester from about 1830 one or two Eakets family arise. John or Thomas Eakets may be the first to use that variation. There are about 10 males with the surname.

At Bisley, Gloucestershire Thomas Ecott married Ann Pierce in 1690. Thereafter through 1800 there are Ecot, Eycot, Eacutt, mixed spellings. There were probably only three families of which Samuel Ecot and Ann Wallis are most prominent.

At Woodchester from 1736 - 82 Jonathan Eycott of North Cerney was a miller. Perhaps he learned his skill at the Trinity Mill at Bagendon. Then James Eycott who married Susannah Fowler in 1766 begat children whose names became Eccott notably Job 1771 and James 1773 and other children were Ecot, Ecoat, and Eycot. It is not proven that James is Jonathan's son.

From time to time Eycotts lived at Gloucester city, mostly in the 1800's. A few lived at other locations in this area. Records appear in about 15 locations.

The Eycott/Eacotts of Tetbury

At Tetbury there are a number of records especially from the 1700's. Richard Eacott Son of William and Sarah was born in Tetbury in 1710. William died in 1760 and was believed to have been 99 years old in that year which means he was born in 1661. There are two Williams who might be this one. Both were born at Stratton near Cirencester. In 1664 William was born to William and Joan. Then in 1670 William was born to William and Elizabeth. This William under the name was counted in a census in 1735-6 when he was 74 and his wife Sarah was 63. Richard 31 was there as were Samuel age 13 and James age 12.

Names at Tetbury: Eycott, Ecott, Eacott, Eccourt, Eckut are all mixed in the spelling.

It seems old William, whose wife Sarah Ecot died in 1750, was a man of some substance who had a house on Charlton road on the south side of

Tetbury. His family seems to have been one with some issues. In 1719 Jane Wells charged Richard Eycott with defamation. However the known Richard of William was only 15 at the time which raises the question if a person so young could have been so charged in those days. Later in 1728 Jane Eycott and Margaret Mitchell were both charged with adultery. Did Jane Wells marry Richard and then cheat on him? By 1736 Richard was now making child support payments of 1 shilling a week payable every 4 weeks for the upkeep of a child and in addition was making added payments in January and later in December for shoes for a child. These were duly recorded in the overseers records for obligations to the poor.

By 1743 Richard was made a tythingman for Tetbury, a position where he was responsible for keeping the peace similar to a police constable of today. William's daughter married Jonathan Avery a fact revealed in his will of 1751 and proved by his son Richard in May 1760 who saw to it that his sister was paid her 1 shilling while he inherited all the rest.

"To my daughter Elizabeth the wife of Jonathan Avery one shilling
To my son Richard Eacott ... all the rest of my money chattells rights and credits, and appoint him whole and sole executor" Was this simply a sign of the times or a temperamental falling out?

Richard Ecot died Feb 27 1767 age 63 at Charlton presumably in the two storey Cotswold stone house, still standing, that he inherited from his father.

There were other Eacotts about the town as well. Nearby at Beverstone a Richard Ecut was father to Jane Ecot in 1696 after which he went to North Cerney where a son Thomas was born in 1698. He may have come back to Tetbury. A Richard Ecut married Mary Jones in 1701 in Beverstone. Had he lost his first wife and remarried or is this another person? And is this Jane the same Jane Eycott who was 30 years later accused of adultery or was it the married Jane?

Samuel Eckut born 1713 in Ampney Crucis married Mary Wallis of Tetbury born 1724 in the church at Leonard Stanley in 1751. Samuel Acott married Ann Powell in nearby Long Newton in 1716 and William Acutt married Anna Oaksey in Long Newton in 1717. The connection to Samuel Eckut is not known.

Samuel Wallis Ecott descended from Richard of Ampney Crucis, and Samuel Eckut who lived in Bisley and later Tetbury. Samuel Wallis Ecot was baptized August 9 1752. His sister Mary was baptized March 4 1759. Nineteen years later on December 15 1778 Mary Eycott (Scott) of Stanley, who is living in and chargeable to the parish of Tetbury, named John Newcourt as father of her male bastard. He is to pay 8 pence a week or keep the child and he is to pay 1 pound four shillings a week for the child's future needs. Notice the price per week has risen from a shilling a week when 40 years earlier Richard was charged with child upkeep. Also it is stated that Mary has to pay nothing if she decided to keep the child and not place it in an orphanage.

James Ecot baptized his daughter Jane on April 6 1755. Twenty nine years later, October 18 1784 Jane Ecott (Scott) named Jeremiah Bowles, labourer, as father of her child.

Returning back to 1762, Samuel Ecot (Eckut) buried his wife Mary in February and then later in the year on May 7 he is a member of the court leet. It is a local court set up to hear misdemeanours and petty crimes. We don't know when Samuel died but we do know more about his son.

On November 27 1781 Samuel Scott (Ecot) now a militiaman, a private in the South Battalion of the Gloucestershire Militia, was named by Elizabeth Whitfield of Tetbury as father of her male child, born 18 Dec 1781. This was shown in The Churchwardens and Overseers of the Poor records.[45] Two years later on January 11 1783 Samuel Wallis Eycott was married to Elizabeth Whitefield (born 1762 June 25), daughter of John. In this case Samuel, being in the militia, was as an enlisted man not allowed to marry. This may account for the unusual record of a delayed marriage. Mary Eycott, daughter of Samuel and Elizabeth, was christened on 12 Sep 1784 in Tetbury, Gloucestershire, and she married on 3 Apr 1805 in Woodchester, Gloucester, to John Lusty who was christened on 30 Sep 1781 in Kings Stanley, Gloucestershire. A record of the Lusty family tree has been made.

Saul Lusty in 1819 was the owner of a corn mill built in the 1500's at Stonehouse where the Eycotts also owned mills.

---

[45] *Reference P328a OV 5/4 dated 09 Jan 1783.*

The Eacotts of the Purton, Wiltshire Area

Thomas Neel of Pyriton was granted oversight of Eycott Manor by Margery Le Brun in 1346 because Thomas Burton age 11 had inherited the land. This establishes an association between the Churn parishes and Purton. Purton is also near South Cerney, Wroughton, Wooton Bassett, Swindon and other communities to form this cluster. The Purton link may relate to persons living at Wooton Bassett and Swindon, a total of 36 persons.

Purton has a long history as a village and the name means something like place of the pear tree.

In 1577 John Ackett was married to Jane Parnell at Purton. If there were Eacotts living there for the next 100 years, it is not known.

In the records of Purton apprentices for 1684 the overseers for Purton church were Robert Plomer and John Eatoll which may be a misread of Eacott, a frequent problem when examining old records.

A will of 1684 for William Ecut of Eysey Manor (Kempsford-Castle Eaton area), labourer, whose wife was deceased, left his goods to sons William and Nicholas and daughters Ann, Margaret, and Elizabeth. However Kempsford is more east than South of Cirencester. It is thought the name evolved to Eacott in the will of Anne Eacott.

As mentioned above the greatest concentration of Eacotts, which is the spelling used in virtually all the families in this area of Wiltshire, is in Purton and adjacent Purton Stoke where in 1701 William Ecut was born. From that time on Eacotts are known in this area until the 1900's.

Did the Eycott's move to Purton because of the connection to North Cerney? Did they come down the Roman road, Ermin Street from Cirencester? We do not know where or when the first Eacotts came to this area. We can only speculate from the North and Cirencester or South from Warminster.

The family who lived at South Cerney and Shorncote were known as Eycott but they lived quite close to Cirencester and were there from the late 1600's to mid 1700's when at least one Richard Eycott became Richard

Eacott (1739-1810).

The Eacotts in the other 8 communities in this greater Purton group were one or two persons or in the 1800's families. The Eacott spelling was almost the only one used. Known to have an Eacott connection were Broad Blunsdon where Henry Eacott and Sarah Hunt were married 1819 and may have lived or they may have relocated to Cricklade by 1835. Nearby Haydon Wick was home to James Eycott born 1716 whose will of 1768 would have interested Henry born 1845 and his sister Rosanna. At Crudwell nearer to Tetbury than Purton in 1700 lived Samuel Acott. Again farther away well east of Purton at Highworth an Eacott family lived in the late 1700's and early 1800's. They may have been more connected to the family at Kempsford. All the rest lived in and around Purton-Purton Stoke, Swindon, Wooton Bassett, Wroughton.

Wooton Bassett, Purton, Purton Stoke and Cricklade are on the same road. In the days before the railway came to Swindon and made it a city, one can imagine these as a connected group.

Cricklade was a Saxon market town on the northern border of Wiltshire. Purton Stoke is a small village strung out along the road. It was home to a medicinal mineral spring that was later turned into a small spa. Purton village is on a ridge and has been settled since prehistory. It is best known as the birthplace of the first Astronomer Royal. Wooton Bassett was also a small village strung out along the road. In 1800 there were 1200 people in the market village.

Wroughton to the east was a small country village, home in the 1800's to the John Eacott and Mary Neat family. Descendants lived there in the 1800's.

Swindon had Eacott families in the 17 and 18 hundreds when the town was known for its quarries. A number of stone masons lived there. The town in 1800 had about 2000 people but when the Great Western Railroad came in the 1840s, it became a busy industrial railway centre.

During the 1830's a severe depression and crops failures affected Britain. Many people were desperate and so took action to help solve the problem. As there were many in distress around Purton, someone had the idea of assisting people to emigrate.

The local parish church in Purton had an active connection to Canada in that the church congregation had sponsored missionaries to Canada in the early 1700's. The first S.P.G. Missionary went out in 1702 on the Centurion. A book on church history written in 1927 said this of the year 1837.

" In the years following the Napoleonic Wars much poverty and consequent misery was obtained. It is said that no less than 500,000 persons died from starvation. Purton felt its share of bad times and it was thought well to encourage emigration to Canada. A deed dated 22 May 1837 contained an agreement between church wardens and overseers in Purton and a Mr. Robert Carter of 11 Leadenhall St.,London."

Twenty one persons from Purton were sponsored to Canada to land at Montreal. They and their luggage were to be landed free of charge and food allowances were given as well as medicine and wine. Such things as wooden bowls, platters, hook pots, etc. were specified for each person over 14 and a special supply list for each person under 14 was given. All taxes were met and the fare was seven pounds five shillings for an adult. Children under 14 were half fare. A second lot of persons were sent out in 1844. Some of the names of those sent were Sealy, Maule, Cutts, Tuff, Turner, Baker. One wonders if Charles Eacott, the first known Eacott in Canada (1830), may have experienced these problems and set out from Purton just before this group of immigrants and someone earlier may have sent word back of the conditions abroad. There is more about Charles Eacott in the Eacott Reynolds Families book.

Near Purton, Wooton Bassett's leading citizen, the mayor, John Eacott, died shortly after publishing a sale of items in December 1791. He died age 75, Thursday, Jan 27 1792 and his obituary read in part *"...to the poor, a kind matter, esteemed and respected. A valuable neighbour and honest man much lamented, died Monday."*

It is possible this person may be the son of John who was a son of Berkeley. If so, he was born October 20 1717. The Mayor died leaving his wife Mary. He had a number of nephews and nieces in the Smith family, a John and James, but no children of his own.

His will said *" I also give and devise from after the decease of my wife the house and premises now occupied by Joseph Humphries situated in Wood Street aforesaid unto my niece Ann (sister of the said John Smith) and to her heirs...."*

A second John Eacott of Wooton Bassett also died about the same time as the mayor and is buried in the same churchyard. This John was fortunate enough to have a family. John and Mary had John 1758, Mary 1759, Martha 1764, Thomas 1766, Elizabeth 1768 and then John must have lost his wife and his son John and soon married Jane who provided another son John in 1770.

One of these two Johns was a plumber and glazier who had a brother Thomas also a plumber and glazier in the town of Chippenham. This Thomas died in 1788 leaving a son Thomas and daughters Elizabeth and Susanna.

A plumber and glazier in the 1700's was a skilled trade. The craftsman worked in lead. Lead was used to fit bits of window glass together as we see in church windows today. He also crafted lead plates for roofing, hooks and fasteners, gutters, well fittings and pipe and created coffin lining. He was not the plumber of today as there were no indoor water supplies and toilets. He was like the carpenter, a person who had a large role in building houses. Unfortunately the risk of lead poisoning would have been high in this craft.

The second John at Wooton Bassett was aged 64, a decade younger than the mayor. One of these John Eacotts was the local coroner in Wooton Bassett in 1754, 1776-7 and 1791-2. It was likely the mayor as it was a common practice at the time for a mayor to have this additional task. The other John, since he could make lead linings for coffins, could also have been a coroner. It could add to his income. John's bills for his services were presented for claim in the just mentioned years.

One of these two John's had been an elector in 1772 for a knight of the shire. He voted for candidate Goddard. This voter also was likely the mayor.

Wooton Bassett or Bassett's Wood was an agricultural town with no weaving history or manufacturing. It was a market town on a main road so there were quite a number of inns and ale houses. Unemployment was often an issue. In 1846 a labouring man reported that about two-thirds of the population of the parish were only occasionally employed and the other third, although employed about the farms, could only work in good weather.

The highest wage was 8s. a week or very occasionally 9s. and the usual rate was 6s. to 7s. Such was the town where John Eacott was the mayor.

Just south of Swindon and east of Wroughton a 19th century home to some Eacotts was Liddington where there were Eycott properties owned by two different Eycotts which were sold to the Duke of Marlborough to enlarge his estates at Liddington. "The history of the Medbourne Doynel estate then becomes obscure but in 1617–18 the lands at Medbourne were said to be held of the lord of the capital manor of Liddington. By the 18th century the estate had become broken up into at least four small freehold estates and at the end of the century three of these were held by the Eycott family. Two parcels of land were bought by the Duke of Marlborough from S. and J. Eycott in 1771, while a third, called Larges Close, was purchased from J. Eycott in 1772. In 1776 land which probably represents the remnant of the estate known as Medbourne Farm, was sold by Thomas Warman to the Duke of Marlborough."[46] The S. Eycott may have been Samuel Eacott of Swindon.

North east of Swindon at the hamlet of Coleshill John Acott baptized his children from 1698 to 1719, sons John 1698, William 1702, Edward 1704, Joseph 1708, Benjamin 1713, daughters Ann 1700, Hannah 1719. There was a John Acott son of John and Anne born north of Coleshill at Fairford in 1675. Further back another John was born 1645 at North Nibley in the Cromhall area. The connections are not known and there are no other Acotts at North Nibley and Fairford. So they are both a one off. It appears that Benjamin Acott remained at Coleshill because he married Martha and had sons Thomas 1741, Oliver and Edward 1743, John 1749 and daughter Mary 1747. Oliver has been researched and exists on several family trees. It is thought this Acott line is a variant of Ecott but some Acott families were Huguenot French refugees and those Acotts would have been a variant of the word Acourt, meaning a person of the court. The only clear examples are some London Acotts part of the Spitalfields French community there. The Huguenot connection here is unlikely because the family given names here are more like English than French style names.

---

[46] *Victoria County History Wiltshire vol 9 pages 65-75*

The Eacotts of Chippenham area

Thomas Eacott the brother of John lived at Chippenhan where he too was a trained plumber and glazier. Like other apprentices his parents paid for his 7 year training. In his chosen field most who entered training went on to become master of their craft. In 1765 Thomas was appointed a commissioner to hear the pleas of debtors. So he was a person of some status locally. Eacotts lived at Chippenham, nearby Kington and Lacock from 1750 to 1850.

The Eacotts of Trowbridge area

Trowbridge the county seat is an old town that became a centre for woolen manufacturing. The town's industries boomed in the early 1800's and its population of 6000 in 1800 doubled by 1830. During this period nearly a dozen Eacott weddings took place at Trowbridge. The earliest in 1792 of John Eycott and Hester Player was followed by William Eacott and Phobe Wait in 1799. William worked as a weaver for T and T Clark a large mill employing many people. William may have been active as a Baptist church organizer for a William Eacott is listed in 1812 and 1817 as a cloth worker and along with two others is connected to a Baptist meeting house in Trowbridge. Nearly all the Trowbridge people were Eacott spelling. For a time a few were mixed spelled with Ecot at nearby Westwood. At least one Eycott spelling persisted until 1880. There is some slim evidence that there were Purton connections as in 1810 a Jane Eacott of Purton married M.T. Hale at Trowbridge and Betty Taylor who was born in Purton in 1795 married in Trowbridge in 1814.

Trowbridge is along the same road as Westbury and Warminster and in the past would have been a good days walk.

Mathew Eacott and his wife Ruth Chapman were raised in Trowbridge. There were several Eacott families in the town. Mathew was born about 1824-6 as was his wife. It is difficult to determine exactly who his parents were.

Some choices for Mathews grandparents are William Eacott a weaver who left a 1790 will and James Eycott who was born 1793 who could have been a grandparent or parent. Mathew's parents James and Betty Taylor were married 1814.

Like many others in the area Mathew worked in the cloth mills. His children were all born in Trowbridge, Amelia 1847, Henry John 1848, Benjamin 1851 and Mary 1854.

Sometime after 1854 and before 1860 The family made a momentous decision to emigrate to America. Where the funds for this came from is unknown. With them went Ruth's sisters Hannah and Sarah Chapman. What the reasons were and why the destination we do not know. What is known is that they were living in Lowell MA in 1860 when the census was taken. Mathew was now a provisions dealer working for himself.

The rest of his story can be found under The United States Eacotts. See Mathew Eacott family.

The Eacotts of Devizes area

Devizes is a market town and historically a weaving centre as well as home of a regional jail. In 1664 Richard Ecott married Elizabeth Clark and his will in 1685 informs us that he was a bodice maker. A bodice was a form of corset or girdle. His sister perhaps married John Evans in 1667. The Ecott spelling persisted until the mid 1700's when Richard Eacott married Mary Curtis. In 1844 Stephen Eacott was imprisoned there. Eacotts lived in the area until the 1900's. This is one of the few places in this part of Wiltshire where there is Ecott spelling. Other than Trowbridge there is no other Eacott settlement very close. Like Chippenham and Trowbridge these Eacott appear to be town dwellers not farmers.

The Eacotts of Warminster and Area

An interesting fact about the Eacotts of Warminster and area is they almost don't exist anywhere but in the towns of Warminster and adjacent Sutton Veny. None of the surrounding communities had Eacotts. They were agricultural workers or town dwellers but not land farmers.

In the 1200's the Sutton (Veny) Manor was held by the Cromhale family. Then about 1350 there was a property switch with land at Cromhale (Cromhall) GL. This establishes a potential connection between the two locations. As well the Thynne family owned another manor in the parish in later centuries. The Thynne family owned land at North Cerney and Woodmancote so both of these places could be this Eacott source.

The Eacott name (by that version and usually that version only) appears in Warminster in 1600. At Warminster it is possible to suggest a connection with nearby Longleat whose owners had a connection with Woodmancote or with the line of Edward Ekott (born 1570) from Winstone and North Cerney. The Edward name introduced in the 1500's is not common in other branches of the early family. Edward Ecott of Winstone died in 1612 and his wife Margerie died in 1630. She left a will giving her property to son William Eacoot and her daughter Mary. Their other sons were Richard and Thomas. Whether they are connected to Warminster is not known. A Mary Ecott married in Warminster in 1641. John Eacot married Jane in 1666.

By the 16th century the fame of Warminster market was well-established and the clothing and malting trades, which along with the market were to be the economic mainstays of the town until the 19th century, had begun.

In the early 1600's at Warminster we have John, Richard and Thomas. The first Eacott in Warminster seems to have been John Eacott who baptized Anne at St Deny's in 1603. Richard Acott's son Henry was born there in 1609.

The Warminster line continues for many years and 54 names are recorded over 150 years.

Just north of Warminster at Westbury, Thomas Ecut left his will in 1627 naming his mother Elizabeth and a wife Rachel who was with child. This also may connect with Warminster and North Cerney. Did the child survive? Was it a boy or girl? What became of Rachel?

All but the most important houses in the town were probably of timber at this time. In 1638 thirteen out of fourteen houses in the town belonging to the manor of Furnax were of timber and thatched with straw or reed. The most substantial buildings in the town were perhaps the inns with which the town was well supplied for the convenience of visitors to the market. In

1686 Warminster stood fourth for accommodation among Wiltshire towns with 116 beds and stabling for 328 horses and it was said that there were 51 inns and alehouses in the town in 1710. The value of the principal ones may be judged from the price of £1,000 paid for the 'Red Lion' in 1636.

In 1751 it was described as a 'Populous place with good inns'. The population grew somewhat. In 1665 there were 354 householders in the town which indicates a total of perhaps 1,800 people. In 1781 the town within the turnpike gates contained 539 houses and 2,605 inhabitants. [47]

There were a number of tiny farm plots given to vegetable growing in the Warminster area and there were wool weavers until the early 1800's when larger mills away from Warminster caused the industry to collapse. As Warminster had no streams with decent water power, industry did not thrive there.

John Eacott born about 1640 - 45 married at Warminster in 1668 and had sons William and John. It is not known where John Sr. was born.

An early record for Warminster shows John Eacot and Edward Eacot as paying tithes as householders in 1665.[48] There is no birth record for any Edward in the possible life span of this person with an Eacott style name. This Edward is the second known Edward after the one born in 1570. Thus he may be named after his grandfather or father. These were two adult males who must have been born 25 to 50 year earlier 1615 to 1640. Warminster in 1665 was a prosperous wool town and a cloth making center. It was also known for malting and particularly for its grain market. There were 350 homes and about 1,800 people in the town. The restoration of the King had taken place. London was being hit by the last outbreak of the plague but otherwise stability now existed in England. A century later in 1781 there were 2600 people living at Warminster.

These two Eacott families would have been well known in such a small community. What they did for a living may not be known but what is certain is that they owned property, their homes. The wills for Edward

---

[47] Victoria County History, Wiltshire *vol 8*

[48] *History of Warminster by J.J. Daniel 1879 , pg 116*

Eacott Sr., husbandman of Warminster 1701 and John Eacott Sr. gardener of Warminster 1710 would be plausible evidence that they are the same as recorded in 1665.

Now a husbandman such as Edward would have meant that in his time he was a freeman a small landowner below a yeoman in status yet a farm owner, perhaps with an interest in animal keeping. His house in town meant he had some land nearby he could walk to each day perhaps with a house that would be rented or the farmed property was part of the village. How Edward acquired the property is not known. Did he come from elsewhere to buy it or did he marry and acquire it from an aging father in law? It would not have been unusual to relocate during the Cromwell era and the Restoration because of the upheaval in England.

John Eacott Sr. being a gardener possibly meant he was employed by a large estate. There were several in the area most notably Longleat and Stourhead. These were estates which were being greatly modified as formal estate planning became popular after the restoration. There would have been work opportunities on these estates including that of head gardener where the title would be applied. Otherwise he would be classed as agricultural laborer and likely not had enough money to warrant a will.

His will of 1710, 45 years later, means John could easily have been in his early 30's when he was first recorded.

We know something about a few other Warminster Eacotts.

Uriah Eacott joined the 1st Dragoons known also as the Royal Dragoons in 1800. He reported his age as 15 but when he was discharged in 1828, he was 39. Did he join up at age 11. Since it was a cavalry unit he must have known how to ride a horse. Furthermore this was a very elite military unit and entry must have been an accomplishment especially as a youth. This was a premier cavalry unit and saw lots of action against Napoleon mostly in Spain and most certainly he was at Waterloo. He was discharged in 1828 and became a Chelsea pensioner later in life under the name Escott. He would have owned his royal scarlet uniform but may not have been a resident of the hospital in order to be a pensioner. All former soldiers and non commissioned officers could apply for the pension.

The Royals served in the Spanish Peninsular under Lord Wellesley, later Duke of Wellington. They acted as rearguard during the retreat to the Torres Vedras lines in 1810 and their charge at Fuentesd'Onor in 1811 was a major contribution to that victory.

By the end of the war in 1814, The Royal Dragoons had advanced into Southern France and in order to save the expense and casualties of a sea voyage, they were given permission to march through France to Calais.

The 'Hundred Days' campaign saw The Royals in Flanders again and their successful charge at Waterloo on 18th June,1815, with the Union Brigade was largely responsible for maintaining the Allies' weakest flank until the belated arrival of the Prussians.

Once discharged Uriah could marry and did so to Sarah Loyde. They had 2 daughters and a son, Eli Joseph who married Matilda Tabor and emigrated to Geelong, Australia where his daughter Sarah Dorcas was born in 1857. Uriah's daughter Dorcas 1838 worked as a servant in 1861. Sarah Elizabeth 1830 lived until 1880.

Uriah's Cousin Job Acott (aka Eacott) of Warminster joined the 13th Foot, a Somerset regiment while it was recruiting in Bath in 1817. He was born about 1791. In September 1822 the 13th Foot was moved to Chatham in Kent where it was brought up to strength for service in India. While there it was reconstituted as a light infantry regiment in December and was retitled as the 13th (1st Somersetshire) Regiment (Light Infantry).

The 13th Light Infantry arrived in Kolkata in May and June 1823. Soon after arrival, Burmese forces attacked Cachar, a territory under British protection. War was formally declared on 5 March 1824. There was a lot of fighting action along the Irrawadi River and the 13th took part in the campaign that lasted until February 1826, when a treaty was signed with the King of Ava agreeing to cede territory and pay compensation to the British East India Company. That war over, they returned to England and Job left the service. He married about 1830 and had 4 boys and a girl. Emma 1831, Robert 1834, Samuel 1836, Joseph 1838, and Henry Joseph 1841. In 1861 Job was listed as a retired laundress. So he may have run a laundry business in Warminster. Robert may have gone to sea. Son Samuel became Ecott and was a railway policeman in Warwickshire in 1861.

There is another connection to Warminster that impacts the Eacotts. In the mid to late 1840's a resident became a convert to the Mormon religion and actively preached. Some people and possibly some Eacotts converted to the newly founded American religion which at the time was not yet 20 years old. This was somewhat remarkable in that this happened in a small English town thousands of miles away from America.

In 1821 in nearby Sutton Veny there was one male a John Eacott and in 1831 that male also had a son. Unfortunately in 1821 John Eacott was caught stealing £ 23 from Stephen Gosney of nearby Heytersbury. In those days such a sum was considerable. However it seems all was made right for the next year 1822 a John Eacott had married Hannah Paine. Most of the Eacotts at Sutton Veny were farm workers. The first Eacott marriage at Sutton Veny were Edward Eacott and Alice Noak and William Eacott and Sarah both in 1763. In 1786 John Eacott (Eccott) married Jenny Williams.

Or perhaps it was a different John Eacott who stole from Stephen Gosney because there was a pretty desperate John Eacott living in the area. If so the other John Eacott perhaps was never tried for this because he was up on an armed robbery charge that got him deported before the Gosney case could come to trial. We just don't know.

Westbury had a few Eacotts and Ecot. William Ecott born in 1705 had rather early in life written his will, 1736 at Westbury. Fortunately it did not need to be read for some time as he died 40 years later in 1776. It is possible but not likely he was father of Catherine Carr's John. The John Eacott in the next story married Catharine Carr at Westbury in 1802.

But first let's take a look at the social conditions in England in the first part of the 1800's. Life had gotten a whole lot more difficult. Firstly the population was booming faster than jobs could be produced.

With the Industrial revolution at its height, new industries and technologies were transforming everyday life.

For the owners of the new factories and businesses, men like Henry Eycott had opportunities which seemed endless. However, for the workers in the factories and their families, life was often grim.

It was a time of rising crime and increasing squalor as people packed into the slums of the ever expanding cities. In rural areas, changes to agricultural practices left many laborers without sufficient work to support their families. To feed their families, many turned to crime. The courts were busy processing these desperate people as criminals who would be deported.

In 1800 there were 5,000 trials in England and by 1840 there were more than 20,000.

In 1794 a weeks wages would buy 14 loaves of bread whereas by 1818 the same person could only buy 9 loaves. The weekly wages varied for agricultural workers from 6 to 9 shillings a week for much of the 1820 to 1860 time period. The pasture areas provided the seasonal labor and could offer a man 40 to 50 acres to cut in summer. Another way of providing stable employment conditions was to mechanize as much as possible of the summer work, reducing the exceptional demand and so releasing labor completely from agriculture. It was not until the 1860's however that much was done in this direction but in a generation a revolution took place. Good mowing machines, self-delivery reapers, hay elevators, loaders, hay turners, and side rakes joined the existing horse rake, hay tedder, and small collector. The reduced demand for labor showed itself in boys and girls going out to work later in life. In 1867 the age to work was nine (earlier in most areas in England) instead of seven or eight as it had been in 1843. By 1867 women too went from being universally expected to earn an income when married to being 'less disposed to work than formerly'. Improvement in wages came about due to mechanization and a smaller working force. Steam-plough engine men, for instance, drew 18s. to 21s. a week.

Another possible solution was to get more work out of men during the seasonal pressure. The usual incentive was piece-work and unlimited drink. The drink was a recognized perquisite. It was provided only at hay time and harvest. Work would begin at 3 o'clock in the morning and continue until 8 o'clock at night with a break during the mid-day heat. Women too would lease (glean) from 2 a.m. to 7 p.m. People, however thirsty or avaricious, could work no harder.[49]

England was overpopulated and farm work was simply less and less

---

[49] *Victoria County History, Wiltshire vol 14.*

available.

Over the same time the laws became much more humane. The last person burned at the stake was in 1784. After that if you were guilty of any crime, you were usually hung or let go unless you had money in which case you might be able to work a deal to pay a fine. The last person hanged for cutting down trees and other minor things was in 1814. The last person hanged for shoplifting was in 1822. The last person hung for being found "gay" was in 1835. Children were dealt with the same as adults. So instead of being condemned to death it became easier, more humane and cheaper to transport people and deport them somewhere, often Australia. A sentence could be from 2 to 20 years but was often 7. The term was not significant since being deported meant you had to eventually pay your way back home to a place where nobody wanted you and besides it was quite nice in Australia. Less than 5% of those transported ever went back to England. What about jails? They were not popular as they were expensive. In fact people had to pay to be in a jail such as a debtors prison.

Poaching (illegal hunting) was a common crime in rural areas as was petty theft in urban areas. The crowded cities also provided opportunities for thieves to ply their trade.

Here are some Eacotts who were arrested. Their crimes look like acts of desperation. In the latter half of the 1700's there were other family members who made themselves infamous by having problems with the law. Benjamin Eacott in 1760 was ordered transported from England for dealing in barley and malt[50]. Jane Eacott went to jail in 1783 for picking the pockets of John Majors in Winchester, Hamps. James Eacott was sentenced to death for stealing a sheep March 19 1792 but on March 22 he was given a reprieve. In 1838 Frederick Eacott went to jail for 2 months for destroying game on the property of the Marquis of Bath. William Eacott of Warminster stole a silver tea spoon from Thomas Harris and went to Devizes prison. On April 13 1843 Mary and Thomas Eacott were convicted of stealing faggots (a bundle of sticks) at Trowbridge. Stephen Eacott went to jail for a month because he left his family chargeable to the parish. He could not feed them. Willian Eacott of Sutton Veny got 2 months for poaching on Nov 14 1844. Thomas Eacott went to Devizes prison for 6 weeks for poaching at Blunsden

---

[50] *Manchester Mercury Mar 25/1760.*

and St Andrews.

And there were also victims. At Warminster, in 1782, John Bromhand Eacott in an unusual theft had his feather bed and bolster stolen.

Even for those with work in the factories, the change from reasonable prosperity to poverty could be swift. It only took an outbreak of disease or an injury at work to leave a family without the support of the main wage earner. Older children had to earn a living and help with household tasks. Evidence of these things is seen in the information about the Eacott family that moved to Wales.

The winters in the early 19th century were exceptionally bitter. In 1801 everything froze for 13 weeks and the number of families applying for support rose sharply. The settlement laws made it difficult for people to move around to find work as they had to have a certificate from their parish agreeing to take them back if they became chargeable to the state. People would be deported from one county to the one where they were born if they had to be fed and housed.

The poor laws had been created much earlier to help the destitute but as more and more families required support from the parish, discontent with the poor law grew. The payment for the poor law came from taxes on property owners but, in reality, these were often passed on to the tenants that rented the properties, causing more hardship. So while we don't know the exact details, the next stories arise from these desperate times.

The Story of John Eacott and Catherine Carr

This is a love story, the stuff of 19th Century novels. Here are the adventures of this remarkable couple.

John Eacott was of the Parish of Westbury, Wiltshire. He was born about 1774 probably in Purton, Wiltshire. He married Catherine Carr at Westbury, a spinster of the same Parish. They were married in the parish church by banns *"on sixth day of July in the year one thousand eight hundred and two."* Banns were also published in Purton. Banns were traditionally published in the home churches of both parties. A John Eacott, aka Ecott, Hackett, or Hakott was born 1771 to 1774 in the village of Purton,

Wiltshire. At the age of 27 he courted and in a proper wedding married Elizabeth Catherine Carr also of Purton and Dilton near Westbury. Other than that this information connects Purton to the Warminster area the significance of this fact is not known. We can assume that by the age of 27 he had established himself with employment to feel secure enough that he could support a family. Besides a church wedding, while not expensive, did cost something. Since they were married by banns an expensive licence was not needed. John would have proposed and gained permission from Catherine's parents. Catherine might have woven a ring made of her own hair as a token of her affection and presented it to John. Hopefully both parties felt the marriage was between two persons of similar status in the world. Catherine would go to the wedding in perhaps her only dress, likely of dark or black color. She likely had a cap or hat for her head and since it was July she likely had a few flowers in her hair. For the morning ceremony only the close families would be in the church with the minister and a clerk. John would present her with a plain metal ring, not necessarily gold but that would have been welcome. Everyone knew that all her worldly possessions would now be his and in return he would be responsible to keep and care for her. After the wedding they would leave the church to be greeted by neighbors and friends and a celebration would take place. Until 1823 a woman could not marry until she was 21. But in that year the age was reduced to 14. In practice marriage was delayed until the future husband had established himself enough to care for his wife and family. Their age of marriage was typical for the time. Catherine would have felt herself fortunate to marry as war and disease had reduced the male female balance in the population as there were more women than men. There were a lot of old maids about! An old maid was an unmarried woman over 30.

Catherine Carr was born 13 July 1775 in Dilton, Wiltshire. England. Dilton was a village just west of Westbury. John was 28 and she was 27 on their wedding day.

What occupation John had is unknown but he was listed as a laborer. Why his children came later in their marriage is also not known. By the time Selina was born John was 44. He must have come upon hard times as he was a desperate man and he made some very unwise choices. They had three children. Mary Ann christened 7th February 1806 Saint Denys, Warminster, Wiltshire, England.

Henry born about 1815 and Selina christened 12th February 1818, St.

Denys, Warminster, Wiltshire, England .

After the wars with Napoleon were over, a very great depression set upon England and with the return of soldiers and the loss of war related industry, it may well have been that John found himself in a very dire situation of being unemployed. Many were without work at this time. Married with two small children and a preteen daughter he may have found himself desperate to provide and feed his family. He was a man in his mid 40's and enters history by being caught for stealing and sentenced to 6 months in jail in 1819.

He would have been taken to court by the victim who often was his own prosecutor. Likely two magistrates and a jury would hear the accusation and the defendant was expected to explain away the evidence against him to prove his innocence. If you were not articulate or convincing or the jury did not like you, since at least some of the jurors would likely know you, you were in trouble. Trials were held 4 times a year. No policeman would be involved as there were none until 1856 but there was a local constable, often an unpaid appointment who had to be paid by the accuser to apprehend Eacott to appear at the trial.

John next acts like a mature man driven by desperation. After his release he was even less employable and likely a pretty much broken man, quite unable to provide for his family. In February of 1821, in the depths of winter, he undertook to rob again, this time at gunpoint, for what appears to be some food. This time the law was harsh and the inept thief was caught again. Was he a habitual thief, a no good fellow or the victim of hard times and desperation? No matter, his penalty was deportation to Australia and separation from his young family for stealing 4 bushels of wheat and a sack of grain from John Hasell and William Glass.

Assizes 25/16/6 Sentence: Guilty ! and this is the decision of the case.

The jurors of our Lord the King upon their oath present that John Eacott late of the Parish of Warminster in the County of Wiltshire laborer on the fourth day of February in the first year of the reign of our Sovereign Lord George the Fourth by the Grace of God of the United Kingdom of Great Britain and Ireland King Defender of the Faith with force and arms at the Parish aforesaid in the County aforesaid four bushels of wheat of the value of thirty shillings and one sack of the value of four shillings of the goods and chattels of John Hassall then and there being found feloniously did steal take and carry away against the peace of our said Lord the King his Crown and dignity and the Jurors aforesaid upon their oath aforesaid do present that the said John Eacott on the said fourth day of February in the year aforesaid with force and arms at the Parish aforesaid in the County aforesaid four other bushels of wheat of the value of thirty shillings and one other sack of the value of four shillings of the goods and chattels of William Glass then and there being found feloniously did steal take away against the peace of our Lord the King his Crown and Dignity.

Witnesses: John Hasel.
William Carter.
William Wilkins?
William Pearce.

On the 10th August 1821 at the Wiltshire Assizes, John was sentenced to "Life" for burglary and was transported from Falmouth on the 5th September 1821 on the ship "Mary II".The ship was 540 tons and the Master was Charles Arkell. The ship arrived in Sydney Australia on the 23rd January 1822 after being at sea for 140 days.

Separated from his wife and small children his life was in ruins. She was left in England presumably without means of supporting two small children.

This is not the end of the story. We know a lot more about the life of this John Eacott. His 140 days at sea was well documented. What was life like on a prison ship sailing half way around the world. England had a rough way of dealing with those who had created a problem in society but kept records which illuminate.

Here is the surgeon's diary from the "Mary II". He was John Rodmell.

He Writes :

26 July 1821 - 28 January 1822

July 26th Joined the Mary at Deptford as Surgeon and Superintendent of Convicts. ...by end (?) to be embarked on the ships arrival at Portsmouth. Carpenters from the Dockyard at Deptford were employed fixing the prisons until the 11th of August at which time they were completed. August 12th the ship dropped down to Gravesend - on 16th weighed anchor and came too again at the Nore. 17th got underway, but was obliged to anchor again in consequence of very light winds and ebb tide off the Buoy of the Girdle. 18th got underway with light airs and at 7pm came to in the Queens Channel. 19th weighed and made sail for the Downs, came to in 6 fathoms water at 3pm. Rec. fresh beef and vegetables, at 6pm got underway and made all sail for Portsmouth. 21st came to anchor at the Mother Bank. 22nd got underway for Spithead, at noon came to anchor in 7 fathoms. A sloop with 176 convicts, a guard, two women & 3 children came alongside as soon as the ship was anchored. ......

A list of the prisoners, guards and wives is found in pages which have been omitted. There were 37 guards assigned to this ship.

Amongst the prisoners was: John Eacott

General Remarks Mary II Surgeon's Journal
The Mary arrived at Port Jackson on the 23rd of January 1822 with 176 Male convicts on board after a passage of 129 days from Plymouth and which were landed at Sydney together with the guard on the 28th of the same all in the most perfect health. Several cases of sickness, as will be seen by the journal, occurred but which I am happy to say had a favorable termination.
The ship sailed from Portsmouth on the 9th of September but in consequence of strong Westerly winds setting in when off the Lizard it was deemed advisable to put into Plymouth, not being able to make any progress from the state of the weather at that time, but on the contrary had every prospect of losing what had been gained. On our arrival there, a report was made of the circumstance to Sir T B Martin who happened to be at that port investigating the state of the Dockyards. Sir Thomas directed that the ship should be completed with water and that the usual supply of Fresh Beef and Vegetables should be demanded for the prisoners and Guard. These orders were come into effect without lots of time and everything was kept in readiness for our departure the first favorable opportunity. On the 19th we weighed anchor with a light breeze from the Eastward. After we had been at sea a few days the irons were removed from the whole of the convicts taking of course all

necessary precautions to counteract any attempt at insubordination which might possibly be contemplated, but which I was not at all apprehensive of. The Mary was constructed with a Poop a circumstance that I conceive of importance, as affording a most commanding position for the guard a part of whom was constantly under arms in that situation during the day. It was from this circumstance principally that we were induced to remove so great a restraint knowing well from my own observations that such a measure would contribute greatly to the healthy condition of the prisoners, and which the event seemed fully to justify and I must not omit to state that they evinced much gratitude for the attention which was shown to their comfort both as regarding personal freedom and the due issue of provisions agreeably to the orders of Government. In order to remove all doubt from their minds as to the proper quantities being issued they were not only furnished with a scale of allowance but two of them were constantly to be present when the Steward made the distribution. With respect to the provisions supplied by His Majesty's Government for the use of the convicts every possible care was taken to guard against the substitution of an inferior species, which might be on board for ships use. In obedience to my instructions I used to attend the opening of provisions for the purpose of taking the mark, number and contents of each cask, and although it happened on two or three occasions that the Steward omitted to acquaint me when such circumstance took place I requested that the heading of the casks might be produced for my satisfaction. When the issue of lemonade first took place it was considered a very grateful and satisfactory beverage but after a time it did not seem to be taken with that avidity, which it had been, and bowels complaints had also made their appearance. I certainly attributed it to some irregularity in the mixing of the lemonade and accordingly, without previously suggesting my suspicions, I requested that some might be brought for my tasting the following day, but instead of bringing it from the pot as was intended I ascertained immediately that a portion had been mixed for me in due proportions a tacit acknowledgment that what was about to be issued was not in conformity to the directions which he had received. The steward was reprimanded by the Master and admonished to be more careful in the future, and I have every reason to think that he fulfilled the duties of his station afterwards with correctness. I have omitted to include above in what the irregularity consisted. It was in the withholding of a portion of the sugar whereby the lemonade was made unpleasantly acid and occasioned in some instances much intestinal irritation. It was seemed advisable to put into Port Praya

(?) Island of St Jago on our passage out in order to complete the water, but it was not accomplished with that facility that could be wished owing to the unsettled state of the local government. A supply of fruit and vegetables was procured for the guard and the convicts. We arrived at Port Praya on the 13th of October and sailed for our ultimate destination on the 18th of the same month. Everything went on smoothly during the voyage, indeed much more so than could be expected from the character of those embarked. It was found only necessary to inflict corporal punishment twice in the course of the voyage and that in a moderate degree for thefts amongst themselves. A school was established under the superintendence of the Rev. Mr. Hassall and myself in that part of the ship appropriated to the Boys and which was generally well filled by those desirous of instruction. Many of them who were unacquainted with the alphabet very soon learnt it and at the termination of the voyage could read with tolerable facility. Divine Service was performed every Sunday by the Rev. Mr. Hassall who was a passenger, mostly on deck, but when the state of the weather would not admit of it, the same wasperformed in the prisons. Although I am directed to perform Divine Service I think the Board will admit the propriety of conceding that point to a professional man when there is one present and desirous so to do. I am unable to point out any changes or attention that would be more conducive to the health and comfort of the convicts. The arrangements at present both with respect to the fitting up of the prisons, the mode of victualling and the comforts and necessaries supplied in ease of sickness are such as to leave apparently no room for improvement, and are fully adequate to attain all that could be wished. It seems right that I should say something respecting the issue of spirits to the guard, but only with reference to quantity, half a pint of rum was issued agreeably to instructions mixed with a proportion of water as is usual in His Majesty's Navy and sometimes it was made into Punch by the addition of lemon juice and sugar. It was served to them at twice, the first issue took place immediately after dinner and the last late in the afternoon. This was continued for some time but from the intoxication and disorder that frequently took place it was deemed in consultation with the Officer of the Guard and Master of the ship, absolutely necessary to suspend a portion of their allowance of spirits, which was accordingly done. In future they performed their duty as became good Soldiers and I believe were very glad that such a resolution had been adopted for they were remunerated for such privation much beyond their expectation on their arrival in the Colony of New South Wales.

John Rodmell, Surgeon and Superintendent.

Of particular interest is the Rev. Hassall who just happens to have previously known John Eacott, the prisoner.

Here are more details of the voyage, the ship's journal.

Mary II Journal

Portsmouth August 22, 1821
Embarked on board the Mary 176 convicts from the Leviathan and York hulks all apparently in good health. One man was reported to be subject to epileptic fits but that did not seem a sufficient reason for rejecting him. Also guard of the 46th Reg with L't Sutherland.

ALL the convicts came from either the "Leviathan" or the "York".

7 November
All the prisoners on deck, cleaned and aired below. Issued wine to the convicts. At 11am made the land about Cape Leda (?) on the Brazil Coast. A bed was issued to George Fisher one of the convicts. Opened a cask of pork, contents 80 pieces. Thermometer in hospital 83^0, in the cabin 80^0. 8 on the sick list.

8 November
At sea. James Fletcher, Lee, Thorpe, Rae, Kelly, Lovett and Bolten are doing well. Continued the bitter infusion. Prisoners on deck. Cleaned and aired below. Issued lemonade as usual Number on sick list 8. Opened a cask of beef.

9 November
At sea. Henry Winchester one of the convict's rec'd a severe contusion of the testicles with some laceration of the scrotum by a fall down the main hatchway - much swelling & inflammation immediately succeeded the accident accompanied with much pain. Linen wet in Lotio Plumb Supticet was applied to the part frequently and had a suspensory over all. An opiate in combination with Antimony was taken at bedtime. In the course of the night a very considerable distension of the scrotum took place apparently from an effusion of blood, forming the part into an immense elastic tumour. Discontinued the cote application and sub'd the

part with the linen Ammon C - three times a day. Took a purgative of the submunate (?) of mercury and Islop (?) Fletcher, Lee, Thorpe, Rae, Kelly, Lovett, Irwin and Bolten are doing well. Prisoners on deck. Scrubbed and washed bottom boards of their sleeping places. Served out lemonade as usual. Shook and aired the bedding. Number convalescent 8, sick 1.

10 November
Henry Winchester had a tolerable night etc (blood letting from scrotum) Cleaned and aired below. Lemonade. Casks - beef and sugar

11 November
Cleaned and aired below. Rev. Mr. Hassell performed Divine Service in presence of the guard, convicts and ship's company. Issued lemonade in the forenoon and half a pint of wine each man after dinner. Cask of flour opened.

12 November
Cleaned and aired below. Corporal Andrews of the Guard complains of some pain in the head and irritability of stomach and bowels. Purgative of the Submunate of Quicksilver and Islop was given. Edward Kenny of the Guard affected in the same manner. Temperature in the prisons 82½⁰, Cabins 80⁰.

Similar entries the next two days.

15 November
"All the convict boys and many of the men devote a part of the day to instruction under the immediate superintendence of the Rev. Mr. Hassall." Temperature in the prisons 81½⁰, Cabins 78½⁰. Casks: Flour, Pease, and Beef

Similar entries the next few days. Details of Winchester's treatment were included.

18 Nov: Only 4 on the sick list
19 Nov: Cask of Raisins
20 Nov: Temperature in the prisons 78⁰, Cabins 74⁰.
21 Nov: Casks - Pease, oatmeal, flour
22 Nov: Cask of Suet.

24 November
The hoses of the prison water closets were not (or 'put'?) in order.

25 November
"A blanket was issued to Stephen Reynolds one of the convicts having lost his first one overboard".

26 Nov: 3 on sick list

28 Nov: Temperature in the prisons 76½⁰, Cabins 68⁰.

1 December
Thomas Smith one of the convicts so nearly detached the third finger of the right foot (sic), in the act of cutting wood, that I deemed it advisable to remove it altogether, a tolerable flap of inlegunits(?) was preserved to cover the bone.

2 December
The Rev. Mr. Hassall performed Divine Service in the prisons, the weather being too wet to admit of it on deck.

3 December
Issued pair of Flannel Trowsers and a flannel waistcoat to Lovett & to Richard Dixon. Temperature in the prisons 70⁰, Cabins 65⁰.

4 December
Prisoners on deck for a short time this morning but did not remain in consequence of the weather being moist and disagreeable. Issued blanket, pair flannel trowsers & flannel waistcoat to John Tomlinson also 1 bed & 1 blanket to Daniel Holland. Issued a bed to John Richardson.

5 December
The weather has been much colder the last 48 hours attended with considerable humidity of the atmosphere. Several of the convicts are complaining of catarrhal affections, which in my opinion are attributable to a deficiency of warm clothing more particularly in the article of woollen trowsers or woollen breaches and worsted stockings. The duck trowsers and other clothing are beyond a doubt very proper on most occasions in making of this passage yet as often happens before we enter the tropics and after we emerge from them that the weather is cold

comparatively speaking and other susceptibility to its impressions is much increased. Some of the convicts on their embarkation had warm breaches and stockings but it was by no means uniform. Issued lemonade in the forenoon and win e in the afternoon. Inspected the clothing and bedding of the prisoners. Temperature in the prisons 66^0, Cabins 60^0.

6 December
Prisoners on deck, Cleaned and aired below. Issued a blanket each to William Barnett, William Solomon's & Andrew Gallagher. A shirt each was issued to Thomas Catron, John Hughes, Peter Wilberham, George Ashcroft, Henry Stevens, Daniel Douglas, William Lawley, Christopher Densons, James Weaver, George Mills, George Hills, John Simon, Robert Anderson, James Newton & Henry Coton.

8 December
Issued flannel waistcoat to Stephen Reynolds, flannel shirt to John Lovett. Temperature in the prisons 65^0, Cabins 60^0.

9 December
Majority of prisoners on deck, those laboring under catarrhal affections remained below. Weather bad so prayers were held below.

10 December
Carpenter employed stopping a leak in the prison.
23 Dec: Issued wine and sherbet to the convicts.

25 December
Issued ½ pint of wine to each convict in commemoration of the day. Sick - none, convalescent 4.

26 Dec: Issued a blanket to Thomas Lewis convict.

24 January
Sydney Cove
All prisoners on deck. Cleaned and aired below.Reported myself to the Lt. Governor & also waited on the Colonial Secretary. None sick. Fresh Beef and vegetables issued to the convicts. Temperature in the prisons 76^0, Cabins 74^0.

25 January

Sydney Cove

All the prisoners on deck. Cleaned and aired the prisons. Prisoners are all healthy. People and boats are employed returning the remains of the Public Stores & Provisions. Issued vegetables to the convicts. The guard was relieved yesterday by a detachment of the 48th regiment. Temperature in the prisons 77^0, Cabins74^0.

26 January

All convicts healthy. All prisoners on deck. Cleaned and aired below. At 10.30 the Colonial Secretary came on board and mustered the convicts after which clothing was issued to them. Boats are employed (as of yesterday) Served fresh beef and vegetables to the convicts.

27 January

All healthy. Rec'd orders for the prisoners to have themselves in readiness for disembarkation tomorrow morning.

28 January

At 6 am all the prisoners were disembarked and at 10 o'clock were inspected by His Excellency the Governor who was pleased to express himself highly satisfied with their appearance.

What then became of John Eacott, convict, deported, now in New South Wales, Australia. After removal from the ship he was sent inland to Parramatta for redistribution and assignment to someone who took responsibility over him, a tenure for life to another individual, a step above slavery. However after seven years he was no longer classified as a prisoner and given a Ticket of Leave. Once a convict had his or her ticket of leave they were allowed to work for themselves, marry or to bring their families to Australia. However, tickets of leave did have conditions attached. They had to be renewed yearly, carried at all times and Ticket-of-Leave men, as they were known, were also expected to regularly attend religious services. They were not allowed to carry firearms or leave the colony. Once the sentence was completed, or in the case of a life sentence when a sufficient length had been served, the convict would be granted a pardon, either conditional or absolute.

"As the distance of 14 miles between Sydney and Parramatta was too great to be traversed conveniently in one day by parties of convicts on foot and their escorts of soldiers, a log stockade was built half-way

along the track to serve as an overnight guardhouse and staging depot. This was constructed at a place called Longbottom, the word "bottom" there having its old English meaning "low lying land or swamp" applied to the drainage basin at the head of Hen and Chicken Bay, i.e. present day Concord Oval and surrounding area. An area of 936 acres was reserved in the surroundings of the stockade as a Government farm, but no sustained effort was made to cultivate it."

"At first a log stockade was erected and there the prisoners were detained for a night on their way from Sydney to Parramatta or vice-versa. As a rule they were handcuffed together while on the road. But the more desperate characters (bushrangers etc.) also wore leg irons, so that their march was a slow one; and the rest at Longbottom Stockade was doubtless, a welcome one. Later on a more substantial lockup was erected, and that is still standing. It consists of three cottages, built on sandstone foundations, with brick walls 18 inches thick."

From here John Eacott eventually found himself assigned as a convict to, of all people, the Rev. Thomas Hassall or Hasell (known as the Galloping Parson) at his property "Denbigh" near Cobbity, NSW (now a suburb of Sydney). The relationship between John Hassall and Thomas Hassall is not known. They may have been brothers or even the same person. It seems likely Eacott knew them from Warminster before he attempted to rob John. Whatever the true facts are it does seem very unusual that Eacott was placed with Hassal. Perhaps it was a set up.

It was here that John spent the rest of his life. No doubt he now became a regular church attender and he may have been fortunate to have such a man as Hassall as his overseer for in later life he was a tenant farmer for the Reverend Hassall, an indication of a good relationship and responsibility. This assignment was likely no accident. After John was given a Ticket of Leave he remained employed with the Reverend. The ticket also allowed him to be joined by his family.

In the meantime his wife Catherine, an educated woman with small children, had lost her husband, seemingly forever. However she was not the sort to abandon hope. In some manner she was able, after a few years, to manage passage to Australia with two of her children, Henry and Selena. The fact she undertook to go out to Australia to be with her deported husband says a great deal about the strength of their relationship. This was a remarkable journey and commitment for her. It is likely she had an assisted passage, meaning that she was given financial help from some source, likely the Crown or a benefactor. One could speculate that the Reverend who was considered a person of pleasant personality and kindness had a hand in this. There was also official support to bring out the families of convicts particularly females of which there was a shortage. A convict with a ticket of leave, essentially meaning he had completed his sentence, could make this application. Without this ticket such an application was rare. Eacott had a life sentence but he was given a Ticket of Leave in 1830 # 30/564 . Besides having a ticket he had to show that he could support his family. A convict was essentially a slave to his master. However, a convict's wife could apply to have the convict assigned to her, thus making her husband responsible to her. In this way families could be reunited. This does not appear to be the situation in Catherine's case as she had arranged employment for herself. Yet it does appear that John Eacott or someone was able to get the Crown to give passage and in order for this to happen he must have had the support of the Reverend to whom he was assigned.

On the other hand Catherine may have petitioned herself to be sent out as a settler independent of her husband as she seemed a capable person with skills.

Catherine 53 with son Henry 13 and daughter Selena 10 arranged passage on the "Borneo"in order to join her husband. We do not know what became of their older daughter who could have been married or working. They departed from London on the 11th of May 1828. The Borneo was also a convict ship carrying 73 female convicts in addition to other passengers who may have mostly been families of convicts. Catherine was not alone in being a female with a family on board the ship. During the journey, that stopped at Madeira for supplies, she made the acquaintance of Prudence Perkins Bankin and her daughters, Mary Ann and Sarah from Essex. One of the convicts would have been known to all the children. Sarah Barnes, 14, was the youngest female convict ever to be sent to Australia. The first part of the journey would have been pleasant and among new friends getting to know each other.

Note: It is known that Catherine's mother, Elizabeth Bigwood Carr, died in Australia and whether she and her husband John Carr were on this ship is not known. Elizabeth died at Macquarie Grove.

Richard Bankin had been sent out in 1815 as a convict for burglary of a barn. No goods were found on him and his hanging charge conviction was changed to 14 years transportation to Australia. Unlike Catherine's husband he would soon be a free man getting his Ticket of Leave. In 1825 Bankin had petitioned Governor Brisbane to bring his wife and daughters out to Australia. This was granted and 4 years later they were anxious to be reunited. So the passengers were a mix of convicts and families joining others sent before. We can imagine Catherine and Prudence having long discussions about their lives and the future awaiting then in an unknown land.

After rounding the Cape of Good Hope Sept 27, 1828 the ship suffered badly in a fierce storm and had to make port at Hobart Tasmania on October 8, 1828. The trip took 150 days, much longer than usual and this was the first (and last) voyage to Australia of the Borneo. Sickness also plagued the journey. Three of the convicts had fallen ill and died.

Prudence also became ill on the voyage and was taken directly from the sick bay on the boat to Hobart Hospital where she died a couple of weeks later on 24th of October. She was buried that day in Hobart Cemetery and so Richard never saw her again after he left England.

The grieving daughters resumed their journey to meet their father with Catherine and the others arriving in Sydney, December 28, 1828.

Catherine, shaken by the loss of a fellow traveler who failed to meet her husband, would have been even more anxious to join John whom she had not seen for over 7 years.

Her keen eye on arrival led her to record her impressions of her first days in Australia .She was a literate, cultured, observant woman who was not of the lowest classes. How the passage was paid for is not factually known but she had some assets in spite of the fact her husband had been deported years before. Her remarks below indicate she was indeed an exceptional person.

Journal of Catherine Carr:

It was just as twilight darkened into the night of an evening in early summer of the year 1828, that the good ship Borneo in which we had made our passage from London, dropped anchor in the very spot, a few fathoms off shore abreast of the King's Wharf.

Of course my reason for emigrating to NSW was the hope of bettering my condition and joining my husband. I had been informed, and I found it correct, that very much higher wages than those given in England were earned by mechanics in this colony: consequently I had no occasion, upon arrival, to regret on this account the step I had taken.

After laying out what money I had on clothing, a few standard books to read on the voyage, and such sea-necessaries of the eatable and drinkable sort as were not supplied by the ship, I thought myself very fortunate in obtaining a good passage in the Borneo.

Initiated into that frightfully pernicious but common habit of the colony, drinking rum neat out of wine glasses, we went out, dark as it was, for a stroll down the town. My companion was another passenger off the vessel, and had visited Sydney twice before; and as the ships generally stopped 5 or 6 weeks there, he had had every opportunity of becoming well acquainted with the place.

At this period Sydney was but ill lighted; only a few lamps were scattered throughout the whole length of George Street, which, from the King's Wharf to the end of the houses at the foot of the Brickfield Hill, can scarcely be less than a mile and three-quarters. As we walked down George Street we found Sydney, according to the custom during the first hour of a summer's night, all alive, enjoying the cool air. The street was clear of vehicles, and parties of inhabitants, escaped from desk and shop, were passing briskly to and fro, in full merriment and converse. At the main barrack-gate the drums and fifes of the garrison were sounding out the last notes of the tattoo. In Sydney the barracks occupy a noble sweep of ground in the very centre of town, the best spot, in fact, for general commercial purposes that it contains, a spot that really ought, without further delay, to be resigned to the corporation for those many important uses to which it could under their direction be applied.

Leaving the long line of the barrack wall behind us we at length reached the market place. The fine building that now occupies the spot under the same name, was then not even in projected existence; but the settlers drove their drays into the open air amidst the old shed-like stalls that here and there stood for the occupation of dealers; and the whole was surrounded by the remains of a 3 rail fence. As we wandered through the rows of drays and carts, I could not but remark of striking difference between them and the contents of the carts of any general market for the produce of the land at home.

There was no hay, but its place was abundantly supplied by bundles of green grass, much of it almost as coarse as reeds, and evidently produced by a very wet, rank soil. In other carts we found loads of such vegetables as the country and the season yielded; some of these, we were given to understand, were grown in the Kurrajong Mountains, no less distant from Sydney than 40 miles. In several carts we found sacks of last year's maize; and in a very few, last year's wheat.

Two drays only were loaded with new wheat, and these, we were told, were the property of rich settlers. It was very much the custom of the poorer settlers at this time, and indeed is so still, to sell all or the greater part of the wheat they grow, and live upon their Indian corn. This I was much surprised at before necessity, at a future period, had compelled my palate to reconcile itself to the peculiar flavor of maize-flour, cooked in its various modes; but once used to it, I have always since eaten it with much relish, and have consequently ceased to wonder at its common use by others. It is a common assertion, that the poor Australian settler (or, according to colonial phraseology, the Dungaree-settler; so called from their frequently clothing themselves, their wives, and children in that blue Indian manufacture of cotton known as Dungaree) sells his wheat crop from pure love of rum; and having drunk the proceeds, then of necessity lives the rest of the year on maize. But this seems to be only partially true. The fact appears rather, that wheat being the most costly grain, many eat maize from economy, selling the wheat to procure meat, tea, sugar, tobacco and clothing; and few persons who have tasted the deliciousness of a corn-doughboy eaten with the salt pork which constitutes so large a portion of their animal diet, will consider their taste altogether perverted.

After our cursory look at the market - if look it could be called which was performed in the dark - we went into 'The Market-House". I really forget whether this was its name by license or whether it was merely so called on account of being the principle rendezvous of the market people. It, however, was a regular licensed public house; but I should suppose at this time there were nearly twice as many unlicensed grog shops, as licensed public houses in the town of Sydney, in despite of the constables and a heavy fine. In the large tap-room of the Market-House we found a strange assemblage; and stranger still were their dialect and their notions. Most had been convicts; there were a good many Englishmen and Irishmen, an odd Scotchman, and several foreigners, besides some youngish men, natives of the colony.

Amongst them were present here and they're a woman, apparently the wife of settlers. The few women were all sober and quiet, but many of the men were either quite intoxicated or much elevated by liquor. The chief conversation consisted of vaunts of the goodness of their bullocks, the productiveness of their farms, or the quantity of work they could perform. Almost everyone was drinking rum in drams, or very slightly qualified with water: nor were they niggard of it, for we had several invitations from those around us to drink. I could not however, even at this early period of my acquaintance with this class of people, help observing one remarkable peculiarity common to them all - there was no offensive intrusiveness about their civility; every man seemed to consider himself just on a level with all the rest, and so quite content either to be sociable or not, as the circumstance of the moment indicated as most proper. The whole company was divided into minor groups or twos, threes and fours, and the dedeen (a pipe with stem reduced to three, two one or half an inch) was in everybody's mouth. I think there was not an individual in the room, but one female, who did not smoke more or less; during the brief time we sat there. Their dresses were of all sorts, the blue jacket and trousers of the English lagger, the short blue cotton smock-frock and trousers, and so forth, beyond my utmost power of recollection. Some wore neck handkerchiefs, some none. Some wore straw hats, some beavers, some caps of untanned kangaroo-skin. And not a shin in the room displayed itself to my eyes had on either stocking or sock. Of course I speak here only of the very lowest class; such as were derived from the lowest rank at home. And who, whatever advantages they had had in the colony, still continued unexalted by improved opportunities, unstimulated by hope, and making no efforts beyond what were necessary to supply their mere animal wants. To the same mart came down others in various degrees superior, many, particularly among the young natives, of plain but solid worth; but this was not the place to meet with them.

Catherine who has undergone great trial and found her way back to her husband must now have had high hopes of having a better life.

After arriving she found employment with the McArthurs at "Macquarie Grove". What sort of employment is not known. She had mentioned she might have been a mechanic, a term with different meaning then, more of a trades laborer. We can't assume she lived with her husband since the job was a few miles away from where he was. The reunion was a brief one. Sadly, less than a month after her remarkable journey, she fell ill and died January 23, 1829. Selina was 11 years old, motherless in a distant land with a father she did not know.

The children may have gone to live with their father but not for long.

John Eacott was now a tenant farmer to Rev. Thomas Hassall at his property "Denbigh" near Cobbity. The Hassalls and Cowper families were near neighbors and it is possible that William Cowper and Selena would have met at the little church called "Heber Chapel" at Cobbity. The convicts would have been compelled to attend church on the Sabbath as part of their rehabilitation. For them this would have been a welcome relief as time away from there arduous duties. Unlike other clerics who were cordially hated by the convicts population Thomas Hassall was said to be disarming and friendly. This can be born out by the fact that in later life John Eacott was a tenant farmer to Thomas Hassall up until his death in 20 October 1840. At his death he was about 60-65 years of age and was buried at Cobbity, Pomeerie Grove, Narellan NSW.

Selina Eacott married William Cowper when she was about 16. The newly wed Cowpers through their connection with the Hassall family moved into the Goulburn area where their daughter Mary Ann was born in 1836 at Goulburn Plains. In 1838 when their son John was born, they were at Long Swamp, Binda. William was leasing 640 acres of land from Francis Oakes and he described his occupation as sawyer. Their third child Elizabeth Catherine was born in 1846. She had been named after her great grandmother Elizabeth (Bessie)Carr and her grandmother Catherine Eacott.

Selena remarried and died in 1906.

I have no record of what became of Henry, John Eacott's son although a married Joseph Henry died in Victoria Province AU in 1888 age 69.

Australia, a land populated by the prisoners deported from various parts of the Empire, turned out to be a positive experience for many. Sadly Catherine and John were unable to share in that together. The records of how they arrived is a remarkable poignant story of the settlement of Australia.

Warminster was also the starting point for our next story. This time a settler going to Western Australia.

The Eacotts of Mandurah, Australia

Thomas Eacott of Sutton Veny, who lived in the same general vicinity as John the convict, became interested for some reason in the settlement of Sir Thomas Peel. Peel put together a scheme of questionable worth to take settlers to the western side of Australia and set up a colony there. One might think the idea was popular in Britain as it would preempt any attempt by the Dutch to claim the land. Peel's influence with the Home Secretary, his second cousin, got the scheme which was supported by the Australian governor, Sterling, passed. Nevertheless, the British government determined that land should only be granted to settlers who could demonstrate their capital worth, either in terms of skilled laborers sponsored to emigrate or in terms of equipment and livestock.

Three pounds invested would gain 40 acres of land. Grants would also only be made to those settlers who reached the colony by the end of November 1829. Thomas Peel assembled 300 emigrants but, due to a variety of reasons, reached the colony in December, thus missing out on his promised grant of all the south side of the Swan River south to Rockingham. Sterling instead offered Peel an equivalent grant of land starting south of Rockingham and extending through the present town of Mandurah and to the east to the Murray region.

Peel's emigration scheme was disorganized and Peel himself ,when faced with difficulties, did not cope well. When one of his chartered ships carrying his settlers foundered in Cockburn Sound, Peel retreated to Garden Island and left the settlers to fend for themselves. They camped in the sand hills at Clarence, now the Henderson shipbuilding yards.

Why Thomas Eacott elected to commit himself, his family and his investment to this scheme is unclear. What the allure of an empty far away land was for a married man with family who knowingly severed his contacts with family and friends and abandoned his native land is not known. Conditions in England in the late 1820's were better than at some other times but corn laws were causing high prices and small landholders were being absorbed into large estates. A rising population and dislocation of jobs to cities created an atmosphere of tension. Still there was Canada and America, not so far away. How Thomas got into this scheme is also not known.

But he and his wife, Elizabeth, and daughters, Anne and Harriet, their belongings and possibly some cattle and other livestock boarded the "Rockingham" to seek their future in a new and distant world.

Many of the settlers were to get a land grant title for working off their indenture. Presumably they had the farming skills to sustain themselves.

Once the matter of Peel's grant was settled, he shifted with some of his people and erected some of the first cottages in Mandurah. His own cottage was on the corner of Mandurah and Stewart St. close to a wetland but the cottage was demolished long ago and the wetland filled in. Relations with the local aboriginals became strained almost immediately. In July 1830 George McKenzie was murdered which led to the posting of a portion of the 63rd regiment. This regiment was an instant boost to the population. Gradually other settlers made their way to the region. These settlers included Henry Edward Hall and his family, Captain Meares and Captain Erskine. Some of Peel's settlers including John Tuckey and Thomas Eacott were given part of Peel's grant when Peel was shown incapable of managing it himself. This grant would indicate that Eacott had some status in the colony.

Urban settlement commenced in 1830 with the arrival of Peel and some 50 of his settlers. By the end of that year, cottages were built and the first half acre had been cleared and seeded. Peel settled on the north bank of the estuary, close to a wetland which provided rich fertile soil for the gardens. Fresh water and fish were also in abundance.

Peel's lack of organizational abilities and apparent disinterest in his settlers bred an intense dislike and many settlers returned to Perth as soon as they were able. The 1837 census showed an adult population at Mandurah of 16 people . The sale of some 10 000 acres of his prime land at Dandalup to Francis Corbet Singleton in 1839 led to the establishment of Pinjarra as the major social and administrative center for the region. Others followed Singleton creating a new social elite away from Mandurah.

The settlement remained sparse for years. Because of its geographical isolation, the strained relations between settlers and the aboriginals which ultimately led to the massacre at Pinjarra and the above mentioned problems with Peel, Mandurah did not grow quickly in its early years. The only two buildings still extant from this early period are Hall's Cottage on the southern side of the estuary and Eacott's Cottage now in the grounds of the Mandurah Senior High School.

The Eacotts arrived on the " Rockingham" which foundered in a storm, was grounded and much of the cargo was tossed overboard to get the ship afloat. The passengers in life boats also got tossed into the sea so the arrival in Australia was a wet messy affair although the shallow water meant much was salvageable. Only Thomas, Elizabeth and Anne arrived safely. Harriet apparently died on the journey.

They arrived in the second week of May 1830 and by the end of June 1830, which is the middle of an Australian winter, 34 people were dead, including Elizabeth Eacott, who had died in childbirth.

Thus Thomas and his daughter Anne were left to deal with an unhappy situation. He remarried and had 10 more children.

Ann, it was believed, eventually left Australia and settled in America.

The Eacott families in Australia may not all trace themselves back to these founder families but today there are more Eacotts to be found there than in any other country except England.

Mandurah in Western Australia recognizes their pioneer Eacott with a park, a street and an historic home from 1842.

The Welsh Eacott Group

The Eacotts were not Welsh at all. The earliest Eacott in this family was a certain William Eacott. He lived his life at Warminster, Wiltshire. There were several Eacott families there and there is no specific record as to who his parents might have been. He may have moved there from some other place. A William born in 1807 in Warminster was listed in the 1881 census as a widower. He married Mary about 1830-31 and they had 6 children; Caroline 1832, Jacob 1834, Harriet 1836, Jacob 1839, Elizabeth 1841, Emily 1846. Only one son appears to have survived. Both were named Jacob. Jacob was not a common Eacott name but a few years earlier William and Christian Eacott of Warminster had named their son Jacob as well. It appears there was no earlier Jacob in the family. These Eacotts were congregationalist church members.

William Eacott born 1811 in Wiltshire died 1883 in Chertsy, Surrey was father of Jacob.

Jacob born Feb 10 1839 grew up in Warminster and acquired the trade of brick mason. As a young man he set off to find employment in the booming coal and iron industry in Wales. The Blaina and Nantyglo Iron works, the Beaufort Coal and Iron Works, and the Aberystruth mines were booming in the late 1850's and work was there for the willing. He found employment as a mason at Aberystruth a position he held until at least 1901. He met his future wife Mary Davies born about 1846 who was a local Nantyglo girl. They had 4 boys and 5 girls; Edward 1862 Thomas 1864, Harriet 1865, Mary A. 1867, William 1870, Emily 1871, Jacob 1873, Elizabeth 1876, Hannah 1879.

This was a working class family where income was very tight and education was not a priority as long as one could read and write. Like most other working families the children began working early although they did get some schooling. In 1881 son Jacob was a collier machine man. Thomas, Edward and William worked as hewers in the Aberystruth mines. Harriet 15, and Mary 14 were workers in a Blaina tin factory. These were jobs that were not only dirty but posed serious health risks. Girls working with tin were exposed to toxic poisoning and the coal workers to lung disease. Women and children were paid less than men but also worked 12 to 14 hours a day. Talking, looking out a window or leaving a post meant a fine or a beating.

These factory jobs were unpleasant at best.

As they grew up the boys all lived near their parents who lived at Upper Puddlers Row, Blaina(1881). Jacob died in 1913 in Bedwetly, Monmouthshire, Wales.

In 1870-72, John Marius Wilson's Imperial Gazetteer of England and Wales described Blaina like this:

"BLAINA, a village, with iron-works, in Ebbw-Vale, Monmouth; on the Western Valleys railway, 2 miles SSE of Nantyglo. It has a station on the railway, and a post office under Tredegar. A church, in the Norman style, was built here in 1845. The circumjacent tract of country is highly picturesque."

About the time the children were born, iron had been the main local industry but in the 1870's coal mining increased while iron was in decline. Most of the miners lived in company housing and were forced to deal with the company store for goods. A system open to great abuse by the owners. Some of the pits that opened in this era were - Rose Heyworth (1872), Waun Lwyd (1874), Gray and Vivian (1885), Six Bells (or Arrail-Griffith 1889), Marine (1889), and the Llanhilleth (1891). It is not known where the Eacotts worked. Today these scared hillsides have ceased to produce coal or iron and have returned to a pastoral nature.

I have been able to trace one branch of this family with the following results.

Thomas Eacott, Jacob's second son, married Annie who was from Wolverhampton. It is not known how they met but they settled at Blaina and had a large family. Because of the numbers and proximity of the other Eacotts who lived nearby, it is difficult to tell whose kids are whose.

Edward, the oldest, at 19, was a hewer in the mines in 1881. 20 years later he was still there, a collier. He may have married Mary from Brecon Brynn. However his life underwent a radical change after 1901. Recruiters from Canada had come to actively encouraged miners from Wales to emigrate. There was a need to settle Western Canada and immigrants were paid for their passage. He liked the idea and so he emigrated to Canada in 1904 to the new mining town of Coleman, Alberta where the Western

Canadian Collieries had recently begun coal mines. Edward his wife Jane Elizabeth Davis and daughter Violet Lottie born 1902 arrived in 1906 from Wales. Edward's sister, Elizabeth Mary, who married James Light decide they also wish to leave Wales. The Light family set off for Canada about 1911 but the father and the three small Light boys James 8, Edward 7, Elwyn 5 return to Wales in 1914 while the mother Elizabeth Mary moved on to California.

Edward and Elizabeth had a son, Challis, born Jan 23, 1910 in Coleman AB. Edward in 1911 no longer a miner was working as a self employed merchant selling fruit. He was 50 and Jane Elizabeth was 45. Lottie was 9 and Challis was 1. Edward died in Coleman in 1919 and is buried in the town of Belleview, Alberta. After he died Jane Elizabeth moved to Prideau Street, Nanaimo BC where age 55 in 1921 she worked as an agent. She died in 1927 in Bellview AB. After his mother died, young Challis set off on his own perhaps looking for his older sister or his aunt in California.

Challis had a thirst for adventure as a young man. During the depression he climbed into a railroad box car and headed off to California where he worked under an assumed name, Peter Bruce Miller. He entered the USA legally on July 22 1935 at Eastport, Idaho and did so again March 4, 1940. Still looking for adventure he decided to join those who went off to fight in the Spanish Civil war and volunteered in an American Unit in the International Brigade.

Five brigades of international volunteers fought on behalf of the democratically elected Republican (or Loyalist) government. Most of the North American volunteers served in the unit known as the 15th brigade, which included the Abraham Lincoln battalion, the George Washington battalion and the (largely Canadian) Mackenzie-Papineau battalion. All told about 2,800 Americans, 1,250 Canadians and 800 Cubans served in the International Brigades. Over 80 of the U.S. volunteers were African-American. In fact, the Lincoln Battalion was headed by Oliver Law, an African-American from Chicago, until he died in battle. The American battalion suffered 700 killed or died. Most volunteered in 1936/37 and went to France as it was not possible to go directly to Spain at the time. In 1939 with the advent of Second World war and the defeat of the democratic forces in Spain the brigades ceased operations.

Challis then returned to Canada and enlisted in the Princess Patricia's and served in the second world war first in the Italian campaign from Sicily up the peninsula to Monte Cassino. He was then transferred to England and took part in the Invasion of Europe. His unit fought in the Netherlands and liberated Amsterdam and Apeldoorn.

After the war Challis lived in Surrey BC where he was a letter carrier for the post office. He died in 1990. His son Challis was also a letter carrier and Vancouver bus driver before he died. Challis the third became a member of the Canadian Navy.

The Eacotts of Bisley and Chobham, Surrey

Southwest of London lies the small village of Chobham and the smaller village of Bisley. Sometime before 1740 John Ecutt and his wife Ann became resident at Chobham where he bought a house, lands and premises from Robert Stimpson. It is not known from whence they came. Perhaps Ann was a local girl. John evidently had some money to buy property. Why here? There was no surge in industry in the late 1700's or other work attracting reason to draw him to this place. Their children William 1760, Sarah 1766, and John 1766 were baptized at Chobham St. Lawrence Anglican church. This may have been to meet the law since later Eacotts were baptized at the Chobham Baptist church. Not all were Baptist dissenters because some went to live in nearby Bisley around 1800 and attended other churches. Thomas Eacott who had been born in 1780 came to Bisley and married Mary Martin in 1801. He was an agricultural labourer who in retirement lived at Noah's Ark residence with his wife Mary and son Thomas (born 1825). This family were Chobham Baptists. Marcy Eacott (William Glashier) and William Eacott (Sarah Emlyn or Glaser) also were married at the Bisley Anglican Church of St. John the Baptist 1806 and 07 respectively. It appears their father William Acot was church warden at the time. Ann Eacott died in 1799 leaving her estate to son William. His will of 1842 showed he had a lot of land in the Bisley parish which went to his 4 children, William, Stephen and Ann wife of John Harding and Sarah wife of Daniel Gosden. For most of the 1800's the Eacott name was well known in Bisley. In 1819-29 William Eacott was churchwarden and from 1840-3 another William Eacott had the position. 1854-6 Stephen Eacott, a farmer, was warden who lived with his wife Mary and 4 children at Chatters Row. He farmed 24 acres nearby. His hired man lived with them. Lastly William Eacott was warden in 1865. William Eacott and his wife and son George ran a pub "the Yew Tree" at Bisley in the 1870's. John Eacott born 1808 was a retired butcher living in Bisley in 1881.

Another person Sarah Eacott wife of William in her old age lived with her daughter Sarah (Daniel) Gosden.

William Eacott a farmer and beer retailer (or publican) held 13 acres of land at Bisley in 1871.

Only 2 Eacotts were ever buried at Bisley, Henry age 27 in 1838 and Hariett age 36 in 1858.

Sometime after 1886 the Eacotts are no longer connected with Bisley as George the Inn Keeper and the farmers son Albert George were the last record of Eacotts at Bisley.

In the 1800's around Kingston on Thames, Robert Eacott 1810 -1875 of Long Ditton and possibly Kingston had a family. Thomas Eacott born 1810 lived at Kingston. Near there at Wimbleton were Eckett and Eckitt persons and at Ham the Echett and Eckett spellings appear in the late 1800's. These people are possibly a related group choosing different spellings because all are within a 3 to 4 mile area.

The Eacotts of London

Eycott and Eacott appear in London mostly after 1700. London and Middlesex county were not early locations for Eacott families.

The earliest records from the 1500's to the early 1700's have a smattering of name choices, not necessarily an Eycott/Eacott derivative. Robert Haicot was baptized 1589 in Stepney. Then there are Lidia Acott 1592, Michaell Awcotte 1601, Wm Acoute 1607. Then a little later a family of Hawcott lived at Ludgate from 1607, Mary Hicote 1632, William Icott 1694 at Holborn. There is no pattern or consistency or known connection to Eacott/Eycott.

One interesting note is the baptism of Roxam Acots in 1637 whose father Henry Acots was a French Protestant Walloon living at Spitalfields. After the termination of the edict of Nantes in 1685 in France, French Protestants were denied all rights and thus were being forced to convert to

Catholicism. Many fled, some to Canterbury and London particularly to Spitalfields. In order to flee France these refuges had training and money to assist them. In particular there were many weavers especially of silk who established a French community at Spitalfields where they flourished. Thus the surname Acotts is in some cases a French import and not a variant of Ecott/Eacott and could be French if it came from the south east of England during the late 1500's early 1600's. Similarly Lidia Acott 1592 from Essex could be a Walloon Huguenot Protestant. It is helpful to look at the given names which typically differ from those given to English children.

So when Frances Acott was baptized in 1707 at St. Leonards Shoreditch by John and Mary Acott there is a distinct possibility they were of French descent. Whether any Acott family later used Eacott is not known. However some have family lore that they were thought to have come from France.

Clearly some Acott names are an alternate derived from Ecott or Eacott while others come from Acourt or similar French origin. For that reason I have not followed up further on that variant in this work.

James Eycott was married to Mary Constantine in 1732 at St. Paul Covent Garden. We met him earlier as he was from Cirencester.

Mary Wiltshire Eacott was born in 1770 at St. Alban Wood Street, London to William and Eleanor Eacott.

These are the earliest known London Eycott/Eacott residents. After 1800 the London names are those who have come to London to seek their fortune.

The Irish Eycott - Eacott

It has not been possible to create a separate story for the family in Ireland. Many records were destroyed during the uprising. Eycotts lived in Dublin from before 1700. William Eycott was a silversmith there and may have been part of the Berkeley Eycott group. A Berkley Eycott was born to Richard Eycott on July 22, 1712 in Dublin. After that there is little material until the 1800's when the Eacott version is known in a few places. One Eacott was thought to be a well known writer. Several others in America cite Ireland as their place of birth. Cornet player Robert Kirkpatrick Eacott was promoted to Cornet Vice of the 7th Regiment of Foot from the 20th Regiment Light Dragoons in July 1839. Others lived in County Kildare and Dublin.

Before crossing the Atlantic to look at America it is interesting to look at what can be learned from the British census material for 1881 and later. These are the Eacott families for which those living today can more easily find their own records.

England After 1850

Notes on various Censuses

Census of England 1891

The following Eacott derivation names were found in a study of the 1891 Census for England

Eacott 258
Eckett 171
Ecott 56
Eccott 50
Eycott 39
Eacot 10
Total 584

No persons in England at that census were known to have these spellings: Eacutt, Eccot, Eycot, Ekutt, Ekott, Eacoot, Ekett, Eakett, Eakott, Ecot , Ecket

Census of England and Wales 1901

It can be assumed by this time that the spelling of the name had become formalized due to increased education levels. Using all variations which appeared in the records prior to 1901 and some which didn't, this is the result of all thinkable Eacott variations.

Eacott	404	Eacotts	1	Aycott	24
Eckett	204	Eyckett	1	Icott	1
Eccott	82	Ecot	3	Acot	3
Ecott	46	Eacret	14	Acott	356
Eycott	25	Eakets	27		
Eacot	3	Eacret	14		

No persons were known to have these spellings in 1901:

Eacut, Eacutt, Eccot, Eycot, Ekutt, Ekott, Eacoot, Ekett, Eakett, Eakott, Eccutt, Eccot, Ecat,Eacit, Eakett, Eckut, Eycatt, Eycodd, Eycot, Eycote, Eacert, Ecoate, Ecots, Ecotts, Eyecot Ecute, Ecut, Ecreat, Ecreet, Ecote, Eacot, Eacett, Eyecote, Eyecot, Eyecott, Aket, Akett, Eacett, Eakett.

The Eacott name in 1901 is found mostly in Southern England and adjacent Wales especially Gloucestershire, Wiltshire, Somerset, Berkshire. The Eccott name is largest (30%) in Hampshire and London (25%). The Ecott name is in Southern England but more south easterly than Eacot, 30% Bedfordshire 30% Essex, 20% Croydon. The Eacret name is in Ireland or Manchester and thus may not be a derivative of Eycott. The Eakets are found in Gloucestershire mostly around Cheltenham (90%). The Eycott name is found in greater London 30% and south coast. The Aycott name is mostly in London, Surrey, often in same communities as Eacott.

The Eckett name is found across southern England and the midlands often in the same places as Eacott, however 50% of Eaketts are in the London area.

Of note is the fact that very few of any of these names occur outside the southern half of England.

The prevalence of the name with a likely "EH" sound rather than an

"AY" or an "EE" sound as in ECK, ECC, EAK accounts for the accent emphasis that occurs in the useage of Eacott which appears in all soundings. Some using the Eacott form actually say the name as Eckett or Eccott. A simple spelling change lines up easily with Aycott, Acott, Ecott, Eckett and may reflect local accentuation. Eacret may derive from another source than Eycott.

Census of England 1881

This census has more free data than the 1901 census. Thus it is easier to identify family groupings. In 1881 England was at the height of Empire and the Victorians. It was also the most industrial country in the world.

The examination of the Eacotts from that time show they were largely agricultural or related workers. The second largest group were servants (mostly women). A few were miners, some shop keepers. The industrial workers were varied but railway related work seems the largest source of jobs. The vast majority could have been identified as working class. The distribution of people in the 1901 census was reflected in the 1881. Not a lot of movement took place.

The census included age, place of birth, marital status, street address, occupation and where living. This is available online (search: 1881 Census England). The records entered by me do not generally include street address.

There are discrepancies between the 1901 and 1881 data in name changes, as Eacott to Ecott, frequent year of birth variations by as much as 5 years and sometimes place of birth differences. Some of these are in the specifics such as a neighborhood or estate given instead of the municipality. While there are people who will appear unknowingly more than once in the records, there are others who clearly were not recorded in 1881 that were recorded in 1901 and who existed in 1881 and likely the reverse applied in 1901. There seems to be a lot of errors. People who were in my data base prior to the entering of census data should have shown up as matches but many did not.

The original Eycott Name was no longer found in the North Cerney area. Only 18 Eycott names were in the census and they were in fewer than 5 families.

Name and Location Study (from 1881 census)

An analysis of the variants of the Eycott name based on the census material using males born before 1850 and a few unmarried older females gave the following information which indicates the earlier sources of the names:

The **Eycott** name was found in London and in Stroud Gloucestershire and a few were also living at Aldershot in the 1870's.

The **Eckett** name was mainly in two localities about 12 miles apart Reading and Basingstoke. 20% on the west side of Reading and 22% on the west side of Basingstoke. London area had 33% of the Ecketts. The remaining families were scattered in isolated places in Berkshire, Surrey, and Somerset.

The **Eccott** name was 80% located on the east side of Basingstoke within a 5 mile radius. After 1850 there were Eccotts at Shefford near Chaddleworth.

The **Eaket** name was all in Gloucestershire.

The **Ecott** name was in several small villages south of Bedford, Bedfordshire and in the vicinity of Cromhall, Gloucestershire.

The **Acott** name, the largest group, is concentrated along the B2015 corridor from Tunbridge Wells to Maidstone in Kent, over 50%, especially at Yalding. This is a small area about 10 miles by 2 miles. About 15% of the Acotts were in London and 7% each in Oxford and at Maisey Hampton, Gloucestershire. Most of the rest were in Kent. So the name was extremely localized. Among the 9 older Acott men over 60 years (born before 1840) 4 were not born in Kent. These were born in Maisey Hampton, Gloucester, Oxford, and Somerset The Genealogic records and name associations don't generally include Acott as a variant and the reason is the connection to the French Acourt name brought to England by Huguentot refugees. However, only as a German name does it appear in America in the 1880 census. Although German immigration to England was rare, it could be a German name confused with Eacott.

The **Eacott** name is found in more diverse places than the other names; however, 90% of all the names were 5 miles north of , to 15 miles south of the modern M4 highway from London to Bristol. 60% of Eacott name sites were in Wiltshire; 18% Warminster; 14% Chaddleworth; 8% Cromhall; 8% Wroughton; 14% other Wiltshire places; 10% in Surrey, South West of London. The rest were elsewhere in Southern England.

The statistical base for census records of those males born before 1850 is 65 Eacott;54 Eckett; 73 Acott; 23 Eccott; 6 Eycott ; 13 Ecott.

Before 1800 my database has very few Eckett or Acott names. Before 1700 most were Ecott or Eycott. Some early names such as Ecut did not exist in the census. The fact that Acott and Eckett have very few occurrences before 1800 indicates they were likely derived names, not original.

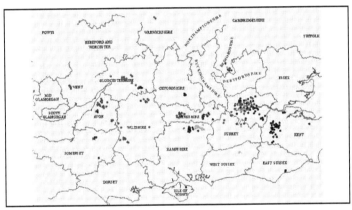

The map shows the distribution by dots for the surnames just discussed for males over 20 years of age across southern England in 1880. The names are mostly concentrated in very small local areas.

There are a few people outside the area of the map for example a family in Derby another in Yorkshire. Importantly many of these places had no Eacott or variation names prior to 1700.

Glimpses of the Past

Small frozen moments of time can be dusted off and picked out of the sawdust of the ice house of history. These are seldom blocks of information but tantalizing chips that the different census gives us.

More questions than answers arise as the chips melt away from our knowing. Nowhere is there an iceman to deliver the blocks. I shall try here to illustrate the news fragments of the spring day when all the census records were collected.

It looks on the surface as if a father or a couple of brothers perhaps settled around Reading and Basingstoke, having come some miles from the west and began using the Eckett spelling of the name. On the east side of Basingstoke someone translated Eacott or Eycott or even Eckett into Eccott and the spelling took. Someone, perhaps from Maisey Hampton in Gloucestershire, relocated to Yalding and the name Acott took hold or they may have been the Huguenot Acourt families. Just who moved and when is a question likely never to be answered.

A little more clear is the arrival of **Jacob Eacott** in the coal mining valley by Blaina, Monmouthshire from Wiltshire. A bricklayer by trade he likely found the prospering of the coal industry in Wales a good work opportunity. He married, settled down, and raised a large family of boys who went off to work in the coal mines that fed the engine of industrial expansion in Britain. Some of his cousins back in Wiltshire went to work in the railway factories working steel and boiler plate. Others worked in the railway systems, some as clerks, porters etc.

The biggest employment for the various families was in agricultural jobs. Of the 37 known **Eccott** occupations in 1901 thirteen were doing such things as picking watercress, gardening, keeping game, or other farm jobs. Among the rest were a railway plate layer, a carpenter, several general laborers and a couple of men who were navvy (laborers) on the railroad, a ganger platelayer in the gas works and a railway porter. The ladies were servants or cooks, laundry workers or dress makers.

Of the some 117 male **Acotts** examined, more than 30 were essentially farm labor although some said they were farm carters or horseman. A dozen were bricklayers or helpers, one a stone mason and another a sculptor of stone marble. In the transportation trade there was a brewers drayman, a railway engineers assistant, railway clerks (2) a porter, a milk carrier, tram driver, builders carter. The wealthy estate owners employed Acotts as footman, coachmen, groom, head kennelman for fox hounds and gardeners.

John Acott of Oxford was a comic opera actor. Horatio was an assurance superintendant. Horace a drayman, Herbert an Irvam Trade (?), Peter a police officer, Richard an Innkeeper, Walter a Royal Engineer Sapper who built bridges, cleared roads etc., while another Walter was a coin clerk. One William was a leather dresser who turned hides into colored and polished leather and another William a mangle man who pressed clothes in a machine. There were shop keepers, merchants, butcher, baker, fruiterer and several apprentices including printer and brass foundry apprentices and finally a very fit George was a pianoforte remover.

Among the approximately 100 **Eckett** workers half a dozen were domestic servants and only 8 were agricultural workers or farmers. Because a number lived in London, urban occupations prevail. 8 were in construction as cabinet maker, painter, carpenter or bricklayer. There were half a dozen dressmakers or laundresses. Some were birdcage, basket or packing case makers. Another 8 worked in some capacity for the railroads. There was an innkeeper, electrical instrument maker which in 1880 was cutting edge technology, undertaker, clergyman (2), police constable, beer seller, school mistress, piano teacher, tea buyer, printing machine manager, waiter, journalist, fishmonger(2), civil engineer and an artillery gunner. Over all the education level among these people was fairly high.

The **Ecott** trades included carpenter, bricklayer , butcher, dressmaker, tailor, machinist and a few agricultural workers. There was also an engine stoker who shoveled coal into a furnace, a soldier, and a bank clerk. There was nothing very unusual in these jobs

The **Eaket**s, all of Gloucestershire, had 3 stone masons, a painter, and laboring jobs.

Aycotts worked as boiler stoker, boiler maker, cheesemonger assistant, newspaper reporter, wood carver, laundry, boot maker.

Eycott careers included 3 house painters, teacher, coffee house keeper, naval chief officer, matron, and one cricket at Chopper Willow.

The **Eacret**s were mill workers.

Finally the **Eacotts**, 3 dozen were domestic workers, cooks, servants etc. Another 3 dozen were agricultural workers mostly not otherwise specified, some were gardeners, herdsman etc. 7 were farmers on their own land. 8 worked in the coal mining industry, another 8 worked on the railroad. 6 were in the grocery trade, and six were bricklayers. One was a brick maker. 5 were clergy or similar, 6 were seamstress or dressmakers. 3 teachers, 3 cabinet or chair maker, 2 bank clerks, 2 train drivers. More than a dozen were industrial laborers. A few were shop keepers and one a professional bailiff, another a candy shop owner, a bristle merchant, china sales agent, boiler smith and a number of people with odd sounding jobs, cigar box cutter, compositor who arranged type for a printing machine, a chimney sweep, a town crier who made public announcements, iron monger, a telephone wire man who was installing the very first telephones in England, a tent maker, a paper folder (?), corset machinist, brass trimmer, a wheel chairman (?). There were also a soldier, 2 seamen and a nurse. Apart from the seven Eacott owned farms there were few landed families. Whatever status the Eycott/Eacott name may have had in earlier centuries it is clearly a name held by very ordinary people at the turn of the 20th century.

What was happening in family life? During the last years of the 1800's the population of Britain had increased greatly. In 1500 there were about 2 million People by 1600 4 million and by 1800 there were around 8 million. At the turn of the century millions had migrated and yet there were about 50 million in Britain. Large families abounded. Most children went to school but by the age of 14 most boys held jobs and many girls of 16 were domestics and factory laborers.

By 1880 some modern jobs were evident such as telegraph messenger, electrician, shorthand writer, news reporter. There were a goodly number of middle aged unmarried women mostly working as domestics. Some women aided by daughters were taking in laundry. Families owing or renting were adding to the family income by taking in renters. A great many households had one or two unrelated people living with the family. They must have been busy places because they would be sharing meals and living space with several children. Some of the farms were being managed by widows aided by their sons. A very few people were pensioners or listed as living on their own means. Some people were unemployed including a school master who had recently returned to England after having lived in Germany and Switzerland where some of his children had been born. At least one of his children eventually lived in Argentina.

Fitting together puzzles showed that one boy of 5 placed in an orphanage eventually was educated and became a dentist. Another person, a recently widowed grandfather, was present for the birth of his daughters child during the time of the census. Some people lived and worked on great estates employed by high ranking people such as a senior magistrate.

There seems to be a lot of bricklayers among the various families as well as some carpenters but more bricklayers. Was this something of a family trade or just a reflection on the building industry needing more bricklayers than carpenters. While there are a few in the military, the numbers are very small. Likewise, the number of well educated persons is also quite small. There are no lawyers, doctors and almost no persons of rank or senior management. However there are several theological people, a few bank clerks and some teachers. Most people would be considered employees rather than employers. Those who were employers in 1880 were very small business people.

Other Locations

A will of 1684 for William Ecut of Eysey Manor (Kempsford-Castle Eaton area), labourer, whose wife was deceased left his goods to sons William and Nicholas and daughters Ann, Margaret, Elizabeth.

In Berkshire at Tilehurst (1742-1812) a line of Ecket names occur. The same occurs derived from Eycott at Ampney Crucis (1709-49). At Yattendon Berks. Eacotts are listed (1745-48) and later at Brightwalton (1775-1824). These latter two are directly connected back to Cirencester and Berkeley Eycott.

There are a number of marriages occurring in different places without any additional entries.

Eacotts in the United States

There are only a handful of Eacott who came to America before 1850.

Before 1776 Martha Eacott arrived, likely deported, as a bonded passenger. Then in 1782 Hannah Eacoff married Ralph Pule in Chester PA. In 1810 John Eakett was in Sharpsburg MD.

In the United States the census reports only tell part of the story. There was not much before 1830 and in that census a John Acott lived in Philadelphia and a William in Franklin TN. Richard Ecott lived at Stow MA and later Dexter NY. William Escot was in Hebron CT. Henerey Eicket was in Jackson Ohio. Philip Eskoat and John Eskcott were in Manchester MA. This John had been in the 1820 census as Easkott in the same place.

In addition Michael Eacott was in Hamburg NY in 1830. John B. Ecotr was in North Carolina and George Eacrat was in Pennsylvania and John B. Eycot was in Illinois. Nothing more is known of these people.

By the 1840 Census there were a few more people but not much more detail. William Eacott and Thomas Eckott (sp?) were in Westmoreland PA. Richard Ecott in Orleans NY. Abraham Echet in Greene NY. Jacob Ecket in St Louis MO. Adam Eicheat in Philadelphia PA. Andrew Escutt was in Charlestown MA and Joseph Escott in Kent co. MI. The spellings were pretty flexible so in later census the same person may surface with a different spelling. Another issue with the alternate spellings is the fact that the alternate such as Escott, Eakett or Eaket, Acott and Ecot unless specified as English can often be German born in their origin.

No other alternative spelling versions were listed although it is known there were some. These will be brought forward later.

The Escott family of Walker, Kent co, MI is likely English. The family shows up in the 1860 census. Escotts in England are rarely if at all derived from Eycott, Eacott. The Eakett family of Pendelton KY are from Germany. The Adam Ecott family of Ulster NY are also German.

Frederick Eakett of Zanesville OH was from Ireland. The Aucott family only known in Philadelphia PA were from England. The Acket family of Oakland MI and Wisconsin origin is not known.

Another family is George Eaket born 1842 and Sarah Eaket born 1839 in Liberty, Ohio

Eacott Families of New England

Mathew Eacott Family

Mathew Eacott(1826-1877) and his wife Ruth Chapman (1824-1894) (Father Joseph mother Ann Reynolds) were raised in Trowbridge, a cloth manufacturing town in Wiltshire. There were several Eacott families in the town. His father was identified as James Eacott.

Some choices for Mathew's grandparents are William Eacott a weaver who left a 1790 will and Richard Eacott of Purton. James Eycott who was born 1793 is a possible parent. However the likely choices for his parents are James born 1794 and Betty Taylor. They married in Trowbridge in 1814.

Like many others in the area Mathew worked in the cloth mills. His children were all born in Trowbridge, Amelia 1847, Henry John 1848, Benjamin 1851 and Mary 1854.

The family made a momentous decision to emigrate to America. They arrived at Boston on the 14th September 1855. Where the funds for this came from is unknown. With them went Ruth's sisters Hannah and Sarah Chapman. What the reasons were and why the destination we do not know. What is known is they were living in Lowell MA in 1860 when the census was taken. Mathew was now a provisions dealer working for himself.

By 1870 the decision to emigrate had paid off. His business had prospered and between his real estate and personal wealth he was worth $9,000. Henry and Benjamin were likely working in the family store.

Ten years later Mathew has died, 1877. Benjamin is working for his brother Henry who is a meat and provisions dealer, (butcher shop). Henry has also married his wife Florence and live in their own place. The rest of the family lives at number 8 Third Street, Lowell MA. It was a frame home likely next to the store. Also by 1880 there is a boy Fred Silcox age 8 living with the family. Amelia has married Ebenezer Chapman.

As the 1890 Massachusetts census was destroyed by fire, there are no records.

By 1900 there is no record in the census for any more Eacotts of this family. Henry J died in 1893 at Lowell age 45. His wife Florence born a Pilsbury, remarried George Lane 3 years later in 1896. Benjamin does not show up in any known records.

James Henry Eacott Family

James Eacott, age 18, arrived in Boston MA aboard the "North America" from Liverpool in 1852. This would mean he was born in 1834. There is no record of a suitable James born about this time. We do know that James Henry of Lisbon Falls, Maine claims to have been born in England in 1835. So perhaps young James in order to travel alone added a couple of years. It is also possible that James was the son of another James (1817) who emigrated about the same time. Perhaps he went first or perhaps was following.

Still this does not connect to any birth records. Each of the suitable James born in that era can be accounted for later in England.

However Mathew Eacott was from Trowbridge and came to Lowell MA a few years later with his family. In addition Elizabeth Louisa Eacott born 1832 - 1885 daughter of James Eacott and Betty Taylor of Trowbridge came to Lowell MA. with her husband John Huntley. They also came from Trowbridge. So they are brother and sister.

It is possible that another relative William Eacott emigrated as well. William 1815-1890 son of James and Eliza of Trowbridge died in Lowell MA.

James Eacott (1816-17) was the brother of Elizabeth Louisa Huntley. His father James was baptized in Purton Wiltshire 17 August 1794. James married Betty Taylor of Pool Keynes, a village between Purton and Cirencester, on Aug 23 1814. His wedding was likely attended by his brother Charles about the same age who emigrated to Canada in 1830. (See the Eacott Reynolds Families book)

James found work in the mills of Trowbridge where his children were born. In 1851 James was living in an end unit of a row house at 125 Union Street, Trowbridge. He was employed as a dyer in a cloth mill. His wife Sarah Alloway (1816 -1851) had just died. Daughter Sarah Anne (1834) was also working at the mill. Son James was not living at home perhaps working elsewhere before emigrating. His children are Sarah Anne 1834; James 1837; Eliza 1838; Maria 1844; Louisa 1845.

We have some evidence why James relocated to America. They were a family of cotton mill workers. Likely James had responded to the advertising and recruitment efforts of the Amoskeag Mill Company of Manchester NH. It was set up as a model manufacturing company in what amounted to a company run town. Amoskeag was to become the largest mill company in the world. In the 1850s agents went to England to buy the latest new specialty machines and hired the weavers and dyers who had the know how to run them.

"Wonderful conditions at Amoskeag in Manchester New Hampshire" read the ads published in newspapers and posters. A picture of a worker with a fistful of money accompanied the advertisement. The Amoskeag Mill was producing among other things denim cloth that was bought by Levi Straus to make jeans. All this must have appealed to James who needed a change in his life.

It is recorded that James Eacott born 1816 married Catherine McCarty, a widow, daughter of Mr. Mrs. Harrison on 22 Oct. 1855 in Lowell MA. Whether he is the same person in this story is likely, but read on.

By 1860 James Eacott and his family had established themselves in Manchester, NH

In 1860 James was 38 (1817), remarried to Mary 38 and was working in a clothing mill as a spinner. Son James 23 (1837) was a carder. Daughter Eliza 24 (1836) was a fancy weaver and Louisa 16 (1844) was a spooler. Their week was long, 73 hours work over six days a week. They went to work in the dark and came home in the dark much of the year so gas lighting on the streets was a big help. A few years later his son had by 1864 relocated to Dexter, Maine. James died in Manchester on 22 Mar 1866.

James Eacott (1837) had now established himself by 1870 in Dexter

Maine where he now works in a small town in a smaller mill. He is working in a woolen mill in Dexter as is Eliza. Their home is valued modestly but his savings are greater than most of his neighbors. Daughter Dora 14 and son James 6 (1864) are in school. Sometime in the next few years James (1837) disappears. There is no death record known. By 1880 his wife Eliza and children are living in Lisbon, Maine where the children are working in a woolen mill. In 1881 Dora fell ill and died and is buried in Lewiston, Maine.

In the subsequent years Eliza remarried a Plummer who also died. The family remains in Lisbon Maine. In 1900 son James H. (1864) 35 was working in electrics and he and his wife Emma were living with his mother. Emma Holland came from England in 1880 and they were married in 1892. Their son is James H. (1895). By 1910 James has entered the dry goods business. Over the next 20 years James 1864 has retired. The family has relocated to Hartford, CT where in the early years of the depression James H (1895) is a book keeper for a general contractor. His parents arc with them. He is a WWI veteran who was working as a stenographer for Lewiston Bleachery and Dye work when he was drafted into the army in July 1917 and then was discharged March 1919. He married Madilynn in 1922 and their son James was born in 1924. By 1940 James (1864-1941) is living as a patient in a nursing home near Lewiston, ME.

In 1942 James who was born 1895 (died 1982) is working for Bartlett Brainard and Co in Hartford CT and he registered for the draft a second time. James his son is 18. This James served 3 years in WWII 1943-46 (he lived1923- 2001).

William Eacott Family

Yet Another New England family was that of William Eacott, (1814 or 16) and his wife Eliza who brought their family out from Ireland about 1847 to Lowell MA. It was the height of the potato famine. While they may have come from Ireland, they were born in England If there is a connection to the other Eacotts in Lowell, it is not known. William was a pedlar but also did real estate. In 1860 he had a house worth $2000 and $1000 in cash. He had seven children. Henry (1839) was a mill hand. Henry's sisters were Sarah Ann (1837) Eliza (1841) Elizabeth (1843) Ellen (1846) Louisa (1849) Jemima (1851) and Emma J (1856). The last 3 were born in Lowell MA. There was also a Charles J born in Lowell in 1853 who died in 1860 of convulsions.

He was perhaps the first Eacott in Lowell. William Eacott had been there for at least 5 years when he took the oath to become a citizen on September 13 1856.

The document in part read " *I William Eacott, do solemnly swear, that I do renounce and abjure all allegiance and fidelity to every foreign prince, potentate, state and sovereignty whatsoever, particularly to Victoria , Queen of the United Kingdom of Great Britain and Ireland whose subject I have heretofore been, that I have never been of any orders of the nobility, nor born with any hereditary titles and I will support the Constitution of the United States.* "

In 1861 Henry Eacott, his only son, now a painter, decided to join the Union army. He enlisted on Aug 23 at age 22 in Co. G, 19th Infantry Regiment 28. He left Massachusetts for Washington, D.C. on August 30. Camped at Meridian Hill until September 12, 1861 he then moved to Poolesville, Md., September 12-15. He was on guard duty on the Upper Potomac until December. He took part in operations on the Potomac October 21-24 and saw action at Ball's Bluff October 21.He moved to Muddy Run December 4 and had duty there until March 12, 1862. Then he moved to Harpers Ferry and on to Charlestown and Berryville March 12-15 when he was ordered to Washington, D.C., March 24 and then to the Peninsula March 27. He took part in the siege of Yorktown April 5-May 4. Then he was involved in a rapid series of serious action West Point May 7-8 and battle of Fair Oaks, Seven Pines, May 31-June 1. Seven days before Richmond June 25-July 1. Oak Grove, near Fair Oaks, June 25., Peach Orchard and Savage Station June 29, White Oak Swamp and Glendale June 30. At the battle of Glendale union troops were retreating and were attacked. Not routed they managed to stabilize a poorly led force attacked by an enemy with equally poor strategy. Along with 297 others Henry, William's only son, died that day. He died in the field hospital of a recorded but unreadable two word cause. He may have been married by this time because an Alice Eacott, daughter of Dominick and Ann McDermott, married Charles Webster 22, a soldier at Lowell MA in 1863. We have no other known Alice Eacott in America so she may have been William's wife. Alice Eacott died 1909.

William's daughters married. Sarah Ann married a Quant in 1857- died

1905. Ellen or Helen N married John Breed 1867 and died age 28 of trauma. Eliza married John Norris 1862. Louisa married 1. A Holmes 2. Ebenezer Dustin. Elizabeth married Edwin Stackpole. In 1880 the Stackpoles lived next or with William who still had daughter Jemima 29 at home with his wife Eliza.

Also in Lowell MA in Ward 1 was Agnes Eacott 22 born 1838 in Canada. The relationship among these people is not known.

In Manchester New Hampshire James Eacott born 1817, his wife Mary born 1822 in England lived with his son James H. born 1837, daughters Eliza 1836 Louisa born 1844. They arrived in America after 1852. Dora J. Eacott age 3 (1857) was in Dexter, Maine. This may have been the family of James Eacott born in Trowbridge, Wiltshire Dec 29 1816 to James Eacott and Betty Taylor. His Grandparents would have been Richard Eacott and Sarah Clarke of Purton and thus would have been cousin of Charles Eacott who went to Canada about 1830.

James' family in England consisted of his wife Sarah Alloway who he married in 1833 when he was 17. She may have died in 1851. The children of this family were Sarah A 1834, Eliza 1838, Maria 1844, Louisa 1845 and James 1837. While not exact the similarities are very strong. There is no marriage record for Mary and James.

The Early Eacotts of the Rest of the USA

New York

At Dexter, NY (near Brownsville, Waterdown, Orleans) Richard Eacott arrived with his family. Richard was born about 1778. His wife Maria was born about 1791. Now it so happens that at Trowbridge, Wiltshire on Dec 24 1815, one Richard Eacott married Maria Litman. Perhaps they migrated to Stow, Massachusetts with their daughters Maria (1818) and Hannah (1822) between 1822 and 1830. He is in the census as having a son and daughter under 5 which is inconsistent with two daughters, he was 50-60 and his wife 30-40. It would also be likely they are related to the Eacott families in Massachusetts.

A daughter Dorcas was born 1830 in that state, likely at Stow. Richard died in New York state in Orleans (near Dexter) age 62 in 1840. His daughter Hannah never married and died 1859 age 39. His daughter Dorcas married James Bigwood, a woolen factory owner. Their daughter Addie Bigwood married Burt Alverson, a leading citizen of Dexter in 1907.

Richard's oldest daughter Maria (1818) married William Hilliker who also came from England, quite possibly Trowbridge as well. Their son William Eacott Hilliker was born July 26 1842, served in the Union army 1864/5 with the 2nd Connecticut Artillery. He joined in June 1864 just after the regiment had suffered a major defeat and loss of men. The regiment next participated in the beginning stages of the Siege of Petersburg. It was transferred to the VI Corps to participate in the 1864 Shenandoah Campaign during which it suffered even more heavy losses. In December the regiment was sent back to the Army of the Potomac. It fought in the breakthrough at Petersburg and the Appomattox Campaign. After the surrender at Appomattox Court House, the 2nd was sent to North Carolina to assist Maj. Gen. William T. Sherman in forcing the surrender of the Army of Tennessee. In May the remaining members of the 14th Connecticut Infantry were assigned to the regiment. After participating in the Grand Review, the regiment garrisoned several forts around Washington. The 2nd Connecticut Heavy Artillery was mustered out on September 5, 1865.

William returned to Dexter and married Sarah Countryman in 1877. He died at Dexter, NY 1921.

Pennsylvania

William and Catherine Engle (1783-1872) married at South Whitehall Twp, Lehigh Co. PA (Allentown) about 1811.

William was born in England and Catherine in New Jersey. They had twin sons Thomas and William Eacott who were born in 1812.

William Sr. was likely born between 1775 and 1790. There are several Williams who can not otherwise be identified in this period and so there are two William Eccotts at Warminster, two Eacotts at Swindon, one Acot at Deverill near Warminster and one Eacott at Chippenham. All other Williams can be traced as living in England. Is William Sr. one of the above?

~~~

Twin **Thomas Eacott** (1812 - 1865) married Hannah Folk (1800-1840) on July 7 1832 in Longswamp Twp Berks Co. PA (Reading Pa). Thomas lived in Lehigh PA and Hamilton, Ohio. Children were Marianne Katherine 1833- 1914 born Reading PA.,William Henry 183, Ellen Jane 1837, Maria 1841, Catherine Ann 1843 or Kate, Thomas 1846, Pierce 1853-53, Maylou 1854 and Caleb 1848.

Marianne (1833) married Benneville Miller and lived at Urbana Ohio. Edward Eacott Miller was their son. Eacott Benton Miller 1888-1954 is related somehow. He was a major in WWI in the Philippines.

During WWII Lt. Col. James Eacott Miller was A-1 or 5th in Command of the IX Bomber Squadron which served in the Mediterranean and the European Theaters of War. This group was composed of B-26 bombers.

Correspondence in the Byroade papers at the University of Arkansas contain this reference: *"Byroade papers contain a pamphlet copy of a secret memorial of General Tanaka of Japan regarding the impending World War, signed by Lt. Col. Eacott S. Miller, P.S.;"* This was inside information about Japan's plan for war with the USA.

Caleb (1848) married Hattie ? and their children were Harriet 1874, Thomas 1876-76, Bill 1880, Marie 1884, Frank 1880. In 1880 Caleb came in on one of the first trains at Rock Creek, Gunnison, Colorado one of the coldest cities in the lower 48 states and a mining town. His occupation was listed as tinner. A Caleb is living in Jacksonville FL in 1900 born 1851 whose wife is now Clara and daughter Marie (1884). He died 1917 in Jacksonville, FL

William Henry: At the time of the Civil War in America, William Henry Eacott was living in Butler County, SW Ohio. He was involved in the reserve militia and wrote in July 1861 requesting that his men wished to become a full volunteer regiment. As 2nd Lt. Of Company B, 35th Ohio Regiment he tendered his resignation on June 30, 1863. Whatever became of that is not known because at age 27 on Aug 12 1864 his service ended. He would have been in the Union forces at Chickamauga among other places. His brother in law was Capt Thomas Stone of the same Regiment.

Catherine Ann 1843 - 1913 married William R. Coppage. She was grandmother of Dr. John Eacott Manahan born 11 Dec 1919 at Charlottesville, VA died 1990. He was married to Anna Anderson the false celebrated "Anastasia". Manahan's mother was Lucile Becker 1894-1963 and his father was Dr. John Levi Manahan 1887-1966, Dean of Education, University of Virginia 1920.

~~~

The other twin, **WilliamEacott** (1812) also born at South Whitehall,PA. William settled in Ligonier Twp, Westmoreland Co. PA (east of Pittsburg) before 1840. In 1840 census he had 1 boy and girl under 5, 1 male age 15-20, 2 females 20-30, and 1 50 - 60, likely his mother. He died A couple of years after migrating from Pennsylvania. He settled at Platte, MO now a suburb of Kansas City. He died at Leavenworth, KS in 1846 leaving a family and his wife **Jane Harr** who was from Janesville, Lancaster PA (1813 -1885).

William's children were Kate or Catherine Elizabeth born (1837 - 1900) at South Whitehall, Thomas Armstrong (1838) , John Henry born 1840, Cecilia born 1842. Mary Caroline was born Platte, MO in 1845 not long before her father died. She married Thomas Henry Hutchison 1843-1916 and she died 1932 and is buried at Leeds, MO.

In 1850 William's widow **Jane** was maintaining a house full of five children ranging from 4 to 13 years of age. She had a live in man from Belgium and a relative, possibly a sister in law or her mother in law, Catherine Eacott born 1803 (fake age ?) living nearby in Weston, MO where she was a housekeeper for a farmer and his family. Later Catherine Engle Eacott came from Pennsylvania to live at Weston where she died in 1872 age 89. Jane was also being courted by Hardin Steele a prominent local person.

Jane married Hardin Steele in 1850 and had other children. Hardin thus became stepfather and father-in-law to Catherine (1837).

Catherine or Kate born 1837 and Asa Steel(e), son of Hardin by a first marriage, were married by 1860 and had 3 children William, Julie, and Emma. Also living with them was John Henry (now 19)and his sister Mary(now 13). John Henry went to Kansas City and worked as a harness and saddle maker. When the civil war broke out, the Steele family were quick to align with the confederate cause.

John Henry Eacott married Thankful R. Hanna (born1844) in 1871 at Jackson, MO, a town in the SE of the state. She was one of 9 children of

A.L. Hanna. Thankful died and by 1900 John Henry was working as commandant of the Confederate Home for old Soldiers near Dover MO, a village east of Kansas City. The home is now a state park. Henry was a confederate veteran himself having served in the 12TH Regiment of Missouri Cavalry out of Jackson county. The action of this group is not well documented although it operated in Missouri and Arkansas against federal troops in skirmishes. It must be noted that John Henry and Thomas' first cousin William of Ohio was a Union officer.

Thomas Armstrong Eacott, William's other son, (1838) bore a family name that may have no blood connection because it was common at the time to give appealing second names that appear like family names.

In 1862 Thomas decided to join the confederate cause perhaps because his Steele relatives were involved. He joined the 2nd Missouri Confederate cavalry unit in what was called "New Company C". This unit began as the 4th Missouri Cavalry Battalion and was increased in strength to a full regiment by August 1862. They were known as the "Butternut Boys" . Its first battle was at Iuka, Mississippi on September 19, 1862 as part of Armstrong's Cavalry Army of West Tennessee and also with McCulloch's Cavalry under Lee and Forrest. During his time in "New Co. C" he was nearly always on the move in Tennessee and Mississippi with his longest posting in the defense of Vicksburg. A major battle at Selma, Alabama April 2nd 1865 resulted in 2700 Confederate casualties with under 400 Union. Its last operation was against Wilson's Federal Cavalry in Alabama where it was surrendered by Gen. Richard Taylor on May 4, 1865 (Citronelle, Alabama). As the war was soon over, he did not spend much time as a prisoner of war. During his maneuvers in Mississippi he may have met and got acquainted with his future wife, Mary Beth Sandlin born 1844.

For a time they moved about the country first in Tennessee where Nina was born 1868 and then to Mississippi where Cora Blanche was born in 1871. Finally they settled at Brownwood, Texas where Claude 1876, and Thomas Kate Jan 11 1879 were born. Now there is a record that one Thomas A Eacott died October 5 1865. That could not be so because he survived a gun battle in 1876 where a William Gilleylen had a shot gun and was seeking to take Eacott's life. He tracked Eacott down and shot at him three times on the night of January 20th 1876. In return Thomas Eacott shot and killed Gilleylen after which he went to the sheriff to give himself up.

Thomas died 13 Mar 1880 and then in 1885 his wife died leaving the children as orphans.

From then until 1897 there were a series of court appearances where the younger two girls were passed around under different guardianships to safeguard them and their modest estate claim.

Cora, known more as Blanche was of age, over 14, and was able to choose her own guardian but sister Thomas Kate was only 8 in 1893 when there was a found need for guardianship with the Cook family until she was 14. She then chose to live with her married sister now Blanch Madison. Nina the oldest girl married first J.M. Cook 1885 then a May and had a son Eacott May who was born 1887 and died 1940. Nina lived mostly at Bell Texas. She died age 92 (1960) while in Israel. Claude 1876 died Oct 1957 while living at Goldthwaite TX . Thomas Kate married Shelly Arthur Whithead and had two sons. They were recorded in Oklahoma in 1900. Thomas Kate died August 1969 in Burnet Co. TX.

Illinois

Albert William Eacott (1862-1935) was the son of **James R. Eacott** (1837) and Elizabeth (1835) born in Maisey Hampton, Gloucestershire. He was the second oldest of nine children of a bricklayer. His father in 1901 lived at Poulton and died in Swindon in 1918.

James' children were Edmund James, James, Richard, George, Mary Jane, Robert, Priscilla and Tom.   Like his father he was a bricklayer. He married in 1887 and his first wife Nellie died. Albert emigrated to Chicago, IL in the 1890's. He married Ethel Kebby in 1912 who was 22 years younger. Nellie was mother of George Lamot Eacott (1892-1970), Victor Eacott (1898-1972), Albert Eacott(1907). Then Ethel became mother of Sidney Leonard Eacott(1914-1951) and Reginald Eacott (1916-1916). The family lived for a long time at 2036 Warren Avenue in a mixed race neighborhood where they took in boarders to supplement their income.

George L. began work as a bricklayer in Chicago. He married Alice June in 1914 and had sons Fred Lamont Eacott (1915-2000) and George Albert Victor Eacott (1917-1994) and a daughter Dorothy Eacott 1928. In 1930 he was doing well as a car dealer but by 1940 was listed as a mostly unemployed bricklayer again and no longer owned his own home.   George

Albert married Margaret Lange and lived in Wichita TX. To them Richard George was born 1943. They lived in Galesburg Ill.

Victor married Rachel and lived in Chicago until at least 1940 and also was a bricklayer early in life. He died in Birmingham Alabama 1972. Another son Albert was also a bricklayer. **Sidney** married Margaret McSweeny 1938.

In addition there was a **William E. Eacott** born 1888 in England who immigrated in 1892 and moved to Douglas, Nebraska. In 1910 he was a painter for a theatrical company in Omaha and was married to Mary. Children Mary 1918 and James 1919. By 1930 his wife and daughter had died and he was caring for his son James D. who was born in 1919.

In the 1920 census of the USA there were only 4 Eacott family surname groups in the USA.

A reminder, the contents of this book were focused on Eacott families up until the mid to late 1800's. However some information extends into the 20th century if it was thought helpful to complete a story.

The Eacotts of Canada

The Bernardo Home Children

Between 1869 and the late 1930s, over 100,000 juvenile migrants were sent to Canada from the British Isles during the child emigration movement. Motivated by social and economic forces, churches and philanthropic organizations sent orphaned, abandoned and pauper children to Canada. Many believed that these children would have a better chance for a healthy, moral life in rural Canada where families welcomed them as a source of cheap farm labor and domestic help.

After arriving by ship, the children were sent to distributing and receiving homes, such as Fairknowe in Brockville and then sent on to farmers in the area. Although many of the children were poorly treated and abused, others experienced a better life here than if they had remained in the urban slums of England. Many served with the Canadian and British Forces during both World Wars.

Thomas John Barnardo (1845 - 1905) was an Irish philanthropist and founder and director of homes for poor children usually known as Dr. Bernardo's Homes.

The lot of widowed mothers with children or whose husbands abandoned them and even parents who had more children than they could care for simply abandoned or gave them up for adoption.

These were people who had known real poverty. Elizabeth Eacott age 32 with Robert 7, Elizabeth 3 and infant Susan Jane removed themselves from the Medway Kent Chatham Workhouse where they had been housed until June 14 1888. We do not know the circumstances as to why they were there or where they went. There were other examples of Eacott families in similar circumstances.

During the latter part of the 1800's and well into the 1900's schemes were used to send orphans and other children from Britain to Canada and Australia. These were called Home Children. One such scheme was carried out by Dr. Bernardo. This is the story of two Bernardo boys who were Eacott and sent over to Canada.

Alice Cunningham married **Thomas Eacott** who was a boiler maker in a railroad engine factory in Swindon Wiltshire.

Alice Emily Cunningham was born about 1861 to Mary and George William Cunningham. He was a painter and paper hanger in Westminster London. Alice had an older brother George and 2 younger sisters Harriet and Mary. She met Thomas George Eacott who was a boiler maker born to William and Harriet Eacott in 1853 in Swindon. His father was also a boiler maker, a skilled trade. Thomas had brothers James and Thomas.

Alice and Thomas were married 13 September 1885 at St. Mary Lambeth, London. Frederick William was born 1886, Reginald Charles 1889, Cecil and his twin Jessie 1895 and William 1900. There were others. In 1891 their father Thomas was convicted of burglary and sentenced to one year in prison at Devizes. His crime was he stole a ham and some cloth to wrap it in.

Part way through his sentence the officials using the Criminal Lunatics Act of 1884 had him sent to the Devizes Roadway Lunatic Asylum. So there was something quite mentally wrong with him. He was still or back there in 1901 although he must have had some association with his wife as both Cecil and William were born during his incarceration or when on release. In 1891 we do know that Alice and her newborn Violet Eacott were in Marylebone, London but Frederick and Reginald were living in Battersea with their uncle William Ghagan, his wife Mary and their 19 and 7 year old daughters. Frederick was 5 and Reginald 2. In 1893 sister Eva was born.

As Frederick and Reginald grew they came to learn their uncle did not want them nor did their mother. The solution for these adults was to send the boys to Dr. Bernardo's home where they spent time until passage to Canada could be arranged.

In 1900 **Reginald Eacott**, age 11, all dressed in his new suit of clothes was sent off to Liverpool with 100 other boys to be shipped to Canada. A band played as they were marched aboard the 'Tunisia" in Liverpool. Each group of children had an escort party to handle arrangements. The crossing took several days, most of it in rough water. He landed at Quebec and it was arranged for him to go to Rutherford, Ontario to work on the farm of Herbert M. Shaw. Shaw was paid a fee to maintain the boy who was an indentured servant until he became of age. The sending agencies felt they were giving these children a better life by sending them away. Many children were seen as the scum of the earth and abused and treated as virtual slaves. Yet others were taken in as part of the family. They were expected to go to school but many did not. In this case Rutherford was very near where his brother had gone a few years before. What is not clear is what became of Reginald Charles because he was not with the Shaw family in either 1901 or 1911.

His passage and clothing were supplied by the organization that helped him leave England. He was born 1889 and arrived alone age 11 in early 1900 after a life of having been sent here and there. We don't know how long he stayed with Shaw as there is no record. The Shaw's were a young couple in their 30's. Reginald's English family lost contact with him. Once placed in the hands of these child care organizations a parent had to pay up for the expenses incurred if they wanted them back so basically they were abandoned forever.

Frederick William George Eacott his older brother also went to Canada at the age of 8. Born in 1886 he sailed on the S.S. "Laurentian" destined for Toronto in 1894. He was placed with William and Flora Jordan an older farm couple living in Dawn Twp. near Bothwell, Ontario. Jordan had been born in England in 1836. The Jordan's were likely appreciative, well meaning Baptists. Young Eacott was using his middle name William. Whether he knew of the other Eacotts in the Bothwell area is not known. We loose track of him but it is recorded that a Frederick William Eacott took out homestead papers in 1911 in Saskatchewan. A Frederick William was living in Omaha Nebraska in 1930 unemployed. He was a widower with an 11 year old son James.

Their brother **William Henry Eacott** was born Jan 27 1900 in England about the time Reginald was sent to Canada. William said he never knew he had older brothers.

After Thomas died in the early 1900's Alice married Frederick Watts. The wedding was 29 July 1912 but in the census of 1911 they had been living as husband and wife at # 24 Wayford St. Battersea for 8 years. Watts was a house painter. Cecil now 16 was working as a milk boy and William 11 was in school. There is no evidence of Violet in 1901 although in 1903 she and Cecil were attending Mantua school in 1903 and living with their mother at 21 Yelverton Rd. In 1911 she was living on her own working as a domestic and later that year married Henry Arthur White in London. In 1915 Cecil joined the Gloucester Regiment # 19662 and served in France until the end of the war leaving as a lance corporal. He was wounded in the chest. At age 19 he was 5 foot 2.5 inches tall. He died 1968.

I have not been able to follow Reginald Charles in Canada or elsewhere.

I was provided with some family lore on this story but have not been able to verify it.

What makes this story particularly poignant are the circumstances of Alice Cunningham, the children's mother. Her grandfather was alleged to have been First Lord of the Admiralty in 1800's (not a Cunningham) and her parents were well to do (painter /paper hanger/builder). Her mother was an educated woman who was fluent in French. Thomas her husband was a boiler maker's journeyman and was comfortable as he owned two rows of Terrace Houses in Swindon. When Alice married Eacott, she was disowned for her actions and as he proved a poor father (he was locked away for lunacy) so she was reduced to being a charwoman (Census 1910) while raising 7 children. (including Violet 1891-1978, Jessie Leslie 1895-1988, Eva Angela 1893 - 1981) The eldest had to fend for themselves after the divorce. (no evidence for divorce). Such was the nature of the Victorian mind. The children were simply cast aside.

Other Bernardo children were **Charles Eacott** born 1890 who sailed on the S.S. Cambroman in 1900 age 10. He was sent to Russell, Manitoba. **Frances Eacott** a girl of 9 born 1903 sailed on the S.S. Virginian in 1912. **William Eacott** born1905 age 7 also sailed on the Virginian in 1912 perhaps with his sister. No idea if they stayed together or where they went. **Fred Eycott** age 15 born 1878 sailed 1893 on the S.S. Sardinian to Montreal. Each of these children were considered a burden to the mother country and presumably to their parents. What thoughts must have been in the minds of these kids who by their lot in life had to be brave. How did the mothers of these children feel? One must question the morality of removing children from a parent and transporting them by the thousands abroad.

The Line of Challis Eacott

Challis was covered earlier under the welsh Eacott line.

The Simeon Eakett Family

A Simeon Eakett was likely born Simeon Eacott Feb 4 1827 at Purton, Wiltshire to William and Harriet Eacott. Some of their other children were William 1832, Sarah 1829. A Simeon Acot age 14 arrived at New York from London April 15 1840 on the "Catharine" accompanied by several family members William age 10, Harriet 19, Sarah 8 and Elisa 38. They were listed as bound for Canada likely to meet their father. It is clear from other records his mother was Harriet. She was not aboard this ship. Elisa could be the mother here of a different Simeon but Simeon is not a common name.

They arrived in the district of Brock where in 1842 Elisa Acot arranged to be married in Hamilton.

So is Simeon Eakett, also Eacott and Acott. There is no other birth of a Simeon in England by any similar name within 10 years and the family members on the ship match up fairly well.

In 1851 Simeon Eaket 25 with his mother 62 and sister 23 are living in Brock District where he has taken up a farm in Puslinch Twp. This is the same Township where Samuel Eakett came to settle. In a few years he acquired a modest 50 acres (usual farm was 100) of Canada Land Company land in the Huron tract and settled in Morris Twp near Brussels Ontario. He married Amelia Dunn and reported his fathers name as Robert. (May have been William Robert or similar).

In 1861 he is where he will remain for the rest of his life in Morris Twp. He built a log house there in 1852. Amelia was 32 and their children were William 9, Mary 6, and John 4. Simeon reported his age as 35. Ten years later he reports his age as 40, changed his origin to Scottish, and became a Presbyterian from Church of England. There are now two more children Charles 9 and George7. He was now married to Mary age 40. Simeon appears to have changed his identity while remaining in the same spot. How much can one trust the census material?

Twenty years later 1891 he is widowed, age 63, once again English and now a member of the Brethren Church. His son Alex 20 and daughter Annie 18 are with him. He died later that year in Dec. 1891. As he likely came from Purton, he may have had much in common with Charles Eacott who arrived in Canada in 1830 and also with the Samuel Eakett family.

Other Ontario Families

Robert Eakett is also born at Arkell in August 1861 to John Eakett and Ann Hewer. They move to Algoma district in the 1880's and had a number of children.

Also at Arkell were **William and Elizabeth Starkey Eakett** who are in the Arkell cemetery. Their daughters Margaret Jane 1869 and Fanny 1871 were born there. This may have been the Willliam who arrived with Simeon.

Robert Eacrett settled in Hay Twp in Huron County in 1853. He came from Ireland. He was a teacher in Zurich ON in 1870's and Christopher and R. Eacrett had 50 acre farms at Rodgersville. Robert was 61 in 1861 and married to Margaret 51. Their daughters in 1861 were 20, 16, 12 all born in Ontario. So Robert arrived by 1840. Christopher may have been his son. Robert Eacott a farmer in 1921 lived in Hay Twp on north half lot 13 con 2. He was born in Ontario age 60 and married to Margaret age 51. Hid father was Irish and his mother was Scots. Daughters were Eclice 20, Sybil 16, Aldythe 12.

Isaac Eacott 1845 -1911 came to Canada with his 4 sons, Alfred, Samuel, George and settled in Hamilton. The 4th son John went to Vancouver. Descendants of this family live in various parts of Ontario.

Another **Isaac Eacott** born April 12, 1812 possibly son of William Eacutt and Hannah of Chaddleworth Berks. settled in Osnabruck ON before 1850. His wife was Sophia and his sons were Edward Eacutt 1848 and John s. Eacutt 1856. He also had 5 daughters. Whose sons were Floyd Eacutt 1892 and Leon Eacutt 1894?

The Line of Samuel Eakett

No Samuel Eakett birth can be found to match his reported birth of December 1817. However Samuel Eacott was born to Thomas in Warminster, 19 Oct 1818. Another Samuel Eacott was born to William of Purton in January 1815. Finally there was a Samuel Richard Eacott who was born in 1813 at Shoreditch in London.

Samuel Eakett married Francis (Fanny) Dory (1822-1899) in 1855 in Ontario Canada. They began their marriage at Puslinch Twp. under the name of Eacott. Their children William 1843, Harriet 1845 and Joseph 1847 were baptized in the Wesleyan Methodist Church under the Eacott name. They lived in the vicinity of Arkell (Guelph) as did other Eaketts.

Later they move to Egremont Twp. Grey County where he died in 1872. In 1871 census his children were Samuel 13 (1858-89), Fanny 10 (1860-1947) m. Francis Bye (1861-1931), they moved to Sault St. Marie ON and some of their family later crossed to Michigan, Sault St. Marie, Harriet

(1849-1890) married a Bye before 1863, and moved to Jackson, Bremer, Iowa, William 9 (born 1856- date source unknown, census says 1862) was lost to history.

Samuel's son Samuel Eacket 1858-89 was married in 1880 in Wellington Co. ON. George Edgar Eakett 8 in census, 1862 -1944 was born Cedarvale, Grey, county and married at Mount Forest in 1884 and lived in Grey co ON. This family has a genetic match to the family of Charles Eacott 1794 below. Mary age 6 at the census is not in other family records.

Samuel's untimely end at age 56 left his family in a mess. Egremont at that time was sparsely settled and occupied farms were far apart so his wife and children had no close neighbors on their road to help them.

William and Elizabeth Eakett lived in Puslinch Twp. where Margaret Jane was born 1869 and Fanny was born 1871. Was he Simeon's son? Both Samuel and William are listed as early Wesleyan Methodists for Puslinch.

The line of Charles Eacott

We now come to the family line of which I am a direct descendent. There is extensive coverage of this line in the book "Eacott Reynolds Families" printed by Lulu.com

Charles was born in Wiltshire sometime between 1790 and 1797 to Richard Eacott of Purton. He became a Talbot settler in 1832 in Euphemia Township Ontario. He married Margaret McCabe from Ireland in 1836. Here he raised his sons John 1837-77, Henry 1840-1929, and daughters Jane 1843 - 1917 and Sarah 1849 - 1903. All were farmers. Henry had oil wells on his farm and lived in Bothwell after he retired. John died at an early age leaving his wife Maria Willis and children Charles, Henry and Margaret. She remarried. Henry married Elizabeth McCauley who died on their 55th wedding anniversary. They had several children.

Revery

Why work on a project for decades? Why assemble the parts of a giant puzzle? When I began this project in 1980 there was no known evidence for DNA variation and the evolution of gene families. One's surname and family records defined who we were. Today a surname is a title of a tiny fragment of a Y chromosome. A fragment that in scarcely a dozen generations is so diluted that one is lucky to share a single centimorgan with that surname. In fact to the date of this writing I have not one single example of an Eacott/Eycott genetic match but I have hundreds upon hundreds of surnames linked to my genes. They come from all over Europe and beyond.

From this I am acutely aware that I am related to everyone I meet. My cousins all. Yet the kinships I have sought out in this work convey a certain mystic attachment. Sometimes in the late of evening while pouring over the little bits of discovery that parts the mists of time, I feel the presence of someone who seems to want mc to explore their story. I visualize persons and scenes and places long since gone. It is almost like some of my genes are recognizing themselves having descended across time and space. So I continued to root around the internet or old books to glean a new element of a life long since lived. Then I welcomed them to the pages of this book so we may know them.

I have tried to be scientifically and historically accurate and in so doing enriched my understanding of the past. The Eacotts were not kings and queens. They didn't shape a lot of history. But in exploring them over centuries I have a new understanding of various moments in history with an Eacott connection. A connection to an odd name that has survived among a few people to this day.

Why did I write it? Because I wanted to and because it explains who I am. Hopefully, the reader will have found it satisfying to learn of the Eacott surname family because genetically you are probably related in some way!

If genealogy interests you, there is a master GED file of thousands of names and relationships gathered by me under the Eacott file at Ancestry and on Family Tree Maker. It is possible to construct a detailed ancestry similar to the one for Berkeley in the appendix for other Eacott family lines. There are many dead ends. There are a lot more stories to be uncovered. If you are looking for your Eacott related ancestor they may be in the master file that stops about 1900 for most families. It is assumed that after 1900 there is so much data available that almost anyone can trace back to then.

Most people did not make it into this book because I did not know their story. If I had it would be here. However the reader may wish to add pages of their own family discoveries!

I would welcome submissions of new material, suggestions and corrections for revisions for future editions. This is a work in progress!

APPENDICIES

You will find much repeated, yet elaborated on material in this next section. There are several unique genealogical resources to help better understand why some things in the book are the way they are.

Appendix A
The Eacott Name

Like other names the Eacott name evolved over hundreds of years. The earliest record of the name is in the form of EYCOT. Eycot was an ancient manor along the river Churn in the county of Gloucester, England. It was recorded in the great census ordered by William the Conqueror in 1086 AD. The name was then briefly recorded as Aicote. There were no persons of that name recorded at that time. In a manuscript of Worcester (Hemming's Cartulary) from the late 11th century the name of the manor is recorded as EUGKOTE. The name was given to an area granted in a Saxon charter from the late 800's early 900's.

Before the 12th century it was not common for people to use surnames. When in the 12th C. last names became popular because of French influence, they were names which indicated a place, an occupation, a physical description or a relationship. Just under half of all English surnames are named for a place. This seems to be the case for the Eacott name.

At the time of the Domesday record the area where the Eacotts lived had been influenced for over 400 years by Saxons who became to be known as Anglo-Saxons. The Anglo-Saxon language became the basis for Old English. This language had connections to Denmark and adjacent Germany as well as to the Norse languages.

If the name is Old English, which seems likely, the meaning can be made reasonably clear. "Cott or Cote" means a small hut or habitation or a shelter for sheep or birds as in dovecote. The Indo European root is *"ku"* from which the words coop, cubby are also derived. In the Cotswold area a cot, specifically, was a stone sheep shelter.

In feudal times the squire of a knight would be provided a cot and some land which he held by right of cottage or tenement.

"EY" can mean several things.
   It can mean " ever " as in "for aye"
   It can mean " egg " as in birds egg
   It can refer to water in several ways; running water, an island, or marshland. The most common Saxon use was for an Island.

Thus the following meanings are possible:
   " One who always lives in a small house"
   " One who lives at the egg house or hen house"
   " One who lives in a house by the stream, or by or on an island or marshland"

It seems very probable that the last meaning is the most likely because the manor house at Eycot was located on the west bank of the Churn R. and there are old reports of there having been an island and a marshy area nearby.

However, the word EYOT if related refers to the raising of nestling falcons placing the name in association with that occupation. The actual word Eacott is a later invention.

Eldon Smith in " New Dictionary of American Family Names" 1973 says that Eacott Means " Dweller in a cottage by the river". Old records show EA and EY interchangeable in the name. This was possible in Old English because EA, EY, and EG all refer to water in some manner and the use does not change the meaning.

Barber in " British Family Names", 1903, says Eacott is derived from the Anglo-Saxon - Echeard; Danish - Ecert or Eigaard; German - Eckardt; Flemish - Eekhout; or from one of several Norse names beginning "EY"

Another possible origin comes from the name of a Frenchman who was awarded the lordship of Duntisbourne Abbot and who leased from Hugh Donkey the manor of Bagendon. His name was Gilbert de Eskecote. Later there were persons from that area with the name Estcourt. It is not known if Gilbert ever lived in the area of Bagendon. However the name is similar enough to offer some confusion especially if some of his locally born offspring took a version of his name and modified it. Yet it must be remembered that Eycote already existed as a place nearby and had been since the 900's. Eycot was also known or sounded as Eugkote about 1086 so precision cannot be exact.

The name prior to 1400 in the few references known noted an individual as being so and so "de Eycote" or " of Eycote". From the 1500's a few EA names existed derived from EY, EC and EK versions. The EA form was not popular and in Bagendon and Cirencester did not ever exist. Ea versions occurred in North Cerney, Rendcomb and areas adjacent to the north.

Up until 1750 the vast majority(over 80%) of recorded names were Eycott. From 1750 there is a mixed transition with increasing use of Ecott and Eacott. At that time the Eacott version was becoming the most common one in Wiltshire. After 1800 the Ey version is scarce everywhere and virtually vanishes by 1830 with Eacott being the more common version.

Local Variants
The EA version, found also as ECott in the Cromhall-Alveston area, was common also in Purton-Swindon and Warminster areas of Wiltshire. By the time of the 18th century census a pattern existed in a belt from London to Bristol with versions of the name concentrated mostly in specific locals. Eacott was the most widely dispersed yet still mostly in Avon, Wiltshire, Berkshire and London. Eakets were in Gloucester, Ecott in Bedfordshire and Gloucester, Ayott in London and Bedford, Eycott in London, Berkshire and Yorkshire. Eckett was only used in London, Reading, Basing towns and Acott in London, Kent, Gloucester and Oxford. Those who used Acott in London and Kent were likely Hugenot Protestants from France and not descended from Eycott. The Eccott variant spelling was only in London and Basingstoke. These variations on the name account for nearly all people with an Eacott variation.

Other Variants
Up to 1800 language was quite flexible. As a result most names were recorded quite as they were said in the local dialect. Records show the same family with members whose names were spelled variously. The files of the Church of Latter Day Saints relate Eacott to Eycott, Aycott, Acott, Eckott, Eckett, Ecott. Eakets, Eccott. Sometimes with only one "t" in a variation. A few others Eacoote and the very early Eycote are no longer found. Haycott, Hickett, Icott, Eyecott are in the LDS files as a variant. However in the 1881

census of the UK there were only 5 male Hicketts of 23 in Worcester, York and Middlesex. There were 2 Eyecott female servants in Middlesex, 2 male Haycotts in Kent and Sussex. No Eccot and no Icott were found. Whether these are variants is not proven. Some names that might look like a variant have no evidence that they are. Estcourt, Eastcott, Escott, Earthcott, Elyot, Amscott are some of those names with no proven link to an Eycott based name. Some names occur outside Britain, in Europe, Americas, Australasia that are similar but not linked. Eekhout, Ekert, Eacherd, Ekardt, Ecert are examples of these names which might sound similar but are not the same family except where there has been, if any, an isolated spelling error.

Record Transitions
There are ample records showing the interchangeability of Eycott, Eacott, Ecott and so forth in a number of families.

Church records seldom go back before 1538 when it was ordered that parish records of births, baptisms, marriages and deaths be kept. Many of the previous records were destroyed with Henry VIII's dissolution of the monasteries at the same time. From that time there were parish records and a local bishops record. They were sometimes at variance. These rather early references respecting North Cerney from the parish register exemplify the point.

Dec. 4 1661 Elizabeth wife of Richard Eacott Sr. buried ... only Richard Ecott appears in other records.
Feb 22 1664 Richard sone of Richard Eacott Sr. Baptized
Dec 24 1676 Jonathan son of Joseph Eacott baptized
        1682 Joseph Eycot is buried and for some years there are no more Eacotts only Ecotts and Eycotts

The bishops register shows this entry:
Dec 24 1676 Jonathon son of Joseph Ecot baptized
So depending on who made the entry on the register Joseph was an Eacott, an Eycott and an Ecott.

How to say the name!

The pronunciation of the name had importance in the spelling. An Old English grammar book says "EA" is a diphthong vowel. That is a vowel where each of the two letters is said. Just how one does that is very awkward. The letter E was pronounced as in "NET" while the A got less emphasis. To find the relationship with EY use the Y sound from "Yes or young" and the EA and EY are difficult to distinguish. Egg also comes from the EY sound. Thus the first sound in the name in ancient times was more like "EHy" or"EHa" with the last letter being made soft. The original pronunciation may have been more like "EHcott" or "AYHcott.

The 11th century word EUGKOTE might be a close sound variation. In more recent memory the name in Alveston (near Bristol) was said as AYE cott, and is recalled by the local place name in North Cerney as "Ache-it" (as in tooth ache) remembrance in the first settlement area in Ontario was also "Ache-it" Most current users seem to prefer EE-cott or EH-cott.

In the Saxon times the alphabet used was the runic alphabet with 29 letters. The 28th letter was EA with an accent over the E. It was written as a W with a line down from the mid centre point, resembling a Neptune's spear.

The EY version of the name existed continually until the mid 1700's in the Churn valley and in scattered places but since then seems to a have died out nearly everywhere. Other versions of the name are rare before 1700.

The "cott" Suffix

Another element that may have some significance about the name is the observation of the suffix "COTT". An examination of this in British place names shows that the "COTT" ending existed in a very specific band extending in an arc south and east of the Bristol Channel from north Devon, Somerset, Gloucester to Oxford, inland from the sea. From Bude in the west, north of Exeter and along the A30 are such places as Eastcott, Natcott, Elmscott, Brazacott, Patchacott, Southcott, Tetcott, Luffincott, Kellacott, Upcott, Middlecott, Northcott, Bennacott, Accott, Hiscott, Uppincott, Beccott, Knightacott, Golsoncott. Outside that belt there are very few Cott or Cote names of communities except in Somerset.

In Somerset, although more scattered, are: Cattacott, Draycott, Carlingcott, Nightcott, Woolcott, Ashcott. Then from Bristol into Gloucestershire: Earthcott, Eycott, Horcott, Buscot, Calcot, Murcot, Earlingscott ending in a line from Warwick to Oxford. In this north area

"COTE" endings are also more common. The area is known as the Cotswold includes many of the "Cott" places.

What, if any meaning can be taken from this observation remains to be seen. It may or may not conform to an ancient area that gave reason to apply this suffix in this area. This could be a clue as to the linguistic origin of the name.

The pre Roman language in the entire area was Brythonic, a Celtic based language related to Welsh and Cornish. There appears, so far, to be no indication that Eycote had linguistic connections with this language.

Appendix B
More on Genetics

Scientific research throughout the world has shown that all our paternal lines are connected somewhere in the past and that these connections can be traced by reading the yDNA. As with maternal genealogies defined by mtDNA, men tend to cluster into a small number of groups, 18 in total, which can be defined by the genetic fingerprints of their yDNA. In native Europeans, for example, there are 5 such groups. Among Native Americans there are 4 and among Japanese people there are 5 and so on. The men within each of these groups are all ultimately descended from just one man, their clan father. Obviously, these ancestral clan fathers were not the only men around at the time but they were the only ones to have direct male descendants living today. The other men around, or their descendants, had either no children at all or only daughters. These clan fathers also had male ancestral lines and these ultimately converge on the common paternal ancestor of every man alive today. This man, know as "Y-Chromosome Adam", lived in Africa 60,000 – 80,000 years ago.

How far back can the Eacott DNA be traced in England? An interesting question. From the few samples of Eacott Y chromosome DNA it appears that all male Eacott belong to the genetic marker group R1b (hg1) This means they belong to the major western European genetic group of which about 70% of males in Southern England belong . The haplotype is also known as the Western Atlantic Modal haplotype. These were Paleolithic ice age hunters, Cro-magnon man who 35 000 years ago moved from Southern France (cave painters) into Spain and then to England and western Europe and northward before the last ice age. They were known as the Aurignacian culture. Using the archaeological record it can be seen that the Aurignacians left the Asian homeland in the Gulf area of Pakistan, moved along the Zagros Mountains region and entered Anatolia about 47,000 years ago. They crossed the then dry Straits of Bosphorus and migrated through present-day Bulgaria up the Danube River to present-day Hungary and Austria and into Germany. Another branch had split from their Austrian relatives and migrated to Italy from the west via the Riviera across the Pyrenees Mountains to El Castillo in Northern Spain by approximately 37,000 years ago. From there they moved into Southern England.

Atlantic Modal Haplotype gene code (AMH) DYS388, DYS390, DYS391, DYS392, DYS393 = 12 ,24, 11, 13, 13. That is DYS388 marker is 12 etc. About 3 dozen markers and their code numbers are used in creating matches.

This is a haplogroup chain for the Eacott name

The Eacott ancestors migrated out of Africa and ......
F -M89 - 76000 to 60000 years ago crossed Red sea into Arabia.
K-M9 - 50000 years ago moved to steppes of Iran and central Asia
RM207 - 35000 years ago the ice age and they hunted big mammals
RM343 - 27000 years ago remaincd around Iran until end of ice age
              11500 years ago moved between Black and Caspian sea
RM269 - 10000 in Ukraine and now farming and herding, Bronze age
RU152 - 8000, this is a sub group of RM269 and this group is related to Nial of the Nine hostages a 4th century king of Tara, Ireland. 320 generations ago. Following is the haplotype identity trail as it is currently thought to exist. It shows each genetic change and group narrowing. Additional Y chromosome testing may add more sub types after RZ36.

```
R P297 - RM 478
      RM 269  - RPF 7558
              - RL23
                    - R51
                        - RP311- RM405
                                  - RP312 - RDF19
                                          - RDF27
                                          - RDF99
                                          - RL21
                                          - RL238
                                          - RU152 -RL2
                                                   -RPF6601
```

So far, all Eacott tested males carry this much and more of this pattern. An alternate pattern would shown Germanic or Viking roots.

Thus the genetic roots of the Eacott, like most in southern England, are based on settlers from the ice age mixed with other similar males who arrived from France bearing the same genes.

Yet when one traces their ancestry backwards an individuals DNA will share under 1% with an ancestor going back only 6 grandparents. You will share that small % with 128 great grandparents.

Appendix C
Notes on the Domesday Records
http://www.domesdaybook.co.uk/contents.html

The Domesday census ordered by William the Conqueror in 1086 AD was taken to determine what he had gained in his victory and to determine what taxes could be levied. The information that follows was taken from "Domesday Book # 15, Gloucestershire" edited by John Morris and published by Phillimore Publishing, Chichester England in 1982. The original text was reorganized and printed in 1783 by Abraham Farley. Translations are from his Latin work.

In the census there were 78 main land holders, including the king, in Gloucestershire. Of this group 24 were churches, abbeys, and bishops. The accounts which follow are intended to give some idea of what the Churn valley was like at the time of the Norman invasion.

A hide was an area of land about 120 acres. A plough was a team of oxen and a plough. The hide was a unit of land for taxation purposes and the carucate a unit for measurement and cultivation. "Value then" meant at the time of the conquest twenty years before. A free man did not owe allegiance to any lord. A reference to a person would mean adult male.

The Kings Lands (1)
In Cirencester, five hides - 31 villagers with 10 ploughs, 13 slaves, 10 small holders, 2 free men,.

Also in Cirencester was Hullasey 3 ½ hides, 4 villagers, four small holders.

In Brightwells Barrow Hundred Brictric held Fairford. 21 hides, 56 villagers, 9 small holders.

In Rapsgate Hundred, Wulfward held Chedworth. 15 hides, 16 villagers, 3 small holders. The sheriff added 8 villagers and 3 small holders.

Lands of Thomas, Archbishop of York (2)
In Rapsgate Hundred, St. Oswalds held a manor of 4 hides in (North) Cerney before 1066. St. Oswalds still holds it and has two ploughs in lordship; 6 villagers and 2 small holders with 5 ploughs.1 slave; a mill at 7s; meadow, 2 acres.Value then 100s; now 4 pounds.

Lands of the Church of Worcester (3)
The church held (Great) Colesbourne itself, and Swein from it.
He could not withdraw. (change lordships) 8 hides which pay tax.
Walter son of Roger (Roger of Pitres, sheriff of Gloucester)

The church held Eycot itself, and Alric from it. It lies in Bibury.
(lands) 1 hide. In lordship 2 ploughs;
2 villagers and four small holders with 2 ploughs.
2 slaves: meadow, 8 acres; a mill at 64d.
The value was 20s; now 30s.
Ordric holds it from the bishop.

-Latin Original-
Ipfa aeccla ten Aicote .7 Ailric de ea. In Begeberie jacet.
Ibi una hida. In dnio funt. II. car. 7 II. uitti 7 IIII. bord cu
II. car. Ibi.II. ferui 7 VIII. ac pti. 7 molin de. LXIIII.
den.
Valuit. XX. fol. Modo: XXX . folid. Ordric ten de epo.

In Bibury Hundred
The church held Bibury itself 21 hides, 19 villagers, 2 small holders, 3 ridingmen who have 4 hides; a priest who has 3 hides.
11 slaves male and female.

Land of St. Mary's of Pershore
In Rapsgate hundred the church holds Cowley

Land of St. Mary's of Lyre
In Rapsgate hundred the church holds Duntisbourne (Leer).
Roger of Lacy gave the land to the church. Edmer held it before 1066.

Land of Roger of Lacy
In Rapsgate Hundred
Duntisbourne (Abbots) Gilbert holds from him (Gilbert de Eskecot)
Kenward, a Thane of King Edwards held it and could go where he
would. (could choose any lord)
 2 villagers, 2 smallholders, 2 slaves, value 40s.

In Cirencester Hundred
Stratton - 5 hides, 15 villagers, 7 smallholders with a priest, 5 slaves.

Land of Roger of Berkeley
In Rapsgate Hundred
He holds Coberley, 10 hides, 19 villagers, 4 smallholders, 4 slaves.

Land of Osbern Gifford
In Rapsgate Hundred
Osbern holds Brimpsfield 9 hides. 16 villagers, 6 smallholders, a priest,
8 male 4 female slaves.

Land of Gilbert, son of Thorold (52)
In Rapsgate Hundred
North Cerney. 7 hides, 2 thanes - Elaf and his brother,
held it as two manors and could go where they would.
In lordship 4 ploughs, 7 villagers, and 6 smallholders with 5 ploughs,
 6 slaves; a mill at 8s; meadow, 6 acres; woodland 2 furlongs long
and one wide.
4 of Gilberts men-at-arms with their men have 7 ploughs and a
mill valued at 8s. Value of the whole manor before 1066 was 14 pounds
now 12 pounds.

Rendcomb. 5 hides which pay tax. Aelfric held it. I lordship
1 plough; 3 villagers and seven smallholders with 3 ploughs.
7 slaves; a frenchman who holds the land of 2 villagers.

A mill at 8s; meadow, 4 acres.
The value was 7 pounds now 100s.

Rendcomb. Walter holds it from him (Gilbert). 3 hides which pay tax.
In lordship 2 ploughs; 4 villagers, 3 small holders with 2 ploughs. 6 slaves; a mill at 5s; meadow 3 Acres.
The value is and was 6 pounds

(Gilbert was also Gilbert of Bouille. North Cerney also included Calmsden and Woodmancote. Rencomb was classed as Upper (later Marsden) and Lower (later Rendcomb))

Land of Ansfrid of Cormeilles
In Rapsgate
Elkstone. 2 Leowins held it as 2 manors 4 ½ hides in Colesbourne 1 ½ hide. Alwin held it as a manor.
These 3 thanes could go where they would. 5 villagers, 2 smallholders, 4 slaves on one manor, 5 villagers 2 smallholders at the other. At Colesbourne 2 villagers and 2 smallholders

Syde. 3 hides, 1 villager, priest, 3 smallholders, 6 slaves.

Land of Hugh Donkey (63)
In Cirencester Hundred
Hugh also holds Bagendon, and Gilbert from him. 3 hides which pay tax.
Wolfward held it. In lordship 3 ploughs; 5 villagers with 3 ploughs; 6 slaves
A mill at 10s; meadow, 8 acres.
The value was and is 4 pounds

(Gilbert de Eskecote sublet from Hugh)
There are several cross references about this time which tell of the manor of Eycot and the curious fact that it was a detached part of Bibury hundred and not part of Rapsgate hundred.

"Eycot occurs in precisely the same position as the normal hundred head, though not in capitals or rubricated, and signifies that this holding was in Bibury hundred, not Rapsgate hundred." Eversham Manuscript K (folios 57r-62r) which is a hideage schedule of all holding in

Gloucestershire done as circuit returns.

Later evidence shows that another four hides made up Eycot and were included in the 21 hides of Bibury Manor. Surveys locate the four hides as being held by three riding men at Eycot in Rendcomb (Red Book of Worcester - pp 412, 414, 417, 439 ; a church record of the Bishop of Worcester)

Again, Worcester B MSS, Hemming's Cartulary (an 11th century manuscript published in 1723)
" *To Begabira (Bibury) elong 21 hides; in Begabira and Abolingatun (Ablington) 15 hides; in Beorudeslea (Barnsley) 5 hides and in Eugkote (Eycot) 1 hide*"
Folio 39r Hearne text pp 84-84

Also, Worcester B MSS. Colesbourne folio 140r Hearne text pp 310-11
"In Rapsgate Hundred. The church holds Colsbourne itself and Swein from it; he could not withdraw 8 hides which pay tax. Walter son of Roger holds it from the church. The church holds Aicote (Eycot) itself, and Alric from it. It lies in Begeberi. 1 hide. Ordric holds it from the bishop" In the margin level with Aicocte is written Aicote in red ink.

The Meaning of the Domesday Record of Eycot

The manor of Eycot, also spelled Eycote, Eyot, Aicote or Eugkote, was located in the middle of Rapsgate hundred and normally would have been the meeting place for the hundred. Oddly, it was a holding of the Bibury hundred which became part of Brightwells Barrow hundred. It was thought to be quite small in area, 1 hide (120 acres or so). However, four more hides existed which were held by riding men (a form of government administrator) who lived at Rendcomb. Eycot was then comprised of 5 hides (over 600 acres). Even with five hides it was not a large manor.

Before 1066, in Saxon times, it was owned by the bishop of Worcester who leased it out to Alric. Alric leased or owned at least 8 other properties in Gloucestershire. It is not known if this was one or several persons of that name. It was certain that he held 1 hide in Eycot. The other four were listed in the Red Book of the bishop as being in Rendcomb and Alric may also have leased giving a sub lease to 3 riding men or Radmen. These persons had a higher status than a villager. Originally they were escorts or messengers for the king. They were found on royal or church lands and were entitled to work their own holding free from the demands of the lord. They did have to give work to the lord but did not have to provide full military service. The villagers held some land, more than a smallholder. The smallholder had little more than a garden and a few animals. At Eycot manor there were three riding men and on their land presumably there were some people living. Any of the Radmen or the villagers could have become ancestors of the Eycotts because they were eligible to be taxed and would acquire an identity for that purpose and hence get a surname.

The record says that Alric had ceased to lease the land and in 1086 Ordric was leasing it from the bishop. These were men with Anglo-Saxon names. On this land there were 2 villagers who might have farmed about 12 acres or more, four small holders with a house and garden and two slaves who probably worked for the villagers. There was a meadow of 8 acres probably along the river which was used by everyone. The two villagers appear to have each had a team of oxen and a plough. There was a small mill attached to the manor which had a modest value of 64 pence or just over 5 shillings. This was similar but less than the value of the mills at Rendcomb and North Cerney.

The land while it had increased a third in value in 20 years was still less than a third the value of Rendcomb and only 15% the value of the other. North Cerney was 10 times more valuable than Eycot and Bagendon was 3 times more valuable. Eycot was a very modest possession of the bishop.

The total inhabitants for Eycot, Rendcomb, North Cerney, and Bagendon added up to 83 or so. This figure represented adult males so a total population for the area was likely 200 to 300. There were perhaps 20 to 25 persons living at Eycot.

The principal landlord in the area was Gilbert, son of Thorold who held part of North Cerney and Upper and Lower Rendcomb.

Appendix D
Notes on Victoria History of Gloucestershire (Vol. 7)

The following explains the structure and importance of the ancient land division known as a hundred. Afterwards the early history for each of the local communities, parishes and manors, associated with the early Eycott family is examined.

Hundreds

In England a hundred was the division of a shire for administrative, military and judicial purposes under the common law. Originally, when introduced by the Saxons between 613 and 1017, a hundred had enough land to sustain approximately one hundred households headed by a hundred-man or hundred eolder. He was responsible for administration, justice, and supplying military troops, as well as leading its forces. The office was not hereditary but by the 10th century the office was selected from among a few outstanding families.

Hundreds were further divided. Larger or more populous hundreds were split into divisions (or in Sussex, half hundreds). All hundreds were divided into tithings, which contained ten households. Below that, the basic unit of land was called the hide which was enough land to support one family and varied in size from 60 to 120 old acres or 15 to 30 modern acres (6 to 12 ha) depending on the quality and fertility of the land. A hundred could very loosely be compared with the modern township. Eventually the smallest administrative unit became a parish, based on the local church area. A parish could have tithings.

Above the hundred was the shire under the control of a shire-reeve (or sheriff). Hundred boundaries were independent of both parish and county boundaries although often aligned, meaning that a hundred could be split between counties (usually only a fraction) or a parish could be split between hundreds.

The system of hundreds was not as stable as the system of counties being established at the time and lists frequently differ on how many hundreds a county had. The Domesday Book contained a radically different set of hundreds than that which would later become established in many parts of the country. The number of hundreds in each county varied wildly. Leicestershire had six (up from four at Domesday), whereas Devon, nearly three times larger, had thirty-two.

Hundreds gradually dropped out of administrative usage and by the 19th century several different single-purpose subdivisions of counties, such as Poor Law Unions, rural sanitary districts, and Parliamentary divisions, sprung up, filling the administrative role they had previously played. Hundreds have never been formally abolished.

The French brought the manorial system to England and areas of land under a lord were called a manor. The lords dwelling and his personal lands, his demesne, a small village and the lands of the villagers comprised the manor.

A parish, originally a defined area with a local church, generally measured to determine the number of persons who could be assembled in the church or who formed an agreed on community. Gradually this area acquired civil status as the church was requested to keep records which interested the government. Parish boundaries were adjusted from time to time and the civil role kept increasing. Since 1894 every parish with 300 people or more has a parish council to deal with local government matters. It is not a religious body and can be equated with the role of a township.

Brightswell Barrow and Rapsgate Hundred
Eycot Manor was located in Rapsgate Hundred but was legally a part of Bibury Hundred which was absorbed into Brightwells Barrow Hundred. Later Eycot was absorbed into Rendcomb parish and manor. This may have proved awkward since Eycot was across the Churn river from Rendcomb and no bridge existed in those days.

Brightwells Barrow Hundred was located a few miles east of Cirencester, starting at Bibury and circling to include Aldsworth, Eastleach, Lechade, Fairford. As part of Bibury Eycote was well out of the area as it was in the middle of Rapsgate hundred. No explanation for this has ever been found. Rapsgate was north of Cirencester east and west of the Churn River forming a triangle North Cerney to Chedworth to Elkstone and Syde.

Bibury Hundred
In 1086 Bibury manor included Aldsworth, Barnsley, Arlington, Ablington, Bibury and the more distant Eycot. It was assayed at 40 hides (5000 acres). In 1221 these places became part of Brightwells Barrow Hundred [Pleas of the crown for Gloucester., ed Maitland 1884]. Eycot was included until the 14th century. [record of Gloucester Subsidy Rolls for 1327, 14]
[Exchequer, Kings Rememberances E 179-113-131a r 4]
A separate frankpledge continued for Bibury Hundred under

jurisdiction of the Bishop of Worcester.

Brightwells Barrow Hundred was one of the seven hundreds of Cirencester given in 1189 to the church by the king. This action was later to be the cause of much friction between the merchant citizens and the church and state. [V.C.H. of Gloucester Vol XI pp 152-53]

A biannual hundred view of frankpledge (a meeting of citizens with the lord to settle local matters) was held at the junction of Droitwich Lechlade Saltway and a route from Fairford in the early 15th century. These gatherings, there being no hall for the event, were held in the open perhaps with the lord under an open tent.

The church at Bibury was established well before 899 AD not far from the site of a Roman villa. The Bishop of Worcester had an estate of 15 Cassati (hides) by the river Coln and in 718-45 AD bishop Wilfrith leased 5 cassati there to his daughter.

The next section deals with local government matters.

Bibury Hundred was placed under the lordship of Brightwells Barrow Hundred at the order of the court on a request from the vills including those of Eycot. The bishop however kept many liberties and a period of legal wrangling took place after 1276 about who could pass ordinances about bread and ale assize, view frankpledge and regulate tenants. The duty of a free tenant to attend court was commuted (ended) in 1399. Edward II confirmed the rights of the bishop of Worcester to pass these rules. The Abbot of Cirencester complained about this decision. [Court Roles for Bibury survive for 1270, 1382-90, 1432-77, 1496-8 and later. Some of these may deal with Eycot.] The court was the court leet for tithings of Bibury and Eycot. It dealt with assize (standard sizes for bread, ale, pleas of debt, bloodshed, hue and cry, sale of meat, fishing, maintenance of roads and ditches, and tenurial matters. After 1626 fence viewers and sheep cleaners were also appointed by this court.

After 1151 the bishop of Worcester permitted Oseney Abbey to act and benefit on his behalf. The association of Eycote with Bibury fades away with the meshing of Eycot with Rendcomb. Thus from early times until after 1442 legal proceedings for Eycot are with the Bibury records.

The Churl ,who owned Eycote before Domesday, Alric, had a hide of land (40 to 120 acres depending on the value) which before the Norman invasion classed him as a small free landholder. To qualify as a thane or lord he needed five hides.

Rapsgate Hundred
Rapsgate Hundred in 1086 consisted of Brimpsfield, Chedworth, North Cerney, Colesbourne, Cowley, Elkstone, Rendcomb, Syde, Coberley, and part of Duntisbourne. In all 78 hides, and 1 yardland. Rapsgate was also one of the 7 hundreds of Cirencester given in 1189. An exemption from frankpledge for Rendcomb was secured by the abbey in the 13th century. Thereafter the earls of Gloucester held a court which also included Calmsden and Woodmancote tithings.

The biannual view of frankpledge was held at Rapsgate on the ancient Cirencester Colesbourne road in the south of Colesbourne. Marsden had a separate frankpledge. Among other duties the tithings were liable for wardstaff which was replaced by a 3 shilling wake. Johannes Eycote is named in respect of this duty in the 1300s.

In Rapsgate Hundred we are interested in Eycot manor, Rendcomb, North Cerney and Woodmancote. It is here where the earliest records of the Eacotts exist.

North Cerney Parish and Manor
North Cerney parish has boundaries which existed in 852 AD [Saxon Charters and Field Names of Gloucester., G.B. Grundy 1935]

In 852 Beorhtwulf, king of the Mercians, granted to Alfeah 12 hides of land in Cerney and Calmsden, evidently including the whole of the later parish of North Cerney. Eycott was likely granted about the same time.

Gilbert, son of Turold, owned the manor in 1086. At that time the woodlands were in the northwest of the parish by Woodmancote. Old Park was created later by the owners of Rendcomb.

The Manor of North Cerney was held by the bishop of York from 1086 to 1545 when it was exchanged to the crown. (Henry VIII's dissolution) It was then sold by Henry in 1552 to Sir Thomas Chamberlayne, then resold to William Partridge in 1578 in whose family it remained until 1620-30 when William Poole purchased the manor. The Pooles owned it into 1700s.

Church records for North Cerney exist from 1568.

The population for North Cerney hamlet was 36+ in 1086. In 1327 twenty six were assessed for the subsidy. In 1381 forty five were listed for poll tax. In 1551 there were 145 communicants in the church and in 1563 there were 18 households. By 1603 there were only 110 communicants. In 1650 there were forty families. In 1710 there were 190 inhabitants and 42 houses. Currently there are about 600 persons.

Sir Thomas Vyner 1588-1665 who became Lord Mayor of London was born at North Cerney. Thomas Vyner was a brother and uncle to Eycotts and Lord mayor in 1653. (See Will of Thomas Ekott 1583) He was knighted by Oliver Cromwell. Sir Thomas (born 15 dec 1588 - d. 1665) was a goldsmith of London and Comptroller of the Mint. He married Anne, daughter of Richard Parsons, Honor, daughter of George Humble and in 1661 Alice Bat. He had four daughters by Ann and 2 sons with Honor. His sister Mary was wife of Samuel Moore, goldsmith of London and his half brother William Vyner of East Coope, Warwickshire, was father of Sir Robert Vyner (1631- 1688) who died at Windsor Castle. He was knighted at Whitehall in 1665 and made baronet in 1666. He was sheriff of London at the time of the fire 1666. With his great wealth he bought and made the crown jewels of Charles II, the same ones used today, and furnished £ 300 000 to the Restoration Navy.

The manor house at North Cerney was usually rented before 1500. Another part of the property, 7 hides, was rented for two marks and journey service to the king by the thegns, Eliaf and his brother in 1086. The lordship was held by Gilbert, son of Turold, who subsequently passed it along with Rendcomb, Calmsden, Woodmancote to the earls of Gloucester. Most of the land of Woodmancote, Calmsden and Rendcomb was subleased to the De La Mares. By the early 1500s North Cerney and Woodmancote were regarded as separate manors.
[Inquisitions Post Mortems series II, C 142/80 no. 23 i - located in Gloucester record office].

Woodmancote Manors
Woodmancote began in the 1200's and in 1327 it had 7 taxpayers [Gloucester Subsidy Roll 1327, 10, list for Rencomb includes

Woodmancote] [Ancient and Present State of Gloucester 1712, R. Atkyns]. By 1710 there were recorded a medieval chapel, 13 houses and two Woodmancote manors.

Woodmancote manor was sold to Thomas Taylor in 1566 but Mary, widow of Edward Stafford, was named lady of the hamlet in 1608. [Smith, Men and Armour - Names of all able bodied men fit for service in his majesties service in war in Gloucester compiled by John Smith in 1608, reprint 1902 - Complete Peerage XII (I) 184-5]

Later Woodmancote figures in with Rendcomb and North Cerney manors litigation between the Pooles and Guises.
[Gloucester Record Office - Guise family records of Elmore and Rendcomb. D326/L 11-12]

The Guises acquired 500 acres in Woodmancote and owned it as part of Rendcomb Park in 1837
[Gl. Rec. Off. T10 and Bigland Papers - 3vs 1791-1889.]

Cerney House estate was formed as a new estate from lands leased on long term by Sir Thomas Rich, grandson of Baron Richard Rich, exchequer of Henry VIII, known as Green's and Vyner's. These farms were owned by Woodmancote manors. The Rich family held the land from the early 1600s to 1761 when Thomas Tyndale acquired it. The second Woodmancote manor passed to the De La Mares with Rendcomb before 1200. The land passed to the Leigh family by marriage. While at Cerney House Sir Thomas Rich's daughter Bridget was born in 1596. It is not clear why the Rich family lived at North Cerney since the family held extensive lands in Essex.

An agricultural depression in the 1300s resulted in the tenants giving up their plots of land or perishing in the plague. There was a depopulation and drop in used land. In 1341 ten tenants had abandoned tenancies which had existed in 1291. Wool production was off due to murraine, a serious disease, and a shortage of grazing land. All 11 small holdings had lapsed in rent to North Cerney manor. In 1341 there were 6 yardlanders, 4 half yardlanders, 3 Mondaymen, 4 cottars. Only four tenants leased land. There were 3 freeholders. [Gl. Rec. Off. D621/M7 - Inquisition Post Mortem No. N rec. com. 409]

Later the lands were grouped into compositions of holdings and by

1713 there were 6 large land holders with 33 to 114 acres who held the land for 3 lives (99 years) and 9 cottages with statutory 4 acre holdings. [Gl. Rec.Off. North Cerney man 1713-32, leases 1715-89]

The lands of the Earl of Stafford were mostly at Woodmancote with some at Rendcomb and North Cerney. In 1566 all the tenant lands still with the manor lay in four large farms at Woodmancote. [C3/260/29 G.R.O. : D 293/4; Inquisition Post Mortem Gloucester 1625-42, ii, 103-4]

Woodmancote had 4 open fields, Burcomb (west) Morcomb (north) and later 2 fields on the South slopes above the Churn. The meadowland was only 8 acres but was considered very valuable. (six times the value of arable land). Later this river bottom land was considered the best in the county. While sheep raising was important, crops brought in more money in 1535. The Tame family of Fairford and Rendcomb and the Pooles were big sheep raisers.

Rendcomb Parish and Manor

Rendcomb was named after the coomb or three sided valley near the hamlet. It was isolated on the east bank of the Churn until 1824 when a road link was built across the river. Previously it only had a link to the White Way to the east. Rendcomb Park was established in 1544 and by 1676 held 250 acres.

In 1086 there were 39 inhabitants at Rendcomb and Eycot [Domesday Book Rec. Com. i, 164v, 168v]. In 1327 there were 19 for the subsidy. In 1381 there were 36 for the poll tax.
In 1551 there were 61 communicants in the parish and in 1563 there were 12 households.
In 1650 there were 18 families.
In 1710 a total of 120 inhabitants.

In 1086 two estates at Rendcomb were owned by Gilbert, son of Turold. 5 hides had formerly belonged to Aluric and 3 to Walter, his son-in-law. These estates passed to the earls of Gloucester by the late 12th century and were subsequently sublet to the De La Mare family. In 1255 Earl Richard de Clare reserved 2 plowlands for himself. That land became Rendcomb manor. From 1387 until 1503 the manor was held by Thomas and Robert De La Mare and their descendants. In 1503 Edmund Tame of Fairford obtained it and by marriage it passed to the Staffords in 1547.

Richard Berkeley of Stoke Gifford obtained it in 1564. The Guises purchased it in 1635 but a Berkeley continued to live there until after 1661. During the period when the Berkely family held it, Elizabeth I visited (1592). Sir Thomas Roe lived at Rendcomb during the time his mother Dame Eleanor Berkeley owned the Manor (1608). As a rule the Berkely family were only visitors. The De La Mares and the Tames had actually lived at the manor. The Guises built a new house there.

Colesbourne
The parish church was built in the 11th century. In 1569 the rector of the church also held livings (a sum of money from collections, tithes etc.) at Rendcomb and Tetbury. One Rector was Richard Hawker and another was Hunphrey Horton.

Marsden
Once known as Upper Rendcomb, this manor was at one time held by the Berkeley family

Eycot Manor
All the land west of the Churn in Rendcomb made up the ancient manor of Eycot. Today the Rendcomb parish boundary is that of the manor. [Historia and Cartularium Monasterii Sancti Petri Gloucester. ed. W.H. Hart; Rolls series no. 33 three vols. 1863 - 87 ii 41] Whether the boundary for Eycott is the same as previous to 1732 is not known.   There were 8 inhabitants for the 1327 subsidy. [Gloucester Subsidy roll 14]In 1381 there were 12 for the poll tax.[E 179/113/35a r 2a]There were still a few tenants there in 1442. [Gloucester Record Office D678 Sherbourne estate court rolls] No later records have been found.

The manor house was recorded as Eycot farm to 1732 [GRO D326]. The farm buildings at Eycotfield were the only buildings on high ground in 1837.[Gloucester Diocese Record T1/147]. In 1930 a house was built on the high ground.

In 1096 one hide was held by Ordric (Ordvic) from the bishop of Worcester via Bibury. [Domesday book 164v] An intermediate lordship between the bishop and tenant in demesne was held by Gilbert de Mynors (Miners) and Roger de Mynors at different times in the 1100's. Gilbert de Miners was born at Eycot about 1087 and died after 1127 at Eycot. From Roger it passed to Roger Mucegros [Red Book of Worcester 414-15, 439].

In 1209 and later the land was said to be held directly by the bishop and assessed 1/3 knights fee [Book of Fees i.39, Feudal Aids ii 248] Early holders of the manor were Reynold and Richard of Beckford who made a grant of tithes in Eycot to Gloucester Abbey before 1100. [Gloucester Cathedral Library register Abb Froucester B pp 83-4] [Hist. & Cart. Mon. of Glou. rolls ii 41 cf. reg. Regnum Anglo Norman ii, 104] At some time in 1100's the manor was held by Robert Russell in the name of his wife Basile and his heir William [Gloucester Cathedral Reg.Abb Froucester B pp 83-84] [Red Book of Worcester 439] This was perhaps William Russel who held Eycot in 1209. His widow, Alice, was challenged in ownership by John Russel. Robert Russel got a small estate conveyed to him in 1241. He may have managed to get the manor from her because under law she was entitled to 1/3 of the estate. Her husband had given it all to her.

John Le Brun married Margery, daughter of John Russel, and obtained from Walter Wyth ½ a ploughland in nether (lower) Rendcomb, Woodmancote and North Cerney as well as Eycot. This was in 1303. In 1312 his widow Margery granted Eycot to Thomas Neel of Purton. A contingent remainder in the grant was that the manor was for the benefit of John of Burton (Purton ?) and his heirs, one of whom was Thomas Burton who held the manor in 1346.

Thomas Burton died in 1375 leaving his estate to his son Thomas, a minor. William Archibald was made the boys custodian. A description of the property at the time is available. [Cal. Inq. P.M. XIV pp 94-95] In 1385 John Atwood claimed the manor was his because of a grant made by John Russel to his ancestors Robert and Margery Crook in the reign of Edward II. John Atwood was awarded seisen (ownership under rightful title) from Burton. The following year the land was granted to John Pouger who died in 1405. In 1410 his son John settled an ownership dispute with John Warre, nephew and heir of the younger Thomas of Burton. The land returned to the Burton heirs. By 1421 the land was in the possession of the Abbey at Winchcombe. Warre's sister Catherine and another Burton heir, Robert Andrew challenged the Abbey who had to settle with them for ownership.

After the dissolution of abbeys by Henry VIII, in 1536-40, the manor passed into the hands of Edmund Tame whose widow Catherine held it after his death. It then became included with Rendcomb and was owned by the Staffords. It was likely included in the sale to Richard Berkely in 1564.

They kept Eycot as a residence until about 1690. The capital messuage (main set of buildings or main dwelling) may have been what is now known as Lodge Farm or Rendcomb Farm. It was to Rendcomb that Elizabeth 1st came to visit in September of 1592 as Berkeley was then a member of her court. This Richard was not a leading Berkely when he was born but did own Marsden and at the time he bought Rendcomb, he also bought Calmsden. He was appointed Lieutenant of the Tower of London under Elizabeth and was a privy council member. Some of his family had Catholic leanings but he navigated politics astutely. Berkeley built his main residence at Stoke Gifford. In 1647 Sir Maurice Berkeley of Rendcomb and his relative Richard Berkeley had their estates taken from them as they had raised against parliament and had not paid their fees for 1644 and 45. Parliament granted them a pardon in 1647 after they had paid the fees and fines. These events were during the civil war.

Bagendon
The material for Bagendon in the Victoria County History Series, Vol 16, has not yet been released (as at 2019).

Appendix E
Lordship and Ownership of Eycot Manor

800's   existence known on Saxon charters and owned by the Bishop of Worcester

1066   Bishop of Worcester   lease held by Alric

1086   Bishop of Worcester   lease held by Ordric
1 hide; 4 additional hides were held by 3 riding men(absentee owners) thus Ordric technically qualified as a lord or thegn.

1100's Bishop of Worcester leases to Robert de Moynors (Miners)
held by Reynold of Beckford
leases to Roger de Moynors
held by Richard of Beckford
leases to Roger Mucegros
held by Robert & Basile(wife) Russel

1209 Bishop of Worcester
Land is held by William & Alice(wife) Russel who is the son of Robert Russel

1241 John Russel................... (in dispute by) Robert Russel

1303 to daughter Margery Russel who is the wife of
1312 John Le Brun

1346 Margery grants lease to Thomas Neel of Purton but it is for the use of Thomas Burton

1375 Thomas Burton Jr. age 11, inherits

1385 Robert Atwood cites claim via ancestor Robert Russel and he gets the land away from Burton then promptly he grants the land to
1386 John Pougher

1410 John Pougher Jr. inherits

1421 John Warre makes claim via Burtons takes land from Pougher and gives it to Winchcombe Abbey where claims to rightful ownership of the lease stop.

1534 King Henry VIII dissolves Abbey ownership and Henry takes ownership.

1540 Edmund Tame of Fairford and wife Catherine (Stafford) acquire land from the King as a result of the dissolution. Eycot becomes a part of Rendcomb Park estate.

1547 The Stafford family holds the land.

1564 Richard Berkeley of Stoke Gifford acquires.

1635 The Guise family assumes ownership but Richard Berkeley is an unhappy tenant and refuses to leave. Richard Berkeley is fined for cutting trees down.

1647 Maurice and Richard Berkeley of Rendcomb are pardoned by Parliament for not paying fees in 1644-5. They were supporters of the King and not Parliament. This is some time after the Guises were also claiming ownership. However, until 1690 Berkeleys did remain on property.

Descendants of the Guises then control the estate until 1864.

1864 Rendcomb Estate is established and the owners include the Goldsmid family and others.

1914 The estate of 4,700 acres is broken up into several holdings.

1984 Carron Mann owns a small holding along the Churn R. which may   be the site of the original manor. Eycot house(1934) occupies
        another possible site.

No record exists of an Eycot in ownership or in residence on this land at any time in recorded history. None of the records from the 1300's when "de Eycot" exists name such a person. This may be due to the fact that the name was first used by a person from there and not of there.

The Eycots earliest records are next door in Woodmancote, Rendcomb, North Cerney and Bagendon although they may have been villagers, slaves or small holders at Eycot, they were never the landlords. Margery Le Brun and her husband have control of Eycot at the time that John of Eycot is a townsman in Cirencester and he held land at Bagendon.

Someone, someplace owns the Lordship of the manor of Eycot to this day. The lordship conveys no status or title but does formally exist.

A Description of Eycote Farm 1375

At an Inquisition Post Mortem taken after the death of Thomas Burton respecting the disposition of his estate the following information is recorded.

" Inquisition Post Mortem taken at Cirencester on Saturday
the Feast of S.S. Tiburcius and Valerian, 1375 thus:- Thomas
de Berton was seised in his demesne as of fee on the day he
died, of the manor of Eycote, held of the King, by reason of
the temporalities of the Bishopric of Worcester being in his
hand, as of the manor of Bibury, by knight service and the
payment of 12d. and six bushels of corn at Martinmas, with
suit of court at the said manor of Bibury twice a year.
There is a capital messuage there with a garden worth nothing

*a year, beyond the reprises; 60 acres of arable land, worth
10s and not more because the land is hilly; 60 acres of
arable land worth nothing because they are lying
uncultivated; 5 acres of meadow worth 10s. a year; a parcel
of underwood, worth 12s.; 23s.1d. of the rents of the tenants
at will. The pleas and perquisites of the court are worth
nothing beyond the reprises. The said Thomas also held a
messuage and a half virgate of land in Rodmerton from Henry
Borden by knight service and the payment of 12d. a year,
worth 4s. a year clear. The said Thomas died on Friday after
the Feast of St. Gregory the Pope last past. Thomas his son
and heir was eleven on the feast of the Annunciation last
past."*

Thomas Burton or Berton had acquired Eycote in 1346 and owned it until his death mentioned above. During this period of time England went through a great depopulation caused by the Black Death which began in 1349 and raged for many years. There were many farms abandoned and this was due to death and the lack of people to purchase the crops.

The quotation from above says that on the day he died he had possession of his land, the manor of Eycote which the King had entrusted to the Bishop of Worcester who was lord of Bibury and Eycote was owing allegiance to Bibury. So Burton had to give service as a knight to the Bishop or King when required. He also had to pay 12 shillings and six bushels of grain each year at Martinmas (Nov.11) and had to appear at the court at Bibury twice a year to present information for the Bishop. There was a main farmhouse with a garden that produced only enough for the occupants. There were sixty hill acres which could be ploughed but were not so made no money. The five acre meadow, likely along the river, was good grassland. There was a wood lot as well. The tenants paid rent of 23 shillings one pence. The manor court did not make any money other than meeting expenses settling matters among the tenants. Thomas also was lord of property in Rodmerton. His knight Henry Borden paid 12 pence a year on land valued at four shillings. His son Thomas Jr. was eleven years old. The son's estate was entrusted to William Archibald. When Thomas was about 20, John Attwood went to court to prove an earlier owner had left the farm to his family. He and his relatives got it back with William Russel among them and they gave it to the Abbey at Winchcombe which kept it until Henry VIII dissolved the abbeys. Edmund Tame of Fairford got the land in 1540. Thus young Thomas was done out of his inheritance.

A Description of Eycot Hamlet from History of Rendcomb

In the Middle Ages the parish contained a small hamlet called Eycot, the centre of a separate manor which apparently comprised all the land lying west of the Churn. The hamlet had a chapel by the beginning of the 12th century [84] and 8 inhabitants were assessed for the subsidy in 1327. [85] and *c.* 12 for the poll tax in 138I.[86] There were still a few tenants at Eycot in 1442 [87] but no later record has been found of the hamlet though the manor-house, which was absorbed with the rest of the manor into the Rendcomb estate, was recorded by the name Eycot Farm until 1732.[88] The name of the hamlet, derived from a cottage near an island or water - meadow,[89] suggests that the site of Eycot was down by the Churn and it seems likely that the manor-house survives as the oldest part of Lodge Farm (renamed Rendcomb Manor in the 20th century) which stands by a ford near the north end of Rendcomb park. If that is the case, the final disappearance of the hamlet may possibly be associated with the creation of the park some time before 1544. In the late 18th century Lodge Farm, so called by 1777, was the centre of farm which included Eycot field, evidently a former open field of the manor and most of the other land on that side of the river. The house dates partly from the 17th century but has an early-19th-century wing and some 20th-century additions in Cotswold style. The farm buildings at Eycot field were the only buildings on the high ground on that side of the river in I837 but *c.* 1930 a large Cotswold-style residence, called Aycote House and designed by Norman Jewson, was built for the owner of a small estate established in that part of the parish after the break-up of the Rendcomb estate.

[82] C. H. C. Osborne, J. C. James, and K. L. James, *Hist. of Rendcomb Coll* (Oxford, 1976),   23—4,29, 121, 152—7.
[83]Ex inf. the headmaster, Mr. R. M. A. Medill
[84]*Hist. &Cart. Mon. Glouc.* (Rolls Ser.), ii. 41.
[85] Gb:. Subsidy Roil, 1327, 14.
  E179/I13/35a rot.2a
[87] Glos. R.O., D 678, ct. rolls 94.
[88]4 Ibid.D$_3$_6/Tio.
[89]"P.N.Glos.i 161.
[90]4 Taylor, *Map of Glos. (1777)*

Bagendon

The "History of Bagendon" was published by Rev. George Edward Rees M.A. in 1932. Rees was rector of the church and lived in the hamlet at different times from the 1880's to 1930's . He saw Bagendon as a part of the British nation in his detailed remembrances. Much of what follows comes from his work.

Its history is ancient. Roman artifacts have been dug from the churchyard. Its location attests to its being part of the Dobunni community. As a Christian settlement it predates 680 AD when it became part of the Bishop of Worcester's See. These folk were likely Romano British. The church was built below the level of the adjacent creek on low land that regularly flooded. This oddity plus the discovery of Roman artifacts on the site indicate it might have been a Roman worship spot prior to a building being erected. The local Saxon settlers likely worshiped at the far end of the parish around Woodmancote where their gods included Thor and Woden.

In general the settlers were a group of free neighbors who engaged in agriculture. Land tillage was by lot on a temporary basis and in common they shared a team of oxen. Meadow land was held in common. Winter and spring grain, beans and a long fallow was the usual rotation. Land was set in long strips for tillage but over half was untilled and unfenced. Everyone was entitled to get wood and feed swine on acorns and other nuts. The Saxon land strips existed until the enclosure act of 1792. A map of this exists including the field names.

At Domesday, 1086, Ulward was the Thane of Bagendon and there were 5 yeomen and 5 slaves. Until 1792 there were still 5 freemen holdings.

At Bagendon there was a mill, Trinity Mill, and it has existed for hundreds of years. It is now in an outdoor museum. Bagendon was held after William the Conqueror by Hugh Lanse(Donkey). Gilbert of Thorold held North Cerney, Rendcomb and other places. The other adjacent land owner, Roger de Lacy, joined with them taking sides with Robert of Normandy who was unsuccessfully challenging to become William's successor. As a result they lost their lands in 1088 to Robert Fitzhamon, Earl of Gloucester who got North Cerney. (The word Cerney may be derived from Saxon CERNE which means stone.) North Cerney remained in the Gloucester family hands for centuries.

Bagendon was also taken from Hugo L'Anse, same reason, and given to the Chandos family. The sublease for Bagendon eventually went to the DeBagendon's from about 1100 until 1382. The Chandos were fighting knights and kept a fortified castle, first at Hereford and later Sudeley.

The Chandos held land mostly on the welsh border (13 manors there) and had obligations in Scotland and France. Thus they were often in battle and demanded the services of their knights. This meant that the free men of Bagendon would have been forced often to report to duty. At this time the population of the parish numbered around 60 persons. Richard de Bagendon in 1254 was at the siege of Hereford Castle defending the Chandos family. Sir John Chandos, Captain, helped sail the army to fight at Agincourt. The Chandos line produced mostly daughters who married into the Brydges and Berkeley families.(During the wars of the Commonwealth Cromwell's Roundheads destroyed the tombs of the Chandos family.)

Again the de Bagendon family lost control of other manors they held after the battle of Evesham in 1265 where parliament attempted to check the king's rule. Later in 1286, 16 years after the battle Richard's son also Richard had to pay the debts of his ancestor, a sum of 2 marks per year. This debt was to be passed onto yet another descendent, Richard de Bagendon. Richard decided to become a priest. This broke the chain of debts. However in 1304 Richard was suspended for fathering William de Bagendon, a bastard. He was suspended for 6 months for not owning up to the fact when he became a priest. In 1318 Richard, already his father's chaplain, became Rector of Bagendon. At this time there had been a cattle raid from the next valley and Richard rounded up his parishioners and led them into a raid to steal cattle from the Duntisbourne people and burned down their rector's house. Richard sold the stolen cattle at the Lechlade market. The buyers got into trouble when it was found out and Richard went to trial. He paid a fine and since he was a priest, he was let out of jail. He continued on as priest for many years, survived the Black Death, and died after 1354. He was the last of the de Bagendon knights. After him the manor was transferred to the wealthy Company of Weavers in 1382. King Richard gave it to the Cirencester Weavers Guild who placed the church in the hands of Holy Trinity Church at Cirencester where it remained for some time. This action also removed the feudal obligations of military service of the residents to go to fight the wars of the Chandos family.

Nov 18, 1382 a licence was granted after petition of Richard Playn and others to found a chantry for 2 chaplains at Cirencester for the cost of 40 marks. Richard was acting on behalf of the Weavers Company. This was part of the action of the weavers to escape the control of the abbot by the wool men and weavers. In the 1400's Bagendon Church like North Cerney and Cirencester was rebuilt with the money from the wool business. The weaver's company was closely controlled and their daughters married into each others families.

In 1349 the plague killed many people and times were bad. There were no vegetables in the winter and salt became too expensive for the meat. There was no money so pay became in the form of food.

Bagendon Church, known as St. Margaret, was for over 150 years affiliated with St. Mary's in Cirencester. It was uncertain if the church was dedicated to St. Margaret of Antioch or the Queen of Scotland. Margaret died in 1093 and canonized in 1250 about the time the church was built.

Moorwood farm about 1440 was held by William of Nottingham.

Thomas Seymour, a Chandos, brother- in-law of Henry VIII, lived at Sudeley Castle and was lord of Bagendon. His niece Elizabeth (ER I) stayed with him as a princess age 15. She returned as queen to visit in 1592. Thomas was beheaded in 1549 and the Marquess of Bath, John Thynne, acquired the land. He also got the church land after the dissolution. Thynne lived at Longleat where he built that manor (1611) and also built Moorwood at Woodmancote. His son John succeeded him in 1580. His daughter married the Lord Mayor of London, Rowland Hayward. The Thynnes had sufficient power to influence elections for seats in parliament.

The parish register for Bagendon dates back to 1630 and the leading families were Eycotts of the Moor (Woodmancote) and the Bowles of Bagendon. They were referred to as Mr. and Mrs. being thus small gentry.

In the 1740's William Pitt (prime minister) was lord of Bagendon and his son after. In 1792 with the enclosure act the half of the land of Bagendon that was common pasture land became enclosed for cultivation. This was the first change since Domesday. The manor rights were sold by Thynne to Pitt. The church was given to Jesus College, Oxford. The last rector appointed by the Thynnes was Rev. John Bythesea of Wick House in Wiltshire. Moorwood at Woodmancote went to Squire Haines.

"History of Bagendon"

"History of Bagendon" George Edward Rees, Bagendon 1932 published by Oxford Press

In this book the following references are made to the Eacott - Eycott family. The record of information ends with 1880.

Introduction: Bagendon is a parish 3 miles long and up to 2/3 of a mile wide. It has ancient earthworks from pre Roman times; an ancient inn at the crossroads with a gibbet and a record of a political duel; there is a Norman church; a woods dating back to king John. The parish had once been featured in an early act of Parliament. Some famous people were connected with Bagendon including a queen's husband and a royal gaoler.

Moorwood is an old demesne adjacent to Woodmancote. Bagendon manor house was known as the mansion. Moorwood was built by a member of the Thynne family who also owned Longleat. The Haines family refaced Moorwood in a Georgian style. The house in 1980's was occupied by captain Robinson.

At Domesday there were about a dozen households (60 persons) at Bagendon and in 1712 there were 13 houses and about 60 people. And as at Domesday about half the land was cultivated.

The first bishop of Worcester was appointed by 680 AD and his land included Bagendon. Before the Norman conquest the land was held by a thane called Ulward. Under this lord were five yeomen and five serfs. The land was divided equally into occupied and unoccupied property and held equally by the lord and the yeomen (churls). This arrangement lasted until the enclosure act of 1792.

At Domesday Hugo L'anse (Hugh Donkey) succeeded Ulward (Woolward). Gilbert from Hugo held Bagendon, North Cerney, and Rendcomb but not Eycot. In 1087 Hugo and Gilbert took sides with Robert of Normandy against king William. In 1088 William gave their lands to others. Robert Fitzhamon got North Cerney and for centuries it belonged to the Earls of Gloucester. Bagendon was given to the Chandos family (Sudeley Castle) who lost it during the time of Henry VIII. The de Bagendons were subifudators (subleasers) from the Chandos. Later the king gave the land to the company of weavers of Cirencester who in turn gave it to the priests of Cirencester about 1382. On November 18, 1382 the transfer of land was entered as an Act of Parliament at Westminster. The property in later times, after 1450, was owned by some of these families; Twynyho, Prelatte, Arnold, Tame, Nottingham and Morton. Some of these were transfer by marriage. Sir William of Nottingham held Moorwood and Woodmancote in the 1440's.

[Pg 59 reference] "*In the north east corner of Bagendon church yard near the Norman Coped slab is a massive flat stone that once rested over Frances Ashmeads body on the north side of the church, the only interment there. She married John Ashmead Jr. and lived at the Bear (Inn). Becoming a widow she went to live at the Moor where children were born to her and Mr. Eycott. She died in 1776 and the "cockley" stone upon her grave is like that still quarried at Moorwood and Beech Pike. Tradition calls her Madam Ashmead and her burial all alone in the cold shadow of the church is in contrast to ....*"

Sir John Thynne added to the two manor houses and rebuilt them as mansions after 1792. The patronage of the Thynnes was mostly to Wiltshire men. They appointed the priests from as far away as Wooton Bassett. The Tynnes owned Longleat and via the Seymours were involved with Elizabethan royalty.

[Pg 78] "*The old parchment registers (1630-1740) show how few labourers were hired; the names are chiefly of those who held the small tenements or the demesne lands. The demesne houses at Bagendon and Moorwood were occupied by small gentry and yeomen; in the early days the name Eycott belonged to Moorwood and Dowle to Bagendon; these names appear for many years in the records....For ten years before 1660 there were three rectors, the last appointed by Cromwell, who were Puritans. There is not a single entry to show these men baptized, married or buried anyone. But from then on the strength of the Puritan names is shown Job, Erasmus, Lydia, Jesse, Abigail, Rebecca, Abraham, Emmanuel. In these registers the designations of the chief inhabitants were Mr. and Mistress, kept for the Dowles and the Eycotts except for Madam Frances Ashmead, but her title was equivocal. The farmer is called a husbandman, and there*

were a cordwinder, a rough mason, and two clothyers, a daylabourer and
a shepherd, an almsman and an almswoman, a poor batchelor and an
ancient maid besides several parish clerks."

Other records include the churchwardens book from 1776. At Jesus
College, Oxford is a map of Bagendon. (An ordinance reproduction has been
made). There is a reference in the Hockaday manuscript - an index of
Gloucester parish registers, deed and enclosure awards of 1792 and the
Bagendon enclosure award of 1792.

" *Three parishes meet at the corner of Moorwood and at that point*
there is a no man's land not included in any of them. This curious fact is not
an accident. There is an old Saxon custom of leaving some land for the
sylvan gods."

Moorwood was bought by Nathaniel Haines son John about 1800. He
enlarged the house and lived there. At the same time his uncle Edward redid
the manor house. There are curious external resemblances between them.

In 1572 Thomas Eycott was one of the churchwardens. There were but
7 households so a sermon was given only once each quarter. There was no
cup for the service only a chalice.

During 1713 William Huntington M.A. became the curate and before
his induction Berkeley Eycott and William Chandler were sequestrators. In
1714 an attempt was made to exchange five acres of Berkeley Eycotts land
in North Field with some church land held for the benefit of the repair of
the ancient mill. Nothing was done until 1792.

Thomas Eycott, yeoman, of Bagendon, his wife Mary and children
Thomas Jr, Elizabeth, Rebecca, Mary reputed to be papists took the oath of
Allegiance to king George in 1715. Thereafter Thomas Eycott was
appointed constable of Badgington (sic). This meant he was the primary
government official for the parish and thus was sworn not to be a Catholic
which would have denied him any government position.

[pg 164] Place Names

The Moor - the old name of the house now called Moorwood.
Usually the abode of men of substance, Eycott, Agg, Small, Haines,

Longworth, Robinson.

Moorwood - the most ancient wood mentioned in King John's reign and the last property disposed of by the Marquis of Bath.

North Field - an extensive waste on the north before the enclosure act.

Parson's Grove - given out of Moorwood for repair of the mill. When the monks left the parson got control.

Egg's Piece - belonged to Agg or Egg of North Cerney and had connections with the Vyner family.

Great Wood Piece - Moorwood.

The church book of 1778 shows Eycotts no longer renting seats.

Testators of Bagendon - from 1427 to 1500 the names were Nottingham, Turner, Prelatte, Tywnho, Tame.

In 1525 the will of Thomas Foxley was witnessed by Syr Lawrence Warburton, Wyllyam Eycott and Haylyn Bradeley.

Other wills listed in History of Bagendon
1500 -1600 Haines, Tame, Hobbes,
1581 Richard Eycott of North Cerney will,
1583 Thomas Ekott will,
1629 Robert Eacott will,
1717 Berkeley Eycott will,
1730 Thomas Eycott will,
1732 Thomas Eycott will, and other persons.

The Eycotts of Woodmancote

It is not known when the Eycotts came to live at the hamlet of Woodmancote which is on top of the hill that drops away to the old Eycot manor. The early references to the family locates them in respect to the churches at Bagendon, North Cerney and Rendcomb. Woodmancote is located at the place where the three parishes meet. This included an ancient plot of land deliberately claimed by no one, a form of no mans land at the point where the parishes met. Eycotts had strong connections with Bagendon and North Cerney churches but not so much with Rendcomb across the river.

The feudal lordship of the land at Domesday 1086 indicated that Hugo L'Anse (Hugh Donkey) held BEDWEDENE(Bagendon) and Gilbert (son of Turold) sub held it from him. They rebelled against the king and the land was taken from them and given to the de Chandos'. In 1283 Richard de BATHENDEN(Bagendon) held it from Robert de Chandos. In 1346 (Testa de Neville) Roger de Chandos held the land. There was a double ownership, perhaps father and son. The division of ownership separated Bagendon and Moorwood manors. LLanthony II shows that in an earlier time the parish had been divided in two. King John's charter, July 30,1199 refers to Robert making a gift of wood from Moorwood and Roger the Younger joining in the gift of wood to the mill. In 1383 Sir John Chandos was the lord(a baron).The De Bagendon were the knights. By 1543 the lordship was taken over by the Marquis of Bath, Sir Thomas Thynne.(said as thin).

Woodmancote in the middle ages had its own chapel. The church was located in chapel field. At an unknown time it was abandoned. The wheel cross from it is located on the vestry of Bagendon church and a part of the North Cerney churchyard cross is made from a fragment of the chapel.

The Moor was not the only manor house at Woodmancote. The Moor belonged to Bagendon parish. The second manor went with North Cerney parish. It was dated to the 16th C. The hamlet of Woodmancote was recorded in the 13th C. There were 7 taxpayers in 1327. In 1710 there were 13 houses. The Woodmancote manor house was bought by Thomas Taylor in 1566 and was claimed by his descendants and by the Stafford family. Lady Mary Stafford was named lady of the village in 1608. Later the Pooles and Guises lay claim to the lordship. A third part of Woodmancote, also called the Manor of Woodmancote, went to the De la Mare family and subsequently went to Rendcomb at the time of the Tames ownership.

Thus when references occur about the Eycotts, it is uncertain just where at Woodmancote they lived, other than at the Moor. In Rees' book he reports Eycotts living there until at least 1776. (Francis Ashmead lived with an Eycott at the Moor until her death that year). By 1832 the Haines lived at

Moorwood.

There is an earlier record of John Eycott of the Moor being married to Alse who died in 1631.

The following is an account of some land transactions which show what became of the land held by some Eycotts who were at the time thought to be Roman Catholics.

In 1680 Thomas Eycott gave his lands to Richard. He gave land between Cross Piece and Moorcomb Piece which was bounded on three sides by land owned by the Stevens. In 1708 Thomas secured a mortgage for 700£. At the same time Berkeley Eycott held other property at Bagendon. In 1723 John Eycott gave up his rights to Thomas, his brother. In 1747 Robert Saunders bought the land from Thomas Eycott at the time he, Robert, married Thomas' daughter Elizabeth Eycott. In 1753 Elizabeth Eycott gave to her daughter Elizabeth Saunders her share of the estate. The marriage to Saunders took place at Tyndale but she later lived at Little Farringdon Berks. The land next passed to Wm. Bolt in 1777 and back to Robert Saunders of Little Farringdon in 1807. In 1812 Wm. Croome purchased parcel #809 and in 1832 he is listed as owning a farm house.

At the time of the registration of papists in 1717 this record exists:

Woodmancote QRNC 1 (22) -John Eycott held two houses and several arable parcels of land, meadow and pasture ground with appurtenances in Chedworth, also 1 yard lands of common pasture of diverse sorts and cattle. He held two closes in Woodmancote, one called Dorothy's Leaze and one Linkham's Piece. He was required to pay his sisters Robertta and Martha 3£ each for these until they are married and subject to a mortgage made by Thomas his late father with Jonathan White for a principal of 100£. This was signed by John.

[QRNC (21)] Another registration by a Thomas Eycott of Woodmancote who held four yardlands of arable meadow and pasture as well as a house. His sisters Robertta and Martha held a cottage which was apparently rented to a William Sherrall. There was a mortgage on the farm for 700£. This Thomas or another of the same name was constable of Bagendon in 1715. That means he was appointed to keep the peace in the community and was really the only local government official.

It would appear from this that Thomas in 1680 left his land to his son Richard who passed it on to his son Thomas. This man had two sons John and Thomas and two daughters. John may have lived at Chedworth and arranged to place his share at Woodmancote in his brothers hands, 1723. Thomas was to have no sons but did have a daughter Elizabeth, named after her mother. She married Robert Saunders in 1747 and the Eycott name left the property. Other Eycotts may have lived at Bagendon for a few more years but by 1778 there were no more Eycotts on the church rolls renting seats.

The will of Thomas 1715 says that he had two sons Thomas (the eldest) and John. John was the executor of the will and Robert Moran of Fairford was the trustee. Thomas had three daughters, Rebecca, Elizabeth and Martha. Thomas's wife was Mary. John was given a house and grounds in Chedworth and was also given Dorothy's Leaze and Linkham's piece. Thomas (the eldest) in his will of 1740 says he was a Catholic, a batchelor and he gave his estate to his nephew William Eycott of Cirencester. Thomas also gave his sisters Rebecca and Martha a freehold estate at Woodmancote with a cottage there until they were married.

William Eycott of Cirencester might have been the son of John Eycott of Cirencestor a Catholic Goldsmith with an estate at Bagendon. His mother was Mary, his wife Elizabeth and sons Richard and John who had a freehold estate at Chedworth.

In 1730 the will of Thomas, made and read that year, listed his son Thomas as the executor. He had three daughters Dorothy, Rachelle and Hester. This Thomas also lived at Bagendon and may have been the one listed as constable in 1715. The father of this man might have been a Richard (if he was in his 80's(84)) or it may have been Berkeley (if he was 35) or it may have been another person.

John Eycott of Cirencester in his will of 1751, whose wife is Elizabeth, leaves his estates in Bagendon to his son John who is executor and gives his son Richard 250 £ when he reaches age 21 and the same to his son Thomas when he came of age also. These boys would also gain estates in Bagendon. Henry Timbrell and Richard Worstlar were witnesses.

Appendix F
Notes on a Visit to North Cerney, Bagendon and Area, 1984

My family and I, John Eacott, visited several locations associated with the Eacott-Eycott name during July and Aug.1984.

At Rendcomb we visited the church but found no legible tombstones. Rendcomb manor is now a college and the hamlet shares the church with them. The west side of the property drops off steeply to the Churn river directly above the manor site of Eycott. There is a good view over the slopes of Eycott manor. Below the College and along the west side of the Churn river is a parcel of a few acres of land which belongs to Carron Mann, a Bristol jeweller. They live in the renovated 16th century Lodge farm or Rendcomb Lodge as it is now called. They pointed out some depressions in the land which may outline the foundations of some ancient buildings. Just back of the house is a small stream lined with trees. Its banks have been modified by the construction of a fish pond 150 years ago. In the past this land was likely quite low and likely prone to flooding. From this point the lands of Eycott manor can be seen rising toward a hill ridge to the west.

The property known as Eycothouse was built in the 1930's and the son of the present owner said the site had been an old rabbit warren and there were still some old ruins located there.

At North Cerney we visited a village fete (fayte) and met a number of local persons. At another time we attended evening service at the church. People there knew of the Eacott-Eycott name but no one had ever met a living person called by those names. A stained glass window in North Cerney church was labeled with the name BICOTE and was elsewhere identified by the church records as an error that should read Eicote. There were no stones we could read in the churchyard. There were some old chests and lecterns in the church dating to the 1600's and some references attribute them to the gift of the Eycotts. The church is west of the river, across from the village. There is no resident minister but Miss Peggy West a lay reader is quite active in the affairs of the church.

Local people know the name as AY COTT or A COTT or "Ache-it" in their pronunciation.

At Bagendon, the church was nestled at the bottom of a slope. There are few buildings at Bagendon and it appears very little has changed there for a very long time. Tombstones were not readable here either. The road to North Cerney and the two roads to Woodmancote wound over a hill and along a ridge of land.

Woodmancote hamlet sits on a high spot where the roads from Bagendon and North Cerney converge. The Moor, the old manor identified with the Eacotts, was on the south side of Woodmancote perched near the head of a ravine or sharp little valley which opened out to the south. The yard of the place was dominated by a huge Lebanese cedar planted four or five hundred years ago according to the owner, Major E.R.W Robinson. He and his sons operate a farm of several hundred acres(sheep and grain). The Major was interested in local history and said the Saxon word for island, EYOT was pronounced ATE. He also said there were remains of a minor Roman farm and an iron age fort located on his lands over toward the Eycot manor lands.

Major Robinson also told us that excavations would be taking place at this site in September 1984 by Steven Trow, 12 Lloyd Square, London. The site is known as the ditches. The Robinsons had no knowledge of the Eycotts but it is quite possible the cedar was planted by an Eycot.

The entire area was very hilly with houses nestled in the small valleys mostly in little villages. The hills had a golden color from the ripe grain. The homes were built of stone of the same color. A very pretty area.

Further south we visited Purton, in Wiltshire and learned that the church congregation had sponsored missionaries to Canada in the early 1700's. The first S.P.G. Missionary went out in 1702 on the Centurion. A book on church history written in 1927 said this of the year 1837. " In the years following the Napoleonic Wars much poverty and consequent misery was obtained. It is said that no less than 500,000 persons died from starvation. Purton felt its share of bad times and it was thought well to encourage emigration to Canada. A deed dated 22 May 1837 contained an agreement between church wardens and overseers in Purton and a Mr. Robert Carter of 11 Leadenhall St.,London."

Twenty one persons from Purton were sponsored to Canada to land at Montreal. They and their luggage were to be landed free of charge and food allowances were given as well as medicine and wine. Such things as wooden bowls, platters, hook pots, etc. were specified for each person over 14 and a special supply list for each person under 14 was given. All taxes were met and the fare was seven pounds five shillings for an adult. Children under 14 were half fare. A second lot of persons were sent out in 1844. Some of the names of those sent were Sealy, Maule, Cutts, Tuff, Turner, Baker. One wonders if Charles Eacott, the first known Eacott in Canada (1830) may have experienced these problems and set out from Purton just before this group of immigrants sending word back of the conditions abroad.

Once again I visited the area in 2006. Both North Cerney and Bagendon churches showed more care and attention than they had in 1984. The communities looked almost exactly the same. Only the nearby Cirencester road bypass had altered the scenery. We had the opportunity to visit with the son of major Robinson as the major died the year after our first visit. A minister now serves the two churches.

Appendix G
The Earliest Known Eacotts

From 1100 to 1500

The earliest known user of the name Eycote was Simon de Eycote who on October 17th 1316 was made master of the Hospital of St. Giles, at Kepier, near Durham. The See of Durham being vacant the king, acting as the Bishop, displaced Hugh de Montalto and made Simon de Eycote master in his stead. The mandate of this appointment was made to the brethren and sisters of the hospital although there never seemed to be any sisters attached to the place. Hospital had a different meaning in those days. It was essentially a place for the poor, an almshouse and for pilgrims going to Durham Cathedral and resembled a monastary as it was self contained. There were 13 brothers and a master. Six of them were chaplains. The chaplains each got 2 new boots each year the others got 1 pair of shoes with thongs. The accommodations were not very good but the queen had stayed there a few years before Simon had his appointment. That was not long after Robert the Bruce from Scotland had trashed the place. The queen left about £20 to pay for her nights lodging and help the funding for the place. These were nervous times to get such an appointment as in the months before he took over, their lands had been raided by Scots who claimed the area as part of Scotland. At any time Simon was apt to be attacked. The hospital was founded and funded by Bishop Flambard in 1112. During the time Simon was the Master the area was involved in serious wars with Scotland. It held substantial lands.The hospital was closed in 1546 when Henry VIII dissolved the monastaries. The master was exempted from some church duties but Simon would have been an experienced church official, likely a priest. Simon ruled over the hospital for 4 years at which time the appointment was withdrawn and Montalto was reinstated. At the same time Montalto gave Simon £10 worth of land in Amerston, Harworth and elsewhere. Whether Montalto rebought his position or simply paid off de Eycote as compensation is not known. Simon was likely a member of some religious order and could readily be moved about England. He most certainly was born in the 1200's likely about 1275 but it is not known if he is of the same Eycote as all later ones. Much later Eacotts are again associated with the Durham area but Simon was the only very early Eacott not to be in the Cirencester area for hundreds of years. It is unusual that the first should be so removed from the rest but as he had a position with some status, he may have been the local boy who got educated and left home. [VCH, County of Durham vol 2, 1907 pp 111-14]

It can only be guessed at as to whether or not the manor of Eycot had any residents who actually assumed the name. When the use of surnames came into vogue in the 1200's, it would be likely that one would go by the name " de Eycote - of Eycot". It can not be established either that ownership rather than tenancy indicated a name choice. However, the manor seems to have had strong church connections from Saxon times. It is most likely the de Eycots were folks who at Domesday were one or more of the 2 villagers, 4 small holders or 2 slaves. Alternatively it could have been Ordric and or Alric who sub let from the church. Alric however controlled other lands, some presumably more desirable. In the 1300's the Eycots seemed to have some modest rank in the order of things so it is likely they would have come from the ranks of the villagers a century or so earlier.

These villagers were likely descendants of long settled families with genetic ties to Saxons, Romano- British, and Celtic ancestors.

At the time of Domesday there were 367 settlements in Gloucester. Eyot or Eycott, or Eycote or Aicote was one. There were about 8,000 people in Gloucester. In the Churn valley the population was relatively high at 10 per square mile.

In 1327 the following persons were listed for Eycote as being on the subsidy roll: John Acton, Richard Walker, Richard Geffrey, Richard Cave, Simon Dauwe, Agnet Drois, Richard Page, Richard Dygon. There were no Eycotts. The Subsidy Roll of 1327 was a poll tax to raise money from people who might have some. There were 8 at Eycott. Thus only reasonably well off adult males, yeomen, clothiers, craftsmen, merchants and others of some wealth would be on the roles. The Eycott name occurs only in North Cerney and Cirencester in that year. No variants on the name existed. The earliest couple of references to persons are de Eycote meaning they took their origin from Eycott but by this time did not dwell there. At the time the use of surnames was still evolving and was only a hundred or so years in use which means this is about as far back as one can trace an individual bearing an Eacott name.

The subsidy role use of surnames is about the earliest possible document to do this. The surnames helped the tax collectors identify who to tax. John of Eycott would not have lived at Eycott because this did not distinguish him from others living at Eycott. The name tells where he came from, not where he lived. If a person were mobile or took on a trade, he might change his name again. Surnames were not a guarantee of consistency in those days as they were an individuals identifying term not necessarily a family name. However, by the early 1300's the person himself, his father or grandfather had been identified as having come from Eycott.

John of Eycote, a person who considered himself connected somehow to the manor of Eycott, although he didn't live there and possibly never did, enters history. He had family at North Cerney where he farmed likely raising sheep but John was also a man of the town of Cirencester. Perhaps he was a guild man, a weaver or more likely he was a wool merchant. He was not happy with things. John was likely born in the last years of the 1200's or the early 1300's, owned his own land and had business dealings in Cirencester. For the times he was middle class.

He becomes known to us in 1342. Johannem de Eycote was a signer of a petition to King Edward III on 15 March 1342 given at parliament at Westminster. This information comes from documents of the Abbey at Cirencester known as the Cartulary of Cirencester. The records of the Abbey began in 1131 and ended in 1539 and were in Latin or French.

In 1169 King Richard gave the Abbey considerable land holdings. In the 1200's the Abbey made deals with others holding land in the vicinity to come before the Cirencester court for a fee. Both the king and the church held courts.

During the 1300's a bitter dispute broke out between the townsmen and the church officials which eventually involved the king. The town was a prosperous wool trading center and the abbot got involved with taxing the wool trade and claimed the right of tallege over his tenants whenever the king himself levied a tallege. In 1214 the barons compelled king John to recognize that he could not take tallege in Cirencester because it was the right of the church to do so. By 1312 the king was again taking tallege and so was the church. So double taxes were collected. The townsmen got the king to charge the abbot with wrongly collecting the tallege. The matter was resolved after discussion in Parliament and the king recognized the churches claim on the land.

The dispute between the townspeople and the church continued. The townsmen wanted to have a measure of self rule and argued that the church had never legally been entitled to own the town. In 1342 resentment broke out and a group of men drew up a petition to take to the king. At first they appealed to his own self interest by suggesting that past and present abbots had wrongfully taken revenues belonging to the king. They also accused the abbot of moral turpitude and malversation of endowment intended for the poor.

The dispute with the Abbot of St. Marys with the prosperous wool men of Cirencester who wanted a guild was a standoff because the abbot did not need to borrow funds from them as did the king. So the merchants were not able to force him to grant a charter giving them a mayor and council. This close knit group of weavers, the Cirencester Weavers Guild, existed for centuries. They were a wealthy group and had various land holdings. The Weavers obtained Bagendon for a brief time but turned the church holding over to the control of the church at Cirencester. Johannem de Eycote was probably one of the guild.[51]

In a revision these charges were dropped and 42 townsmen including Johannem de Eycote were called before the king and council. The main purpose of their complaint was to make the point that the abbot had suppressed the borough and had illegally enclosed the sixty acre pasture called the Crundles which had been the common pasture of the borough. They said the abbot had suppressed their Reeves court, hounded his critics and had by means of trickery obtained and destroyed a charter given them by Henry I which made them a free town.

Robert Barbast, accompanied by 42 others including John Eacott, appeared before the king with their petition. In April the abbot was summoned to appear and make answer to some of the grievances which were listed in the summons. There was considerable evasiveness on the part of the abbot who did not produce all of the required documents. The evidence today seems to indicate the abbot and the abbey did not have a good claim to owning Cirencester. However at the time the wealthy abbot was able to make a deal with the king. The townsmen remained unhappy for generations and when Henry VIII dissolved the Abbey, the destruction was particularly thorough.[52]

Called before the king at Westminster by the Sherrif of Gloucester 15 March 1342 were, among others, Robert Barbast, John of Weston, John Estoft, John Canynges, Willelmum Erchebaud, Thomas Payn, John of Yeuele, John Brymesgraue, Willeimum Rothewelle, Robert of Cerne, Reginald the Harpour, Peter of Derham, Lucam le Chapman, John the Smyth, Robert Langford, John of Cricklade, William Somer, Nicholas the Coyffestere, William Edmond, Peter of Stratton, Walter Caumberlayn, John of Otynton, Richard of Scarnyngge, John the Peyntour, Thomas the Valk, Reginald the Goldsmith, John of Eycote, Richard the Deghere, John Waleys, John the Deghere, John Lucas, Robert of Auebury, Thomas the

[51] *Reference*   *"Cirencester Weavers Company" - W.S. Harmer*
"Gu ise Diary" - Barker
"Hi story of Gloucester" - Bigland
"Hi story of Weavers Company of Cirencester" - St.
Clair Baddeley

[52] *Vol I Cartulary of Cirencester by C.D. Ross, Oxford University Press 1964, items before and after # 125.*

Gussh, William Cotyler, Thomas the Coteler, Richard of Stonehouse, and several others. The list shows where these residents hailed from or what they did as well as persons who did not use "the" or "of ".

From this we learn that Johannem de Eycote was a townsman of Cirencester and that he must have been a fairly prominent person in the community in order to be in a position to make a petition. At this time there were only about 500 people living in Cirencester. So it was actually only a small village, one in which the great issue of the day was the appearance of the plague that would depopulate it and lead to the abandonment about this time of the manor of Eycote. The petitioners were likely most of the influential adult males of the area around Cirencester.

In 1381 a Poll Tax return for Cirencester listed 574 adults. 62 surnames are not readable. No Eycote is listed although one name Richard Yaneworth is bracketed as Enekot. Apart from labourers(36), there were 19 brewers, 10 merchants, 9 cobblers, 11 tailors, 5 weavers, 5 smiths, 4 bakers, 4 fishermen, 3 butchers, 2 goldsmiths, 2 tilers, 2 masons, 2 skinners, 1 clerk,, 1 carpenter, 1 draper, 1 harper, 1 bagger, 1 glover, 1 inn keeper, 1 spicer, 1 mercer, 1 saddler, 1 wool monger, 1 draper, 1 tanner. (about 90 listed occupations) A number of the surnames are directly linked to the occupation. Wives, domestic servants (55) were also tax listed. The occupations say a lot about the nature of the town at that time. Presumably the Eycotes were now living at North Cerney and Bagendon and they frequented the town for their beverages, shoes, fine clothes and hired the skills of others where needed.

The third Eycote was Robert who owned a messuage (or estate) according to a deed from 22 May 1383, the location of which is not certain as he was simply noted as holding land adjacent to another property. He was however a person who had escaped the plague.

A little later, still very much in feudal times, 1394, we learn of another John Eycote. He appears on a duty list for persons who had to serve wardstaff, an obscure custom in which persons, knights of the lord, were appointed to stand guard duty. This list of names, their village and place of duty is listed.[53]

---

[53] *Cartulary of Cirencester item # 741] under a "View of Wardstaff in the Seven Hundreds of Cirencester 1394".*

"visus baculi vocatus wardstaff apud Cirencestr' tentus
die sancti Michealis anno regni regis Ricardi secundi KVIII"

(examples)

Daglynworth	Johannes	Sleye (Peryscroys)
Stratton	Johannes	Shepherd (Crowethorne)
Bagynden'	Johannes	Eycot (Berefordebrugge)
Wyggewolde	Henricus	Ameneye (Wyggewolde)

Hundredum de Respigate

Northserneye	Johannes	Muleward (apud TresCruces)

This means that John Eycote of Bagendon had to stand guard duty at Bear ford bridge (Perrot's Brook). It shows how names got rearranged - Bearridge or Bearford became Perrot. This John was a yeoman, a freeman with a land useage held under his lord. The land would have been at Bagendon and thus he may have dwelled at Woodmancote. Was he the son or grandson of Johannem of 50 years before who has survived the plague? Then another couple of decades later do we learn that he dies and leaves his land to his son Thomas?

In 1421-37 [54] is a list of suitors in land transactions. Listed under Bagendon for this time " To Thomas Eycot for the term of his life the house and land of Johannic Eycot lately of Hunfridi atte Mere of Boyndene - presented in writing." This meant that John left his property to Thomas. John owned his property with the permission of his lord Humphry More of Boyndene. This may have been the same John Eycote who had to stand guard duty 20/30 years before. [55]

Bagyndene
" Thomas Eycote ad terminum vite sue pro terra et tenemento
Johannis Eycote nuper Hunfridi Atte More in Bagyndene per
scriptum. "

From a view of frankpledge in the seven hundreds of Cirencester (probably early 1400's).The medieval system of keeping the peace was

---

[54] *Cartulary of Cirencester # 740*

[55] *item # 740 pg 628*

known as frankpledge under which all males over 12 were allotted to groups of about 10 known as tithings who were collectively responsible for the good behavior of one another. Each such group had a chief, the 'tithing-man', and periodically the tithing-men were summoned to the *court leet* of whichever feudal lord held 'View of Frankpledge' for his tenants.

In this instance there is a memorandum that the hundred of Respigateis owed payment twice a year from the place beside the wood of Eycote called Respigate. (Rapsgate)

> *" Hundredum de Respigate"*
> *Memorandum quod visus hundredi de Respegate debet teneri bis*
> *per annum in quodam loco juxta boscum de Eycote vacato*
> *Respegate, videlicet, ad terminum sancti Martini et ad*
> *terminum de Hock', per summonicionem ballivorum abbatis de*
> *Cirencester per eosdem ballivos. Ed ad eundem visum venient*
> *omnes decennarii villarum subscriptarum bis per annum cum*
> *eorum decenis ad presentanda omnia que ad visum pertinent,*
> *videlicet"*

The next reference to an Eycote is to be found in the North Cerney church window placed by John Bicote (Eycote) in 1465. He was the assistant minister (curate) of the church and may have been the son of Thomas who acquired land from John (his father ?). In those days glass was very expensive and these Eycotts were pretty well off. Was it the money from the wool trade? Was this a son of the Thomas we met above?

We also connect Eycots to Cirencester, Bagendon, and North Cerney at this time.

The establishment of the Eycott name by farmers and possibly wool merchants at Bagendon and North Cerney from 1300 to 1500 gives Eycott/ Eacott a family name that is very rare to trace back this far. These were yeomen farmers, free men. They held no titles and there is no record of any heraldry or coat of arms at the College of Arms in London relating to the Eycotts. This is the information we have before 1500.

The Years 1500 to 1600

1316   Simon de Eycote   Master of St Giles, Kepier Hospital near Durham

1342   Johannem de Eycote   Cirencester - petition

1383   Robert Eycote   A landowner, an estate, location not specific

1394   Johannem Eycote   Bagendon - bridge duty

1416   John Eycott   Rendcomb - witness grant

1430? Johannem Eycote   Bagendon - land to Thomas

1430? Thomas Eycote   Bagendon - inherits farm ?

1465   John Eycote   North Cerney - minister

There is now a gap in the records picking up again with..........

1525   Wyllyam Eycott   Bagenden - witness to a will

1569   Ales Eycot   North Cerney -baptized daughter of John (?)

Start of church records

1572-83 John Eycot   North Cerney - 7 girls born

1575   Robert Eycot   North Cerney - girl, Ellen

1578   Thomas Ekot   Bagendon - girl Alse(Alice)

1581   Richard Eycott   North Cerney - his will

1583   Thomas Ekott   Bagendon -his will

1588   Mary Ecott   Elkstone - her will

1589   Robert Eycott   Rendcomb -wife Christian

1589   Thomas Eycott   North Cerney - son John

1590   William Eycott   North Cerney - son Richard

1594   Thomas Eycott   Brimpsfield -will

1599   Edward Ecott   Winstone wife Margery Eacoot

Edward Ecott died in 1612 and his wife Margerie died in 1630 she left a will giving her property to son William Eacoot and her daughter Mary.

1575 or before, Henry Eacot , who married Sarah of Lydiard Millicent was born, had 3 sons

1577 John Ackett was married to Jane Parnell at Purton Wilts.

Several of the persons named above for 1580 - 90 have more children than are indicated above.

Eacotts from 1600 - 1800

There are numerous records of the Eycotts - Eacotts from 1600 onward. However in 1608 in his

" Men and Armour " Smith who took a record of all men in Gloucestershire age 20 to 60 fit for military service recorded no Eycotts in Rendcomb, North Cerney, Bagendon or Woodmancote. Yet less than twenty years earlier there were several grown Eycott men. There is listed one Thomas Coots as age about 40, a fairly short man who was suitable to be a cavalier. At this time Lady Mary Stafford was the Lady of Woodmancote and Lady Eleanor Berkeley was the Lady at Rendcomb. In the absence of any Eacotts we must assume the name Coots was in error. Of course there may be other reasons they were not listed such as the holding of beliefs that would not make them suitable for military duty for the crown.

At this approximate time, 1603, Thomas Ecott baptized two daughters at North Cerneyand a Thomas was buried there in 1604. There were no children living with that name at that time.

William Eacoote was baptized at Winstone in 1607, son of Edward and Margerie. Thomas Ecott was born in 1607 as was Joseph Eycot. In 1610 John Eycott married and John Ecott died. None of these people appeared in Smith's book. Why?

From 1619 we have the Rendcomb will of Joan (Jane) Ecott whose brothers were William, Thomas and Richard Eacott whose son was Thomas. Her sisters were Susan Chamberlain and Margaret Broade and her mother-in-law was Susan Jefferies. Joan directed her body to be buried in Rendcomb churchyard.

1623 John Eicot was churchwarden at Bagendon.

1630 John Eacott was born to Richard, a rough mason, at North Cerney. At this time name interchanges were quite common. Parish and Bishops registers were even at variance with the same person and event. Alse and John Eycot lived at the Moor in the 1630's.

From 1430 until the late 1700s there were 141 Eycot and variations recorded at North Cerney, 15 at Rendcomb, 56 at Bagendon. From after 1683 there were 46 Eycots (only Eycots) at Cirencester. Records went back in most places to just before 1600.

The Eycots did not leave the Churn valley until after 1600. Their first regular appearance outside the upper valley was at Warminster in 1665, Cirencester in 1683, then South Cerney 1696 and Cromhall 1697 although the Rev. Nathaniel Eycott was preaching in Thuxton, Mitford Hundred, Norfolk in 1655-7 for the sum of 22 £ per year. He may have been brother of Joseph born 1607. In early 1700's they spread more into Wiltshire and a few other areas such as London. The Eacott name as such became common at Cromhall and the parishes which adjoin it to the south and around Warminster.

The reasons for the movement out of the Churn valley and the locations where they appear is difficult to determine. However, when examined, there are lordships connected to the places where Eacotts went, the Berkeley family around Cromhall and the Thynne family at Warminster. In addition other names which are associated with Bagendon and North Cerney such as Guise show up in the same places.

Family connections of note from this group include William Ecott of Cromhall who married Sarah Guy, daughter of Philip Guy of Gloucester. He was a descendant of John Guy the colonizer of Newfoundland. From his will of 1625 we find that this Governor of Newfoundland and former mayor of Bristol (1618 - 19) had a farm at Gauntes Earthcott in Almondsbury Parish, a tenement in Bristol, land known as Seaforest in Newfoundland and 1/16 part of the prisage wines of Bristol.

William and Sarah had a son William who married Mary Drew in 1767. Their son William born 1776 reportedly went to the West Indies.

All told the Eacott records for Cromhall 1697-1849 include 90 persons, with another dozen at Wickwar and Charfield. At Alveston there were 47.

In Wiltshire the Eacotts (by that version) appear in Warminster 1665 and Purton in 1703. At Warminster it is possible to suggest a connection with nearby Longleat whose owners had a connection with Woodmancote. The Warminster line continues for many years and 54 are recorded over 150 years. The Purton connection may relate to persons living at Wooton Bassett and Swindon at total of 36 persons.

Just north of Warminster at Wesport, Thomas Ecut left his will in 1627 naming his mother Elizabeth and a wife Rachel who was with child.

Warminster
The first record for Warminster shows John Eacot and Edward Eacot as paying tithes as householders in 1665. (History of Warminster by J.J. Daniel 1879 pg 116). There is no birth record for any Edward in the possible life span of this person with an Eacott type name. These were two adult males who must have been born 25 to 50 years earlier 1615 to 1640. Warminster in 1665 was a prosperous wool town and a cloth making centre. It was also known for malting and particularly for its market. There were 350 homes and about 1,800 people in the town. These two Eacot families would have been well known in such a small community. What they did for a living we do not know but they owned property, their homes.

A will of 1684 for William Ecut of Eysey Manor (Kempsford-Castle Eaton area), labourer, whose wife was deceased left his goods to sons William and Nicholas and daughters Ann, Margaret, Elizabeth.

In Berkshire at Tilehurst (1742-1812) a line of Ecket names occur. The same occurs derived from Eycott at Ampney Crucis (1709-49). At Yattendon Berks. Eacotts are listed (1745-48) and later at Brightwalton (1775-1824).

Eycotts and Eacott occur in London from 1710 in small numbers. There are a number of marriages occurring in different places without any additional entries.

Tetbury
1719 Jane Wells charged Richard Eycott with defamation.
1728 Jane Eycott and Marg Mitchell charged with adultery.
1760 William Eacott of Charleton in Tetbury parish left his will to his son Richard Eacott and his daughter Elizabeth wife of Jonathan Avery.

Who was this man of means?
Lincoln's Inn was one of the 4 courts of law to which barristers belonged. John Eycott was a lawyer and he dwelled in the accommodations provided for them in London.
1751 April 19 – John Eycott of Lincoln's Inn, Middlesex,

Gentleman

From North Devon Chichester family papers

1821 May 10 – John Eycott of Lincoln's Inn, Middlesex, Gentleman
From Lowndes Family of Chesham, Buckinghamshire a limited administration granted to Willoughby Rockham.

(Eycott was a man of means. Why he is in these papers is not known although the last item appears to be giving power of attorney to care for him.) He must have lived a good long life close to 90 years of age.

At Cromhall in 1776 William Ecutt, who had remarried, left his son John, eldest, the messuage and tenement and also left other possessions to other sons William, Robert and Philip. He owned 2 other cottages.

Stonehouse

At Stonehouse during the period from about 1770 to 1840 the father and perhaps grandfather, Henry Eycott and son, Frederick Eycott were active clothiers owning and operating mills. The Manor of Frocester in 1803 was put on sale by George, Earl of Warwick. Leonard Parkinson bought the manor and much of the land. Henry Eycott of Stonehouse purchased another part but sold it to Parkinson in 1806. The Stonehouse Upper Mill was owned by Messers Eycott by 1776 who worked the mill which has 3 stocks and a corn mill. During this time woolen broadcloth was being produced throughout this area and a special skill in coloring the cloth was employed. Mills were generally quite profitable. Bond's Mill the lowest in the parish was built in 1714 and in 1784 the Eycott's had 4 pairs of fulling stock at the mill.. Henry leased the mill to William Wood in 1832. His son Frederick leased it to William Wise in 1840 after a power loom had been built in 1837. Another estate at Nostend was owned by Henry from 1813 to 1830. Nostend was mostly Clutterbuck land. Frederick had 139 acres at Nostend in 1839. Is this the same Henry who led the Gloucester Militia in the early 1800's? Clearly they were a prosperous and influential family at that time. (Victoria History of Gloucester vol 10)

Henry Eycott and Family of Stonehouse (near Stroud)

1800 – boundary between Stonehouse and Eastington. Henry Eycott of Bond's Mill proposed to cover ditch between Stroud Old River and Stanley Brook erecting merestones on the course of the ditch.

1800 – Joseph King stole loom from Henry Eycott, clothier

1804 – legal file of Mrs Anne Clutterbuck Eycott, Stonehouse and William Fryer of Eastington

1817 – Wool was stolen from Samuel Clutterbuck and Henry Eycott, owners. Joseph Eycott was informer (alias Lewis)

1823 – marriage contract between Catherine Eycott of Bond's Mill, Stonehouse, spinster and William John Wood of Stroud.

1831 – John Fletcher stole conies from Frederick Eycott and was fined.

There are also a few other personal notes available apart from statistics of births, deaths and marriages.

In 1632 Richard Ecot of Bagendon, a roughmason died. In 1710, April 19, John Eacutt was a juryman at Southam Manor, Court leet. The business was to order some ditches cleaned and repaired. In 1715 Thomas Eycott was appointed constable of Bagendon. This is interesting in that the Eycotts then living at Woodmancote were considered Papists (Catholics) and could not hold such an office at the time. They were registered as persons whose loyalty could be in question. In 1734 rioters destroyed the toll booths of Cairncross House (near Stroud) and F. Eycott of Oakfields was hired to rebuild the gates. This could be the father or grandfather of the Eycotts of Stonehouse.

1655-7 Nathaniel Eycott listed on survey for trustees of Maintenance for Preaching Ministers

He received £ 22 a year from his patron Robert Long Esq. At Thuxton Rectory, Mitford Hundred, Norfolk. This was an effort in Cromwell's time to address inequities in preachers incomes largely by fining the wealthy bishops.

1736 – James Ecott, the younger, labourer, gets a deed for property at Rodbourne Cheney.

1768 – James Eycott of Haydon Wick, his will, provides for care of his property at Rodbourne Cheney. Bills for thatching and repairing Eycott property from 1778 to 1783. His bequest was rolled into a trust later to create the Wayte Educational Charity.

In 1735 John Eccutt; Thomas Goodall, baker; Phillip Moor all of Uphaven were charged with stealing a furnace belonging to Roger Jarvis and were tried in Wiltshire.

In 1736 William Ecott served on a jury at Westbury Wilts.

Martha Eacott (alias Bryant) was sentenced in March 1759 to 7 years banishment to America. She was taken from jail in Wiltshire directly to the boat where she was shipped out by shipping contractors. She would have to work off her transport as a semi slave. The crime is not known but theft would get such a sentence.

1778 Thomas Eacott of Chippenham, plumber and Glazier died. His son was Thomas and daughters were Elizabeth and Susanna. His brother was John Eacott of Wotton Bassett who was also a plumber and glazier. Chippenham – Deed to Eacott 1784-1805

1792 John Eacott, Yeoman of Wotton Bassett dies. His wife Mary but no children. Nephews were John and James Smith and Neices Sarah, Ann and Mary Smith. (I also give and devise from after the decease of my wife the house and premises now occupied by Joseph Humphries situated in Wood Street aforesaid unto my niece Ann (sister of the said John Smith) and to her heirs....)

In 1797 Henry Eycott was appointed an officer in the city of Gloucester, Troop of Gentlemen and Yeomanry, a cavalry group organized to defend England against an invasion by Napoleon. He was not listed in an 1803 reorganization.

In 1810 William Eacott was a weaver for 2 years with J&T Clark of Trowbridge Wilts.

Most of the Eacotts were probably farmers like most of the population before industrialization.

The dispersal of the Eacotts was not very extensive. There are only very casual entries for all areas of England except Gloucestershire and Wiltshire. A few in Berkshire and a few later on in Surrey. All of the rest are a single marriage or a family with one or two baptisms. Many counties have no Eacotts or variant in the records. Most of the entries are after 1750 and particularly 1800. Only one or two are before 1700 and are marriages.

Of the dozens of parishes in Gloucester and Wiltshire, only 12 in Wiltshire and 25 in Gloucestershire record Eacotts. Most but not all parishes have been documented to 1600s or earlier. Only 27 parish records contain 5 or more entries.18 contain more than 10 and 8 contain more than 15.

These are the most important early sites and the number of names listed and the number of years documented people lived there.

Place	Number People	Time Years	From	To
Rendcomb	15	416	1416	1832
Bagendon	56	390	1394	1788
North Cerney	141	320	1430	1751
Winstone	13	60	1583	1634
Colesbourne	13	88	1664	1751
Cheltenham	7	85	1710	1795
Cirencester	46	110	1683	1795
Ampney Crucis	13	40	1709	1749
Cromhall	90	300	1697	1997+
Alveston	47	150	1767	1911
Purton	11	180	1703	1888
Wooton Bassett	12	40	1778	1772
Swindon	14	19	1779	1798
Warminster	54	215	1655	1880
London	12	150+	1710	1860+

Appendix H
PARISHES in GLOUCESTERSHIRE and WILTSHIRE
with Eycott, Eacott before 1800

1. North Cerney
2. Bagendon
3. Stratton
4. Cirencester
5. Rendcomb
6. Chedworth
7. Colesbourne
8. Elkstone
9. Side
10. Winstone
11. Brimsfield
12. Ampney Crucis
13. South Cerney
14. Cheltenham
15. Stonehouse
16. Stroud
17. Cherington
18. Purton
19. Highworth
20. Cromhall

21. Charfield	22. Wickwar
23. Alveston	24. Iron Acton
25. Chippenham	26. WootonBassett
27. Swindon	28. Baydon
29. Warminster	30. Westwood
31. Kings Stanley	32.Lydiard Tregoze
33. Withington	34. Gloucester
35. Minchinghampton	36.Sutton Veney

And these additional locations not defined by parish prior to or shortly after 1800.

London, Bisley Surrey, Tilehurst Berks, Yattendon Berks, Brightwalton Berks,Tetbury, Devises, Chobham, Long Newton, Trowbridge. Shortly after 1800 Westwood, Berkely, Preshute, Castle Eaton.

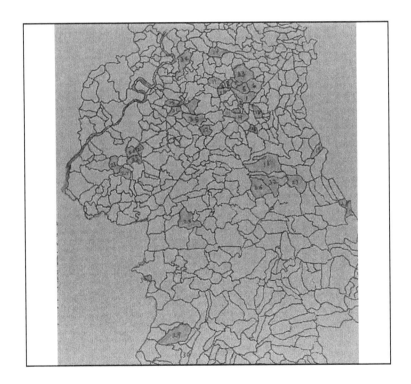

Appendix I
Who were the Ancient Eacotts?

Small bits of information exist to tell us who the ancient Eacotts were. From 1200 to 1600 they were small estate holders at Woodmancote, Bagendon, Rendcomb, North Cerney and adjacent parishes. During the 13 and 14 hundreds they must have suffered from the ravages of the plague, likely only one or two families survived this period. They were people of some social standing and influence. They interacted and married into families of some station in life.

In earlier times they took part in protests against the power of the local church and attended the Kings court to voice this concern. Only a person of the rank of small gentry or better could indulge in this. Again they had to serve legal duties as shown by the guard duty at Bagendon bridge.

In the 1400s one was assistant curate at North Cerney and had the money to install a stained glass window. Only a family of some means could have done this.

During the wars of the Roses the Eycotts were likely influenced on the side of the Yorkists since their rose badge appears in the North Cerney church.

Two local families of note, the Rich and the Vyner families, were neighbours of the Eacotts. A Rich was Henry VIII's minister of finance and a Vyner, whose mother was an Eacott, was connected to the Lord Mayor of London during Cromwell's time in 1600's. The small landowners along the Churn specialized in Cotswold sheep. The wool from these sheep was prized in Europe and the local farmers became quite well off from the sale of wool. The wills of Thomas and Richard in late 1500's were the wills of persons who were quite well off. The giving of brass pots and pewter indicated wealth. Pewter was owned only by those with money. Lesser folk used wood and only the very rich had silver.

The Vyner family became wealthy as goldsmiths and some of the Eycotts were known to be goldsmiths in Cirencester in the 1600s. There had to be wealth to even consider being a goldsmith. The craftsmen who belonged to this guild were very solid middle class artisans.

In the early 1600's Elizabeth I paid a visit to the Berkeleys who owned Rendcomb as well as Berkeley castle. Lady Berkeley used it as one of their summer homes. Such a visit would have been the opportunity for a state occasion and significant local people would have attended. Very likely the Eacotts would have been there. Some time later, Berkeley Eycott was a well known local person living at Cirencester and Bagendon. He was a warden of Bagendon Church. The full extent of the relation to the Eycott and the Berkeleys is not known.

At this same time in history, 1608, Smith undertook to record all men fit for military service. The absence of Eacotts is puzzling. Were they left off because of poor records, special permission, suspect loyalty or !!?

We also know that an Eycott in the 1600s was a rough mason who presumably built walls and foundations and perhaps buildings.

During this time the family may have had sympathy with the Roundheads and Cromwell during the civil war. Local first names were popular puritan names and the relationship to the Vyner family may have had some impact since the Vyner who was Lord Mayor of London was a contemporary of Cromwell.

By 1700 the Eycott line at Woodmancote were owners of a fine manor house. A huge Lebanon Cedar, one of the first planted in England, is located near the house. The first cedar was planted in 1638 and a few others were planted before 1730. This line was held in question as to their loyalty to the crown since they were registered as papists or papist sympathizers at the time of the Jacobite uprisings. Yet at the same time an Eycott was also appointed constable of Bagendon, a position of loyalty to the crown.

During the 1700s the movement of Eacotts away from the Churn valley seems to be related to taking up farming. The line which moved to South Cerney and thence to Purton may have been farmers. South Cerney was a quarry and weaving town and some may have been masons and weavers. The only known Eacott weaver was a William who worked for J&G Clarke in Trowbridge. Yet there were Eycotts who owned mills at Stonehouse near Stroud. There were stone masons and builders living near Stroud hired to repair gates after a riot. At least two of the Wiltshire Eacotts were plumbers and glaziers.

There appears to be some sort of relationship with Longleat and the Marquis of Bath. The Woodmancote manor passed under the feudal protection of the Marquis of Bath in later times. The woods at the manor were the last feudal rights given up by the Marquis whose family name was Thynne. The Woodmancote manor was remodeled by the same architect who worked on Longleat. In the 1700s Eacotts began living at Warminster which was adjacent to Longleat. It is not known how or why they came to be there.

At Cromhall and Alveston the Eacotts seem to have been predominantly farmers. In this area lands have become known with Eacott names. Eacott's Moor is located near Alveston.

At Stonehouse during the period from about 1770 to 1840 the father, and perhaps grandfather, Henry Eycott and son, Frederick Eycott were active clothiers owning and operating mills.

In Berkshire the line from Chaddleworth has provided a line of Eacotts who were often inclined to become active ministers and missionaries. This group has members whose work spanned the globe in the days of empire.

The London and Surrey groups have some records of having been shopkeepers and publicans.In more recent times in the 1800s the Eacotts included farmers, preachers, a farrier in Somerset, horse trainers, dentist , chemist , police officer, builders, printers.

The work of the Eacotts who live or have lived in this century include preachers, shopkeepers, an actor, builders, office workers, teachers, doctors, administrators.

If any traits are handed down it would seem there is high level of social skill and an ability to build things among the Eacotts.

If one looks at the arithmetic, any living Eacott would have in the year 1700 (about 8 generations back) 256 grandparents. Going back to 1500 or 15 generations there would be 32,800 grandparents and in 1375, 20 generations back there would have been 1 million grandparents. So, in theory every person in England in those days would now be an ancestor of an Eacott.

Prior to 1900 there had lived, from the earliest records to 1900, about 700 Eacotts, mostly in Gloucester and Wiltshire. Today there are about four family groups in Canada, four in USA, some in Australia, 1 in New Zealand and a couple of dozen in Britain. All told there are probably 300 Eacotts alive in the world today. About 50 in Australia, 40 in Canada, 24 in USA, 150 in Britain.

Appendix J
Index of Places associated with Eacotts

Place	first	last	Spelling Variants	Numbers Involved
Eycote	1066	1400	about 80 families	
Bagendon	1394	@ 1793	Eycott, Ekot	56 names
Rendcomb	1416	1832	Eycott, Ecot,Eacutts	15 most Ey, Ec
North Cerney	1430	@ 1751	Eycot,Ecott,Eacott	141 mostly Eycott
Winstone	1583	1643	Ecot,Ekot,Eacoote,Eacott	13
Elkstone	1588		Ecott	1
Awre	1606		Eycote	1
Woodmancote	1608	1725	Eycott,	3
Horsley	1663		Eycott	1
Colesbourne	1664	1751	Ecot, Eacott,Eycott	3 most Ecot
Stratton	1664		Eycott	2
Daglingworth	1680		Eycott	
Cirencester	1683	1795	Eycott	46
Brimsfield	1688		Eycott	1
South Cerney	1696	1746	Eycott,Eacutt,Ecut	6
Cromhall	1697	Still	Eacott.Ecott, Ecutt	90+
Charfield	1700	1780	Eacot, Ecott Ecutt	5
LongNewton	1701		Ecot	1
Warminster	1703	1880	Eacott	54
Purton	1703	1888	Eacott	11
Chedworth	1705	1730	Eycott	3
AmpneyCrucis	1709	1749	Ecket,Eycott,Eckut,Eycott	13
Cheltenham	1710	1795	Eacott, Eycott Ecoate	7
Shorncote	1710		Eycott	1
London	1710	1997	Eycott, Eacott	12
IronActon	1711	1781	Eycott Eccott Ecott	4
SherbourneHp	1712	1756	Eccut Eckett	3
Tetbury	1713	1807	Ecute Eycot Eacott	5
Baydon	1715		Eacott	2

Cleeve	1720		Eycott	1
Yanworth	1725		Eycott	1
WootonBas	1728	1772	Eacott	12
Devizes	1730		Ecott	1
Cherington	1734	1750	Eycott	6
Uphaven	1735		Eccutt	1
Stroud	1738	1795	Eacut Eycott	14
AmpneyStMar	1738	1787	Ecot Eccott	2
Highworth	1739	1771	Eacott	3
TilehurstBk	1742	1812	Ecket	18
YattendonBk	1745	1748	Eccot Eacott	3
Chipingham	1747	1779	Eacott	7
Kempford	1750	1754	Eycott	2
Alveston	1767	1911	Ecott Eacott	47
Bratton	1768	1820	Eacott	3
Brightwalton	1775	1824	Eacott	13
Wickwar	1777	1867	Ecot Eckut	5
Swindon	1779	1798	Eacott	14
Withington	1789		Eycott	1
Minchinghmp	1789		Eycott	1
Trowbridge	1792	1839	Eycott Eacott	8
Gloucester	1797	1832	Eycott	4
Stonehouse	1797	1884	Eycott	8
BisleySurry	1800	1820	Eacott	@ 12
Westwood	1808	1819	Eacot Ecot	3
Berkley	1817		Ecott	2
Preshute	1818	1826	Eacott	3
Bristol	1820	1840	Eacott	4
CastleEaton	1824		Eacott	1
Tythington	1841	1910	Ecott Eacott	2
FramptonCott	1875	1980	Eacott	1

Other places of origin after 1875 have not been included.

Appendix K
The Eacotts in Relation to Historic Events

54 BC, Written history in England begins with the arrival of the Romans. It was recorded that the local inhabitant wives shared the men in groups of 10 to 12 men. The women led armies and married Romans. During the Roman era the population reached between 4 and 6 million. There were large scale developments of villas in the Cirencester area. Across England

the prosperity and population did not reach this level again until the 1600's.

The Romans left and the Saxons came between 400 and 600. They did not replace the existing population. They augmented a population in decline.

800's - About this time the Saxon manor of Eycote is created by charter, probably by the bishop of Worcester. Essentially it was land grant to someone.

1066 - William the Conqueror brings 4000 knights to England. 36 Baronies were created that lasted until 1327.

1086 - William orders the Domesday census. Villeins held 45% of the land and another 41% were free men. Yet only 14% of the population held 20% of the land. Cottagers held 5% of the land but comprised 32% of the population. Serfs were 10% of the population and held no land at all. Ordvic held Eycote from the Bishop of Worcester.

1000 - North Cerney, Bagendon churches were in existence

1264 - Bishop of Worcester supports Simon de Montfort against Henry III

1314 - Battle of Bannockburn, England defeated by the Scots.

1316 - Simon de Eycote becomes master of St. Giles Hospital, Durham He was appointed by Edward II

1319 - English defeated in North Yorkshire by Scots, Simon de Eycote ceases to be master returns as Edward II's clerk.

1327 - Subsidy roles for taxation recorded the names of taxpayers in different places. The first large scale records of existing persons. Eycotts are recorded at Cirencester and North Cerney

1337 - Hundred Years War begun. Edward III is king. The wool trade is good with a demand in Europe for the high grade wool. Flocks are now smaller. Villeins often pay cash rather than carry out feudal duties. It is the peak of the feudal times. Parliament is raising money from tax on wool and controlling the king who is spending much on French wars.

1342 - John Eycott signs petition as a townsman of Cirencester to get the abbot out of meddling in their affairs, and also to keep town free.

1346 - Thomas Neel of Purton sub leases Eycote

1348 - plague arrives and repeats in 1361, 1374 and other times. Back of feudal system broken because labour is scarce and expensive. Labourers are at a premium; farms are vacated. The population is cut in half. Cloth manufacturing is begun. Huge flocks of sheep are held by few landowners including the Thynnes and the Bishops. 2 rectors of North Cerney die in plague.

1362 - Norman french abolished in courts etc. English spoken in recognizable form, Chaucer writes his stories

1370's - wills have come into fashion

1376 - Burgesses and gentry hold first Commons, Oxford University is flourishing, clock built for Salisbury cathedral. Wycliffe preaches the reformation.

1377 - Richard II is king.

1381 - Peasants revolt over taxes as there is another set of poll tax rolls.

1382 - Company of weavers of Cirencester are given Bagendon but they give it to priests in Cirencester.

1394 - John Eycott does Wardstaff duty at Berrefordbrugge. (Perrott's Brook)

1413 - Henry V captures lands in France.

1416 - John Eycott witnesses a grant.

1421 - John and Thomas transfer land; John Warre gives Eycote to Winchcombe Abbey.

1429 - Joan of Arc

1430 - Knights loose voting rights which arc now given to all freeholders who are worth 40 shillings (a large sum).

1453 - English loses last of French lands.

1464 - John Eicote is curate of North Cerney church, War of Roses , Church is with Yorkists, Brick and Stone manor houses are in style. Eycote window placed in church.

1470 - Worst of great plagues over. Population begins to rise until epidemic of 1557-9.

1485 - Battle of Bosworth ends war of Roses. N. Cerney church new window has Yorkist badge. There are only 55 peers in the aristocracy and there is no change until 1597.

1509 - Henry VIII is king to 1545.

1510 - A great increase in the value of Cotswold wool for the next decades.

1525 - Wyllyam Eycott witnesses will of Thomas Foxley.

1538 - Churches ordered to keep records of births, baptisms, marriages and deaths. Many earlier records lost because of the Dissolution.

1540 - Edmund Tame of Fairford and wife Catherine Stafford acquire Eycote manor. After Dissolution it becomes part of Rendcomb Park estate. Monasteries all destroyed 1536-40. Feudal laws on land holding abolished.

1551 - There are 881 freemen of the City of London.

1552 - Registration of the poor by parish begun, enforced until 1834 (the poor laws).

1558   - Elizabeth I is queen and 1559 Anglican Church becomes the legal church.

1560   - College of Heralds grants 6000 coats of arms from 1560 to 1640 but none to Eycott or Eacott because the manor is defunct.

1564   - Berkeley family hold Eycote Manor

1566   - Rendcomb parish is established.

1570   - Age of great country houses being built lasts until 1620.

1569/79 - Ales and others born to John, Thomas, Robert. This is a time of great wealth because of weaving and sheep rearing and the start of enclosure of fields. Catholics are rebellious. Drake circles world. 1572 Thomas Eycott is churchwarden at Bagendon, only 7 families attend.

1581/3 - wills of Thomas and Richard show them to have been very well off. The first Ecott.

1588   - Spanish armada defeated and it is time of Shakespeare.

1594/ 1605 - many Ecott references

1600   - By this time about half the population could read and write. Literacy began to decline after industrialization began and population rose rapidly. Population in 1600 was about 4 million. There were few illegitimate births before 17th Century. Marriage was most common among people in their mid 20's.

1603/23 - James I is king, barons and abbots brought low. The gentry and burgesses wield more power. It is a time of mansions in the country and many people are now Puritans and not Anglicans.

1605   - Gunpowder plot, state church (Anglican) enforced.

1608   - Thomas Coots fit for Militia. Eycotts not included in lists so may have antigovernment feelings.

1611   - Marquis of Bath, John Thynne builds Longleat.

1619   - Eacott of Rendcomb, 3 brothers, 3 sisters listed in Joan's will

1630   - earliest Bagendon parish register

1632   - Charles I abolishes Parliament. Richard Ecut, rough mason, dies at Bagendon.

1635   - Guise family assumes ownership of Eycote till 1864.

1638   - Long Parliament meets.

1642/6 - Civil war leads to Kings overthrow. Over 100,000 killed during war. Cromwell takes over with a strong Puritan government. Gloucester a weaving town is a puritan stronghold. Many schools begun. Newton born.

1646/60 - The Commonwealth under Cromwell, Ministers of Bagendon appointed by Cromwell and are Puritans.

1653   - Thomas Vyner, goldsmith, family from North Cerney, is Lord

Mayor of London. Cromhall parish register records begin.

1655 - England divided into parishes and districts under a Major General. Cromwell begins to deport convicts to America. Bristol is now second largest city and remains so until overtaken by Liverpool in mid 1700's.

1661 - Richard Eacott living at North Cerney. Charles II is King. American colonies are growing rapidly and great wealth coming from West Indies. Half the land of England now owned by 160 peers.

1662 - New poor laws force poor to go back to home county. A big increase in number of poor has begun and creates problems.

1666 - Great fire of London, Pepys diary, Richard of Woodmancote is indicted for legal matter.

1665 - The goldsmiths start to become bankers and begin mortgages that lead to many failures in early years of the next century.

1672 - Robert Vyner has become partner in Hudson's Bay Company and also in the newly formed slave trading company.

1673 - Dissenters (Catholics, non Anglican Protestants) excluded from political office.

1681/8 - James II leans to Catholic restoration.

1688 - Royal powers of the king are limited and king rules by invitation of parliament.

1689 - revolution makes parliament supreme, religious Toleration Acts allows freedom of worship to Protestants but only Anglicans can hold office. William of Orange made king followed by Anne.

1696/7 - Eacotts now at South Cerney, Cromhall, and Warminster.

1701 - Act of Settlement and rights of citizens established.

1703 - Eacotts at Purton

1707 - Union with Scotland

1710 - Eycott and Eacott at London and on April 19, John Eacutt was a juryman at Southham Manor. At leet Court the business was to order some ditches cleaned and repaired.

1714 - George I

1715 - North Cerney Eycotts swear oath of allegiance as papists(Catholics). Thomas is made constable of Bagendon, must be influential person. Berkeley Eycott was sequestrator of Bagendon church. In 1714 an attempt to trade 5 acres of Berkeleys land for some church land was made to raise some money for repairs to church.

1719 - Richard of Tetbury charged with name calling.

1727 - George II

1734 - Rioters destroy toll booths at Cairncross house. F. Eycot of

Oakfields rebuilds the gates.

1735 - John Eccutt and two others of Uphaven charged with stealing a furnace from Roger Jarvis.

1736 - William Ecott served as juryman at Westbury Wilts.

1740/50 - Thomas Eycott of North Cerney ends line there and John Eycott of Cirencester is a goldsmith both are Catholic. The lordship of the Woodmancote Manor goes to "Diamond" Pitt father and grandfather of William Pitt Sr/Jr both Prime Minister of England for most of last half of century. They bring in the Closure Acts ending in 1792 the ancient field patterns.

1753 - Marriage Act only Anglican marriages valid except Jews and Quakers. Lasts to 1837

1755 - John Eycott is trading with the Creek Indians in Tennessee and South Carolina

1759 - Martha Eacott deported to America

1750 - Bath is a centre of culture and style

1760 - George III - Industrial revolution begins, migrations to Lancashire, Midlands and the Welsh mines. Cottage industries in villages begin to die as factories grow. Sanitation and science improve life. population of 7 million in 1760 doubles in 40 years. Cotswold loses textile industry to northern mills, fields greatly enclosed

1774 - William Eacott of Gloucester, mason, and wife settle in Jamaica West Indies.

1776 - William Ecutt of Cromhall leaves to several sons an estate with messuage, tenement and cottages. William born this year grows up and goes abroad to West Indies.

1778 - Thomas of Chippenham and brother John Eacott of Wooton Bassett are plumbers and glaziers.

1792 - Closure Act. Narrows strips of Saxon origin land holding eliminated along with the common pasture land. Fields are enclosed so they can be ploughed. Many Yeomen freeholders are tempted to sell their farms and become tenants because of the effects of these laws.

1797 - Henry Eycott appointed an officer in city of Gloucester, troop of gentlemen and yeomen, a cavalry group to defend from Napoleon if invaded

1800 - Henry Eycott running prosperous Bond's Mills at Stonehouse.

1810 - William Eacott a weaver for two years with J & T Clark of Trowbridge

1821 - Thomas Eacott tried in Wiltshire, found guilty and sent to Australia for life.

1830 - Charles Eacott settles in Euphemia Twp Ontario Canada

1830 - Thomas Eacott of Sutton Veny Wilts. arrives in Western Australia on the Rockingham.

1837 - Government takes over registration of marriages.

1841 - First UK census with individuals ages rounded down to 5 or 0. John Eacott, 65 lived in Purton Stoke Wilts. has 2 brothers in America. His age between 65 and 69

1851 - First Census of UK in which significant data is available.

1860 - to 1863 Thomas Eycott, furniture dealer, Gloucester city, lived behind shop which was located in the right angle formed by King St. and Oxbody lane.

1863 - Rendcomb mansion built.

1881 - census records to be available after hundred years has passed.

King and Commoner

William I   1066 - 1087 - Alric

Edward II   1307 - 1327 - appoints Simon de Eycote master of St Giles Kepier Hospital

Edward III   1327 - 1377 - 1342 petition

Richard II   1377 - 1399   (minor until 1389, deposed 1399 -last of Plantagenets) Johannes does Wardstaff duty 1394

Henry V   1413 - 1422 (won Agincourt battle) - 1416 John witness grant. 1421 John/Thomas land transfer

Henry VI   1422 - 1471 (deposed 1461 died in tower) 1464 John curate of North Cerney

Edward VI   1547 - 1553

Mary I   1553 - 1558

Elizabeth I   1558 - 1603 The Tudor rose is featured in the N. Cerney church. Thus the local empathy was with Elizabeth I

1558 to 1603 - Eacott names from 1569 to 1603 -Names: John, Robert, Thomas, Richard, William, Alice, Edith, Elizabeth, Joseph, Mary, Margett, Katherine, Eedie, Eleanor

James I   1603 - 1625

In the record taken in 1608 for men fit for Militia duty a description is given of Thomas Coots, (Eycott-Ekot). This is the only reference to males in Gloucester by this surname. It is obvious that there were others with the family name alive in the area. Therefore they were not considered fit for duty for religious, political or other reasons. James I was son of Mary Queen of Scots. My assumption, the Eycotts opposed the king. Names:

Thomas, William, Joseph, John, Elizabeth, Richard

Charles I   1625 - 1649   (beheaded Jan 30 1649)

Cromwell 1653 -1658   Thomas Vyner Lord Mayor London in 1653

Charles II   1660 -1685   Robert Vyner Lord Mayor of London, Berkeley Eycott goldsmith apprentice in London, Robert Vyner may have been his great uncle.

James II   1685 - 1701 (deposed 1688)

William III /Mary 1689 - 1702

Anne   1702 - 1714

George I   1714 - 1727

George II   1727- 1760 John Eycott at Charleston, trader to Creeks

George III   1760 - 1820

George IV   1820 - 1830   Charles Eacott, to Canada, Thomas Eacott to Australia

William IV   1830 -1837

Victoria   1837 -1901   Census and other records collected.

Appendix   L
Notes on Various Censuses
Census of England   1891

The following Eacott derivation names were found in a study of the 1891 Census for England

Eacott 258
Eckett 171
Ecott   56
Eccott 50
Eycott 39
Eacot   10   Total 584

No persons in England were known to have these spellings in 1891
Eacutt, Eccot, Eycot, Ekutt, Ekott, Eacoot, Ekett, Eakett, Eakott,Ecot Ecket

Census of England and Wales 1901

It can be assumed by this time that the spelling of the name had become formalized due to increased education levels. Using all variations which appeared in the records prior to 1901 and some which didn't, this is the result of all thinkable Eacott variations.

Eacott	404	Eacotts	1	Aycott	24
Eckett	204	Eyckett	1	Icott	1
Eccott	82	Ecot	3	Acot	3
Ecott	46	Eacret	14	Acott	356
Eycott	25			Eakets	27
Eacot	3			Eacret	14

No persons were known to have these spellings:
Eacut, Eacutt, Eccot, Eycot, Ekutt, Ekott, Eacoot, Ekett, Eakett, Eakott, Eccutt, Eccot, Ecat,Eacit, Eakett, Eckut, Eycatt, Eycodd, Eycot, Eycote, Eacert, Ecoate, Ecots, Ecotts, Eyecot Ecute, Ecut, Ecreat, Ecreet, Ecote, Eacot, Eacett, Eyecote, Eyecot, Eyecott, Aket, Akett, Eacett, Eakett.

The Eacott name in 1901 is found mostly in Southern England and adjacent Wales especially Gloucestershire, Wiltshire, Somerset, Berkshire. The Eccott name is largest (30%) in Hampshire and London (25%). The Ecott name is in Southern England but more south easterly than Eacot, 30% Bedfordshire 30% Essex, 20% Croydon. The Eacret name is from Ireland or Manchester and thus may not be a derivative of Eycott. The Eakets are found in Gloucestershire mostly around Cheltenham (90%). The Eycott name is found in greater London 30% and the south coast. The Aycott name is mostly in London, Surrey, often in same communities as Eacott.

The Eckett name is found across southern England and the midlands often in the same places as Eacott. However, 50% of Eaketts are in the London area.

Of note is the fact that very few of any of these names occur outside the southern half of England.

The prevalence of the name with a likely "EH" sound rather than an "AY" or an "EE" sound as in ECK, ECC, EAK accounts for the accent emphasis that occurs in the useage of Eacott which appears in all soundings. Some using the Eacott form actually say the name as Eckett or Eccott. A simple spelling change lines up easily with Aycott, Acott, Ecott, Eckett and may reflect local accentuation. Eacret may derive from another source than Eycott.

Census of England 1881

This census has ample free data. Thus it is easier to identify family groupings. In 1881 England was at the height of Empire under the Victorians. It was also the most industrial country in the world.

The examination of the Eacotts from that time show that they were largely agricultural or related workers. The second largest group were servants (mostly women). A few were miners, some shop keepers. The industrial workers were varied but railway related seems the largest. The vast majority could have been identified as working class. The distribution of people in the 1901 census was reflected in the 1881. Not a lot of movement took place.

The census included age, place of birth, marital status, street address, occupation, and where living. This is available online (search: 1881 Census England). The records entered by me do not generally include street address.

There are discrepancies between the 1901 and 1881 data such as name changes, as Eacott to Ecott, frequent year of birth variations by as much as 5 years and sometimes place of birth differences. Some of these are in the specifics as a neighborhood or estate given instead of the municipality. While there are people who will appear unknowingly more than once in the records, there are others who clearly were not recorded in 1881 that were recorded in 1901 and who existed in 1881 and likely the reverse applied in 1901. There seems to be a lot of errors. People who were in my data base prior to the entering of census data should have shown up as matches but many did not.

The original Eycott Name was no longer found in the North Cerney area. Only 18 Eycott names were in the census and in fewer than 5 familes.

Name and Location Study (from 1881 census)

An Analysis of the variants of the Eycott name based on the census material using males born before 1850 and a few unmarried older females gave the following information which indicates the earlier sources of the names:

The **Eycott** name was found in London and in Stroud Gloucestershire and a few were also living at Aldershot in the 1870's.

The **Eckett** name was mainly in two localities about 12 miles apart Reading and Basingstoke. 20% on the west side of Reading and 22% on the west side of Basingstoke. London area had 33% of the Ecketts. The remaining families were scattered in isolated places in Berkshire, Surrey, and Somerset. I was not able to establish who the Eckett was that changed his name when he came to this area.

The **Eccott** name was 80% located on the east side of Basingstoke within a 5 mile radius. After 1850 there were Eccotts at Shefford near Chaddleworth.

The **Ecott** name was in several small villages south of Bedford, Bedfordshire and in the vicinity of Cromhall Gloucestershire.

The **Acott** name, the largest group, is concentrated along the B2015 corridor from Tunbridge Wells to Maidstone in Ken.t over 50% are there, especially at Yalding. This is a small area about 10 miles by 2 miles. About 15% of the Acott's were in London. 7% each in Oxford and at Maisey Hampton, Gloucestershire. Most of the rest were in Kent. So the name was extremely localized. Among the 9 older Acott men over 60 years(born before 1840) 4 were not born in Kent, these were born in Maisey Hampton Glos, Oxford, and Somerset The Genealogic records and name associations don't generally include Acott as a variant, because it likely is an altered form of the Hugenot french name A'court. However there may be a few Acott not from Kent or London who were from Eycott. Only as a German name does Acott appear in America in the 1880 census, although German immigration to England was rare it could be a German name confused with Eacott.

The **Eacott** name is found in more diverse places than the other names, however, 90% of all the names were 5 miles north of, to 15 miles south of the modern M4 highway from London to Bristol. 60% of Eacott name sites were in Wiltshire. 18% Warminster; 14 % Chaddleworth; 8% Cromhall; 8% Wroughton; 14% other Wiltshire places; 10% in Surrey, South West of London. The rest were elsewhere in Southern England.

The statistical base for census records of those males born before 1850. 65 Eacott; 54 Eckett; 73 Acott; 23 Eccott; 6 Eycott ; 13 Ecott.

Before 1800 my database has very few Eckett, or Acott names. Before 1700 most were Ecott or Eycott. Some early names such as Ecut did not exist in 1881 / 1901 census. The fact that Acott and Eckett have very few occurrences before 1800 indicates they were likely derived names, not original.

I produced a map with colored dots that clearly shows the distribution of males over age 20 in 1881. It appear elsewhere in this book.

Census USA 1880

The Few Acot names in the USA appear to be mostly, not all, of German origin. The Ecott, Eycott name does not appear in either USA or Canada census at this time. The one Eccott family has a German origin. The few Eckett names were also mixed English and German. There are a number of German and Dutch names which are similar, which considering Eycott is of Saxon derivation, is not surprising. There were a few Eacotts scattered about.

Census Canada 1881

One family group of Eckett and a couple of isolated individuals and one family group of Eacott, as well as one father and son, were recorded. Both family groups were farming in Ontario.

The Emigrated Eacotts

Points of Origin

From the evidence it appears that Eacott was derived from Eycot also known as Eycote, Aicote, Eyot or Eugkote. Eycot became or was parallel with Ekot or Ecot. The names all are intertwined in several small parishes adjacent to each other, Rendcomb, North Cerney, Bagendon, Colesbourne and Winstone. The names go back to the 1300's in association with these places.

Commencing with the late 1500's and early 1600's Eacott arises. This variant appears most closely connected with the version Ekott or Ecott and more limitedly with Eycott. All are still with the same parishes. Just before 1700 the name in association with Ecott appears about Cromhall and appears regularly in several parishes south of Cromhall, most notably Alveston. At the same time the name as Eacutt, Eacott becomes known at South Cerney and later about Purton and adjacent parishes in Wiltshire. Elsewhere in Wiltshire a line of Eacotts occurs at Warminster in the 1600's.

Likewise a small group appears in Berkshire, Surrey and London. Other Eacotts before 1800 are almost none existent in all other areas of Britain. Until 1800 nearly all the Eacotts lived in these few places. Notably, the Eacott variant never was strong in the places where the name first appeared.

By the time of census taking in England in the last half of the 1800's Eacott and its variations had this distribution. Eacott was concentrated in Avon, Wiltshire, Berkshire, and London. Eakets were only in Glocestershire. Ecott was found in Bedfordshire and Gloucestershire. Ayott was in London and Bedfordshire, Eycott in London, Berkshire, Yorkshire, Eckett London, Reading and Basing towns, Acott in Lpndon, Kent, Gloucestershire, Oxford and Eccott in London and Basing towns.

The first record of an Eycott abroad was John Eycott, recorded in the south Carolina Gazette as having a license to trade with the Creek Indians in South Carolina and Tennessee, 1750 to 1754.

The first records I have of an Eacott emigrating from Britain was William Eycott (30) of Gloucester a mason who went with his wife to Jamaica in 1774 and John Eycott who went to South Carolina about 1750.

Since 1800 a worldwide migration has taken place.

North America

Before 1830
Martha Eacot arrived before 1776 (book of Emigrants and passenger list). Nothing further.
1750's a John Eycott was a trader in South Carolina to the Creek Indians. Several references
1782 Hannah Eacoff m. Ralph Pyle in Chester PA . Nothing further

1810   George Eacock was included in USA census for Virginia. A George Eacock, a J.M. and a Joseph are listed on a passenger list as immigrants 1583-1940. Nothing further.

1810 John Eakett was in Sharpsburg, Maryland.

1812 Thomas and William twin sons of William and Catherine Engle born South Whitehall Twp. PA . In 1832 Thomas married Hannah Folk , 7 July Longswamp Twp Berks co. PA.

See William And Catherine. Several generations traceable. William may have come from Purton Wilts. and may have been born in 1780 son of Richard, brother of Charles in Canada.

1830 Charles Eacott settled in Euphemia Township, Lambton County and farmed there.

5 Children, 2 boys John and Henry. See Charles and Margaret. Several generations traceable

1830 US Census

Richard Eacott was in Stow, Middlesex county, MA [MA56091227]

Richard Ecott was in New York State. Richard died in Orleans Jefferson County NY   in 1840   age 62   leaving an unmarried daughter Hannah who died 2 dec 1859 age 39. His wife Maria died 21 may 1872 age 84 both in Dexter Jefferson Co. NY. Richard was in census of NY 1840.

Maria appears in 1850 census Dexter, Brownville NY [pg226 nys6a923940]

Maria Eacott was married in MA (1633-1850 marriage index)

Michael at Hamburg, Erie County NY [pg 141 ny56091226]

John B. Eycot recorded in Illinois. Eacotts were living in Galesburg Ill for several decades.

Thomas P. Ecotr in North Carolina

George Eacrat in Pennsylvania

1840 US Census

William at Ligonier Twp., Westmoreland Co. PA

Issac Ecove Ohio

1843 Oliver Eacit married in Rhode Island

1845 Isiac Eacott   died in Canada

1850 Census of USA

Robert Ecourt	PA
Jane Eacott	Missouri
Catherine Eacott	Missouri

1860 Census of USA

Adam Ecott	NY
Peter Ecove	OH
Michael Ecreat	VA
James Eacott	NH
Annie Eacret	Indiana
Elizabeth Eacret	Indiana
Agnes Eacott	MA also 1870
Susan Ecott MD	

1870 Census USA

Emma J Eacott	MA
Elsie June	MA
Eliza Eacott MA	
Benjamin	MA
William	MA
Ruth	MA
Henry J	MA also Civil war records
John Ekett	MA
Louisa D. Ecott	MA
Mary A. Eacott	MA
Matthew Eacott	MA

1880 Census USA

Jones Eycroft	Illinois
Sarah Eacott	Texas Brownswood p 372 TX2844
Cale Eacott	OH
Calib Eacott CO	

John Eycott was a licensed trader in South Carolina in 1750-54. He traveled into Creek territory now Tennessee and carried on trade. [Colonial Records of South Carolina] He was married to Mary Jeys in South Carolina July 29, 1742. John may have been originally from Cirencester. He appears several times in South Carolina records. South Carolina kept detailed records of trading commencing in 1710.

By 1830 Eacotts were living in Canada and the United States. None were recorded in 1790 in the first US census. Charles Eacott settled in

Ontario as a pioneer farmer in 1830.Charles, who was born in Wiltshire, had taken up a crown land grant issued by Thomas Talbot in Lambton Co.Euphemia Twp, Ontario. He may have lived in USA for a time since Talbot made him swear an oath of allegiance. As a settler he had to clear a portion of his land each year, build a cabin and maintain the road in front of his property. He married a neighbor's girl, Margaret McCabe a settler from Ireland in 1835. He was mustered in 1837 in the Kent Militia as a militiaman at a time when a failed rebellion in the colony resulted in a need to round up the perpetrators. As a paid volunteer in Captain William Kerry's Company he signed for his 1pound 17 Shillings and 4 pence. He signed as Charles Ecot. The action of the group was to go to the St Clair River where a rebel attack was expected. They spent the night at a farm near Dresden. A rebel party stopped at the same farm and a skirmish ensued and Kerry was shot and subsequently died. There were 31 in the company, 9 officers and 22 privates including Charles. Charles may have had a brother in USA.

Isiac and his wife Eliza came to Ontario from Britain in 1845. At the same time Samuel and Fanny Eacott were living in Wellington county, Puslinch, Ontario where they were early supporters of the Methodist church. Sadly three of their children met an untimely end in October 1847.

In 1880 Calib was camped on Rock Creek, Gunnison Colorado.

Home Children to Canada

During the latter part of the 1800's and well into the 1900's schemes were used to send orphans and other children from Britain to Canada and Australia. These were called Home Children. One such scheme was carried out by Dr. Bernardo. Two of the Bernardo boys were Eacotts sent out in early 1900's. Reginald Eacott was sent because his father Thomas, a boiler maker, who left his wife Alice Cunningham, would not support him. In January 1902, after a send off with a band, and a train ride to Liverpool and put on board, possibly the "Tunisian", Reginald with a party of 100 other boys was away to Canada. The crossings took several days and the weather caused rough seas. Once in Canada he was sent to work on the farm of Herbert M. Shaw at Rutherford, Ontario. His passage and clothing were supplied by the organization that helped him leave England. He was born in 1889 and arrived alone age 13. His English family lost contact with him. Frederick his older brother also went to Canada at the age of 8. Born in 1886 he sailed on the S.S. Laurentian destined for Toronto. Their brother William Henry was born Jan 27 1900 in England and said he never knew about his older brothers.

Other Bernardo children were Charles Eacott born 1890 who sailed on the S.S. "Cambroman" in 1900. He was age 10. Frances Eacott a girl of 9 born 1903 sailed on the S.S. "Virginian" in 1912. William Eacott born1905 age 7 also sailed on the "Virginian" in 1912 perhaps with his sister. Fred Eycott age 15 b 1878 sailed 1893 on the S.S. "Sardinian" to Montreal. Each of these children were considered a burden to the mother country and presumably to their parents.

Australia

In Australia John Eacott arrived on a prison ship, Mary II, Jan 28 1822. He was from Wiltshire. He was tried in 1821, found guilty, and deported for life. He arrived at Sydney, New South Wales and was sent to Parramatto NSW. Today being a descendant of a prisoner is a mark of celebrity.

In 1828, having been given assisted passage Catherine Eacott and her children Selena and Henry arrived on the bounty ship the Borneo at Sydney harbor.

Soon after Thomas Eacott of Sutton Veny and his wife Elizabeth and daughters Ann Priscilla and Harriet leave for Western Australia on the Rockingham. This Thomas became a pioneer settler in Mandurah in 1830 where his home is preserved as historic. He remarries Charlotte Tuckey in 1839 after misfortune took his first wife and has 10 children. A Street and park are named after him.

Eacotts have been known to have lived in Spain, Argentina, Sri Lanka, New Zealand, South Africa, Ireland and other places in the world.

Appendix M
Lives Lived

Eacotts and their Occupations

As yeomen English, the early Eacotts made their farming count. They met the rules of their lord and early on involved themselves in the wool trade both as farmer and merchant. The records of the 14th and 15th centuries with reference to the name all deal with these issues. The evidence shows that they prospered and perhaps had above average wealth sometimes marrying into solid families as indicated by connections to Henry VIII's exchequer and Cromwell's Lord Mayor of London. Some were goldsmiths like Samuel, Berkeley. A goldsmith was a most prestigious trade.

There was a long tradition of religious connection.

The Church

The earliest is associated with the church at North Cerney where Johannes Eycot was assistant minister in 1465. Later Thomas Eycott was Churchwarden in 1572. At Bagendon an Eycott was often churchwarden.

It was in later times however that Eacotts undertook the ministry. The most interesting line descends from John and then Abraham who lived at Yew Tree in Berkshire in the 1700's. Abraham's son James1805 -1882 seemed to have raised his children in a devoted manner.He was the Rev James buried at Leicester born at Yew Tree. In 1836 he went to the West Indies as a Wesleyan missionary. His 3 sons, Caleb 1844-1911, James W. 1839-1923 , Jabez 1843-1906 all became Methodist ministers while Jabez's daughters Isabel and Brena served as missionaries in India and China respectively. In addition the Rev William Eacott ministered from 1870 until 1907 with the Methodist Church. James W. was buried at Barnard Castle, Durham in 1923. Caleb graduated from University College Durham with an MA in 1870. He served as vicar of King's Norton and was curate of the Chapel St church at Bottesford, Leicester.

Another person Robert Eckett was also a Methodist born Scarborough in Yorkshire 1797 but was raised in London. He died 1862. Robert was a leading Wesleyan reformist and took an active role in the Leeds organ dispute. He agitated for the establishment of the Theological Institute in

1834 but was expelled from the church and joined the Wesleyan Methodist Association in 1839. He planned its foundation and deed in 1840 emphasizing democracy in governance. He played a leading role in the United Methodist Free Church serving 3 times as president. Although he also lived in the north of England as a Methodist, his connection with the Yew Tree branch is not known.

The grandson of James from his son James who migrated to Canada became involved with the Salvation Army. Col. James Clinton born 1899 d. 1981 He served in China with the Salvation Army Overseas Mission as did his daughter Amy (Homewood). Clinton also worked for a long time with prison inmates in Canada. After retiring James Clinton completed his MA in theology from University of Western Ontario, London at the age of 78. His sister Brigadier Emily was also a life long Salvationist joining the social services department in 1929. She spent many years with Faith Haven home for unwed mothers in Windsor Ontario. She celebrated her 100th birthday in 2001. Another brother Frances was also a life long Salvation Army officer.

Anglican Eacotts include Rev. Henry Eacott who was canon of St. Wilfrids Church in Kibworth, Leicester from 1934 to 1943. This church of 1200 was partially renovated and a war memorial created during his time and after his untimely death a lectern was dedicated.

In Australia, Rev. Len Eacott was ordained an Anglican priest in 1983 in Brisbane. He joined the military reserves and was sent in 1993 to Cambodia as part of the UN forces there. In 1999 he was the Senior UN chaplain and involved with the exhumation of persons killed in mass murders. He was made Archdeacon of the armed forces of Australia in November 2002.

The Military

A number of Eacotts have military backgrounds. This is the record as much as has been gathered.

The first mention of possible military service apart from duties as a medieval knight was the listing of Thomas Coots (likely a spelling error) in 1608 as being fit for the militia.

At the time of the fear of invasion by Napoleon, 1797 Henry Eacott was appointed an officer at Gloucester of the Troop of Gentlemen and Yeoman Cavalry.

Uriah Eacott joined the 1st Dragoons in 1804. This was a premier cavalry unit and saw lots of action against Napoleon, mostly in Spain. Most certainly he was at Waterloo. He was discharged in 1828 age 39 and became a Chelsea pensioner later in life.

Another Chelsea pensioner was William Yeacott of the 38th Foot who retired after 16 years service age 45.

Richard Eacott of Bratton Wilts. Was discharged from the 15th Dragoons (light) cavalry of the line,age 34. He served 1801 to 1814.

Job Acott aka Eacott of Warminster joined the 13th foot, a Somerset regiment while it was recruiting in Bath in 1817. He was born about 1791. For the next few years the regiment moved about the UK, Channel islands, Edinburgh and Ireland. It departed for India in 1823 landing in Bengal. In 1824 in Burma there was lots of fighting action along the Irrawadi River. Job was discharged in 1826.

Benjamin Aceott, aka Accett of Great Coxwell Berks. (or Coxhall) born 1771 appears to have been a child of 8 when he joined the 40th Foot in 1779. At the time this was not an unheard of practice. At some point he joined the 1st Royal Veterans Battalion until 1814. When it dissolved, he took his discharge at age 43. The Veteran's battalion was composed of those not quite fit for fighting but capable of other tasks.

Richard Eacott born 1780 in Bratton Wilts. Joined the 15th Dragoons (Light) in 1801 and served until 1814 when he was discharged at age 34. Much of his service was in England except for action in Spain against Napoleon. They were in one serious engagement in 1808. Back in England they did escort duty and quelled the Luddite uprising in the north. Richard may have emigrated to USA.

Charles Eacott of Ontario Canada was a private of the West Kent Militia, Kent County under Captain William Kerry in 1838. He signed his name as Charles Ecot. This group was formed to put down any effort to foment rebellion as had happened the previous year. His pay was 1pound,

17 shillings and 4 pence. Charles was a pioneer settler in 1830 from Wiltshire. His son Henry also served in the militia at the times of the Fenian raids in the 1860's. Charles' great grandson Elgin Murphy was killed at Vimy Ridge in the first World War.

William Eacott was an orderly on the HMS Belle Isle in 1859 and Henry Eacott a private on the HMS Pearl in 1862. Frederick William was a Royal Marine at Plymouth in 1878. At the same time Thomas Eacott was gunner in the Royal Artillery. William Eacott was bugler in a rifle brigade. In 1881 aboard the HMS Asia was an able bodied seaman, Henry J. Eacott born 1860 at Warminster Wilts. and unmarried. H.C. Eycott was a Staff Sgt. 3rd Class with the Army Service corp in 1879. Later H.J. Eycott was Staff Sgt. Major in the same corp in 1906. Lionel Waldenstein Eacott was a trooper body guard for the commander in chief of the Cape medical staff in the Boer war. The Rev. W. was an army chaplain in 1902.

F. Eycott waas a sergeant in the 21st Foot in 1879

The First and Second World War service records include a considerable number of persons. Included here is the Debt of Honour Register for the Commonwealth War Graves Commission. At first glance it looks like just a list but there are some interesting aspects bearing observation.

Surname Rank Service Died Age Regiment Nationality Comment

EACOTT, A J Private 46767 1 November 1918 32 The Queen's (Royal West Surrey Regt.) United Kingdom-died Calais Fr. Age 32, John /mary Ann Bethnel Green London

EACOTT, Charles Arthur Private 6987 20 September 1917 24 Australian Infantry, A.I.F

Age 24 parents William James/Mary Ellen of Longwarry Victoria

EACOTT, Edward Walter Serjeant 18831 7 September 1918 44 Welsh Regiment United Kingdom D. Somme age 44 wife Kate of Larkhall Bethnel Green

EACOTT, Frederick Serjeant 6472308 10 September 1943 29 Royal Fusiliers (City of London Regt.) United Kingdom d. Salerno Italy age29 Alfred/alice Rosina wife Irene Margaret

EACOTT, Florence Mary Civilian 1 February 1945 Civilian War Dead United Kingdom

London wife of Walter of Chingford Essex age 42 .....possible buzz bomb fatality

EACOTT, Frederick R Private 10/3114 29 June 1921 40 Canadian Forestry Corps Canadian

died Vancouver, age 40 son of late Robert/Mary of Huntly Glos

EACOTT, Francis Thomas Private 2168 4 January 1917 27 Australian Infantry, A.I.F Australian died at the Somme age 27 Joseph Charles/Georgina Longwarry Victoria

EACOTT, George Stoker 1st Class D/K 16489 17 September 1939 47 Royal Navy United Kingdom age 47 aboard HMS Courageous ....died at sea at start of the war

EACOTT, Henry Varney Lance Corporal G/7703 4 August 1917 20 The Buffs (East Kent Regiment) United Kingdom age 20 at Ypres William Arthur/Sarah Jane of Erith Kent

EACOTT, HenryWilliam Thomas Private 34958 26 October 1917 27 Royal Warwickshire Regiment United Kingdom age 27 MIA Belgium late Walter/Laura of Reading

EACOTT, J V Bombardier 352779 15 June 1917 32 Royal Garrison Artillery United Kingdom

at Ypres age 32   wife E.M.

EACOTT, Leonard Robert Driver 65011 27 February 1915 24 Royal Field Artillery United Kingdom age 24 of Scarlet Fever Aldershot   john/Charlotte wife Alice Rebecca of Cromhall

EACOTT, R Lance Corporal 15059 1 October 1917 22 Leicestershire Regiment United Kingdom

EACOTT, Sidney Private G/6200 6 April 1916 21 Queen's Own (Royal West Kent Regiment) United Kingdom age 21 in Belgium   AlbertCharles/Ellen was born in London

EACOTT, Thomas Charles Frank Corporal 6146902 18 May 1944 28 East Surrey Regiment United Kingdom at Monte Casino Italy age 28 Charles/Clara

EACOTT-HARRIS, George Henry Civilian 15 October 1940 65 Civilian War Dead United Kingdom age 65 51 Haverstock Rd London ...... blitz bombing casualty

Additional research has not been done on the following

ECOTT, A D Serjeant 1431738 23 July 1944 24 Parachute Regiment, A.A.C. United Kingdom ECOTT, F W Private 302321 21 June 1918 Royal Scots United Kingdom

Surname Rank Service Died   Age Regiment Nationality

ECOTT, J B Private 147974 7 June 1940 25 Royal Army Service Corps

United Kingdom ECOTT, O M Gunner 11571 24 July 1917 Australian Field Artillery Australian

ECKETT, B J Sergeant 1376454 12 March 1943 Royal Air Force Volunteer Reserve United Kingdom

ECKETT, E L Serjeant 1630 12 May 1918 25 Queen's Own (Royal West Kent Regiment) United Kingdom

ECKETT, F C Able Seaman C/JX 198056 18 November 1942 22 Royal Navy United Kingdom ECKETT, F S Driver 522119 25 February 1919 Royal Engineers United Kingdom

ECKETT, L C Corporal 5391784 7 August 1946 24 Oxford. and Bucks Light Infantry United Kingdom

ECKETT, P Bandsman 7602 14 October 1915 Royal Inniskilling Fusiliers United Kingdom ECKETT, S W Private 5745 11 February 1917 The Queen's (Royal West Surrey Regt.) United Kingdom

ECKETT, T W Flight Scrgeant 1895942 27 May 1945 35 Royal Air Force Volunteer Reserve United Kingdom

ECKETT, U T M Lieutenant 21 February 1919 Royal Naval Volunteer Reserve United Kingdom

ECKETT, V G Civilian 19 September 1942 45 Civilian War Dead United Kingdom

Canadian Expeditionary Force - WWI

The following served in the Canadian Army. Enlistment records are online. All the Eacott, Ecott, Acott men were born in England. All the Acott men were born in Kent. Alfred William Eacott and his brother Frederick were in Winnipeg in 1916 and joined up. Frederick changed his mind and did not report for duty. His brother went off to war and came back afterwards to Saskatchewan to join his brother again. Frederick Robert Eacott born in Gloucester was later in British Columbia working as a teamster.

Samuel Eacott had been born in Surrey but his family had moved to Hamilton, Ontario. Edwin James Ecott joined.

The Acott's all born in Kent enlisted across Canada, Charles in

Manitoba 1917, John in Regina, Thomas H in Montreal in 1914, John in Toronto and William in Vancouver with 8 years in the Army already rejoined in Vancouver.

Elgin Murphy son of Margaret Walker (Eacott) joined in Ogema Sask in 1916 and died at Vimy Ridge.

Canada WWII

John Frances (Jack) Eacott joined the Algonquin rifles in 1941 in Timmins ON and transferred to the RCAF. He was stationed in Torbay Nfld as a warrant officer with responsibilities for construction on the base. More of his life is presented later in this book.

Challis Eacott joined Princess Patricia's. See Welsh Eacott's for details.

Australia

There are a few service records for Eycott and Eacott from Australia for WW1. Thomas Roberts Eycott born 12 Oct 1896 at Toowoomba Queensland enlisted in 1914. Several Eacott men all from Longwarry, Victoria signed up in 1915/16. These age 20 something men were laborers, saw mill workers and store clerks and were all related. William James Eacott, Samuel Henry Eacott, Joseph Henry Eacott, Francis Thomas Eacott, Charles Arthur Eacott were the sons of Charles or mother, Mary Ellen Eacott.

Francis Thomas Eacott died at the Somme January 1917. Charles Arthur Eacott died September 1917.

The United States

Military records from the USA are not as forthcoming. However these people have some documentation.

At the time of the Civil War in America, William Henry Eacott was living in Butler County, SW Ohio. He was involved in the reserve militia and wrote in July 1861 requesting that his men wished to become a volunteer regiment. As 2nd Lt. Of Company B, 35th Ohio Regiment he tendered his resignation on June 30, 1863. What ever became of that is not known because at age 27 on Aug 12 1864 his service ended. He would have been in the Union forces at Chickamauga among other places.

Also serving in the Union Army from New York was William Eacott Hilliker a private from Dexter NY who was at the siege of Petersburg.

Signed up Jan 21 1864 discharged 1865.

Serving with the Confederate army in the 2nd Missouri Cavalry Company C was Thomas A. Eacott. He joined "The Butternut Boys" August 1862 and first saw battle at Iuka Mississippi on Sept 19 1862 as part of Armstrong's Cavalry Army of West Tennessee and also with McCulloch's Cavalry under Lee and Forrest. He surrendered May 4 1865 in Alabama. During his time in "New Co. C" he was nearly always on the move in Tennessee and Mississippi with his longest posting in the defense of Vicksburg. He died in October 1865.

WWII

During the D-day invasion on June 8 1944. Lt. Eacott Allen, returning from a bombing run in his P-51B, crashed into another aircraft flown by James F. Scott of 334 fighter squadron. The tail of the other aircraft was cut off and that caused it to dive into the ground killing the pilot. Both were part of the 4th fighter group USAF. Lt. Allen crashed behind enemy lines and escaped. Many years later I was contacted by someone from France who had an interest in finding him as he had been sheltered in their town and they wanted to contact him. Unfortunately, after much searching it was established he had died.

Correspondence in the Byroade papers at the University of Arkansas contain this reference: "Byroade papers contain a pamphlet copy of a secret memorial of General Tanaka of Japan regarding the impending World War, signed by Lt. Col. Eacott S. Miller, P.S.;"

Lt. Col. James Eacott Miller was A-1 or 5th in Command of the IX Bomber Squadron which served in the Mediterranean and the European Theaters of War. This group was composed of B-26 bombers.

Miller, Eacott Berton, born 09/09/1886, d. 02/08/1954, COL USA, RET, Plot: OS PL5, burial 02/11/1954 in San Francisco National Cemetery.

An account of the Viet Nam war involving Lt. Eacott, see appendix S.

Other Professions

There appear to have been a number of educators among the Eacotts and some were in various trades especially the building trades. Back in 1845 there was an Eacott's Circulating Library established in Bristol. Also in Bristol were a cordwainer, a lady straw hat maker and a husband and wife team who went to London and opened a private school for girls.

Other than farmers the first Eacott trade was a 1630 Richard at North Cerney who was a rough mason. At Chippenham and Wooton Bassett in the 1770's Thomas and John Eacott were plumbers and glaziers. While at the same time, William was a mason in Gloucester.

Others were in the textile trade in some form or another.

Landmarks

Eycott still exists on the topographic maps of England as noted elsewher. However other sites exist.

Somewhere in the Lake District of England there is a volcanic rock group known as the Eycott Volcanic Group, middle ordovician, caradoc volcanic succession continental near Keswick in Cumbria. Also in the Lake District is Eycott Hill. There is an Eycott farm on the edge of the Lake District Park, Penrith, Cumbria. How did the Eycott name arrive so far out of its place of origin?

One researcher found that Great Aiket Pike and Great Aiket Moss were places on an ancient map of the area where most names were Viking. So, Eycott was never a person – Eycott was Aiket and Aiket was a place.

'Aiket' is the Viking name for oak-wood. There's a cluster of places with similar names, such as Aiketgate east of Carlisle, Aikton near Wigton and Askew Rigg Farm beside Eycott Hill itself which suggest that many parts of north Cumbria had oak-woods when the Viking settlers arrived in about 900AD.

At Coventry Eacotts are remembered by a street, Eacott's Close.

In Lambton County Ontario there is an Eacott family cemetery plot.

Mandurah in Western Australia recognizes their pioneer Eacott with a park, a street and an historic home.

Appendix N
Some Letters

When this project began in the early 1980's I had no information about even my grandfather. Along the way I met others who were also interested in the Eacott family. One of these persons was Miss E.M. Newton who in 1984 wrote to a number of Eacotts in England. We corresponded and she wrote one day sending me a packet of letters and a note that she was now unwell. I never heard from her again. Here are some extracts:

~~~~~~~

East Ilsley

Nr. Newbury Berks.

14.8.84

.............My grandfather , I believe, was born between 1850-1860 but where, I cannot say. He married at East Ilsley around 1880 and had a family of 2 sons. I know he had an elder step brother, but more than that I cannot say...........................

<div align="right">
Yours sincerely,

F.A. Eacott
</div>

~~~~~~~

21 the Square

Alveston

Bristol

24.8.84

.... I am Olive Louise Eacott (69) and am living in the house I was born in, which my father moved into in 1915 (I believe) and his mother Rosalinda Eacott died in. Her Husband Edgar Eacott was a farmer at Earthcott, died at the age of 35 of pneumonia and is buried in the new churchyard here at Alveston. But most of the Eacotts were buried in the Old Alveston Churchyard. I remember when I was quite young seeing several gravestones there full of the Eacott name. One with painted Cherubs and trumpets at its head was dated 16– or so I think............

Certainly on an old ordinance map my husband found that there were several acres of land at Earthcott that were called Eacott's Marsh.

I should be most interested to hear about the Frampton Cotterell Eacotts because my father told me why our family and theirs never spoke again after a refused request for help when his father died at 35 and left his mother a widow in dire straits with a very young family......

Yours Sincerely

Olive O'Neill

~~~~~~~

Four Oaks

Sutton Coldfield

....................My father came from Frampton Cotterell, also had several cousins round about that area, but never kept in contact. My father died when I was six years of age and many years have passed since then. I am now 76 years.................

I Remain

R.C. Eacott

Appendix O
English Naming Conventions.

Many countries have naming customs or naming conventions. While not always used, the British had a very highly developed system of naming children. When it is used, the naming customs often assists in developing a pedigree. The British naming custom is shown below but be careful – a variation of the naming custom might have been used or the naming custom might not have been used at all.

For the sons:

1. The eldest son is named after the paternal grandfather.

2. The second son is named after the maternal grandfather.

3. The third son is named after the father.

For the daughters:

1. The eldest daughter is named after the maternal grandmother.

2. The second daughter is named after the paternal grandmother.

3. The third daughter is named after the mother.

Subsequent children would be named after still earlier ancestors but generally the naming pattern in their cases would be less structured.

All of this is great if all of the children have been found. But if children have been missed, it can be very misleading.

Appendix P
Poor laws 1691 and Population Movement in England

If one of your relatives seems suddenly to have disappeared, perhaps they were "removed". Under the Poor Law anyone incapable of earning a living was likely to be "examined" and if legal "settlement" to another parish could be established, they would be the subject of a removal order.

Few of the associated "examinations" have survived but where they have there is a surprising wealth of genealogical information to be found. The majority of the removal orders, not surprisingly, were instigated during the winter months between October and March.

Note: From 1691 settlement was established by birth in a given parish, payment of rent/rates, by apprenticeship to a parishioner or by a year of service within the parish. Anyone wishing to move from one parish to another would not be welcomed unless they had a certificate of settlement which confirmed that the original parish would be responsible if he/she needed poor relief. Each woman was allocated a number and apparently had to be recommended by an employer or respectable person. These laws were renounced in the late 1800's.

Appendix Q
Names from the Subsidy Rolls for 1327 listing taxpayers

P. Franklin, *The Taxpayers of Medieval Gloucestershire. An Analysis of the 1327 Lay Subsidy Roll with a New Edition of its Text* (Stroud, 1993)

The extracts taken are about the earliest record of surnames in England. The names are of those whose wealth placed them in a position to be taxed and thus likely fairly well off people. Only adult males would be noted.

The names will be largely restricted to yeoman, clothiers, craftsmen, merchants and the wealthier citizens of the parish and hence shouldn't be viewed as an indication of all names in the parish. (From Bigland)

The selection of places include any in Gloucestershire with strong Eycott connections and places with names that could be corrupted to be Eycott/Eacott. The only actual places with Eycott names are North Cerney and Cirencester.

Bagendon: Ashmead, Guest, Hill, Huntingdon, Parsloe, Poulter.

Charfield: Bishop, Blagdon, Cox, Crooms, Cullimore, Downs, Drew, Eyles, Fowler, Griffin, Halliday, Harris, Hickes, Lodge, Mayo, Millman, Morton, Pain, Parnell, Pick, Pilsworth, Price, Prout, Roach, Rous, Shipway, Stock, Tyndale, Watts, Witchell.

Cirencester: Adye, Ainge, Allaway, Arandel, Archer, Armes, Arnold, Arrowsmith, Ashley, Ashwell, Atkins, Austin, Avening, Badnege, Baily, Baldwin, Ballinger, Baneford, Bathe, Bathurst, Beckett, Benger, Berkeley, Betterton, Blake, Breech, Brereton, Bridges, Brown, Browne, Burge, Burgoyne, Burton, Bush, Byam, Calvert, Canter, Carpenter, Chance, Chandler, Cherley, Cherrington, Church, Cletherow, Cleveland, Clutterbuck, Coates, Coleman, Colen, Compton, Cook, Coxe, Coxwell, Cripps, Cresswell, Croome, Crossley, Damsell, Danis, Dawnay, Day, Deacon, Deighton, Doudin, Ebsworth, Edmunds, Edwards, Ellis, Estcourt, Evans, **Eycott**, Eyles, Fairfax, Ferrebee, Ferrys, Fettiplace, Fewster, Fletcher, Foot, Forden, Forder, Freeman, Fryer, Gale, Gastrell, Gegg, George, Gibbs, Gillam, Glanvill, Green, Greenway, Griffith, Grimes, Groves, Guerney, Gunter, Gurnee, Haines, Hancocks, Harding, Harrison, Hatchet, Hayward, Heard, Hewer, Hewes, Hill, Hillier, Hinton, Hodges, Honour, Hooper, Hopkins, Howe, Huges, Hungerford, Ireton, Jacobs, Jenkins, Johnson, Johnston, Jones, Kemble, Kemish, Kildermore, Kilmister, King, Kirby, Lane, Lawrence, Lewis, Ludlow, Lyne, Mapson, Marner, Marsh, Martyn, Master, Merrett, Millinson, Millington, Mills, Monox, Moore, Morrell, Morse, Moulder, Moysey, Newcombe, Newport, Norris, Note, Oates, Oldsworth, Olive, Onion, Onslow, Osmund, Overbury, Paget, Paine, Painter, Palling, Parsons, Path, Pearce, Peek, Perry, Pew, Poole, Powle, Pratt, Radway, Ratcliff, Raymond, Reeve, Rich, Richardson, Robbins, Robins, Rogers, Rowe, Rowles, Rudge, Saintsbury, Saunders, Seaman, Scruton, Selby, Selfe, Serrell, Shewell, Shirley, Sleech, Small, Smith, Snow, Sollace, Sparkes, Sparrow, Stephens, Steevens, Stiles, Stone, Strange, Stronge, Sutton, Taggart, Tebbat, Telling, Thompson, Tibbet, Timbrell, Tipper, Tombs, Tully, Turner, Tustin, Ursell, Vaisey, Waight, Warneford, Weare, Webb, Welch, Weobly, Wheeler, White, Whitley, Whitmore, Willis, Willet, Williams, Winstone, Witshed, Wodehouse, Wroughton.

Lassbrough: Estcourt, Dutton, Geale, Horfield

North Cerney: Baldwin, Bendall, Blake, Broad, Bryan, Cherrington, Corbet, Eldridge, **Eycott,** Fry, Guest, Haines, Hawkins, Jordan, Lovesy, Millar, Painter, Perry, Radway, Rich, Stephens, Stockwell, Townsend.

Pitchcomb: Bond, Budding, Chew, Chissold, Clissold, Cook, Davis, Escott, Gabb, Gardner, Gill, Harris, Hogg, Jenner, Jones, Mills, Page,

Palling, Pool, Randel, Viner.

Stroud: Adderley, Aldridge, Allaway, Arundel, Aston, Barrett, Baylis, Biddel, Binter, Blake, Bond, Briday, Browning, Bubb, Bucknell, Budding, Busy, Butler, Canton, Capel, Carver, Chandler, Chapman, Chew, Clayfield, Clissold, Close, Clutterbuck, Colborne, Cole, Cooke, Corbet, Cox, Creed, Cripps, Croome, Dallaway, Dangerfield, Daniel, Davis, Day, Delmomt, Dicks, Drew, Dunn, Dyer, Eastcot, Elborugh, Elland, Ellis, Essex, Essington, Farr, Field, Finch, Fisher, Flower, Franklin, Fream, Freame, Freebury, Gabb, Gainey, Gardner, Gibbons, Gill, Glover, Goddard, Godwyn, Grazebrook, Gryffin, Gyde, Haines, Hale, Hall, Halling, Hamond, Heart, Hill, Hodges, Holder, Holmes, Holwell, Hopson, Hughes, Iles, James, Jenkins, Johns, Johnson, Keen, King, Knight, Knowles, Lambric, Lamburn, Leversage, Lewis, Libby, Lloyd, Mander, Mansell, Marle, Marling, Marten, Martin, Mason, Maule, Merritt, Miles, Millard, Miller, Mills, Minet, Mower, Neale, Newland, Oakey, Page, Paine, Parslow, Pates, Peglar, Phelps, Pierce, Playne, Pleydell, Pool, Powel, Power, Price, Pritchard, Reid, Ridler, Rommieu, Saintbury, Scudamore, Seede, Sewell, Sims, Smith, Snowden, Sollars, Sommers, Stanton, Stephens, Stockham, Stratford, Tanner, Taylor, Tuckwell, Turner, Tyers, Underwood, Verender, Vick, Wake, Warner, Washbourne, Wathen, Watkins, Watts, Webb, White, Winchcomb, Window, Winnet, Wintle, Wise, Worden, Wright, Wyatt.

Appendix R
Descendants of Berkeley Eycott

Generation 1

Berkeley Eycott was born about 1655 in Bagendon, Gloucestershire, England to Richard Eycott. He died on 12 Mar 1716 in North Cerney, Gloucestershire, England. He married Mary Shewell on 13 Sep 1688 in North Cerney, Gloucestershire, England. She was born before 1670.

Notes for Berkeley Eycott:

He was in his will listed as Gentleman of Eycot House Rendomb.

Apprenticed to William Cowland, Goldsmith Guild Hall, London in 1670

1564 Richard Berkeley of Stokes Gifford buys Eycot manor. They held it for many years. Lady Eleanor Berkeley was mistress at Rendcombe in 1608 (will prob 5/5424 Ward/729/42).

From Goldsmiths of Gloucestershire:

Berkeley was son of Richard a farmer from Bagendon and apprenticed in 1670 to William Cowland. Unlike his brother William he did not become free of the Goldsmiths but returned to Cirencester to set up business by 1698. Was church warden 1703-05 fined 30 June 1706 for selling substandard wares?

Notes for **Mary Shewell**:

The relatively few Sewells found in Gloucestershire records are sometimes confused with the Shewells as pointed out in a previous article in Soul Search (July 2000). The IGI lists about 60 Sewells events in the county, compared with 330 Shewells. By 1881 the Census returns show just 3 Sewells to have been born in county against 44 Shewells. That the ratio of one name to the other should have changed so dramatically may be fortuitous but as this article seeks to show, there may be explanations.

Between the 16-18th centuries, nearly three-quarters of the IGI events for Sewell and Shewell were associated with the Stroud area, principally at Bisley but also at Miserden, Painswick, Minchinhampton and Nympsfield. Like Stroud, the upland village of Bisley is closely connected with the cloth trade. In the IGI, after 1608, there are 16 Sewell and 70 Shewell events registered at Bisley. Up to 1730 there is a mixture of the two surnames within the same family but after this date only Shewell appears.

In the S aisle of All Saints, Bisley is a rare, if not unique, memorial brass dedicated to Kateryn Sewell, dated 8th January 1515. A woman is shown in Tudor dress beneath which is an inscribed plaque and two smaller brasses displaying her six sons and five daughters. These have apparently been removed from their original position and screwed onto the wall.

At least as early as 1578, the Sewells were tenants of a small manor known as Ferris Court. The manor was sold in 1599 to John Sewell who bequeathed the property in 1622 to his son John (d.1646). The family acquired a coat of arms employing a diagonal band and three owls - reminiscent maybe of the chevron and three bees of other Sewell crests. By 1669 Ferris Court had passed out of

Sewell hands but returning briefly in the 1760-70s. Ferris Court is a very modest building of the 17th century or earlier, now used as a barn, and situated opposite to Home Farm. Marked on the OS map, it is situated on the southern edge of Lypiatt Park about halfway between Bisley and Stroud.

The 18th century historian John Bigland mentions the Kateryn Sewell brass but gives her surname as Shewell. A visit to Bisley proves this to be incorrect. Bisley has a large collection of inscribed memorial plaques and Bigland includes the following:

Walter Sewell died March 8, 1664. Thomas his son died Feb 2, 1694. Joan his wife died Sept 20, 1714.

To add further confusion the Victoria County History totally ignores the name Shewell and refers to Sewell throughout the volume covering the Bisley Hundred.

As the VCH shows, other properties had Sewell connections. In 1647, Calfway Farm, to the north of Bisley, belonged to Walter Sewell of Stroud, a dyer, who passed it on to his son Robert in 1659. In 1671, Robert and Walter Sewell, clothiers, held the estate and it was still in Robert's hands around 1686.

By 1698 it belonged to Robert Sewell, a baker, who was still the owner in 1745 although in the meantime he had moved to Nympsfield. Incidentally, Bigland documents both Shewell and SHOWELL memorials at Nympsfield. By 1770 Calfway Farm was held by John Sewell and retained until 1819 when it became part of the Lypiatt Park estate.

Huckvale's Court, later known as Thrupp Mill, at Far Thrupp (south of Stroud), was according to the VCH occupied in 1608 by Richard Sewell (d.1635). Inherited by his son Giles, it passed in 1677 to Richard Sewell. In 1752 it was known as Sewell's Mill. A John Sewell appears in the 1776 Stroud electoral list as a freeholder. By the early 19th century, however, there neither Sewells nor Shewells in the Stroud Directory nor for that matter do they appear in the 1851 Census for Bisley.

Berkeley Eycott and Mary Shewell had the following children:

i. John EYCOTT was born on 01 Sep 1689 in North Cerney, Gloucestershire, England. He died on 28 Apr 1751 in North Cerney, Gloucestershire, England. He married Elizabeth Jones on 15 Sep 1715. She was born before 1695.

ii. RICHARD EYCOTT was born on 18 Apr 1692 in Cirencester, Gloucestershire, England. He married UNKNOWN. She was born before 1700. He married (2) MARY SADLER on 19 Mar 1726 in Cirencester, Gloucestershire, England. She was born before 1710.

iii. THOMAS EYCOTT was born on 02 May 1695 in North Cerney, Gloucestershire, England. He married Penelope Ebsworth on 06 Sep 1720 in Cirencester, Gloucestershire, England. She was born before 1700 and probably married this Thomas. Other Thomas's born 1690 and 98.

iv. SARAH EYCOTT was born on 19 Sep 1698 in Cirencester, Gloucestershire, England. She married J. Ballinger on 15 Dec 1720 in Cirencester, Gloucestershire, England. He was born before 1700 and probably husband of this Sarah.

v. JOSEPH EYCOTT was born on 28 Dec 1703 in Cirencester, Gloucestershire, England. He died on 28 Sep 1786 in Stonehouse. He married Mary Freeman on 12 Apr 1730 in Quedgeley, Gloucestershire, England (or 7 april 1730 Chedworth). She was born in 1712 in North Cerney, Gloucestershire, England. She died on 18 Mar 1785 in Stonehouse, Gloucestershire, England.

vi. MARY EYCOTT was born on 18 May 1707 in Cirencester, Gloucestershire, England. She married C. May on 09 Jun 1728 in North Cerney, Gloucestershire, England. He was born before 1710.

vii. BERKLEY EYCOTT was born on 05 Oct 1710 in Cirencester, Gloucestershire, England. He married Mary Patch on 08 Feb 1731 in North Cerney, Gloucestershire, England. She was born before 1710 in Siddington, Cheshire, England.

Generation 2

JOHN[2] **EYCOTT** (Berkeley[1]) was born on 01 Sep 1689 in North Cerney, Gloucestershire, England. He died on 28 Apr 1751 in North Cerney, Gloucestershire, England. He married Elizabeth Jones on 15 Sep 1715. She was born before 1695.

Notes for John Eycott:

In his will he leaves his Bagendon estate to his son John.

Thomas and Richard ... other sons were not of age.

No mention is made of Elizabeth, Jones, Joseph, James and Mary in the will. The FT record has no Thomas.

Another record of John Eycott has all his children spelled as Eccot. Will of John Eycott of Cirencester, Goldsmith, 11 May 1737, proved 1751. Had estates in Bagendon. Was in records of English Catholics.

John Eycott and Elizabeth Jones had the following children:

   i.   THOMAS^3 EYCOTT was born before 1750.

   ii.   JOHN EYCOTT was born on 20 Oct 1717 in Cirencester, Gloucestershire, England.

           Notes for John Eycott: Since the year of his birth is the same as that of John Eacott, mayor of Wooton Bassett 1717 to 1792, he may be the same person. See also John Eacott 1728 who was plumber and glazier.

   iii.   RICHARD EYCOTT was born on 07 May 1730 in Cirencester, Gloucestershire, England.

   iv.   JOSEPH EYCOTT was born on 09 Aug 1716 in Cirencester, Gloucestershire, England.

   v.   ELIZABETH EYCOTT was born on 22 Jul 1719 in Cirencester, Gloucestershire, England.

   vi.   JONES EYCOTT was born on 13 Oct 1721 in Cirencester, Gloucestershire, England. He died in 1779 in Cirencester, Gloucestershire, England. He married Elizabeth Tombs on 06 Apr 1758 in Cirencester, Gloucestershire, England. She was born before 1740.

           Notes for Jones Eycott:

He appears on a voter's list about 1770 for Cirencester as a householder owning his own house.

He was also known as Eccott.

vii. JOSEPH EYCOTT was born on 11 Mar 1723 in Cirencester, Gloucestershire, England. He married Elizabeth in Yattendon, Berkshire, England. She was born before 1730.

viii. JAMES EYCOTT was born on 17 Feb 1725 in Cirencester, Gloucestershire, England.

ix. MARY EYCOTT was born on 01 Feb 1727 in Cirencester, Gloucestershire, England.

RICHARD^2 EYCOTT (Berkeley^1) was born on 18 Apr 1692 in Cirencester, Gloucestershire, England. He married (1) unknown born before 1700. He married (2) MARY SADLER on 19 Mar 1726 in Cirencester, Gloucestershire, England. She was born before 1710.

Richard Eycott had the following children:

> i. ANNE^3 EYCOTT was born on 16 Jan 1711 in Cirencester. Married John Wooley of Withington
>
> ii. JOHN EYCOTT was born on 01 Apr 1714 in Cirencester, Gloucestershire, England. He was trader to the Creeks. Married Mary Jey 29 July 1741 at Charles Town South Carolina.
>
> iii. GEORGE EYCOTT was born on 29 Oct 1715.
>
> iv. SARAH EYCOTT was born on 17 May 1716 in Cirencester, Gloucestershire, England. She died on 17 May 1716.
>
> v. SLAUGHTER VICARAGE EYCOTT was born on 11 Dec 1718 in Cirencester, Gloucestershire, England.
>
> vi. RICHARD EYCOTT was born on 04 Sep 1723 in Cirencester, Gloucestershire, England. He married ELIZABETH. She was born before 1725.

vii. MARY EYCOTT was born on 18 Feb 1724 in Cirencester, Gloucestershire, England.

THOMAS[2] **EYCOTT** (Berkeley[1]) was born on 02 May 1695 in North Cerney, Gloucestershire, England. He married Penelope Ebsworth on 06 Sep 1720 in Cirencester, Gloucestershire, England. She was born before 1700 and probably married this Thomas. Others born 1690 and 98.

Thomas Eycott and Penelope Ebsworth had the following children:

i. PENELOPE[3] EYCOTT was born before 1730. She married Richard Charles on 21 Oct 1752 in Hampnett, Gloucestershire, England. He was born before 1735.

ii. ELIZABETH EYCOTT. She married ROBERT SAUNDERS.

JOSEPH[2] **EYCOTT** (Berkeley1) was born on 28 Dec 1703 in Cirencester, Gloucestershire, England. He died on 28 Sep 1786 in Stonehouse. He married Mary Freeman on 12 Apr 1730 in Quedgeley, Gloucestershire, England (or 7 april 1730 Chedworth). She was born in 1712 in North Cerney, Gloucestershire, England. She died on 18 Mar 1785 in Stonehouse, Gloucestershire, England.

Notes for Joseph Eycott: not in Berkeley's will so may not be this line or else died and other Joseph married.

Joseph Eycott and Mary Freeman had the following children:

i. THOMAS[3] EYCOTT was born on 27 Jun 1732 in North Cerney, Gloucestershire, England.

ii. SARAH EYCOTT was born on 20 Apr 1734 in Cherington, Gloucestershire, England. She died on 26 Jul 1744.

iii. HENRY EYCOTT was born on 17 Oct 1736 in Cherington, Gloucestershire, England. He died about 18 Mar. 1801 in Stonehouse, Gloucestershire, England. He married ANNE CLUTTERBUCK. She died after 1804.

He married ELIZABETH. She was born in 1735. She died in 1792 in Stonehouse, Gloucestershire, England.

iv. GRACIANA EYCOTT was born on 09 Mar 1738 in Cherington, Gloucestershire, England.

v. JOSEPH EYCOTT was born on 01 Feb 1739 in Cherington, Gloucestershire, England.

vi. NATHANIEL EYCOT was born on 21 Apr 1746 in Cherington, Gloucestershire, England. He died on 06 Jan 1805 in Stonehouse, Gloucestershire, England.

vii. LUCY EYCOT was born on 21 Aug 1748 in Cherington, Gloucestershire, England. She married Robert Smith on 20 Jul 1788 in Cirencester, Gloucestershire, England. He was born before 1750.

viii. MARY EYCOT was born on 02 Sep 1750 in Cherington, Gloucestershire, England.

ix. WILLIAM EYCOT was born on 20 Feb 1742 in Cherington, Gloucestershire, England.

x. MARY EYCOTT was born on 12 Aug 1753 in Cherington, Gloucestershire, England.

xi. SARAH EYCOTT was born in 1759 in Cherington, Gloucestershire, England. She married John Gill on 13 Mar 1781 in Stroud, Gloucestershire, England. He was born before 1760.

Notes for Sarah Eycott: may be daugther of other Joseph born to Joseph.

BERKLEY[2] EYCOTT (Berkeley[1]) was born on 05 Oct 1710 in Cirencester, Gloucestershire, England. He married Mary Patch on 08 Feb 1731 in North Cerney, Gloucestershire, England. She was born before 1710 in Siddington, Cheshire, England.

Notes for Berkley Eycott: could be Bartley , not in Berkeley Eycott's will so perhaps other family line.

Berkley Eycott and Mary Patch had the following child:

    i. BARTLEY^3 EYCOTT.

    Notes for Bartley Eycott: It is an assumption that Bartley was son of Berkley. Time frame fits.

Generation 3

JOSEPH^3 EYCOTT (John^2, Berkeley^1) was born on 11 Mar 1723 in Cirencester, Gloucestershire, England. He married Elizabeth in Yattendon, Berkshire, England. She was born before 1730.

    Joseph Eycott and Elizabeth had the following children:

    i. JOSEPH^4 ECCOT was born in 1745 in Yattendon, Berkshire, England.

    ii. THOMAS ECCOT was born in 1746 in Yattendon, Berkshire, England.

    iii. JOHN EACOTT was born in 1748 in Yattendon, Berkshire, England. He married (1) REBECCA RAFE on 09 Oct 1774 in Yew Tree, Berks. She was born before 1750 in Wickham, Berkshire, England. He married (2) JANE LAY in Yew Tree, Berks. She was born before 1760.

SLAUGHTER VICARAGE^3 EYCOTT (Richard^2, Berkeley^1) was born on 11 Dec 1718 in Cirencester, Gloucestershire, England. May have died in London

    Slaughter Vicarage Eycott had the following children:

    i. ELEANOR^4 EYCOTT was born in 1752 in Berwick-on-Tweed, Northumberland.

    ii. GEORGE EYCOTT was born in 1754 in Berwick-on-Tweed, Northumberland.

iii.　JOHN EYCOTT was born in 1755 in Nottingham, Northumberland.

RICHARD³ EYCOTT (Richard², Berkeley¹) was born on 04 Sep 1723 in Cirencester, Gloucestershire, England. He married ELIZABETH. She was born before 1725.

Richard Eycott and Elizabeth had the following child:

i. JANE⁴ ECOTT was born on 25 Aug 1745 in Rodmorton.

Richard's siblings JOHN EYCOTT, ANN WOOLEY, GEORGE and SARAH are not known to have children.

ELIZABETH³ EYCOTT (Thomas², Berkeley¹). She married ROBERT SAUNDERS.

Robert Saunders and Elizabeth Eycott had the following child:

i. ELIZABETH⁴ SAUNDERS.

Notes for Elizabeth Saunders:

In 1723 John Eycott gave up his land rights to Thomas, his brother (these were likely sons of Berkeley.). In 1747 Robert Saunders bought the land from Thomas Eycott at the time he, Robert, married Thomas' daughter Elizabeth Eycott. In 1753 Elizabeth Eycott gave to her daughter Elizabeth Saunders her share of the estate. The marriage to Saunders took place at Tyndale but she later lived at Little Farringdon, Berks. The land next passed to Wm. Bolt in 1777 and back to Robert Saunders of Little Farringdon in 1807. In 1812 Wm. Croome purchased the Eycott property at Woodmancote and thus ends the Eycott connection.

HENRY[3] **EYCOTT** (Joseph[2], Berkeley[1]) was born on 17 Oct 1736 in Cherington, Gloucestershire, England. He died about 18 Mar 1801 in Stonehouse, Gloucestershire, England. He married ANNE CLUTTERBUCK. She died after 1804. He married ELIZABETH. She was born in 1735. She died in 1792 in Stonehouse, Gloucestershire, England.

Notes for Henry Eycott: Is he father of Henry of Stonehouse? Did he die in 1801? He may be son of Joseph and Mary.

In 1783 Henry Eycott was a clothier and blackwell hall factor at Stonehouse. Bailey's Western and Midland directory. British Library cw3305537096

Notes for Anne Clutterbuck: her identity assumed as wife of Henry because of legal file 1804 Mrs. Anne Clutterbuck Eycott of Stonehouse and William Fryer of Eastington her second husband.

Henry Eycott and Anne Clutterbuck had the following children:

i. HENRY[4] EYCOTT was born in 1773. He died about 1821 in Stonehouse, Gloucestershire, England. He married MARY. She was born in 1772. She died in 1847 in Stonehouse, Gloucestershire, England.

ii. SARAH EYCOTT was born before 1763. She married James Lewis on 15 Nov 1783 in Stonehouse,   Gloucestershire, England. He was born before 1765.

Henry Eycott and Elizabeth had the following child:

iii. WILLIAM EYCOTT was born in 1806 in Stonehouse, Gloucestershire, England. He died in 1812 in Stonehouse, Gloucestershire, England. He married MARY. She was born in 1772. She died in 1847 in Stonehouse, Gloucestershire, England.

Generation 4

JOHN[4]EACOTT (Joseph[3] Eycott, John[2] Eycott, Berkeley[1] Eycott) was born in 1748 in Yattendon, Berkshire, England. He married (1) REBECCA RAFE on 09 Oct 1774 in Yew Tree, Berks. She was born before 1750 in Wickham, Berkshire, England. He married (2) JANE LAY in Yew Tree, Berks. She was born before 1760.

John Eacott and Rebecca Rafe and/or second wife Jane Lay had the following children:

     i.   WILLIAM[5] EACOTT was born on 30 May 1779 in Brightwalton, Berkshire, England. He married HANNAH. She was born before 1790.

     ii.   JOHN EACOTT was born on 26 Aug 1775 in Brightwalton, Berkshire, England.

     iii.   ELIZABETH EACOTT was born on 20 Apr 1777 in Brightwalton, Berkshire, England.

     iv.   ABRAHAM EACOTT was born on 20 Sep 1781 in Brightwalton, Berkshire, England. He died in 1865. He married (1) MARTHA WIGGINS on 11 Nov 1804 in East Garston, Berkshire, England. She was born about 1780 in England. He married MARY JONES. She was born before 1790.

     v.   MARTHA EACOTT was born on 30 Sep 1787 in Brightwalton, Berkshire, England.

     vi.   REBECCA EACOTT was born in 1784. She married Thomas Frowde on 11 Dec 1802 in Brightwalton, Berkshire, England. He was born before 1785.

HENRY[4] EYCOTT (Henry[3], Joseph[2], Berkeley[1]) was born in 1773. He died about 1821 in Stonehouse, Gloucestershire, England. He married MARY. She was born in 1772. She died in 1847 in Stonehouse, Gloucestershire, England. Notes for Henry Eycott: Cath. Eycott of Bond's Mills, spinster, had a marriage contract with William John Wood of Stroud written in 1823. She is not entered as an attached person because Henry has no daughter called Cath. Henry lives at Bond's Mills.

Henry or his father had married Catherine Holmes who died age 27. Henry was noted as clothier of Stonehouse 1793. Catherine born abt 1766. Daughter of Stroud blacksmith Robert Holmes

1725 - 1793 and Hannah 1766 - 1844. The Holmes are buried at Randwick near Stroud.

Times of London May 30 1818

May 23, at Eastington Gl., H.C. Eycott Esq. married Ann Clutterbuck, only daughter of Wm. Fryer Esq. of Eastington Gl. So is H.C. Charles born about 1800? and is this the same Ann Clutterbuck married to this Henry's father? If so, was she a second wife to the Sr. Henry?

Henry Eycott and Mary had the following children:

    i. ELIZABETH MARY[5] EYCOTT was born on 10 Apr 1794 in Stonehouse, Gloucestershire, England. She married Richard Martin in 1822 in Stonehouse, Gloucestershire, England. He was born before 1800.

    ii. JOSEPH EYCOTT was born in 1795 in Stonehouse, Gloucestershire, England.

    iii. JOSEPH WILLIAM EYCOTT was born on 24 Feb 1796 in Stonehouse, Gloucestershire, England. He died in 1802 in Stonehouse, Gloucestershire, England.

    iv MARY ANN EYCOTT was born on 19 Sep 1797 in Stonehouse, Gloucestershire, England. She died about 27 Jan 1832 in Stroud, Gloucestershire, England.

    v. MATILDA EYCOTT was born in 1798 in Stonehouse, Gloucestershire, England. She died in 1798.

    vi. FREDERICK EYCOTT was born on 29 Nov 1803 in Stonehouse, Gloucestershire, England. He died in 1884 in Stonehouse, Gloucestershire, England.

He married Sophia. She was born about 1812 in Stonehouse, Gloucestershire, England. She died in 1896 in Stonehouse, Gloucestershire, England.

      vii. JOSEPH EYCOTT was born on 27 Apr 1805 in Stonehouse, Gloucestershire, England. He died in 1805.

      viii. WILLIAM EYCOTT was born in 1807 in Stonehouse, Gloucestershire, England.

      ix.   CATHERINE EYCOTT was born about 1800 in Stonehouse, Gloucestershire, England.

      x.   CHARLES EYCOTT was born about 1800 in Stonehouse, Gloucestershire, England.

Notes for Charles Eycott: This may be Henry Charles Eycott who was declared bankrupt. Times of /London May 19 1851 at the insolvent debtors court. Adjourned protection.

Appendix S

Account from Viet Nam 1969 - US Forces

This article was not included in the main text as it took place more recently than the rest of the book. It is however an interesting account.

First Lieutenant Eacott Involved as Pilot During Viet Nam War

On 11 May 1969, while operating northeast of Bearcat, a Spur scout spotted and engaged an unknown size enemy force. In the ensuing battle, the Scout was shot down and both pilot and observer were killed. The two dead crew members were extracted by a Medivac helicopter and the aircraft was destroyed in place by artillery. Air Force fighters and seven Cobra gunships expended on the area, causing the enemy force to split up and retreat with unknown casualties.

History as remembered by:

then 1LT Charles Stutzman, Silver Spur One-Three:

On 11 May 1969, I was riding as observer with 1LT Eacott when the call came out that a Spur Scout had been shot down. I can not remember who the Cobra pilot was but I don't think I will ever forget who the front seat gunner was. It was Captain Donald Duncan who, by the way, is the author of this history. We arrived on location just a few minutes after our Cobra ship since we could only attain about 130 knots while the Cobra could do close to 160. As we arrived, we made several circles around the downed Loach at about 75 foot altitude noticing that it had a faint trail of smoke rising up from the engine area through some of the numerous holes that had been inflicted by the VC. I observed that Sgt. Roderigues was alive but was wounded in the upper leg and was taking cover outside the aircraft beside and rear of the mini gun. He was sitting almost laying down on the ground. We made a few circles around the downed aircraft and looked to see if we could locate any enemy. During this time Roderigues moved his position from rear of the mini gun to in front of it and then back to the rear crawling and kneeling and looking at us and back at the surrounding area but WO Gilbert did not move at all. Eacott made a closer pass directly in front of the downed Loach at about 50 foot, allowing me to check out if WO Gilbert was alive. What I observed through the shot up Plexiglas was that he was slumped in the seat with his head laying back and there was a visible wound in the forehead.

During the next 4 or 5 passes we did not detect any visible VC still in the area. Eacott looked at me and asked if I thought we should land and recover the downed crew. I responded affirmative and we both removed our shoulder harnesses and advised the two Cobra pilots our intentions. The Guns suggested that they make a few passes with suppressive fire to insure that if there were any VC in the area that they would keep their head down as we landed. Duncan began laying in 40 mike and as is the normal with that weapon, the gunner will not know exactly where the first round will land. Then after observing where the first rounds land, one would use an arbitrary spot on the sight as a reference to guess where the next rounds were going to hit. (I had previously learned this fact first hand while riding front seat Cobra.) The only problem was on this occasion is that as 1LT Eacott was making a circling approach to land and had his eyes directed to the downed Loach. I was looking for any VC out my door and I saw the first round of 40 mm impacting just about 100 feet left of my door and our flight path and the 2nd round of 40 mm landed just to the right of Eacott's door exploding in his line of vision as he had started a circling approach to the Loach. I think that Eacott did not realize it was "friendly fire" and thought it was VC fire from below and he opened up with several burst with the mini gun. This is where it really got busy. All the rest happened in a span of only about 1 minute or so (although it seemed to be much longer and it happened as if it was in slow motion). I had seen that it was the 40 mm from Duncan's ship due to it exploding on the tree tops as he (Duncan) walked it on away from us and pounded the surrounding area. With the exception of an area about 300 foot in diameter with the downed Loach in the center, the entire ground started to move as hundreds of VC that had been camouflaged started crawling, moving and running around about 150 feet away from the down aircraft. The best way I can describe it is that it reminds me of an ant pile full of mad fire ants. I opened fire with the Car 15 and found that the observer who I had bumped off the mission had short loaded all his clips with only about 5 to 10 rounds per clip. (I later asked him in a not too nice manner what in the world was his reason for not having full clips of ammo and he said that when they were all full his pack was too heavy to carry. . . go figure!!) I expended every round he had in a matter of minutes and began to throw out grenades until all I had left out of the 40 or so that we started with was smokes. I had even threw out all the Willie Pete, Incendiary and a few CS. I used up all but 5 rounds of both mine and 1LT Eacott's .38 ammo.

By this time other Spur Hunter Killer teams were arriving on station and relieved us. Shortly the Lift Platoon arrived with troops ready to insert. They were orbiting off station (to the North I believe but am not sure). As we had expended all our firepower, we backed off and held back towards the west of the area closer to a refuel area just in case we were needed later.

In a short span of time a large but undetermined number of VC were killed. With in about 30 minutes or so Dust Off rescued Sgt. Roderigues while almost getting annihilated themselves. As I recall, the medic at great danger was able to pull him on board while one of his crew members used his "personal" unauthorized weapon to suppress the VC as they attempted to assault the Dust Off aircraft.

Sgt. Roderigues was flown to the hospital at Bien Hoa and was recovering with a wound to the upper leg which was not life threatening. To everyone's disbelief Sgt. Roderigues died 4 days later due to, of all things, pneumonia. I don't understand how that could happen, but it did.

Looking back at that day, I count it as the closest that I have ever been to loosing my Immortality. First by "Friendly Fire", and I am NOT pointing fingers as CPA Duncan because I have operated the same piece of equipment riding in front seat Cobra and know it's inaccurate way of guessing where the first round would hit and then walking it into the target. Then by the 100's of VC that were so well camouflaged that they were invisible until we started shooting. And even after numerous ships had expended their ammo and a Dust Off landed, the enemy was still large enough to plaster the Dust Off with numerous rounds almost resulting is further American deaths. It was the most intense fighting I had been exposed to up to that point, or would get exposed the rest of my abbreviated tour. Then to the situation of trusting the observer to have a full load of ammo as I went off into war on my 3rd day of transition into Scouts after loosing faith in Hueys when I lost my tail rotor on a night firefly mission. Then if we had landed before Duncan disturbed them with the 40 mm and Eacott hosed down the area with the mini, we would not *have had enough ammo to defend ourselves as we surely would have had to do when the waves of 100's of VC would have assaulted us as we were trying to extract Sgt. Roderigues. I would guess that there were (this is not a Texas stretch) well over one thousand VC moving around on the ground. After Dust Off cleared and the Guns hosed the entire area down with "Red Smoke" ("Nails") (flechettes / darts) as it was, and the Air Force had a hey day defoliating the area with their toys, the DC-3's that had nick names such as "Spooky", "Puff", and "Smoky" could really defoliate. As best as I can recall, the size of the VC unit was reported to be in the thousands.*

Just a few days later the area was swept and not a body could be found, and we all know how that works, the meat hooks and mass graves. We also know the devastation that a few loads of Nails and what "Spooky", "Puff" and "Smoky" could lay down. It puts a entirely different meaning to the term "Awesome" which is a word that it used too easily today by the younger generation.

Appendix T

Eycott-Vyner Connection

Thomas Ekott in his will of July 1583 says he was not a well man. In fact he was to depart this world within the month. In August his will was proved.

Thomas was a husbandman at Bagendon. That is he was a farmer, raising principally sheep. He had 6 daughters all unmarried and a son, Joseph all under twenty years of age. In addition his wife was still of child bearing age. It could thus be guessed that he was between 35 and 50 years of age. Thomas had 5 brothers, Robert (his will 1629), John the Younger, John the Elder, Edward and William. John the elder had children. His wife was Elizabeth. His will includes references to Henry Balden or Baulden.

Richard Eycott of North Cerney, ostensibly in good health, set forth his will in 1581. His children four boys and 2 girls, John, Anthony, William, Thomas and Elizabeth and Katherine . Richard has a brother Phillipe who has some severe difficulties and needs to be cared for. His son Thomas has been delegated to care for him.

Thomas in his will says this, " I make my brother THOMAS VYNER of North Cerney, RICHARD BURTON parson of Badgendon and HENRY BALDEN of Wodmancote mine overseers and give to every of them ten shillings."

During the 1500's the price of wool increased rapidly and Cotswold wool was in great demand in Europe. Literacy was also on the rise and by mid century the old feudal rules on land ownership had been abolished. It was a time of prosperity for the yeoman farmers, particularly in the Cotswolds. The wills indicate ownership of some modest property such as pewter dishes, not wood or clay.

Families by and large didn't stray far from their origins and Bagendon and North Cerney were adjacent villages on the road along the Churn river. Everyone pretty much knew everyone else.

Thomas Vyner of North Cerney is married twice, first to a sister of Thomas Ekott (Margaret born about 1533). They have several children Richard 1566, Joane 1568, Katherine, Robert, Mary, Ann including a son William (31 jan 1568) before Margaret dies and Thomas remarries Ann Ellis (born 1554) also of North Cerney. There are several more children born including, on the 15 of December 1588, a son also Thomas, born at North Cerney. Thomas senior has a sister who has married and moved to London. At the age of 13, 1601, Thomas junior is apprenticed to Thomas's brother in law Samuel Moore who is a London goldsmith. This is a trade with great career connections and available only to the favored child who has access to these connections. In 1604 Thomas junior continues his apprenticeship with William Terry. From 1623 to 1665 he lived at the "Vine" Clements Lane, Lombard St. home of the money managers of London. Thomas moves in a select society and became a goldsmith, banker, and national financier for the Commonwealth and also the monarchy. In 1646 to 1651 he became an Alderman for Billingsgate. In 1648 he was Sheriff of London. An active supporter of Cromwell he was made Lord Mayor of London in 1653. This was real power at the highest level that only great wealth could command.

His nephew Robert Vyner, son of his half brother William whose mother was Margaret   (presumably Ekott), became an alderman in London for Broad St. in 1666. He had been an apprentice of his uncle in earlier years. He had gone into business with his Uncle. Born at Warwick in 1631 he died at Windsor Castle in 1688. He was lord Mayor in 1674. In 1662 Thomas and Robert were the King's goldsmiths and were asked to supply the East India Company. He also was a partner in the Hudson's Bay Company and reputed to be the wealthiest man in England.

With the Restoration of Charles II to the throne, Thomas changed sides like many other influential people of the day and became a supporter of the monarchy again. His reward was instant as he was created a baronet in 1660 for his support. (He had also been knighted by Cromwell.)

Thus when he died 28 may 1665, his funeral was a major event. He had been a leader of the realm and one of his clients was Samuel Pepys' who attended the funeral. Thomas was buried at St. Mary Woolnoth. Thomas' brother Robert is also buried there. Robert erected a statue to Charles II on Lombard St. that is now in Newly Hall in Yorkshire. A third brother George Vyner was given building contracts in London after the great fire in 1666 and worked under the supervision of the great architect Wren. Robert became deeply involved with funding the frivolities of Charles II, lending the king great sums, erecting a huge bronze statue to the King and personally creating the crown and most of the regalia for the coronation (the crown jewels of today). Unfortunately the king later defaulted on the loans and financially ruined Robert. He died in 1688 at Windsor castle.

In the shadow of these self made giants there were opportunities for relatives. Two Eycott relatives, a nephew or great nephew, became goldsmiths themselves in Cirencester and Glouster. Bearing a prestigious name which may have linked them to another of the great families, Berkeley and William Eycott had a birth that gave them a future. Born after the great upheaval of the 1640's when the Puritan power was ascendant, when Roundheads fought Royalists, parliament stood against the king and prevailed in the 1650's, they were reared in a community with strong links to Cromwell. Bagendon parish had clergy appointed by Cromwell and had many Puritan style names in the baptisms. Considering the influential local people who rose to prominence, it can be assumed this was a Cromwell supporting community.

Young Berkeley was about 13 years of age, had some schooling and it was arranged for him to be sent to London to be apprenticed to the goldsmiths in 1670. This was 4 years after the great fire, during which his uncle Robert had been the Sherriff of London and there was much construction in the rebuilding of London at the time. The Goldsmiths new hall had just opened. The guild of Goldsmiths were at the peak of their power. They controlled not only the making of gold plate and jewelry but also coin and the flow of currency. It was before the creation of modern banking and around 1670 the goldsmiths of the city were engaged in the nearest thing to being bankers and money lenders. To be apprenticed meant a secure future. Berkeley Eycott served his apprenticeship under William Cowland. However it appears that he never got around to petitioning for his freedom and thus technically did not become a master smith. Thus it is not known how long he remained an apprentice although 7 years was the usual time it took to reach the level of master by creation of a masterpiece. He did however become a goldsmith in Cirencester. In the year he went to London 1670 Robert was becoming a partner in the Hudson's Bay Company and thus part owner of nearly half of Canada. Then 2 years later he was to be involved with creating the Royal African Company, a slaver organization. When he was apprenticing Robert become Lord Mayor of London 1674. Robert Vyner's famous family portrait of 1673 by J.M. Wright now hangs in the National Portrait Gallery, London [NPG 5568]. Robert had a son Charles, named after the King. Charles died in 1688 shortly before Robert. His daughter Bridget became the Duchess of Leeds. Berkeley and William lived in London at a very favored time.

Additional Notes

1. John Cowland was of reputable parents, apprenticed to a goldsmith, got into fight over a women and killed a man near Drury lane theater in the year 1700. Was he the son of William and thus known to Berkeley?

2. Sir Robert Vyner 1673 a family portrait by J.M. Wright is in National Portrait Gallery London.

3. Sir Thomas Viner was lord mayor in 1653. He and Robert his nephew connected to the North Cerney Eycott family.

4. Sir Robert the nephew of Thomas. Sir Robert was a rich goldsmith and banker with a house at Swakelys, Middlesex. His wife was Mary Whitechurch, the widow of Sir Thomas Hyde. Their daughter became the duchess of Leeds. Sir Robert became lord Mayor of London in 1674, went bankrupt in 1684. He and his son Charles both died in 1688.

Appendix U

References

Transactions of the Bristol and Gloucester Archaeological Society

87 volumes begun in 1876 - University of Western Ontario Library (UWO) London, On ; Gloucester Records Office, Gloucester (GRO)

"The Ancient and Present State of Gloucester" by Sir Robert Atkyns, 1712. GRO

"Historical, Monumental and Genealogical Collections Relative to the County of Gloucester" by Ralph Bigland,1791. Eycotts are mentioned only at North Cerney and Cirencester. These would be people of some substance merchants, landowners, manufacturers etc.

"A New History of Gloucester" by Samuel Rudder, 1779

"The History and Antiquities of Gloucester" by Thomas Rudge, 1803

"Gloucester Studies" by H. P. R. Finberg, 1957

"The Cotswolds" by E.R. Delderfield 1961

"A Cotswold Village" by J. Arthur Gibbs 1898

"The Buildings of England" - Gloucestershire: The Cotswolds by David Very 1970

"Ancient Cotswold Churches" by U. Daubney 1921

"The Domesday Geography of Midland England" by H.C. Darby, Cambridge U. Press, 1971

Domesday Book #15 Gloucestershire by J. Morris, Phillimore Press, 1982

"A Belgic Oppidum" Record of Excavations (Bagendon) 54-56 by E.M. Clifford, Heffer and sons Cambridge, 1961

"The Cartulary of Cirencester Abbey Gloucestershire" by C. D. Ross, Oxford U. Press -2 vols- 1964

Victoria County History for Gloucestershire, Oxford U press, Vol VII 1981 (UWO)

"Saxon Charters of Gloucester" by Grundy 1935 (GRO)

"Men and Armour" by Smith, 1608 (reprinted) (UWO)

"History of Bagendon", by Rees, 1932

"Bound for Australia" Australian convict records, by D.T. Hawkings

Other Sources of Information

Gloucestershire Records Office, Worcester Street, Gloucester GL1 3DW, tel (0452) 21444 write to County Archivist. Fee for a search. Their records include: court documents from 1660, various boards from 1800's, hospitals from 1754, diocesan archives from 1541, cathedral archives from 1188, Church registers from 1538, assorted business, association and club records from 1750. A file exists on Eycott/Eacott and on Woodmancote.

Wiltshire Record Office, Trowbridge

Corinium Museum, Park Street, Cirencester, Gl. GL7 2BX, Tel.0285 5611

Gloucester Family History Society c/o Alan Izod Wharnes Road, Upton St. Leonards Glos.

The Bingham Library, The Waterloo, Cirencester. Local documents and information.

I.G.Y. index, Church of Latter Day Saints. extensive recordsof available parish records for Britain and other nations Any Mormon church with a library has a set of detailed data.

Family Search *https://familysearch.org* Full access to IGY

Ancestry.com or other national sites for searches and family trees.

Www.eacott.info web page is a link to online material by the author.

Red Book of Worcester, old church records, Worcester Records Office, County Hall, Worcester

Manor Court Rolls for Eycott 1421 and 1442 (GRO) D678 court rolls # 61c + 94

Frankpledge view at Bibury for Bishop of Worcester(GRO) D678 Bibury court rolls

Rendcomb Court Rolls 1387-1481 , 30 years, Staffordshire Records office, D641/1/4m/1-11

Inquisitions Post Mortem. Gloucestershire 1359-1413, 88 yrs 1375 rents from tenants at will

Gloucestershire Cathedral Library. Reg Abb. Froucester B, pp 83-84 cf.--several entries respecting church at Eycott

North Cerney leases -(GRO) Woodmancote 1715 - 89, GRO D2525

Bagendon Church Wardens Book 1776 at Jesus College Oxford, also a Bagendon Map

Gloucester Subsidy Roll 1327 (GRO) lists tax payers by manors

Poll Tax for 1381and many other documents are found at www.nationalarchives.gov.uk

Manor court rolls for Winchcombe 1421-1442 some refer to Eycot manor D678 ct rolls 97A, 61c, 91, 62, 94. -no eycot surnames shown.

Eacott - Eycott records at the Gloucester Records Office

1416   Eycott - John of Rencomb, witness grant   D326 T9214 to

1715 Eycott - constable oath of allegiance, Bagendon   Q/so4 p18

1715 Eycott - records of papists and alleged papists holdings and oath of allegiance from Thomas Sr., Jr, Rebecca, Mary all of N. Cerney Q/so4

1715   Eycott - Woodmancote - title to deed   D475/T1

1717   Reg. of Estate   Q/RNC 1(22) also (21)

1735   Eycott - Thomas of Bagendon B4/21 and GDR E 27

1719-20   Richard Eycott, Tetbury, name calling charge   GDR B4/112438

1723   Jane Wells vs Richard Eycott, Tetbury , Jane accused of adultery (Jane Eycott)   GDR B4/1/2440

1753   Eycott - Elizabeth   D475/T.1

1823   Cater(?) Stonehouse, marriage settlement   D1917

                  family pedigree, North Cerney   P70M17

RENDCOMB (including Eycott) Records at Staffordshire records office

Court rolls, 1387-88, 1400-09, 1433-51, 1464-65, 1476-81, SRO D641/1/4M/1-11

Accounts, 1364-65, 1401-02, 1412-20, 1433-42, 1452-53, 1463-73, 1485-1504, 1554-58

SRO D641/1/2/138b, 156, 160-163, 169, 177, 183-186,190, 192-208, 250

Wiltshire Wills

1685	Richard Eacott	Bodice maker	Devizes
1701	Edward Eacott Sr	Husbandman	Warminster
1710	John Eacott Sr	Gardener	Warminster
1720	William Eacott		Warminster
1775	John Eacott	Yeoman	Warminster

| 1778 | Thomas Eacott | Plumber/glazier | Chippenham |
| 1792 | John Eacott | Yeoman | Wooton Bassett |

Appendix V

Useful Bits of Information for Studying Ancestry

One in 3 of the gentry made a will in 1600's.

An index of all wills before 1700 is published by PCC (Prerogative court of Canterbury) British Records Society

18,000 apprentices are recorded from 1641 to 1888 according to the Society of Genealogists.

Militia reestablished in 1757 and each parish had to train some men age 18 to 50. Lists were drawn up and published locally.

"Interred" means a burial was of a Catholic, a suicide, or an excommunicated person.

After 1653 births, not baptisms are recorded in church records. Baptism was usually 3 days later.

1662 the Act of Uniformity stated that all rites and ceremonies had to be done by the Church of England. All elected persons had to attend that church. That church's common book of prayer had to be used. Those who refused were called nonconformists and could not be legally married or baptized except in the established church.

After 1753 marriages were standard entries by license.

1823 England legal marriage age dropped from 21years to 14 for boys and 12 for girls.

Landowners numbered about 3 000 in early 14th C. Each had a coat of arms. A yeoman was a substantial farmer who owned at least some of his land outright. A husbandman mostly held land as a copy holder, originally called a villein, had about 30 acres and grazing rights and paid something to the lord of the manor. A farmer was usually a man who paid rent for his land.

Only a dozen or so gentry families today own the land from which their medieval ancestor took his name.

Title Mr. or Mrs. meant the persons were gentry, that means landowners.

1530 the terms ESQ or esquire was common for the gentry to use. Some who were not, used it as well, but the claim could be tested.

July 1 1837 Births, Marriages and Death records by the British government began.

1841 census, anyone over 15 years of age had their age rounded down to nearest 5. Thus a person 59 would become 55 on the form.

Names

Hereditary surnames in England began in East Anglia between 1250 and 1350. There were people still recorded until well into the 1400's who had no surname. A leading reason to insist on surnames was to enable the collection of taxes from identifiable people.

In the 12th century 30% of the male given names were Henry, John, Richard, Robert, William. By the 13th century this had increased to 57% and by 14th century to 64%.

Common female names in 11th /12th century were Joan, Agnes, Catharine, Mary, Elizabeth, and Anne.

In the16/17th centuries the puritans took names such as Joseph, Samuell, Sara

A name with single family origin is rare. Few can trace back to Domesday and fewer still can trace back to the anglo Saxon era. Eycott is likely a single family name. Only Ardens and Berkeleys can prove descent from pre conquest times. According to "The Berkeley's Family History" they were from Eadnorth.

Places

Cromhall in Glos. was an Abbott's Parish. Records date from 1653. 2.5 miles from Wickwar. Cromhall Abbotts (Cromale) at Domesday was Kings land, now Abbottside Farm. Cromhall Lygon records were lost.

Gaunts Earthcote - Hardicote was the original name, never Eacott.

Rendcomb manor mansion dates to 1863, now a school. It was a Parish from 1566 including Eycott manor. Rendcomb was bought by Richard

Berkeley son of John Berkeley in 1564. Grandson Richard was Royalist in 1640's. Son Maurice was also MP died 1654. Richard died 1661. Berkeley Eycott was born during this time, likely named in honor of one of them. William Berkeley was governor of Virginia in mid 1600's. Richard was his uncle. In 1635 Eycot farm part of Rendcomb was sold by Maurice Berkeley to William Guise. Richard Berkeley the father of Maurice was later charged with committing waste by felling trees on the property.

Purton parish as at 1558 it was in the Archdiocese of Wiltshire. Salisbury diocese was held by Glastonbury Abbey at 1086.

Woodmancote was a tything parish of North Cerney. (tithing, a subdivision unit of a parish)

Cirencester town and Chedworth were on the king's land.

The earliest records of peoples names for taxes are on the Subsidy Roles for Cirencester, Bagendon, Woodmancote from 1327 and 1381. The manor court roles for Bagendon and Woodmancote are in the Red Book of the bishop of Worcester.

North Cerney, catalogue Ref. P70 accessions 8468 and 9453 at the GRO.

Notes and papers were collected or compiled by Canon Turner relating to the history of the North Cerney parish, its activities and some of its families - ref. P70 MI 7 from 15th century to late 20th century. It includes details about North Cerney and Woodmancote manors, (based mainly on Domesday Book), information about church lands, the school, the Reading Room, Friendly Societies, the Cheltenham-Cirencester turnpike road (with photocopy of plan, 19th cent.), lists of churchwardens (16th-20th cents.) and parish clerks (18th-20th cents.), owners of Cerney House (Rich, Tyndale, Holder, Croome and Viner families); extracts of PCC wills 15th-17th centuries, notes and pedigrees mainly covering 16th-19th centuries of the following families: Baldwin, Baradell, Broad, Broadhurst, Brown, Coxe, Crump, Cherington, Dean, Eycott, Hall, Large, Painter, Perry, Savory, Smith, Sparrow, Stockwell, Teale, Telling, Tombs, Townshend and Wilson, sale particulars from 1913 of Rendcomb Park Estate (used for information about inhabitants) and a recruiting poster for clergy entitled 'Do I look like a parson?' (used to store pedigrees).

Appendix W

Henry Eycott and Family of Stonehouse (near Stroud)

STONEHOUSE MILLS AND THE CLOTH INDUSTRY

from Victoria History of Gloucester Vol 10

Henry and Frederick Eycott, Saul Lusty, Clutterbuck and others.

Note: King's Stanley and Leonard Stanley are parishes of Stroud abuting Stonehouse.

From the 16th to the early 20th century the manufacture of woollen cloth was the main source of employment for the inhabitants of Stonehouse. The earliest mention found of a fulling-mill in the parish was in 1469, three were working there by 1517, four in the late 16th century, and seven in the 18th century; the history of the nine separate mills that have been found recorded is traced below. Weavers were recorded in the parish from 1540. In 1608 29 people employed in the cloth trade were enumerated as against 17 employed in other trades and 10 in agriculture: they included 6 clothiers, 12 weavers, 7 fullers, and 4 dyers. During the 18th century over 20 clothiers were recorded at Stonehouse, and 10 weavers of broad cloth there took parish apprentices between 1724 and 1785. Among those employed at the mills, shearmen were mentioned in 1709 and 1788, and a wool-scribbler in 1772. A dyer lived at Westrip in 1767.

In the first half of the 19th century the rebuilding and reorganization of some of the cloth-mills of the parish and the adaptation of the remainder to other purposes reflected the change to a factory system in the industry. In 1833 it was said that the bulk of the weaving in the area was carried on in factories, and in 1839 only one mill, the Oil Mill which apparently ceased cloth production soon afterwards, still depended entirely on outdoor weavers. The distress among the weavers, that was attendant on the changes, was said to have been considerable, but in 1839 their condition was found to be better than in neighbouring parishes, with constant employment at good wages obtainable at the mills. The remaining outdoor weavers, whose average earnings were higher than in most of the other clothing parishes, were then mainly master-weavers usually with two looms. Two weaving-shops in Stonehouse village and one adjoining the Spa Inn at Oldend were mentioned in 1840; there are said to have still been several, some of them attached to farm buildings, in the parish c. 1870. Cloth production in the parish during the later 19th century was carried on by three firms, at Ebley Mill, Stonehouse Upper and Lower Mills, and Bond's Mill, and the industry continued to give employment to a large proportion of the inhabitants until the early 20th century. Between 1827 and 1861 41 cloth-workers were admitted to membership of a Stonehouse dissenting chapel. Those employed in dependent trades of the industry in the 19th and early 20th centuries included shear-manufacturers at Ebley and Cainscross mentioned in 1820, firms of millwrights at Ebley until 1931 and at Stonehouse between 1879 and 1894, a wool-broker at Stonehouse in 1863, a firm of teasel-merchants at Ebley until 1894, and a mill-furnisher at Ebley between 1914 and 1919. A firm of wool-merchants and -sorters was established at Stonehouse from c. 1920 to 1930.

There was a mill at Ebley, near the later Ebley Mill, in 1393. In 1403 a moiety of it passed to John Deerhurst, and in 1426 Thomas Deerhurst and Lawrence Maldon each held a moiety. Perhaps at that time it already comprised a corn-mill and a fulling-mill on the same site for in 1469 John Deerhurst of Hardwicke held a corn-mill called Deerhurst's Mill and a fulling-mill called Maldon's Mill. Maldon's Mill was leased by John Deerhurst to a fuller, Thomas Kynne, and Robert Kynne owned it in 1491. After 1511 Maldon's Mill was leased from the Kynnes and later the Cookes to the Bennett family of clothiers, who from 1505 also leased the corn-mill, Deerhurst's Mill, from the Deerhursts and later the Barrows. John Bennett held the mills in the early 16th century, and his son William after 1536. He or a later William was working the fulling-mill in 1578, and his son Thomas in 1580. Thomas, who built Ebley Court in 1587, died c. 1598, and his son Leonard in 1621, when the mill comprised three fulling-stocks and a corn-mill. In 1621 the Bennetts' mill, usually known as Ebley Mill, passed by marriage to the Selwyn family. From the late 17th century the Selwyns leased it to the Turner family of clothiers: John Turner held it in 1681, Thomas Turner between 1710 and 1721, and another Thomas in 1779 and until 1788 when he became bankrupt. A new corn-mill was built at the mill in the early 18th century.

In 1800 Ebley Mill, which then stood on the north side of the Stroudwater Canal, was acquired by Stephen Clissold who built a large new mill south of the canal c. 1820. The new mill was not used, however, until c. 1825 when it was bought by Robson & Severs who abandoned the old mill and destroyed its mill-stream, and made a large reservoir by the new mill. Before 1839 the mill was leased to John Figgins Marling, and in 1840 it was bought by his brothers Thomas and Samuel Stephens Marling. In 1839 there were 71 handlooms at the mill, although only 42 were working, employing 72 workers, including 30 children; power was provided by five water-wheels. (fn. 26) In 1870 the mill was said to employ c. 800 workers. In 1967 Ebley Mill was owned by Marling & Evans Ltd., and housed the carding and spinning processes for the firm's factory at Stanley Mill. The main part of the mill comprises a long stone block of four stories and attics with grouped segmentalheaded windows, apparently the building of c. 1820, and adjoining it on the north-east a tower and a square five-story block with larger windows, designed by G. F. Bodley and built c. 1862. Another building to the west of similar type and date as the older part of the main block was sold c. 1908, and in the 1940s was used by a hosiery yarn spinner. A third block of similar type was demolished in 1965.

The two mills in Stonehouse manor mentioned in 1086 were probably the mill to the east of Bridgend, later known as Stonehouse Upper Mill, which had been granted away from the manor in 1085, and the mill to the west of Bridgend, later known as Stonehouse Lower Mill, which remained in the possession of the lords of the manor until the 17th century. The manor mill included a fullingmill with two stocks in 1496 when it was granted to William Bence on condition that he built there two new mill-heads, a river-gate, and a rack. After 1507 the mill was held by Robert Collier, and by 1533 it had passed to the clothier Richard Fowler who took a further lease of the mill, then known as New Mill, and ½ yardland in 1542. Richard died in 1560, and his son William, who had bought Stonehouse manor jointly with William Sandford in 1558, received the mill at the partition of the manor in 1567. It then comprised three fulling stocks and a corn-mill. Neither William Fowler's son Daniel nor his grandson Stephen appears to have been a clothier, and the manor mill was being worked by John Jessor in 1647 and 1655. Members of the Fowler family, however, were clothiers at Stonehouse until the late 18th century: Stephen's brother Nathaniel was mentioned as a clothier in 1622 and 1655, and Stephen

Fowler, a clothier and probably Nathaniel's son, died at Stonehouse in 1717; a later Nathaniel Fowler, who was at one time in partnership with one of the Nash family of Bridgend, died at his house in Stonehouse in 1781, The manor mill had been sold away from the manor by 1697 when it was owned by the Lye family who sold it in 1701 to the clothier John Arundel. He was recorded as working it between 1710 and 1736, and the mill was known as Arundel's Mill in 1755. In 1764 John Arundel's son William sold it to William Hill who died in 1784 having acquired a considerable fortune in the clothing trade. The mill passed to Edward Hill who owned and worked it until at least 1805. Lower Mill was rebuilt c. 1810 as a large building of five stories which included weaving shops. In 1812 it was occupied by Thomas and Richard Cooper, and before 1819 by the firm of Cooper and Wathen. Its later history is given below.

Stonehouse Upper Mill, known as Corneham Mill in the 16th century and Sandford's in the 18th, was granted by William of Eu in 1085 to Gloucester Abbey; the abbey's mill-stream running westwards from Ryeford was mentioned c. 1340. Richard Mill was the miller between 1507 and 1517 when Corneham Mill, comprising a fullingmill and a corn-mill, was leased by the abbey to Henry Betts. From 1525 the mill was leased to John Sandford; he purchased the freehold in 1544 from Gloucester Corporation, which had acquired the mill with other possessions of Gloucester Abbey in 1542. John Sandford became one of the most prosperous Gloucestershire clothiers of his time; he exported cloth to Germany and had an agency at Frankfurt-on-Main. In 1549 he bought Leonard Stanley Priory. Later he moved to Gloucester, and in 1554 granted Corneham Mill to his son William, who bought Stonehouse manor jointly with William Fowler in 1558. The mill then descended with the Sandford's estate at Stonehouse, and the family probably continued to work the mill as clothiers until its sale by William Sandford in 1731. The mill then comprised three stocks and a corn-mill. By 1765 the mill was being worked by Ambrose Reddall who still occupied it in 1776. Afterwards it was worked by Messrs. Eycott, perhaps of the family that later owned Bond's Mill, and then by Nathaniel Watts who went bankrupt in 1798 when the mill was assigned to his creditors William Tanner and John Brown. It was probably the mill being worked in 1804 by John Brown and Sons.

By 1839 both Stonehouse Upper Mill and Stonehouse Lower Mill had been acquired by the firm of R. S. Davies which had 18 handlooms at work in them. The mills apparently ceased cloth production when sold by the firm in 1904. At the sale waterwheels were advertised with both mills as an additional source of power to steam. The main block of Upper Mill, built of brick with three stories and attics and a central tower apparently dates from a rebuilding of 1875. Adjoining the mill on the east, presumably on the site of the old house of the Sandfords, is a stone house of c. 1800, which had a classical portico. Formerly known as the Rookery, the house was occupied by R. S. Davies in the mid 19th century but in the later 19th century was apparently used as offices, (fn. 78) which purpose it served in 1967. The buildings of Lower Mill were once far more extensive than the two brick-built blocks of the earlier 19th century which survive; in 1812 they included a mansion with 15 rooms.

Another fulling-mill at Bridgend, called Nashes Mill in the 18th century and later Bridgend Mill, was owned by Humphrey Osborne in 1567; it stood south-east of the road near the bridge. Osborne leased it to William Nicholson a clothier in 1579, and in 1588 sold it to Jasper Selwyn. During the 17th and 18th centuries the mill was worked by the Nash clothing family: it was probably the mill of Giles Nash mentioned in 1637, and a Giles Nash was leasing it from the Selwyns c. 1680. The second Giles died in 1699, Giles son of John Nash in 1719, and another Giles Nash in 1729. A later Giles Nash (d. 1767), who was said to have made a fortune in the clothing trade, gained a wide reputation as a dyer in scarlet; scarlet-dyeing at Bridgend was mentioned in 1773, and 'Nash's scarlets' became famous. The Nashes lived in a house near the mill; it was described as an old house in 1773, and was presumably the Nash Court mentioned in 1838. In 1773 the house and mill were apparently owned by a Mr. Elliot, and in 1804 the clothier John Dimock (d. 1808) was leasing the mill from the Elliot family. Dimock's grandson John Dimock and a Mr. Hitch were working it in 1819. Later it was occupied by Sir Paul Baghott who went bankrupt in 1837, and in 1840 Aaron Evans was leasing the mill from George Elliot. In the later 19th century it apparently functioned only as a large dyeworks. The dyeworks there were owned with Upper and Lower Mills by the Davies family, but from 1856 or earlier until they closed c. 1900 they were worked by the firm of Joseph Gainer.

Bond's Mill, the lowest mill in the parish, was first mentioned in 1714. In 1724 it was sold to four clothiers by John Ball, lord of Stonehouse manor, whose family may have worked the mill for some time earlier; his father, also John Ball, was a cloth factor of Blackwell Hall; a Samuel Ball, clothier, of Stonehouse, died c. 1654 and John Ball a clothier, perhaps

Samuel's son, in 1668. By 1750 Bond's Mill was being worked by Richard Pitt, who purchased it soon afterwards, and Mrs. Pitt, a widow, put the mill up for sale in 1774. In 1787 when it comprised four pairs of fulling-stocks it was being worked by Messrs. Eycott; Henry Eycott was leasing it to William Wood in 1832, and Frederick Eycott to William Wise in 1840. A power-loom was installed at the mill in 1837. Bond's Mill was occupied by Charles Warner in 1863, but by 1870 it had been acquired by the Eastington firm of Charles Hooper, which apparently rebuilt it in 1887 and continued to produce cloth there until 1934.

In 1721 William Adderley, a mercer of Stroud, acquired land at Ebley and built a new mill, later known as the Oil Mill. In 1723 it was being used to produce rape and linseed oil, and in 1725 John Adderley was making oil there. When put up for sale in 1727 it was said to be adaptable as a fullingmill, and it was perhaps in use as such by 1751 when it was owned by the Rimmington family. In 1764 the Oil Mill, described as a fulling-mill of four stocks and two gig-mills, belonged to Mr. Rimmington of Woodchester, and it was apparently the mill at which the partnership of Thomas Pettat of Stanley Park, John Rimmington, and Richard Flight were making cloth when they went bankrupt in 1786; the owner was then Samuel Rimmington. The Oil Mill was acquired in 1791 or 1792 by James Lewis, who worked it until his death in 1826; his sons continued the business until at least 1840. In 1833 the mill gave employment to c. 200 people, including the outdoor weavers. It had ceased to be a cloth-mill in 1856 when it was probably the corn-mill worked by William Hall. In 1885 it was driven by both water-power and steam, and when sold in 1892 it had two steamengines, eight pairs of stones, and two water-wheels. The Oil Mill remained a corn-mill in 1967.

The corn-mill built c. 1500 by John Gibbs on a piece of land inclosed out of Stonehouse Ham was apparently at Ryeford; his son Richard Gibbs held it in 1539. It had perhaps been adapted as a fulling-mill by 1608 when two members of the Gibbs family were clothiers. By 1710 Ryeford Mill was owned by the clothier Giles Phillips, who settled it on the marriage of his son Thomas in 1717; it then comprised three fulling-stocks and a gig-mill. On his death in 1757 Thomas Phillips devised it to his nephew Halliday Phillips (d. 1780). In 1798 and 1804 the mill was being worked by the clothiers Nathaniel Miles and William Taylor. In 1819 it was owned by Saul Lusty, who sold it to Reuben Hyde in 1828. John King owned it in 1840, and in 1853 it was being worked as a cornmill by the firm of Ford &

King; it was then powered by two water-wheels and had six pairs of stones. It remained a corn-mill until c. 1880, the building and site later being used as a saw-mill and timber yard.

From: 'Stonehouse: Economic history', A History of the County of Gloucester: Volume 10: Westbury and Whitstone Hundreds (1972), pp. 276-84.

URL: http://www.british-history.ac.uk/report.asp?compid=15887. Date accessed: 15 June 2006.

Appendix X

Eacott - Eycott Wills

Wills at **Gloucester Records Office** from 1500 to 1800 including storage retrieval number   (compiled 1984)

1583 -000	Ekott Thomas	Bagenden
1588 -151	Ecott, Mary	Elkstone
1594 -152	Eycott, Thomas	Brimpsfield
1619 -110	Ecott, Joan	Rendcomb
1621 -164	Eycott, William	Woodmancote
1629 -128	Eacott, Robert	Bagendon
1631 -154	Eacott, Margery	Winstone
1663 -172	Eycott Richard	Horsley
1670 -149	Eycott Richard	N. Cerney
1683 -075	Eycott Joseph	N. Cerney
1701 -132	Ecot, John	Colesbourne
1711 -263	Eycott John	IronActon
1712 -142	Eycot, Berkeley	Bagendon
1714 -172	Eycott Thomas	Coates
1715 -311	Eycott Thomas	Woodmancote
1730 -197	Eycott Thomas	Bagendon
1732 -162	Eycott Richard	Cirencester

1733 -050	Eycott Thomas	Badginton
1738 -154	Eacut, John	Catswood Bisley
1757 -022	Eycott Elizabth	Cirencester
1764 -012	Eycott Joseph	Cirencester
1772 -148	Eycott Richard	Cirencester
1775 -138	Eycott Elizabth	Cirencester
1776 -036	Ecut, William	Cromhall
1779 -072	Eycott Jones	Cirencester
1781 -089	Eccott, Alice	IronActon
1789 -102	Eycott John	Withington
1811 -000	Ecott Philip	Wickwar

Other wills:

1581	Eycott Richard North Cerney - copy in text
1760	Eacott William Charleton in Tetbury parish

Wills at GRO, Gloucester Record Office 1800 to 1900

1801	Eycott Nancy	Stonehouse
1811	Ecott Philip	?
1825	Ecott Mary	?
1866	Eycott Ann	Clutterbuck
1867	Eacott John	Wickwar
1869	Eacott Jemina	Alveston
1875	Eacott Robert	FramptnCoterell
1879	Eacott Philip	Alveston
1879	Eacott John	Alveston
1894	Eacott Edgar	?
1900	Eacott Robert	Huntley

Wills to 1931 include James 1909, John 1910, Emma 1907,Charlotte 1924, Mary Eliz 1917, Eliz Sarah 1923

Surrey Wills	(compiled 2006)	
Sry 0817	Richard Ecot	1720 Brother
Sry 0894	William Eacott	1795 friend
Sry 0213	Ann Eacott	1797 Widow
Sry 0212	Ann Eacott	1789 Wife
Sry 0212	John Eacott	1789 Testator, Yeoman
Sry 0919	Thomas Eacott	1824 labourer of Bisley
Sry 0678	Miss Sarah Eacott	1840 Daughter
Sry 0678	Mrs Sarah Eacott	1840 Wife of Bisley
Sry 0678	Stephen Eacott	1840 Son
Sry 0678	Miss Ann Eacott 1840	
Sry 0678	William Eacott	1840 testator, Farmer of Bisley

Prerogative Court of Canterbury

All PCC Wills held by the Public Record Office (grouped in the series PROB 11), which are available on Documents Online, cover the period from 1384 to 1858. Until that date, all wills had to be proved (formally approved) by church and other courts. The Prerogative Court of Canterbury, the most important of these courts, dealt with the relatively wealthy individuals living mainly in the south of England and most of Wales (originally the ecclesiastical province of Canterbury).

Description	Details	Date	Catalogue ref

Mary Eycott, Spinster of Chipping Barnet , Hertfordshire 25 June 1782 PROB 11/1091

Sarah Eycott, Widow of Gloucestershire 06 December 1755 PROB 11/819

Mary Eycott of Saint Andrew Holborn, Middlesex 07 May 1751
PROB 11/787

John Eycott, Goldsmith of Cirencester , Gloucestershire 19 October 1751
PROB 11/790

James Eycott, Mercer of Saint Paul Covent Garden , Middlesex 20 February 1746
PROB 11/744

Henry Eycott, Clothier of Stonehouse , Gloucestershire 18 March 1801
PROB 11/1355

Mary Ann Eycott, Spinster of Stroud, Gloucestershire 27 June 1832
PROB 11/1801

Henry Eycott of Stonehouse , Gloucestershire 08 October 1821
PROB 11/1648

William Powlett Eycott, Upholdsterer of Hammersmith , Middleex01 Dec 1843
PROB11/1989

William Eycot, Tailor, North Cerney Gl.   20 Aug 1748

Amy Eacott, Spinster, St Luke Middlesex   24 Apr 1823

Notes from early Wills and Other documents

Joan Eacott 1619 - Rendcomb : Buried in Rendcomb churchyard.

Brothers - Will Eacott, Richard Eacott, Thomas Eacott.

Sisters   - Susan Chamberlain, Margaret Broade. Also Thomas son of Richard Eacott. Susan Jefferies her mother-in-law.

Thomas Eycott 1740 - North Cerney: Catholic, a batchelor to William Eycott of Cirencester his nephew and only next of kin. His sister Rebecca and Martha freehold estate at Woodmancote and have cottage there until married.

John Eycott 1751 - Cirencester: Catholic, a goldsmith of Cirencester. Estate at Bagendon, mother Mary, wife Elizabeth, sons Richard and John, freehold estate at Chedworth payment to sisters.

William Eacott 1760 - Tetbury: Charleton in Tetbury parish. Daughter Elizabeth wife of Jonathan Avery. Son Richard Eacott.

William Ecutt 1776 - Cromhall: Sons John eldest, William, Robert, Philip.

John inherited Messuage and tenement. Also owned two other cottages. He was remarried.

Wills at Wiltshire Record Office, Trowbridge.

1627 Thomas Ecut	Mother Elizabeth, Wife Rachel was with child,Westport		
1684 William Ecut	Labourer	Eysey	

Sons: William, Nicholas; Daughters Ann, Margaret, Elizabeth. Wife deceased

1685 Richard Eacott	Bodice maker	Devizes
1701 Edward Eacott Sr	Husbandman	Warminster
1710 John Eacott Sr	Gardener	Warminster
1720 William Eacott		Warminster
1775 John Eacott	Yeoman	Warminster
1778 Thomas Eacott	Plumber and Glazier	Chippenham,

Son: Thomas, Dau. Elizabeth, Susanna

Brother - John Eacott of Wotton Bassett also plumber and glazier

1792 John Eacott	Yeoman	WottonBassett,

Wife: Mary, Nephews: John Smith, James Smith. Neices: Sarah Smith, Ann Smith, Mary Smith

1853 James Eacott	Shearman	Trowbridge

Prerogative Court of Canterbury Wills

Description	Date	Catalogue ref	Details
Will of Mary Eycott, Spinster of Chipping Barnet , Hertfordshire	25 June 1782 prob 11/1091		
Will of Sarah Eycott, Widow of Gloucestershire	06 December 1755 prob11/819		
Mary Eycott of Saint Andrew Holborn, Middlesex	07 May 1751	prob 11/787	

John Eycott, Goldsmith of Cirencester , Gloucestershire   19 October 1751
prob 11/790

James Eycott, Mercer of Saint Paul Covent Garden, Middlesex 20 February
1746   prob 11/744

Henry Eycott, Clothier of Stonehouse , Gloucestershire 18 March 1801
prob11/1355

Mary Ann Eycott, Spinster of Stroud, Gloucestershire 27 June 1832
prob11/1801

Henry Eycott of Stonehouse , Gloucestershire   08 October 1821 prob 11/1648

William Powlett Eycott, Upholsterer of Hammersmith, Mdlx   01 December1843

prob 11/1989

William Eycot, Tailor, North Cerney Gl.   20 Aug 1748

Amy Eacott, Spinster, St Luke Middlesex   24 Apr 1823.

Appendix Y

Legal Records of Interest

The Guise Family and Its Gloucestershire Properties. Catalogue Ref.
D326 Guise family of Elmore, Gloucestershire.

Deeds: Rendcomb, Colsbourne, Chedworth, N. Cerney,

FILE [no title] - ref. D326/T8 - date: 1636

Exemplification of a fine: Richd. Berkeley, esq., Maurice Berkely knt., Geo.
Hyett, esq., and Edw. Galton, Esq., to Wm. Guyse esq. & Jas. Weele gent.:
manors of Rendcomb & Marsden, (lands in Rendcomb & Marsden,
Colesbourne & Eycott, 'Chedworth Woodlandes', North Cerney &
Calmsden). 29 April, 11 Ch. I [1636] ["No. 13"].

FILE [no title] - ref. D326/T10 - date: 1732

Attested copy "Release in order to a Recovery and Settlement of all Sir
John Guise's Estates in Gloucestershire": Manor, capital messuage,
advowson etc. of Brockworth, with Wooleryes Farm etc.; manor, advowson
etc. of Elmore, with fishing in R. Severn; Manor of Rodley with lands in
Westbury-on-Severn; Rendcomb Park, Manor of Rendcomb, capital
messuage called Eacott (Eycott) Farm; Manor of Marsden, incl. lands called
Sharshall in Colesbourne and Chedworth; Manor, cap. messuage etc. of

Leaden's Court [Highleadon]; land in Newland & Woodruddings [Rudford], formerly of Sylvester Canning, widow; farm called Cowpers Hill in Upton St. Leonards; lands in Brockworth Witcombe & Cranham, & in various other parishes [specified], & disposing uses of other properties, incl. Manor & advowson of Woodmancote & N. Cerney. [Settlement on Lady (Anne) Guise].

Note : By 1732 Eycott was better known as Eacott.

The End of Eycott Ownership at Woodmancote

Deeds and Wills : Catalogue Ref. D475

North Cerney

FILE [no title] - ref. D475/T1 - date: 1680-1827

Messuage and land in Woodmancote; with wills of Thos. Eycott of Woodmancote, 1715 (1817), Robt. Saunders, 1730, with administration 1731, Elizabeth Eycott, 1753, Elizabeth Saunders, 1768, proved 1777, Thos. Tyndale of N. Cerney, 1765, Robt. Saunders of Little Farringdon, 1807-8, proved 1809.

Evidence of Eycotts being Catholics

Gloucester record office. There is also the book of recorded papists 1717

FILE - An Account of the Roman Catholicks who have Estates in the County of Gloucester - ref. Q/SO/4/1 [n.d.]

North Cerney, Thomas Eycott yeom.

FILE - A list of the Papists and Reputed Papists in the County of Gloucester - ref. Q/SO/4/2 [n.d.]

North Cerney: Thomas Eycott Senr. and his wife, Thomas Eycott jun., Elizabeth, Rebecca, Mary, Eycott

FILE - The names of the persons who took the Oaths of Allegiance and Supremacy to His Majesty King George and the Abjuration Oath, p'suant to the statute made in the first year of his said Majesty's reign, Intituled "An Act for the further Security of His Majesty's Person and Government, etc." at the Mashal Sessions, 1715. - ref. Q/SO/4/3 [n.d.]

Thomas Eycott, Constable of Badgington

Other Court Documents:

1751   April 19 – John Eycott of Lincoln's Inn, Middlesex, Gentleman

From North Devon Chichester family papers

1821   May 10 – John Eycott of Lincoln's Inn, Middlesex, Gentleman

From Lowndes Family of Chesham Buckinghamshire a limited administration granted to Willoughby Rockham.

Eycott was a man of means, a lawyer living at a prestigious address. Why he is in these papers is not known although the last item appears to be giving power of attorney to care for him. So far he can not be connected to any line and nothing else is known about him. He was likely not married.

Proceedings of Old Bailey

1. Elizabeth Eycott, victim in trial of in Joseph Bishop, theft : pick pocketing, 5th April, 1827. Joseph Bishop was indicted for stealing, on the 26th of February, 3 canvas-bags, value 1s.; 5 lbs. of volati

2. Samuel Eycott, victim in trial of Joseph Bishop, theft : pick pocketing, 5th April, 1827.

Last days of Eycotts in Bagendon:

1715 – Will of Thomas Eycott of Woodmancote

1717 – John Eycott and Thomas Eycott registered in book for Popish Estates in Gloucester

1735 – probate will of Thomas Eycott, Bagendon

1753 – Elizabeth Eycott wife of Robert Saunders of Little Farringdon.

1736 – James Ecott, the younger, labourer, gets a deed for property at Rodbourne Cheney.

1768 – James Eycott of Haydon Wick, his will, provides for care of his property at Rodbourne Cheney. Bills for thatching and repairing Eycott property from 1778 to 1783. His bequest was rolled into a trust later to create the Wayte Educational Charity.

1860 – several matter of Deeds for Thomas Eycott, furniture dealer, city of Gloucester

Apprenticeship Records

1712   - John Ecott, son of the widow Jane of Upton St. Leonards, a carpenters apprentice

1717   - James Eycott, son of Berkeley, apprenticed to Joseph Shewell a wax chandler

1717   - Richard Eycott, mercer, took John Tymbrnell of Cirencester as apprentice

1730   - James Eycott, mercer, Covent Gardens, London took apprentice.

1758   - Joseph Eycott was apprenticed to Theo James a taylor in Stroud

1760   - John Eycott, cordwainer, Ampney Crucis took appentice.

1766   - John Eacott, plumber/glazier of Wooton Bassett

1765   - William Accott apprenticed to Thomas Sayer, carpenter/joiner of Edmonton Middlesex

1775   - Matthew Acot of Cricklade was master blacksmith

1781   - John Eccott of Shepton Mallet

1785   - Benjamin Acott, master barber and peruke (wig) maker of Cirencester

1794   - Henry Eycott, clothier, Kings Stanley took William A. Clarke.

1783   - William Powlett Eacott

1783   - Jane Eycott was apprenticed to Sarah Colen, mantua maker and dress maker

1804   - Elizabeth Acott, appenticed as a mantua maker in Cirencester

Henry Eycott and Family of Stonehouse (near Stroud)

1799   Henry Eycott of Bond's Mill died. Wife Nancy. Son Henry. Grand sons Henry Charles and Joseph William Eycott. Grand daughters Elizabeth and Mary Ann. Brother Nathaniel whose children were

Thomas, Joseph and Mary (Walker) Eycott.

1800 – boundary between Stonehouse and Eastington. Henry Eycott of Bond's Mill proposed to cover ditch between Stroud Old River and Stanley Brook erecting merestones on the course of the ditch.

1800 – Joseph King stole loom from Henry Eycott, clothier

1804 – legal file of Mrs Anne Clutterbuck Eycott, Stonehouse and William Fryer of Eastington

1806 – Henry Eycott sold his share in Frocester Manor Estate

1813 – Henry Eycott owned an estate at Nastend, Eastington. In 1839 139 acres were transferred to Frederick Eycott.

1817 – Wool was stolen from Samuel Clutterbuck and Henry Eycott, owners. Joseph Eycott was informer (alias Lewis)

1821   Henry Eycott of Stonehouse will 17 December 1821. Wife Mary. Half brother William Stanton, adopted son of first wife. Sons Frederick, William (died 1812) and Henry Charles. Daughters Elizabeth, Mary Ann (died 1806), Catherine

1823 – marriage contract between Catherine Eycott of Bond's Mill, Stonehouse, spinster and William John Wood of Stroud.

1831   – John Fletcher stole conies (rabbits)from Frederick Eycott, was fined.

1866   will of Ann Clutterbuck Fryer of Gloucester, widow of Frederick Eycott of Oakfields, stonehouse effects valued at under £ 450

1884   Will of Frederick Eycott late of Oakfield was proved by widow Sophia and nephew Rev. William Eycott Martin. Nephews Clark and Edward Palling Little. The estate was valued at £ 45,431 which is about 2 million today.

Other Legal Matters

1803 – Survey of lands of Mrs. Catherine Eycot Bulkeley (Berkeley?) at Bisley and Stroud

1813 – Marriage settlement of Catherine Eycott, widow of Bathwick Somerset, 20 February.

1821 – James Eacott , Diane and child removed from Bitton to St. Albans under poor laws.

1824 – James Eacott charged with deserting his family

1635 – Eycot farm sold by Maurice Berkeley to William Guise. However Richard Berkeley was later charged with committing waste by felling trees on the property.

1643-1769 Cricklade – Deed to Eacott from Earl of Radnor

1784-1805 Chippenham – Deed to Eacott

1773 -1883 Cumbria, Greystoke Castle – tenants bonds for Eycott.

Eycott Hill, John Eycott farmed here as at 1901. Geologic landforms, such as Eycott Hill are named after the property which is in the lake district.

Church Fundings

1655-7 Nathaniel Eycott listed on survey for trustees of Maintenance for Preaching Ministers. He received £ 22 a year from his patron Robert Long Esq. At Thuxton Rectory, Mitford Hundred, Norfolk. This was an effort in Cromwell's time to address inequities in preachers incomes largely by fining the wealthy bishops.

1902 – Stipend of £ 130 per annum to Rev. Jabez Eacott

1870 – West Farleigh, Kent a tithe for Rev. Eycott-Martin

Public Record Office now The National Archives

On line catalogue   Kew England   Search run on May 17 2001 Summary of searches done .

You ran a basic search of "Eycott"

There were **17** hits within catalogue entry details. Hits 1 to 17 are shown below sorted by catalogue reference.

PRO Reference	Title/Scope and Content		Covering Dates
C 142/293/3	Eycott, Thomas:	Gloucester	4 James I.
C 142/298/2	Eycott, Thomas:	Gloucester	5 James I.
C 142/307/89	Eycott, Thomas:	Gloucester	7 James I.
C 5/267/33	Sims v. Eycott:	Gloucester.	1711
C 5/372/64	Sims v. Eycott:	Gloucester.	1712
C 9/413/123	Eycott v. Eycott		1681

C 10/320/15   Combes v. Oatridge, Eycott, Freeman & Sirres: Glos   1711

C 10/144/39   Eycott v. Eycott: Glos   1682

C 10/389/34   Eycott v. Balding, Stephens, Eycott, Berkeley, Broad: Glos 1710

C 12/1265/22 Grahl v. Eycott   1789

C 12/1186/46Willett v. Eycott   1761

PROB 5/5424   Berkeley, ...,? gent, of Eycott House, Rendcomb, Glos. Will of person undated

WARD 7/25/59 Eycott, Thomas: Gloucester   7 Jas I.

WARD 7/29/42 Eycott, Thomas: Gloucester   5 Jas I.

WARD 7/33/202 Eycott, Thomas: Gloucester   4 Jas I.

WO 339/27391 Eycott H G, Lieut   1914 -1922

WO 339/55451 Eycott - Martin R

You ran a basic search on "Eacott"

PRO Reference	Title/Scope and Content	Covering Dates
ADM 157/2345	Eacott - Ectin	1865
AIR 80/69	Eacott - Ecott C air force record	

BT 372/741/58 R312409 Eacott F A BT seamen' discharge 30/05/1925 LONDON

BT 372/1564/66 R574484 Eacott J K 05/12/1935 Dagenham   1913-1972

BT 372/1887/48 R638946 Eacott G A 18/12/1933 Bath   1913-1972

C 205/12/38 Sarah Ann Eacott, widow 1881 Jan 26 County: Berks [1880] Aug 3

C 12/572/30   Gibbard v. Eacott   1776

MAF 9/316   Manor of Bisley: G. Eacott   1 8 8 5 , J a n . 1 5   M A F Agriculture award, holding

MAF 9/316   Manor of Bisley: W. Eacott   1885, Jan. 15

PIN 26/4431   Name: Eacott C J Nature of Disability: Myalgia 1916-1923

WO 339/65362   Eacott H WO War Office pension requests   1914-1922

WO 364/5175   Name: Eacott, Cecil G - Earwaker, Charles   1914-1920

WO 374/21611   Eacott, Lieut F S   1917-1922

WO 374/21612   Eacott, Revd H J T   1918-1920

WO 398/66	Eacott Elizabeth - Edgell Winifred	
WO 399/11018	Eacott Isabel	01/01/1914 - 31/12/1920
WO 399/11019	Eacott Mabel	01/01/1914 - 31/12/1920

You ran a basic search on "Ecott".

There were 5 hits within catalogue entry details. Hits 1 to 5 are shown below sorted by catalog reference.

PRO Reference	Title/Scope and Content	Covering Dates
AIR 80/69	Eacott - Ecott C	
BT 372/1505/42	R563108 Ecott J 18/05/1928 Sheppard Bedfordshire	1913-72
BT 372/1876/181	R636776 Ecott G R 18/03/1937 London	1913-1972
MT 41/55	Captain Ecott (Bablockhythe Ferry)	1947
WO 339/46264	Ecott H	1914-22

You ran a basic search on "Eycot"

PRO Reference	Title/Scope and Content	Covering Dates

C 143/44/18   John le Brun to settle the manors of Elkston and Winston on himself for life, with remainder to John son of John de Acton, Ellen his wife, and the heirs of their bodies; remainder to William Malerbe, Elizabeth his wife, and the heirs of their bodies; remainder to the right heirs of John de Acton; retaining land in Eycote [in Rendcomb] and Norton.   13 EDWARD I.

C 143/171/1   William de Eycote to grant a messuage, land, and rent in Barnham and Walberton to a chaplain in the parish church of Barnham, retaining land. Sussex.

17 EDWARD II.

E 326/4082   Grant in frank almoin by John Russel, son of William Russel of Cotes, to the monks of Bruerne, of all his meadow of Eycote, in the west part of the water, adjoining the lower part of Flexhomma, and all his meadow in the east part of the water, with land in Lillesleye, with permission to enclose the said meadows.

A search of **Acott** was conducted but not included. Most entries were for patents in the 20th century.

In 2006 the above search could not be repeated as access had changed.

Table of Contents

The following table is useable only in the print edition.

APPENDIX GUIDE

Books by John M. Eacott

Of Other Times - Early History of Norwich Township - 1980

The Eacott History - similar earlier version of Eacott Name History

McBride Mast Families - genealogical study and stories

Eacott Reynolds Families - genealogical study and stories

Becoming John - stories of growing up in Tillsonburg Ontario

Sunshine Sketches of Nizwa - about living in Nizwa, Oman

The Spook Story - children's book (not in circulation)

The Erin Stories - children's book (not in circulation)

   -- *Most of these books are available at www.lulu.com*--

Made in the USA
Columbia, SC
22 June 2022

62091289R10200